A
Review

A Review of the Bible

Printed by CreateSpace.com
   A Division of Amazon

ISBN - 1452813272

EAN 13 - 9781452813271

This review is taken almost exclusively from the New International Version of the Bible International Bible Society, 1984 or the King James Version except where otherwise indicated

Cover design and book interior by Laurie Wall Bates and Lydia Di Cino.

A Review

of the Bible

ᘛ⬯ᘚ

Carrie Wall

Foreword

First, I want to say, I believe every word of the Bible to be important. By writing this review, I wanted to make it a little easier for you to get the *main thoughts* of the Bible in a week or at most a month.

By reading this review of the Bible, I hope you will have a greater desire to read the complete Bible. This is not meant to educate professional Bible students, but to simplify and use words the average person can understand.

In order to do this I read each Chapter, as if for the first time, using the notes I've written in my Bible and the under-standing from a lifetime of reading, classes and sermons.

I love the truth and hope this will make the bible a little easier to understand and also a quicker read for busy people.

Table of Contents

Old Testament

New Testament

Old
Testament

Genesis

A Review

The first five books of the Bible were written by Moses while wandering in the Wilderness, so far as we know. (Deut. 31:24-26)

(When Moses had made an end of writing the words of the law, they were placed in the Ark of the Covenant.)

Genesis covers more time than any other book. The first seven Chapters cover 1656 years. (Add up the ages recorded in Chapters five plus another hundred years recorded in Chapter 7 verse 6).

In the beginning there was the godhead; God, Jesus and the Holy Spirit. (Gen. 1:2 and John 1:1).

The earth (that now is) was without form and void. Everything was spoken into existence, in six days. (1:31), (Heb. 11:3).

Day 1 – Light, day and night
Day 2 – Separation of waters and an expanse between the earth and sky.
Day 3 – Dry ground and seas, vegetation and their seeds.
Day 4 – Sun, moon and stars
Day 5 – Fish of the sea and birds of the air
Day 6 – The animals of the earth and man (1:3-26)

The earth was created for man and was complete when man was created. On the seventh day, God rested and made the day a day of rest for man until the church was established. After that, the first day of the week is called 'The Lord's Day' (Rev. 1:10).

God made a beautiful garden for man (Adam and Eve) to live in called, Eden. They were vegetarians at this time (9:3).

They could eat the fruits of the garden except for the tree in the midst of the garden. A serpent told Eve the reason God didn't want them to eat of it was because they would be like gods. She believed him, ate some and gave Adam some. Their eyes were opened. Because they disobeyed God, they were put out of the garden and had to work for their living (3:16, 17).

This was how sin entered the world. This also brought about death. For as in Adam all die, in Christ shall all be made alive (1 Cor. 15:22).

Adam and Eve had two sons: Cain and Abel. They offered sacrifices to God. Cain brought some fruit of the ground and Abel brought an animal sacrifice. God was not pleased with Cain's offering (Gen. 4:4-6).

Hebrews 11:4 says, 'by faith Abel offered a better sacrifice'. They *must* have been told what to offer.

Cain was angry and killed his brother. He was sent away.

They had another son, Seth, who was in the lineage of Christ (Luke 3:37).

There were some good people on the earth but as time went on, they became more and more wicked. The Lord was grieved and his heart was filled with pain. He decided to destroy the people he had created (6:5-7).

There was one righteous man, Noah. He was 500 years old before he had a family of three boys, Shem, Ham and Japheth. God instructed Noah on how to build an Ark to save his family of eight before sending a flood of waters to destroy the earth and its inhabitants. The Ark was to be 450 feet long, 75 feet wide and 45 feet high with 3 stories. He was to take seven pairs of every kind of clean animals and birds and two pairs of every unclean. The animals came to Noah. He didn't have to gather them up, but provided food (6:21).

There was no fear as people were not eating flesh as yet. After the flood God said, the fear and dread of you will fall on all the beasts of the earth. 'Everything that lives and moves will be food for you' (9:14).

One reason the people did not believe Noah when he told them God was going to send a flood, was because it had not ever rained. Streams came up from the earth and watered the surface of the ground (Gen. 2:6).

It rained 40 days and 40 nights and covered the mountains. They were in the Ark over a year (Gen. 7:11 and 8:13-15).

God put a sign in the sky, a rainbow, to show he would never again destroy the earth by water. We still see it today (9:14-17).

Noah lived 950 years. All the people today come from the family of Noah, (but he came from Adam and Eve).

The whole world spoke one language at this time. They were making bricks by now and decided to build a tower that would reach to the heavens. This displeased the Lord because he wanted them to populate the earth he had made. He confused their languages and scattered them over all the earth. The tower was called Babel (11:1-9).

Abraham

Abram was born about 300 years after the flood. Noah was still alive (9:29). When Abraham was 75 years old and living in Ur of the Chaldeans, God called him. He said, 'Leave your country, your people and your father's household and go to the land I will show you!' (12:1)

The Promises:

I will make you into a great nation and I will bless you.

I will make your name great and you will be a blessing.

I will bless those who bless you and whoever curses you I will curse.

All people on earth will be blessed through you (lineage of Christ) Matt. 1:2.

Abram took his wife Sarai and his nephew, Lot, and set out for the land of Canaan (Ch 12). They had become very wealthy in flocks and herds and had to separate to have enough pasture land. Given a choice, Lot chose the plain of Jordan. It looked like a good choice, but the people who lived there, Sodom, were wicked. Once Lot was taken captive in a war and was rescued by Abram (14:11-16). Afterwards Abram met Melchizedek (King of Salem) and gave him a tenth of everything (14:17-20).

The Lord spoke to Abram again (3rd call) in a vision, telling him he would have a son. Sarai, wanting to help out, gave Abram her handmaid, Hagar, to bear a child. By this time, Abram was 86 years old.

When Abram was 99 years old, he got a 4th call. Over a period of nearly 25 years, he was called four times.

1. Genesis 12:1-9
2. Genesis 13:14-18
3. Genesis 15:1-21
4. Genesis 17:1-27

This time the Lord changed Abram's name to Abraham and Sarai's name to Sarah. He made a covenant with Abraham:

This time next year, Sarah will bear you a son. The covenant was: Every male among you shall be circumcised for the generations to come beginning at eight days old, whether bought or born. This was a sign of faith. Abraham was 99 years old and Ishmael (the son of Hagar) was thirteen when they were circumcised.

Soon after that, Abraham was sitting at the entrance of his tent in the heat of the day when he looked up and saw three men standing nearby. Immediately he started showing them hospitality, providing water to wash their feet and having a meal prepared for them. Again he was told; this time next year Sarah would have a son. She heard and laughed.

As the men left, they all walked along together. One of the men was the Lord. He said to the other two, 'Shall I hide from Abraham was I am about to do?' What he was about to do was to destroy Sodom and Gomorrah. Abraham tried to save them. The Lord said he would not destroy the towns if ten righteous could be found. The men of Sodom were homosexuals. They even tried to get Lot to bring his guests out to them.

As it turned out, only Lot and two daughters were saved because his wife looked back and turned into a pillar of salt (verses 17 and 26).

The daughters, wanting to preserve the family line, made a pact to get their father to drink wine and lie with them. They did this and two nations came from this; the Moabites and the Ammonites.

Abraham finally has a son! They named him Isaac. He was circumcised on the 8th day. Abraham was 100 years old and Sarah was 90. When Isaac was weaned (two or three years old) Abraham held a great feast. Hagar's son, Ishmael, was mocking. Sarah had Abraham to send him and his mother away.

God tested Abraham by asking him to sacrifice his beloved son, Isaac, as a burnt offering. As he took the knife to slay his son, the Angel of the Lord, Jesus, called out from heaven and stopped him (22:1-14).

Sarah died at age 127 in Hebron in the land of Canaan. Abraham went to find a burying place for her. The place he wanted was a field near Mamre with a cave and trees. He purchased it for four hundred shekels. This later became the burying place for other family members: himself, Isaac, Rebekah, Leah and Jacob.

After Sarah's death, Abraham sent his servant, probably Eliezer (Gen 15:2), to his country, Haran, and relatives to get a wife for Isaac. He was age 37 when she died.

The servant took with him ten camels laden with gifts and arrived near evening at a well where women went to draw water. He prayed, 'May it be that when I say to a girl, please let down your jar that I may have a drink. And she says, drink and I'll water your camels too. Let her be the one you have chosen for you servant Isaac'. This happened just as he asked (Gen. 24).

She was the daughter of Bethuel, son of Abraham's brother, Nahor (see Gen. 11:27). This would make them 1st cousins. She had a brother named Laban (Gen. 24:29).   The girl's name was Rebekah. They all went to the girl's home and told them everything that had happened. Laban and Bethuel said, 'This is from the Lord, we can say nothing one way or the other'. They called Rebekah and asked her, 'Will you go with this man?' 'I will go,' she said.

When they arrived home, Isaac had gone out to the field to meditate. After relating everything that had happened, he married Rebekah. They stayed in his mother's tent and he loved her (24:67). Isaac was forty years old when he married Rebekah and like Sarah, she was also barren. When he was sixty years old, Rebekah had twin boys, Esau and Jacob (Gen. 25:19-26).

Esau was born first and should (as first born) have had he greater blessing, but sold his birthright to his brother for some lentil stew.   Rebekah and Jacob continued to trick Isaac into giving Jacob the blessing. Esau was a hairy man so they covered his hands and part of his neck with goatskins, put Esau's clothing on him and Rebekah prepared the tasty food Isaac had requested. Isaac was almost blind. In verse 27 Isaac had a little doubt but after touching and smelling him, he gave him the blessing of the first born.   Soon Esau returned with his tasty game. When Isaac found out he had been deceived, he trembled violently.

Esau held a grudge against Jacob and vowed to kill him. His mother told him to flee at once to Haran to her brother Laban's house.

That night he spent at a place called Bethel. He had a dream. He saw a stairway reaching from earth to heaven and angels ascending and descending on it. Above it stood the Lord.

He said, I am the Lord, the God of your father Abraham and the God of Isaac. I will give you and your descendants the land on which you are lying. Your descendants will be like the dust of the earth and you will spread out to the east, to the west and to the north and to the south. All peoples of the earth will be blessed though you. I will bring you back to this land (Gen. 28:10-15).

Jacob made a vow saying, 'If God will be with me and will watch over me on this journey I am taking and will give me food to eat and clothes to wear so that I return safely o my father's house, then the Lord will be my God and this stone that I have set up as a pillar will be God's house. Of all that you give me I will give you a tenth' (28:20-22).

Jacob arrived at Paddam Aram where Rebekah's kin lived and saw a well where they were watering the flocks. Rachel came with her father's sheep. Jacob rolled the stone from the well and watered his uncle's sheep. He kissed Rachel and began to weep aloud. He told her he was Rebekah's son. She ran to tell her father and he stayed with them for a month, working for free.

Jacob had fallen in love with Rachel and said he'd work for Laban seven years for Rachel. When the seven years were up, Laban gave him her older sister, Leah. Jacob was unaware of it until morning light. He was told, 'finish the bridal week and you can have Rachel for another seven years' work'.

Leah began to have children. She had six sons and a daughter. Rachel was barren. Each daughter had a maidservant and each one of them had two sons. After about fourteen years, Rachel gave birth to Joseph.

Jacob was ready to return home, but Laban had been blessed because of him (30:29, 30). He wanted Jacob to stay. They made an agreement. Every speckled, spotted or dark colored sheep, lamb or goat would be Jacob's wages.

Jacob took fresh-cut branches, cut stripes on them and placed then in front of the watering troughs. When the stronger animals came there at mating time, Jacob would but the branches before then to 'mark' their offspring. Jacob told his wives the 'Angel of God' (Jesus) had told him to do this (Gen. 31:10-13) in a dream.

After six more years (20 altogether) the Lord told Jacob to go back to the land of your fathers and to your relatives and I will be with you (31:3). Joseph was six plus years old.

They left while Laban was gone and Rachel stole her father's household gods. Laban pursued them and finally caught up with them after seven days (Gen 31:17). They had words but made up. Laban kissed his grandchildren and daughters and returned home.

On their way home, they came close to where Jacob's brother Esau lived. Jacob was fearful he would still be angry at him for stealing his birthright and sent messengers ahead. They returned saying Esau was coming to meet him with 400 men.   Jacob assembled a sizable present for his brother:

200 she goats	20 he goats	30 milk camels
200 ewes	20 rams	20 she asses
40 cows	10 bulls	10 foals

That night, Jacob sent his family across the Jabbok River and he was left alone. A man wrestled with him until daybreak (Gen. 32:22-24). The man said, 'Your name will no longer be Jacob, but Israel'. The man was probably Jesus (Gen. 32:30).

When Jacob met Esau, Esau ran to meet him, threw his arms around him and kissed him and they both wept. Esau didn't want to take the gift. He said he had plenty but Jacob insisted. He told his brother, 'to see your face is like seeing the face of God'.

Esau returned to Seir where he was from and Jacob settled in Succoth for a while, where he built a place for himself and shelters for his cattle. He bought the land from the sons of Hamar, the father of Shechem (Gen. 33:19). Hundreds of years later Joseph's bones they had brought from Egypt during the exodus were buried on this property and his descendants inherited this land (see Joshua 24:32).

They must have stayed in this area a while as Dinah was near Joseph's age. She went out to visit the women of the land.

Shechem, the son of Hamar, saw her and violated her. He wanted to marry her but her brothers (Simeon and Levi) took revenge. They told Shechem if the men would be circumcised, they would intermarry with them. However, on the third day, while they were still in pain, they killed every male, took Dinah, carried off their wealth and families (Chapter 34).

God told Jacob to go to Bethel (where he had the vision of the ladder) and build an altar.

He passed on the blessing of Abraham to Jacob, renaming him Israel (Gen. 35:9-15).

During this time period, Deborah, Rebekah's nurse, died and was buried under the oak below Bethel (Gen. 35:8).

They had left Bethel and were headed toward Ephrath (Bethlehem) when Rachel started labor pains with Benjamin. She had great difficulty and died about 1 day from home (see Gen. 28:10).

When Jacob arrived home his father was still alive. When he died, Esau and Jacob buried him. He lived to be 180 years old. That made Esau and Jacob 120 as Isaac was 60 when they were born (Gen. 25:26).

Esau had 3 wives from the daughters of Canaan (Gen. 26:34, 35). He was the father of the Edomites. When the Israelites were on their way to Canaan, the Lord told Moses, 'you are about to pass through the territory of your brothers, the descendants of Esau, who live in Seir. They will be afraid of you, but be very careful. Do not provoke them to war, for I will not give you any of their land, not even enough to put you foot on. I have given Esau the hill country of Seir as his own. You are to pay them in silver for the food and the water you drink' (Deut. 2:4-6).

Joseph

Joseph was the beloved son of Rachel. Jacob made a richly ornamented robe for him.

When he was seventeen years old, he was tending the flocks with his brothers and brought a bad report to their father about them. He was also a dreamer. In his dream they were binding sheaves of grain out in the field when suddenly his sheaf rose and stood upright while their sheaves gathered round and bowed down to it. This angered his brothers. Even his father rebuked him and said, 'will your mother and I and your brothers actually come and bow down to the ground before you?' Rachel was alive when Joseph had these dreams at age 17 (see Gen. 37:2 and 10).

His brothers hated him. One day his father sent him to see if all was well with them. When they saw him coming, they plotted to kill him. The oldest brother, Reuben, said, 'No, let's put him into this cistern', in-tending to rescue him later. When they saw a caravan of Ishmaelites coming, another brother, Judah, said, 'Let's sell him'. That's what they did. They killed a goat, dipped his robe in the blood and carried it to their father intimating an animal had eaten him. Jacob mourned and refused to be comforted. He's sons and daughters came to comfort him (37:35). He probably had as many daughters as he did sons. They only counted sons then.

The 38th Chapter interrupts the story of Joseph to relate the story of Judah, Jacob's fourth son. He left his brothers, met and married a Canaanite woman and had sons. When a son died, leaving him no off-spring, his brother was supposed to marry her and produce offspring for his brother. Judah's daughter-in-law, Tamar, was waiting for this to happen and when it didn't, she disguised herself as a prostitute when she heard her father-in-law Judah was to pass by that way. (His own wife had died). He hired her with the promise of a goat. He left his seal and staff until the goat arrived. When someone brought the goat, she was nowhere to be found. Later she was found to be pregnant by Judah, her father-in-law. She had twin boys. One, the first born, was named Perez and was in the lineage of Christ (Mat. 1:3).

Joseph in Egypt

Joseph was sold to Potifer, one of Pharaoh's officials. In everything he did, the Lord gave him success. The household of the Egyptian was blessed because of Joseph and he put Joseph in charge of everything.

Potipher's wife tried to get Joseph to be intimate with her, but he refused all her advances. One day as he ran from her, she grabbed his cloak and it came off in her hand. When her husband came home, she told him this story:

'That Hebrew slave you brought us came to me to make sport of me. As soon as I screamed for help he left his cloak beside me and ran out of the house' (Genesis Chapter 39).

Joseph was put in prison. Two men he was in prison with were the King's cupbearer and baker. They both had dreams the same night which Joseph interpreted. The cupbearer was to be restored to his position, but the baker was to be beheaded. The cupbearer forgot about Joseph until two years later, when Pharaoh had a dream. No one could interpret it. Finally, the cupbearer told the Pharaoh about his own dream and Joseph was sent for. Joseph told him, 'I cannot do it, but God will give Pharaoh the answer he desires'.

The Pharaoh's Dream (Gen. 41:17-27)

1. He saw seven cows, fat and sleek. After them, seven cows scrawny and lean. The seven lean cows ate up the seven fat ones, but were no different.

2. He saw seven heads of grain full and good and seven heads withered and thin.

Joseph said, 'the dreams are the same'. There will be seven years of plenty and seven years of drought. Find a wise man to put in charge. They should collect food during these good years and store it up for the years of famine.

Pharaoh appointed Joseph to be in charge of this. He rode in a chariot, wore fine robes and Pharaoh's signet ring. He was thirty years old. Joseph stored up huge quantities of grain, beyond measure. He married Asenath, daughter of the priest of On and fathered two sons, Manasseh and Ephraim (Gen. 41:41-52).

When the seven years of abundance ended, the people came to Joseph for food, even from other lands, not only Egypt.

Jacob, Joseph's father, said to his sons, 'I have heard that there is grain in Egypt. Go there and buy some for us'. He did not send Benjamin.

When Joseph's brothers arrived, they bowed down to him (see Gen. 37:10). He recognized them, but pretended not to. They did not know him. He spoke harshly to them and accused them of being spies and they must bring their youngest brother, Benjamin, to verify what they said. They were talking among themselves, not knowing he could understand.

When they got home and opened their sacks, there in each man's sack, was his pouch of silver!

Jacob said, 'My son will not go down there with you, his brother is dead and he is the only one left.' It had been 20 years.

Finally after everything was gone, Jacob said, 'take a gift, balm, honey, spices, myrrh, nuts, almonds and double the amount of money. Take your brother and may God grant you mercy. If I am bereaved, I am bereaved.'

When Joseph saw them and Benjamin with them, he told his steward to prepare dinner for them. He asked if their father was still living. When he saw Benjamin (his own mother's son) he left them to weep in private. He did not sit with them because Egyptians could not eat with Hebrews.

He had them seated in the order of their ages, the oldest to the youngest. He gave Benjamin five times as much as the rest (Gen. 43).

When they left to go home, Joseph told his steward to put his silver cup and the money in Benjamin's sack. Then he sent men after them and accused them of stealing and brought them back.

Judah had told his father he personally would guarantee Benjamin's safety. He pleaded with Joseph to let him take Benjamin's place (44:18-33). He told him the family's history (Joseph could see they were sorry for selling him). He could no longer control himself and wept so loud the Egyptians could hear him.

He said, 'I am your brother Joseph, the one you sold into Egypt! God sent me ahead of you. There will be five more years of famine. Now hurry back. You shall live in the land of Goshen and be near me'. Then he threw his arms around Benjamin and wept.

Pharaoh and his officials were pleased and directed them to take carts from Egypt for their wives and children, provisions for the journey and new clothing.

When they arrived home, they said, 'Joseph is still alive!' Jacob was stunned but was finally convinced (Gen. 45).

They loaded up all they had. When they reached Beer-sheba, he offered a sacrifice to God. God spoke to Jacob in a vision at night and said, 'I will surely bring you back again. Joseph's own hand will close your eyes (in death)'.

There were seventy sons in all counting Jacob, Joseph and his two sons. With wives and daughters it could have been as many as 200. (CW)

When they arrived in Goshen Joseph went to meet his father. He threw his arms around him and wept for a long time. Jacob said, 'Now I am ready to die'. He was 130 years old then and lived in Egypt seventeen years (Gen. 47:28). They lived in the best part of Egypt, Rameses, but there was still a famine.

When the Egyptians' money was gone, they exchanged their livestock for food. When their livestock was gone, they sold their land for food. Then they sold themselves. They farmed the land for Pharaoh. A fifth was to go to him and four-fifths was for their livelihood and seed.

When it came time for Jacob to die, he said, 'do not bury me in Egypt'. He said Joseph's two sons would be reckoned as his. He blessed Ephraim as the first-born but he was the second son. When the land was divided in Canaan, Manasseh received the largest area.

Before his death, his sons gathered around him and he told them what would happen in days to come.

Then he said, 'bury me with my fathers in the Cave of Machpelah with Abraham, Sarah, Isaac and Rebekah and Leah. He then drew up his feet into his bed and breathed his last.

The physicians embalmed him, taking a full forty days and the Egyptians mourned for him seventy days.

All Pharaoh's officials, members of Joseph's household and his brothers went to bury him. After burying him, they all returned to Egypt.

After their return, his brothers were afraid Joseph would hold a grudge against them, but he told them, 'don't be afraid. You intended to harm me, but God intended it for good to accomplish what is now being done, the saving of many lives'.

Joseph lived 110 years. Before his death, he said, 'I am about to die but God will surely come to your aid and take you up, out of this land, to the land he promised on oath to Abraham, Isaac and Jacob. Carry my bones up from this place'.

After embalming, he was placed in a coffin in Egypt where he stayed the remainder of time they were in Egypt, the forty years of wandering and probably the years after they reached Canaan.

He was buried at Shechem in the tract of land Jacob had bought (Gen. 33:18, 19; Joshua 24:32). Joseph had lived in Shechem (Gen. 37:12, 13)

Exodus

A Review

Moses continued writing…

"Fear not to go down into Egypt; for I will make of thee a great nation… and I will surely bring the up (Gen. 46:3).

The sons of Israel (Jacob) who went to Egypt, each with his family, were: Reuben, Simeon, Levi, Judah, Issachar, Zebulun, Benjamin, Dan, Naphtali, Gad and Asher. Seventy in all. (Joseph and his sons were already there). Sons only were counted, not wives and daughters (see Gen. 46:26, 27). The number of 75 in Acts 7:14 probably includes Joseph's grandsons.

All that generation died and a new king, who did not know Joseph, came to power. The Israelites had increased so much the Egyptians were fearful of them so they put slave masters over them and put them into forced labor. To reduce the population, the midwives were told if it was a boy to kill it, by throwing it into the Nile.

Moses

When Moses was born, he was not thrown into the Nile. His mother got a papyrus basket, coated it with tar and pitch, like Noah did the Ark in Genesis 6:14, and put it among the reeds of the Nile with his sister standing watch.

Pharaoh's daughter and her attendant went down to bathe. She saw the basket, opened it and saw the baby crying. She said, 'this is one of the Hebrew babies'.

Moses' sister came forward and asked if she could get one of the Hebrew women to nurse the baby. Miriam got his own mother to nurse him. Pharaoh's daughter claimed him as her son and named him Moses (2:10).

When Moses was grown up, he saw one of the slave masters beating a Hebrew and seeing no one, killed him, hiding him in the sand.

The next day, he went out again and saw two Hebrews fighting. When Moses tried to interfere, the man said, 'who made you ruler of us? Are you thinking of killing me as you killed the Egyptian?' Moses knew what he did was known and fled the country (2:11-15).

He went to Midian. The priest of Midian had seven daughters. His name was Jethro or Reuel. He married one of them, Zipporah, and had two sons.

Moses was tending his father-in-law's flock when he saw a strange sight – a bush that was on fire, but did not burn up. When he went closer a voice called out to him. It was God.

He told Moses he had seen the misery of his people and had come down to rescue them. He wanted Moses to lead them out to the land he had promised Abraham (17:7, 8), Isaac (26:34) and Jacob (35:9-13) of Genesis. God told him, 'You are to go to the Israelites and say to them, "The Lord the God of your fathers has sent me to you," (3:15).

Go to the elders, then you and the elders go to the King and ask for a three days journey to offer sacrifices to the Lord.

Excuses:
1. Who am I that I should go? (3:11)
2. What shall I say when they ask his name? (3:13)
3. They will not believe. (4:11)
4. I am not a good speaker, I'm slow of speech. (4:10)
5. Send someone else... (4:13)

I am sending your brother, Aaron. He will be your mouth (4:14-17). He is already on his way (4:14). Moses returned to Jethro and asked to go visit his people back in Egypt and he said, 'Go in peace'. Moses took his wife and his son and started out with his rod in his hand.

Evidently Moses had not circumcised his son (see Gen. 17:9-14), because the Lord was about to kill him. His wife, Zipporah, took a flint knife and cut off her son's foreskin (circumcised him).

Moses, Aaron and the elders went to Pharaoh but he refused to let them go. Instead, he increased their work by making them find their own straw to make bricks (Chapter 5).

Moses asked the Lord, 'O Lord, why have you brought trouble on these people?' (5:22).

God said, 'say to the Israelites: I am the Lord, I will bring you out... I will bring you to the land I swore with uplifted hands to give to Abraham, to Isaac, and to Jacob' (6:8).

Moses and Aaron descended from the tribe of Levi (Jacob's third son). Moses was 80 years old and Aaron 83 when they spoke to Pharaoh.

The Lord said to Moses and Aaron, 'Take your staff and throw it down before Pharaoh and it will become a snake.' The Egyptian magicians were able to do the same, but Aaron's staff swallowed up their staffs.

The Ten Plagues

The Lord prepared the Israelites and Egyptians by sending ten plagues upon the Egyptians.

1. All the waters of Egypt turned to <u>blood</u> even in their drinking buckets. The fish died. They dug along the Nile to get water to drink. This lasted seven days.

2. The whole country was plagued with <u>frogs</u>, in the palaces, in their bedrooms, in their beds, in their ovens and kneading troughs. Pharaoh summoned Moses and Aaron. Pray to the Lord to take the frogs away. This he did and the frogs died in the houses, courtyards and fields. They were piled into heaps. Pharaoh hardened his heart again.

3. The Lord said, 'Stretch out your staff and strike the dust of the ground'. It became <u>gnats</u>. Pharaoh would not listen.

4. The Lord said to tell Pharaoh next he would send <u>flies</u>. The houses would be filled, even the ground but the flies were not where the Israelites were. Pharaoh said, you can go, but not far. After the flies left, Pharaoh hardened his heart again and refused to let them go.

5. The Lord said the next plague would be on their <u>livestock</u>. All the livestock of the Egyptians died, but not one animal belonging to the Israelites died.

6. The Lord said to Moses and Aaron, 'Take handfuls of soot from a furnace in front of Pharaoh, toss it into the air and it will cause festering <u>boils</u> to break out on men and animals throughout the land.

7. So that you may know that there is no one like me in all the earth, tomorrow I will send the worst <u>hailstorm</u> that has ever fallen on Egypt. All livestock that is left out in the field will die. Everything growing in the fields was stripped. It did not fall in Goshen.

8. Tomorrow, I will bring <u>locusts</u>. They will cover the ground so that it cannot be seen. They will devour all that the hail left and fill your houses. Now, his officials are trying to persuade Pharaoh to let them go. He asked Moses and Aaron, 'Just who will be going?' He answered, 'Our young and old, our sons and daughters, our flocks and herds'. Pharaoh said, 'No! Have only the men go, that's what you've been asking for'. He Lord sent locusts. Nothing green remained on tree or plant in all the land of Egypt.

9. Moses stretched out his hand toward the sky and <u>total darkness</u> covered all Egypt for 3 days, yet the Israelites had light. Pharaoh summoned Moses and Aaron and said, 'Go,

worship the Lord with your women and children, but leave your flocks and herds'. Moses said, 'Our livestock must go with us. Until we get there, we will not know what we are to use to worship God'. Pharaoh said to Moses, 'Get out of my sight! Don't appear before me again'. Moses said, 'Just as you say, I will never appear before you again.'

10. The Lord told Moses, 'I will bring one more plague. After that he will let you go. Tell the people to ask their neighbors for articles of silver and gold. About midnight, I will go throughout Egypt and <u>every first born son will die</u>. There will be loud wailing throughout Egypt more than has ever been or ever will be again. Among the Israelites, not a dog will bark' (Ex. 7:14-11:10).

Passover

The Lord said to Moses, 'This month is to be for you the first month of your year' (and the beginning of their Passover, our April 14th). They were to take a male lamb, one year old, keep it up from the 10th to the 14th day, kill it and put blood on their doorposts. They were to roast it and eat it with unleavened bread and bitter herbs. They were to eat it with their loins girded (cloak tucked into their belt) sandals on their feet and their staff in their hand and in haste. Each year thereafter, it was to be an annual observance and was to last a week. It was called the Passover or The Feast of Unleavened Bread. The first celebration after leaving Egypt was in the Desert of Sinai, in the first month of the second year, at twilight on the fourteenth day (Numbers 9:1-3). No uncircumcised male was to eat of it.

The Exodus

That same night, the Lord struck down <u>all</u> the first born of Egypt. There was not a house without someone dead.

Pharaoh summoned Moses and Aaron and said, 'Go and also bless me'.

They took their dough before the yeast was added carrying their kneading trough and the articles of silver, gold and clothing the Egyptians had given them.

They left from Rameses and journeyed to Succoth. There were about 600,000 men, besides women and children. Many other people, besides Israelites went with them as well as large droves of livestock. They had lived in Egypt 430 years to the day.

God led them around by the desert road toward the Red Sea. They took arms, also Joseph's bones (see Gen. 50:24-25).

By day, the Lord went ahead of them in a pillar of cloud and by night, a pillar of fire. When Pharaoh realized the people had left, he said, 'What have we done? We have lost their services!'

He took 600 chariots and pursued them. When the Israelites saw them they were terrified and said, 'It would have been better to serve them than to die in the desert!'.

Moses said, 'Fear not, stand still and see the salvation of the Lord' (Ex. 14:13).

Moses stretched out his staff over the sea. All that night, God sent a strong east wind and divided the waters so that the Israelites went across on dry land with a wall of water on their right and on their left.

The Egyptians went after them with their chariots. The Lord made their wheels come off. Moses stretched out this hand again and the waters returned, covering and drowning the Egyptians. Not one survived.

The Israelites feared the Lord and put their trust in Moses (Chapter 14).

For three days after that, they traveled in the desert without finding water. When they did find it, it was bitter. After Moses threw a piece of wood into the water, it became sweet. This place was Marah.

The Israelites started grumbling about food. They remembered he food they had in Egypt. The Lord said to Moses, 'I will rain down bread from heaven for you'. Each morning they were to gather enough for the day. On the 6th day they were to gather twice as much, as the 7th day was a day of rest. It could be boiled or baked. It was called manna. In the evening, they had quail. It was white like coriander seed and tasted like wafers made with honey. They ate manna 40 years until they reached the border of Canaan (see Joshua 5:10-12, Numbers 11:1-34 for more details).

God told Moses to take his staff and strike a rock to bring forth water at Horeb.

Remember, they had brought arms which they had to use at Rephidim. The Amalikites came and attacked the Israelites. Joshua led the battle. Moses held up his hands during the battle. When he grew tired, Aaron and Hur held his hands up. Moses was told to write about it (17:8-14).

Jethro Visits

Moses' father-in-law, Jethro, had heard of all God had done. He brought Moses' wife and his sons to him and was delighted to hear everything first hand that the Lord had done (Chapter 18).

When he saw how much time Moses spent in judging the people he offered a suggestion that Moses should select capable men to judge less difficult cases and only send the difficult cases to him.

In the third month, after they left Egypt, they came to the Desert of Sinai and camped in front of the mountain (19:1, 2).

The Lord said to Moses, 'I am going to come to you in a dense cloud so the people will hear me speaking to you. Have them wash their clothes. On the third day I will come down. Put limits, because whoever touches the mountain will be put to death'.

On the morning of the third day there was thunder and lightning, a thick cloud and a very loud trumpet blast. Everyone trembled. The Lord called Moses to the top of the mountain.

God spoke the Ten Commandments

1. You shall have <u>no other Gods</u> before me.
2. You shall not make unto thee any <u>graven images</u>.
3. Thou shalt not take the name of the Lord thy God in vain.
4. Remember the Sabbath day to keep it holy.
5. Honor thy father and thy mother.
6. Thou shalt not kill.
7. Thou shalt not commit adultery.
8. Thou shalt not steal.
9. Thou shalt not bear false witness against thy neighbor.
10. Thou shalt not covet.   (Exodus 20)

Other Laws

If you buy a Hebrew servant, he is to serve you six years; in the seventh year, he shall go free. If he has married and has a family and does not want to go free, the master shall pierce his ear with an awl. Then he will be his servant for life (21:2-6).

If anyone strikes a man and kills him, he shall be surely put to death. If accidental, he can flee to a place I will designate.

Eye for eye and tooth for tooth...

Restitution must be made if they steal, or harm comes to an animal in their care.

Anyone who has sexual relations with an animal must be put to death...

Do not mistreat an alien, for you were aliens in Egypt.

Do not take advantage of a widow or orphan...

If you lend money to my people who are poor, do not charge interest.

You must give me the first born of your sons.

Do not eat the meat of an animal torn by wild beasts.

Do not follow the crowd in doing wrong.

Do not accept a bribe.

Sabbath Laws

For six years you are to sow your fields but on the seventh year, let the land lie idle. Six days do your work, but on the seventh do not work.

The Annual Feasts

Three times a year you are to celebrate a festival to me.

1. *Passover,* or Feast of Unleavened Bread, for a week in the month of Abib (April) for that is the month you came out of Egypt.

2. *Pentecost,* or Feast of Harvest, for the first-fruits of the crops you sow in the ground.

3. *Harvest,* or Feast of Ingathering, when you gather your crops.

I am sending my angel to go ahead of you and bring you into the land... I will send my terror ahead of you. Little by little, I will drive them out. Do not let them live in your land or they will cause you to sin against me (Chapter 23).

Moses wrote down everything the Lord had said (24:4). He read to them the Book of the Covenant.

Moses on the Mountain

The Lord said to Moses, 'Come up to me on the mountain...I will give you the stone tablets on which I have written the laws and commands'. Joshua, his aide, went with him. They stayed on the mountain forty days and forty nights (24:18).

The Lord told Moses to have the people bring an offering (free will). The things they were asked to bring were: gold, silver and bronze. Blue, purple and scarlet yarn, fine linen and goat hair, ram skins dyed red and hides of sea cows, acacia wood, olive oil for light, spices for the anointing, oil and incense, onyx stones and other gems to be mounted on the ephod and breast piece. These things were to be used in building the tabernacle according to the pattern I will show you in Chapter 25:1-9.

The Ark

They were to make an ark 45 inches long, 27 inches high and 27 inches wide overlaid with pure gold. It also was to have a ring on each corner to put poles through to carry it by.

The Lamp Stand

They were to make a lamp stand of pure gold with 3 branches on each side. Then make seven lamps to sit upon it.

The Tabernacle

The Tabernacle was to have ten curtains surrounding it: six feet wide by 42 feet long. Five were to be joined together by loops and clasps.

They were to be made of linen; blue, purple and scarlet yarn. The tent over the Tabernacle also had curtains. The door of the tent was called the tent of meeting, where Moses and others met with the people. Here, God spoke with Moses (Ex. 29:42).

The altar of burnt offering was to be made of acacia wood, 90 inches long by 90 inches wide and 54 inches high. It was to be overlaid with brass. It was to have horns. (This was to bind the sacrificed animals, Ps. 118:27). All the vessels used in the sacrifices were to be made of brass.

The lamps were to use pure olive oil and to be kept burning.

The Priestly Garments

The Levites at that time were Aaron and his four sons, Nadab, Abihu, Eleazar and Ithamar.

Their apparel when ministering as priests was a breast plate, an ephod, a robe, an embroidered coat, a turban and a sash, made of gold, blue, purple and scarlet linen (28:5). They were to make an Ephod, square and attached to each corner. Two onyx stones with the names of the children of Israel, six on each one from the eldest to the youngest were to be engraved on them (28:6-11).

They were also to make a breast piece, 9 inches square with rows of twelve different precious stones on it, representing each tribe. It had a gold chain to go over the head, like a necklace, and also attached at the waist. It was to be worn when Aaron entered the Holy Place. The Urim and Thummim were in the breast piece. This was a means of making decisions.

Other priestly garments were robes of blue cloth, with bells around it so he could be heard. A tunic of fine linen, sashes and headbands, linen undergarments reaching from the waist to the thigh. They had to be consecrated by washing with water dressing in the above clothing and pouring anointing oil on their heads.

A bull was brought to the front of the Tent of Meeting. Aaron and his sons were to lay their hands on its head and slaughter it.

The breast and thigh of the sacrifice was to be for Aaron's family to eat.

Each day, morning and evening a year old lamb was to be offered at the entrance to the Tent of Meeting.

An altar for burning incense was also to be made from acacia wood and overlaid with gold. It too, had two gold rings for poles to transport it. It was to be 18 inches long by 18 inches wide by 36 inches high and was to keep burning.

A bronze basin for washing hands and feet was to be made. Before entering to the Tent of Meeting, they had to wash with water, both hands and feet (30:17-21).

The recipe for anointing oil was myrrh, cinnamon, cane, cassia and olive oil. This was to anoint the Tent of Meeting, the Ark, table, lamp stand, altar of incense, altar of burnt offering and its utensils and Aaron and his sons. It was considered sacred, not to be used for any other purpose.

The recipe for incense was gum resin, onycha, galbanum and frankincense (equal amounts). This recipe was not to be made or used for any other purpose either.

The craftsmen who were given special abilities by the Lord were Bezalel of the tribe of Judah and Oholiab of the tribe of Dan.

All this information was given to Moses while he was on Mt. Sinai for forty days.

The Golden Calf

Moses was gone so long the people thought something had happened to him. They asked Aaron to make them a god. He asked for their gold earrings, made a golden calf and an altar in front of the calf. He then announced, 'Tomorrow will be a festival for the Lord'. The next day they rose early, sacrificed burnt offerings, sat down to eat and drink and got up to indulge in revelry.

The Lord said to Moses, 'Go down, your people have become corrupt'. He wanted to destroy them and make a great nation out of Moses. Moses talked to God. He said, 'Oh Lord, why should your anger burn against your people?... What would the Egyptians say?...Turn from your fierce anger, relent... Remember your servants Abraham, Isaac and Jacob to whom you swore by your own self'. The Lord did relent.

Moses went back down with the two tables in his hands, written with God's own hand.

When Joshua, who went with him, heard the noise he said, 'There is the sound of war in our camp'.

Moses said, 'It is the sound of singing that I hear'. When he approached the camp and saw the calf and dancing, his anger burned and he threw the tables, breaking them to pieces. He took the calf, burned it, ground it to powder, scattered it on the water and made the Israelites drink it. He was also angry with Aaron, who had told him, 'They gave me their gold, I threw it in the fire and out came this calf'.

Moses said to them, 'Whoever is for the Lord, come to me'. The Levites came. The Lord said for them to kill their brother, friend and neighbor. That day about 3000 people died.

Moses asked the Lord, 'Please forgive their sin, but if not, then blot me out of the book you have written'. The Lord said, 'Whoever has sinned against me, I will blot out of my book'. The Lord struck the people with a plague (Chapter 32).

The Lord said to Moses, 'Leave this place but I will not go with you'. Moses went to the Tent of Meeting. He told the Lord, 'How will they know that you are pleased with me unless you go with us?' God allowed Moses to see his back (Chapter 33). He said no one could see His face and live.

The Lord told Moses to chisel out two stone tables like the first ones and he'd rewrite what He had written. This time he went by himself. He was there forty days and nights without eating bread or drinking water.

When he came down, his face was radiant. They were afraid, so he put a veil over his face (Chapter 34).

They started building the tabernacle and its furnishings. Everyone who was willing brought the gold, silver, bronze, jewelry, linen, hides, etc. Every skilled woman spun with her hands and brought what she had spun.

Bezalel and Oholiab whom the Lord had filled with skill, received the offerings the people had brought and began the work. There was more than enough.

They made everything according to the pattern God had given Moses on the Mount. The Tabernacle, the Ark, the Table, the Altar of Incense, the Lamp Stand, the Altar of Burnt Offering, the Basin for Washing and the Courtyard. The amount of materials used was recorded by the Levites (Ch. 38:21-31).

Everything Completed

The priestly garments, Ephod and breast piece, robes and everything to be worn, the Tabernacle and its furnishings were inspected by Moses and he found everything to be as the Lord had designed it.

The Lord said to Moses, set everything up...on the first day of the first month of the second year.

1. The *Tabernacle* was set up with frames, crossbars and tent.

2. The *Testimony* was placed in the Ark. It was placed in the Tabernacle with a curtain shielding it.

3. The *Table* was placed in the Tent of Meeting and bread was placed on it.

4. The *Lamp Stand* was placed in the Tent of Meeting opposite the table and the lamps set up.

5. The *Gold Altar* was placed in the Tent of Meeting in front of the curtain to burn incense.

6. The *Altar of Burnt Offering* was set near the entrance to the Tent of Meeting for burnt offerings and grain offerings.

7. The *Basin* was placed between the Tent of Meeting and the altar, for washing of hands and feet.

8. The *Courtyard* around the Tabernacle was set up with a curtain at the entrance to the courtyard.

Moses finished the work. The cloud covered the Tent of Meeting and the glory of the Lord filled the Tabernacle.

In all their travels, whenever the Cloud lifted from above the Tabernacle, they would set out.

One year after leaving Egypt the Tabernacle was completed, everything set up and the laws given (40:17). Exodus Chapters 13 through 40 cover one year.

Leviticus

A Review

Moses continues his writing. One year after leaving Egypt, the Tabernacle, Tent of Meeting, the furnishings and the priests clothing are prepared. The cloud covered the Tent of Meeting and the glory of the Lord filled the Tabernacle.

The Lord called to Moses and spoke to him from the Tent of Meeting. He said, 'Speak to the Israelites and say to them "When any of you brings an offering to the Lord, bring as your offering an animal from either the herd of the flock" (bull, goat, or sheep)' (22:19).

Burnt Offerings

Herd: Male without defect, offered at the entrance of the Tent of Meeting. Skin it, cut it in pieces, wash the inner parts and legs with water and burn all of it on the altar.

Flock: Sheep or goat, male without defect, offered on the north side of the altar. Cut it in pieces, wash the inner parts and legs with water and burn all of it on the altar.

Birds: Dove or young pigeon. Wring off its head, drain the blood on the side of the altar, remove the crop and throw it on the east side of the altar where the ashes are. Pull it apart by the wings, but not completely. Burn it.

Grain Offerings

The grain offering shall be from fine flour with oil and incense on it. The priest shall take a handful and burn it as a memorial on the altar. The rest belongs to Aaron and his sons. If baked, use no leaven (yeast) but salt it.

Fellowship Offering

An animal from the herd, either male or female, but without defect. Remove all fat and burn it. The fat is the Lords. They were not to eat any fat or blood (3:17).

Sin Offering

If the priest sins unintentionally, he must bring a young bull, pour its blood at the base of the altar, remove the fat and burn if at the entrance to the Tent of Meeting. The rest must be burned outside the camp. The sin offering was not to be eaten. If the whole Israelite community sins unintentionally, when they become aware of the matter, they are to offer a young bull as a sin offering before the Tent of Meeting. The elders are to lay their hands on the bull's head before slaughter. The priest will make atonement for them and they will be forgiven.

If a leader sins, he must offer a male goat.

If a member of the community (common people) sins, he must offer a female goat. If a person sins because he does not speak up regarding something he has seen or if he touches anything unclean, such as a dead animal, he must confess the sin and bring a female lamb or goat for sacrifice. If he cannot afford a lamb, he is to bring two doves or two young pigeons. Even if this is too much, he can bring about two quarts of fine flour for his sin offering. He must not put oil or incense on this because it is a sin offering.

Guilt Offering

If a person commits something wrong against the Lord, even though he does not know it, he is guilty and must make an offering; a ram from the flock. He must make restitution if possible and add 1/5 to its value. The priest will make atonement for him. These sins might be deceiving his neighbor of something left in his care, lying or cheating, or bearing false witness. The same law applies to the sin offering and guilt offering. If the priest so desires, he can keep the hide for himself (7:8).

The Priests' Share

The breast and right thigh are for Aaron and his sons as their regular share as priests. These regulations were given to Moses on the day the Israelites were commanded to bring their offering to the Lord in the Desert of Sinai (8:38).

Ordination Offering

The Lord said to Moses, 'Bring Aaron and his sons, their garments, the anointing oil, the bull for the sin offering, the two rams, the bread made without yeast and gather the entire assembly at the entrance to the Tent of Meeting.

First Moses washed them with water, then put on Aaron's tunic, robe, ephod and breast piece. He put the Urim and Thummim in the breast piece, the turban on his head with the diadem on it.

Aaron as well as his sons and the Tabernacle were anointed with oil. His sons put on their special clothes; tunics with sashes and headbands.

They offered a bull for the sin offering. Moses slaughtered it as well as the ram for a burnt offering. Another ram was slaughtered for the ordination.

Some of the blood was put on the lobe of Aaron's right ear, the thumb of his right hand and the big toe of his right foot.

They prepared the ram according to the instructions God gave Moses on the Mount. Then Moses told Aaron and his sons to cook the meat at the entrance to the Tent of meeting and eat it with the bread made without yeast.

They had to stay in the Tent of Meeting for seven days and nights until their ordination was completed (Chapters 8 and Exodus 29:1-37).

The Priests Begin Their Ministry

On the eighth day Moses summoned Aaron, his sons and the elders of Israel. Moses said to Aaron, 'Come to the altar and sacrifice your sin offering and your burnt offering and make atonement for yourself and the people, as the Lord has commanded'. He also offered the grain offering and the fellowship offering.

After doing all this in the way it was commanded, he stepped down. Fire came out from the presence of the Lord and consumed the burnt offering and the fat portions on the altar.

The people shouted for joy.

Nadab and Abihu

Aaron's sons, Nadab and Abihu, took their censers (flat pans in which burning coals are carried), put fire in them and added incense, and they offered unauthorized fire before the Lord contrary to His command.

Fire came out from the presence of the Lord and consumed them and they died (10:1, 2).

It seems as if their sins were adding incense to the fire. In Chapter 16 verse 12, Aaron the high priest added incense on the Day of Atonement when he went into the Most Holy Place once a year.

They were carried outside the camp. The people were allowed to mourn.

The remaining two sons of Aaron, Eleazer and Ithamar were told not to leave the entrance to the Tent of Meeting because they too had been anointed and would be taking over as priests.

They were told they could eat the offering, breast and thigh, also Aaron's family was to eat it (10:12-15) but Aaron was unable to eat that day because of the sorrowful things that had befallen him (10:16-2, the death of his two sons.

Clean and Unclean Food

Clean

Land Animals: Those that have a split hoof, completely divided and chews cud.

Water Creatures: Any that has fins and scales.

Birds: Those that have jointed legs for hopping on the ground (locust, katydid, cricket or grasshopper).

Unclean

Unsplit Hoof: camel, Coney, rabbit, pig

No Fins or Scales: Catfish

Birds of Prey: eagle, vulture, owl, gull, hawk…

Flying Insects: any that walk on all fours

Animals That Move About on the Ground: rat, lizard, gecko…Chapter 11

Purification After Childbirth

If a Son – She is unclean for seven days as with her monthly period. On the eighth day, he is to be circumcised. She must wait 33 days to be purified from her bleeding.

If a Daughter – She is unclean for two weeks. She must wait 66 days to be purified from her bleeding.

She is to bring to the priest at the Tent of Meeting, a year old lamb and a young pigeon or dove so he can make atonement for her and then she will be ceremonially clean (Chapter 12).

Regulations About Skin and Disease

When anyone had a swelling or rash or bright spot on his skin that may become an infectious disease, he had to go to Aaron or his sons to examine. If the hair in the sore had turned white, it was an infectious skin disease. If the hair has not turned white, he would be put in isolation for seven days. If the sore has faded at the length of that time, he would be clean. If it has spread, he is unclean.

If someone had a burn, the same procedure would be followed. If someone had a sore on his head or chin, it would be checked for yellow hair.

If a man had a swollen sore on his head that was reddish-white it was infectious. It could be leprosy. He must live alone outside of the camp if it was leprosy (12:1-45).

Mildew

If any clothing is contaminated with mildew and it is greenish or reddish, it must be shown to the priest. If after 7 days the mildew has spread, the clothing must be burned up.

If it has not spread, the article was to be washed twice (13:47-58).

If anyone suspected there was mildew in his house, he must go to the priest. They were to empty the house before he went in to examine it. The house would be closed up for 7 days then re-examined. If I had spread, the contaminated stones were to be replaced, the walls scraped and plastered with new clay. If the mildew reappeared the house must be torn down. If the mildew has not spread, the priest shall pronounce the house clean. He is to take two birds, kill one and dip the other in its blood, sprinkle the house seven times to purify it and release the live bird.

Cleansing From Infectious Skin Diseases

The diseased person was to be examined outside the camp. If the person has been healed it is to be done like the house except the person is to be sprinkled with the bird's blood. Then the person is to wash his clothes, shave off all his hair and bathe with water. He must stay outside his tent for 7 days. After that he must shave off all his hair (head, beard, eyebrows). He must wash his clothes and bathe and he will be clean.

On the eighth day, he is to bring a guilt offering and a sin offering (see Lev. 6:24-30 and 7:1-5) to make atonement from his uncleanness (Chapter 14).

Discharges Causing Uncleanness

When a man has a bodily discharge, the discharge is unclean. Any bed he lays on, anything he sits on, anyone who touches his bed or where he sits must wash his clothes and bathe. The man who has the discharge must make a sin offering and a burnt offering because of the discharge (Chapter 15).

When a man has an emission of semen, both the man and the woman must bathe with water.

When a woman has her regular flow of blood, she will be impure for 7 days. Whatever she lies on, sits on or whoever touches where she's touched must wash his clothes and bathe (see Rachel in Gen. 31:34). She must not have sexual relations during her monthly period (Lev. 18:19).

The Day of Atonement—Yom Kippur

The Day of Atonement is the most holy day of the Jewish year. It is the seventh month and tenth day of the Jewish calendar (16:29-34). Here are the steps Aaron, the high priest, must take before entering the Most Holy Place.

1. He must have a young bull for a sin offering and a ram for a burnt offering.
2. He is to put on the linen tunic, linen undergarment, tie the linen sash and put on the linen turban.
3. He must bathe himself before putting them on.
4. From the Israelites, he is to have ready two male goats for a sin offering and a ram for a burnt offering.
5. Aaron is to first offer his bull for his own sins and those of his household.
6. He is to take the two goats and present them before the Lord at the entrance of the Tent of Meeting.
7. He is to cast lots for the two goats, one for the Lord and the other for the scapegoat.
8. One goat will be sacrificed for a sin offering, the other will be used for making atonement by sending it into the desert as a scapegoat.
9. Aaron is to slaughter the bull for his own sin offering and that of his household. He is to take a censer full of burning coals from the altar, add two handfuls of incense and take them behind the curtain.
10. He is to take some of the bull's blood and with his finger sprinkle it on the front of the atonement cover (seven times).
11. Then he is to slaughter the goat for the sin offering (for the people) and do the same thing. This way he will make atonement.
12. No one is to be in the Tent of Meeting at the time Aaron goes in to make atonement in the Most Holy Place for himself, his household and the whole community of Israel.
13. When he comes out, he shall take some of the bull's blood and sprinkle it with his finger seven times on the horn of the altar.
14. When he has finished, he shall bring forward the live goat, lay his hands on its head, confess the sins of the

people, putting them on the goat's head and send it away in the care of a man.

15. The goat will carry on itself all their sins to a solitary place and be released in the desert.
16. Aaron must then go into the Tent of Meeting, take off his linen garments and leave them there, bathe, then put on his regular clothes.
17. The man who takes the scapegoat off must wash his clothes and bathe.

These were the steps the high priest was supposed to take on the one day a year for atonement for the priests and the people. Their sins were not forgiven, but covered for another year (16:34).

Eating Blood Forbidden

The Israelites were not to sacrifice privately. They must bring their sacrifice to the Tent of Meeting and let the priest do it.

They must not eat blood. It is life. Anyone who hunts an animal or bird must drain out the blood and cover it with earth (Chapter 17).

Unlawful Sexual Relations

The Lord said to Moses, 'You must not do as they do in Egypt or in the land where you are going'. Obey my laws.

1. Do not approach any close relative (for sex).
2. Do not approach your mother.
3. Do not approach your father's wife.
4. Do not approach your sister or half sister.
5. Do not approach your son's or daughter's daughter.
6. Do not approach your aunt.
7. Do not approach your daughter-in-law or brother's wife.
8. Do not approach both a woman and daughter.

9. Do not take your wife's sister as a rival wife (while your wife is living).
10. Do not approach a woman during her monthly period.
11. Do not approach your neighbor's wife.
12. Do not lie with a man as with a woman.
13. Do not have sexual relations with an animal (neither man nor woman).
14. Do not give any of your children to be sacrificed.(Ch 18)

Other Laws

The Lord told Moses to say to the people, 'be holy because I, the Lord your God, am holy'.

1. Respect your mother and father.
2. Observe the Sabbaths.
3. Do not make idols.
4. Do not eat a sacrifice after the second day.
5. Do not reap to the very edges of your field or pick up what's fallen. Leave that for the poor.
6. Do not steal.
7. Do not lie.
8. Do not deceive.
9. Do not swear falsely.
10. Do no defraud your neighbor.
11. Do not hold back wages of a hired man overnight.
12. Do not curse the deaf or put a stumbling block in front of the blind.
13. Judge your neighbors fairly.
14. Do not slander.
15. Do not endanger your neighbor's life.
16. Do not hate your brother.
17. Do not seek revenge or bear a grudge.
18. Do not mate different kinds of animals.

19. Do not plant your fields with 2 kinds of seed.

20. Do not wear clothing woven of 2 kinds of material.

21. When you plant a fruit tree, don't eat until 5 years.

22. Do not eat any meat with blood in it.

23. Do not practice divination or sorcery.

24. Do not cut your hair at the sides or edge of the beard.

25. Do not cut your bodies of put tattoos on yourself.

26. Do not make your daughter a prostitute.

27. Observe the Sabbath and revere my sanctuary.

28. Do not turn to mediums or seek out spiritists.

29. Rise in the presence of the elderly.

30. Do not mistreat the alien living among you.

31. Do not use dishonest measuring standards.

32. 'Keep all my decrees and laws and follow them. I am the Lord' Chapter 19

Rules for Priests

They were not to touch a dead body unless it was a close relative, such as a mother, father, son daughter, brother or unmarried sister.

They were not to shave their heads or the edges of their beards or cut their bodies.

They must not marry women that were prostitutes or divorced.

The high priest must not make himself unclean even for his father or mother.

The woman he married must be a virgin of his own people.

Even if descended from Aaron, no one who has a defect would be allowed to present offerings to God by fire. The defects would include: blind or lame, disfigured or deformed, crippled in hand or foot, hunchbacked or dwarfed, any eye defect, running sores or damaged testicles. He could eat the food but not serve in the sanctuary (Chapter 21).

Who May Eat the Sacrifices

No one who is unclean (has an infectious skin disease, touches something dead, or has an emission of semen, etc.) shall not eat any of the sacred offerings unless he shall bathe himself. When the sun goes down, he will be clean.

The priests' family, a bought slave, a daughter who becomes a widow or is divorced and moves back home may eat. A daughter who marries anyone, other than a priest may not eat the sacred offering (22:1-13).

Unacceptable Sacrifices

When offering a burnt offering, it must be a male, without defect. If it has a defect it will not be accepted.

When a calf, lamb or goat is born, it is to remain with its mother for seven days. After that, it would be acceptable as an offering.

Do not slaughter a mother and its young on the same day (22:17-28).

Appointed Feasts

1. *Passover:* Begins at twilight on the 14th day of the first month. It lasts a week. The bread must be made without yeast. An offering should be made each day. On the first and last day assemble and do no work.

2. *Pentecost:* Seven weeks or 50 days after the Passover, also called Feast of Weeks. It lasted only one day (23:21). They were to bring two loaves of bread baked with yeast, offer sacrifices, assemble and do no work (23:15-21).

3. *The Feast of Tabernacles:* was celebrated on the 15th day of the 7th month and lasted seven days. That week,

the people lived in booths as a reminder of their wilderness wandering. It also celebrated the harvest of the fruits of the land. The first and last days were for rest. Many sacrifices were offered (23:33-43).

The Oil and Bread

The Israelites were to bring clear oil made from pressed olives to keep the lamps on the gold lamp stand burning continually (see Ex. 37). They were to take about a gallon of fine flour for each loaf. They were to bake 12 loaves, making two rows of six loaves. This was to be done weekly and was for Aaron and his sons (24:1-9).

A Blasphemer Stoned

One of the mixed multitude (an Israelite mother and an Egyptian father, Ex. 12:38) fought with an Israelite and blasphemed the Lord. The Lord said to Moses, 'Take the blasphemer outside the camp. All who heard him are to lay their hands on his head and the entire assembly are to stone him'. The laying on of their hands passed the guilt to him (24:10-16).

The Sabbath Year

The Sabbath Day was a day of rest for God and man.

The seventh year was a rest for the land. Do not sow your fields or prune your vineyards. Whatever the land produces may be eaten (25:1-7).

The Year of Jubilee

Count off seven Sabbaths of years (49). Sound a trumpet on the 10th day of the 7th month (the Day of Atonement) and proclaim liberty throughout the land.

Do not sow, do not reap, eat what comes up. The sixth year will yield enough for three years.

In this year, everyone is to return to his own property or family.

If you buy or sell, do it based on the number of years left. The land must not be sold permanently. The land was the Lords. The people were only sojourners.

If one should become poor and have to sell, a near kinsman could redeem it (see Ruth 4:1-10). It would remain in the hands of the buyer until the year of Jubilee.

If a man sells a house in a walled city, he has a year to redeem it. After that, the buyer keeps it permanently. If the house is in open country, it can be returned in the year of Jubilee.

The Levites always have the right to redeem their property. You must not charge a poor fellow countrymen interest or sell him food at a profit.

No Israelite who becomes poor and sells himself should be treated as a slave but as a hired worker until the Year of Jubilee.

Your slaves are to come from the nations around you. They can become your property.

If an Israelite sells himself to an alien, one of his relatives can redeem him with the price based on the number of years left until the year of Jubilee, when he would have to be released (25:8-55).

Reward for Obedience

If you follow my decree and obey my commands I will send you rain, the ground will yield its crops, the trees will yield their fruit. You will eat all your want and live in safety in your land.

I will grant you peace. You will lie down and no one will make you afraid. I will remove savage beasts from the land and your enemies will fall by the sword. I will make you fruitful and increase your numbers.

I broke the bars of your yolk and enabled you to walk with heads held high.

Punishment for Disobedience

But, if you will not listen to me, if you reject my laws and violate my covenant, I will do this to you:

I will bring terror, wasting diseases, fever, that will destroy your sight.

You will plant seeds in vain, be defeated by your enemies, flee when no one is pursuing you.

Wild animals will rob you of your children and destroy your cattle. I will send a plague among you and you will be given to your enemies... I will turn your cities into ruins and scatter you among the nations.

The land will enjoy its Sabbath Year while you are in the country of your enemies...

When their uncircumcised hearts are humbled and they pay for their sin, I will remember my covenant with Abraham, Isaac and Jacob. I will not reject them completely.

These are the decrees, laws and regulations the Lord established on Mt. Sinai between himself and the Israelites through Moses (26:46).

Redeeming What is the Lord's

A vow was not required but if made, it was required that it be fulfilled.

A person could be dedicated to serve. A house could be dedicated. If the person wants to redeem it, he must add a fifth to its value. If he dedicates land, he could redeem it by adding a fifth to the value. The first born animals already belong to the Lord.

A tithe of everything from the land belongs to the Lord. Every tenth animal that 'passes under the shepherd's rod' is the Lords. (This means as the animals pass single file out of an enclosure, every 10th animal is marked for the tithe).

There are the commands the Lord gave Moses on Mt. Sinai for the Israelites (27:34).

Numbers

A Review

Moses continues...

The Lord spoke to Moses in the Tent of Meeting in the Desert of Sinai on the first day of the second month of the second year, after they came out of Egypt. He said:

"Take a Census"

Take a census of the whole Israelite community by clans. List every man by name, twenty years old or more, who is able to serve in the army.

A man, the leader, from each tribe was to assist Moses and Aaron. The numbers from each tribe was:

Reuben	46,500	Simeon	59,300
Gad	45,650	Judah	74,600
Issachar	54,400	Zebulun	57,400
Ephraim	40,500	Manasseh	32,200
Benjamin	35,400	Dan	62,700
Asher	41,500	Naphtali	53,400
			603,550

The families of the tribe of Levi were not counted. They did not go to war. They had charge of the Tabernacle, to take care of it and transport it when they moved.

The Arrangement of the Camp

Each tribe had a special place to set up camp. Each tribe had its standard 'flag'. Moses Aaron and his sons were to camp in front of the Tent of Meeting. They were responsible for the care of the sanctuary. No one else could approach it (3:38). The others were further away.

When they moved, they had a special order as to who was first and last. They started from the east toward the sunrise.

The Lord said, 'I have taken the Levites in place of the first born'. Take a count of them that are 1 month old or more.

There were 22,000 (3:39). Then a count was made of the Israelites one month old or more. There were 22,273, a difference of 273.

Redemption money was collected for the difference, five shekels (about two cents) for each one.

Levite men 30 to 50 years old were to serve in the Tent of Meeting.

Preparation for Moving

The Ark
When it was time to move, Aaron and his sons would go in, take down the shielding curtain and wrap the ark with it, put hides of sea cows over this and a solid blue cloth over that. Last, they put the poles in place for transporting.

Table of Presence
They were to spread a blue cloth over the table, plates, dishes, bowls and jars. The bread was to remain on it. Over the blue cloth they were to spread a scarlet cloth, cover that with hides of sea cows and put its poles in place.

Lamp Stand
They are to take the blue cloth and cover the lamp stand, lamps, wick trimmer, trays and jars used for oil. They are to wrap it and all its accessories in a covering of sea cows and put it on a carrying frame.

Gold Altar

Wrap it in a blue cloth as well as all the articles used for ministering in the sanctuary. Put poles in the altar and the rest on a carrying frame, after covering with hides of sea cows.

Bronze Altar

Remove the ashes and spread a purple cloth over it. Place on it all the utensils that belong to it (fire pans, meat forks, shovels and sprinkling bowls). Spread a covering of sea cow hides and put its poles in place. After everything is finished and they are ready to move, the Kohathites, sons of Levi, are to carry them, but are not to go into the sanctuary and look.

(All this wrapping and preparation may seem too much unless you've seen the conditions that still exist in the wilds of Africa. When we went to visit our daughter's family in Kenya and went to different places of interest, we sometimes had to take our own food in the bed of a pickup truck through places that had no roads, like this country in the early days. If there were dirt roads, you had to go real slow because of the many holes. The Israelites, being in the desert, had lots of sand like we see on the news in Iraq and Afghanistan, so it was necessary to keep the articles clean.) [C.W.]

Eleazar, son of Aaron, was in charge of the oil, fragrant incense, grain offering and anointing oil, the entire Tabernacle and everything in it.

The Gershonites' Duties

Their men, aged 30 to 50, served in the work at the Tent of Meeting. They were to carry the curtains of the Tabernacle, Tent of Meeting, its covering and outer covering of sea cows, curtains for the entrance, the courtyard and altar. Also the ropes and equipment used in its service (4:21-26). There were 2630 men Ithamar directed in this.

The Merarites' Duties

Their men aged 30 to 50, also served in the work at the Tent of Meeting. Their duty was to carry the frames of the Tabernacle, its crossbars, posts and bases, as well as the parts of the courtyard with bases, tent pegs, ropes and all their related equipment. Each man was assigned a specific thing to carry each time they moved. There were 3200 men and Ithamar, son of Aaron, also directed this.

The Kohathites' Duties

The Kohathites were responsible for the care of the sanctuary. They were responsible for the care of the table, lamp stand, altars, curtain and everything related to their use. Their leader was Eleazar, son of Aaron. When everything was covered and ready to move, the Kohathites were to do the carrying of the things in the Tent of Meeting. There were 2750 men. The total number of men to do the work and carry the Tent of Meeting was 8580 (Chapter 4).

Restitution for Wrongs

When a man or woman wrongs another, he must confess the sin and make full restitution, adding $1/5^{th}$ to its value.

Test for an Unfaithful Wife

If a husband suspects his wife has been unfaithful to him, he can take an offering of barley flour and take her to the priest. He shall take some holy water (the only time it is used in the Bible), put dust from the Tabernacle floor into it, loosen her hair, and put the grain offering in her hands while he holds bitter water. The priest then will put the woman under an oath

(If you have gone astray while married to your husband…may the Lord cause your people to curse and denounce
you when He causes your thigh to waste away and your abdomen
to swell). If she drinks the bitter water and this happens, she has
defiled herself. If nothing happens, she is free. This was called
the Law of Jealousy (Ch 5). No case was recorded.

The Nazarite Vow

This vow was voluntary, but if a man or woman wanted to
make a vow for a certain length of time for total consecration to
the service of the Lord, they must:
1. Not eat or drink anything that comes from the grapevine.
2. No razor may be used on his head.
3. He must not go near a dead body, even his family.

If someone dies suddenly in his presence, he must make
five offerings:
1. Two doves or two young pigeons
2. A year old ram as an offering (fellowship)
3. A year old lamb for a burnt offering
4. A year old ewe for a sin offering
5. Grain, drink and bread offerings

He must shave off the hair he dedicated and place it in the
fire under the fire of the ram (the fellowship offering). After that,
he may drink wine. These things were to be offered *after* the
vow had ended. Hopefully none would die in his presence (Ch 6).

Offerings at the Dedication of the Tabernacle

When the Tabernacle was finished, anointed and consecrated, the tribal leaders made offerings. They brought six
covered carts, from every two tribes, and twelve oxen, one from
each tribe. The Gershonites got two carts and four oxen. The
Merarites got four carts and eight oxen.

The Kohathites did not receive any because they carried the holy things on their shoulders by means of poles (4:4-15). For the next twelve days, the tribes, one at a time, would bring an offering. Each offering was the same thing:

1. One silver plate (130 shekels)
2. One silver sprinkling bowl, filled with flour with oil as a grain offering.
3. One gold dish, filled with incense
4. One young bull, one ram, one lamb a year old, one male goat, two oxen, five rams, five male goats, five male lambs a year old, all to be sacrificed.

This was a total of 252 animals (Chapter 7).

Setting up the Lamps

'You shall bring clear oil of pressed olives for the light, so the lamps may be kept burning' (Ex. 27:20). There were seven lamps on branches of pure gold. Without them, it would have been dark.

Setting Apart the Levites

The Lord told Moses to purify the Levites by sprinkling water of cleansing on them, shave their whole bodies and wash their clothes. They made a grain offering, a sin offering and a burnt offering. After this, they could start their designated work at the Tent of Meeting. For this work the age was 25 to 50. They must work no longer after 50 but could assist their brothers (Chapter 8). Everything was in readiness.

The Passover

The Lord spoke to Moses in the Desert of Sinai in the first month of the second year after they came out of Egypt. He said,

'Have the Israelites celebrate the Passover at twilight on the 14th day of this month'. Some could not celebrate because they were ceremonially unclean on account of a dead body.

The Lord told Moses, 'When any of you are unclean because of a dead body or are away on a journey, you can still celebrate the Lord's Passover at the appointed time and way, also the alien living among you can'.

The Cloud

A cloud covered the Tabernacle by day and by night it looked like fire. As long as the cloud stayed, they stayed. When it lifted, they set out. It might stay two days, a month or a year.

The Silver Trumpets

The Lord said to Moses, 'Make two trumpets. When both are sounded the whole community is to assemble. When one is sounded, the leaders are to assemble, when a blast is sounded, the tribes on the east are to set out. The priests are to blow the trumpets'.

The Israelites Leave Sinai

Year 2, 2 months, 20th day. The Israelites leave Sinai and go to the Desert of Paran in the order God designed. Moses asked his brother-in-law, Hobab, to go with them. He knew the area. They traveled three days.

Quail From the Lord

The rabble (mixed multitude) began to complain about the manna. They remembered the good things they had to eat in Egypt. They wanted meat.

The Lord said, 'Tomorrow you will eat meat, not just one day but the whole month'. Moses couldn't see how that could be, because there were so many people. The Lord said, 'Is the Lord's arm too short?'

A wind went out from the Lord and drove quail in from the sea, all around the camp to about three feet above the ground. The Lord was angry with them and struck them with a plague (Ch 11).

Miriam and Aaron Oppose Moses

Miriam and Aaron began to talk against Moses because of his (Cushite or Ethiopian) wife. Some think he had married another wife other than Zipporah whom he had married in Midian. If this is so, it was very soon. Her father Jehtro had recently brought Zipporah and her two sons to him (Ex. 18:5).

The Cushites were descendents of Ham, Noah's son (Gen. 10:6). Miriam was made leprous for one week.

Exploring Canaan

The Lord said to Moses, 'Send some men to explore Canaan'. One leader from each tribe went (12). After 40 days they returned, carrying a single cluster of grapes on a pole. The report: The land does flow with milk and honey (rich) but the people who live there are powerful, the cities fortified and very large. Only 2 who went, Joshua (Moses' aide) and Caleb, said, 'We should go'. The rest spread a bad report (Chapter 13).

The People Rebel

That night, the people wept aloud. They said, 'We shall choose a new leader and go back'.

Joshua and Caleb said, 'If the Lord is pleased with us, he will lead us to that land. Do not rebel against the Lord'.

Again, the Lord wanted to strike them down and make a great nation of Moses. Moses pleaded with the Lord again on behalf of the Israelites and reminded him of his promises. He asked the Lord o please forgive them. He did but said, 'Not one of the men, who saw the miraculous signs I performed in Egypt, will see the land except for Joshua and Caleb. For forty years, a year for each day you explored the land, you will wander. Everyone 20 years or more, who grumbled against me, will fall in the desert. I will bring your children to the land you have rejected'.

Moses' Authority Challenged

250 Israelites men, well-known leaders, came to Moses and Aaron asking, 'Why do you set yourselves above the Lord's assembly?'

Moses said to Korah, 'In the morning the Lord will show who belongs to him…'

The next morning, Korah gathered all his followers and appeared at the Tent of Meeting.

The Lord said to Moses and Aaron, 'Separate yourselves from this assembly so I can put an end to them'. Moses pleaded again, but the ground under them split apart and swallowed their whole households and possessions. The earth closed over them and they were gone, 250 men.

The Israelite community were still grumbling against Moses and Aaron and the Lord sent a plague to kill 14,700 more people (Chapter 16).

The Budding of Aaron's Staff

To stop the wrangling over who the leader was, the Lord told them to bring a staff from each tribe with their names on them. The staff belonging to the man I choose will sprout. The next day, Aaron's staff had sprouted, budded, blossomed and produced almonds. It was placed in front of the Testimony as a sign of the rebellious (Chapter 17).

The Lord said to Aaron, 'Only you and your sons may serve as priests'. The Levites and their families were to eat the best of olive oil, new wine and grain, the first fruits of the harvest, the breast and thigh of the sacrificed meat. They would have no land inheritance but would receive tithes. Of these tithes they must pay a tithe of ten percent (Chapter 18).

The Water of Cleansing

Recipe:

Ashes of a burned heifer, Cedar wood, hyssop and scarlet wool (thrown on the burning heifer)

When anyone touched any part of a dead person they were to take some of the ashes, put them in a jar, add fresh water and sprinkle everything with it on the third and seventh day. Anyone connected with the cleansing must wash their clothes and would be clean after seven days.

Water From the Rock

Miriam died in the Desert of Zin and was buried. There was no water there and the people started quarreling. The Lord told Moses to take his staff and his brother, Aaron, with him and speak to a rock and it would pour out its water. Moses did as directed and said, 'Listen you rebels, must we bring your water out of this rock?' He then struck the rock twice with his staff.

Because he struck the rock when he was told to speak to it, the Lord said Moses would not bring the Israelites into the Promised Land (20:1-12)

The Edomites (descendants of Esau, Jacob's brother) would not allow the Israelites to go through their territory (20:14-21).

Aaron Dies

It was here, near the border of Edom, that the Lord told Moses to take Aaron and his son, Eleazer, up Mt. Hor. He was told to remove Aaron's garments and put them on Eleazer. Aaron died there because when Moses struck the rock, he was with him and did not speak up. The people mourned for him thirty days.

The Bronze Snake

The Israelites went around Edom but grew impatient and started grumbling again. The Lord sent venomous snakes among them to bite them. Many died. The Lord told Moses to make a bronze snake and put it on a pole. Then, when someone was bitten, if he looked at the bronze snake he would live. Jesus spoke of it in John 3:14, 15. Its name was Nebashtan. It was carried into Canaan and preserved until Hezekiah destroyed it (2 Kings 18:4).

Israel Starts Conquering

Israel sent messengers to Sihon, the King of the Amonites; 'let us pass through your country'. They would not and brought their army out and fought with Israel. Israel won and occupied all the cities of the Amorites as far as the Arnon. This was Israel's first victory and the land east of the Jordan that Gad, Reuben and the half tribe of Manasseh wanted as their inheritance (Numbers 32).

Balak Summons Balaam

The Israelites traveled to the plains of Moab and camped along the Jordan River across from Jericho. Moab was terrified.

Balak the king sent for Balaam to put a curse on the Israelites. He asked God what to do. God said, 'Do not go with them and do not put a curse on them because they are blessed'. He refused to go. Balak sent other princes and offered to reward him handsomely.

Balaam told them, 'Even if Balak gave me his palace filled with silver and gold, I could not do anything great or small to go beyond the command of the Lord my God'.

That night God told Balaam, 'Go with them but do only what I tell you'. He went but God was angry that he did. The Angel of the Lord went along causing the donkey to try to stop him. Balaam beat him three times. Finally the Lord opened Balaam's eyes. Balaam said, 'I have sinned. I will go back'. But the Lord said 'Go'.

Three times Balak made sacrifices and called on Balaam to curse the Israelites. Once the Lord said, 'God is not a man that he should lie, nor a son of man that he should change his mind'. Finally Balak said to Balaam, 'Neither curse them at all nor bless them at all'. (Chapters 22-25).

While they were staying in Shittim some of the Israelites engaged in sexual immorality and idol worship with Moab.

Moses said to Israel's judges, 'You must put to death those who have worshipped the idol, Baal'.

When an Israelite man bought a Midianite woman into the family, Phinehas, son of Eleazar, took a spear and drove it through both of them. God had sent a plague upon them and this stopped the plague; 24,000 had died (Chapter 25).

The Second Census

The Lord said to Moses and Eleazar (Aaron had died), 'Take a census of those 20 years old or more who are able to serve in the army'. The numbers from each tribe was:

Reuben	43,730	Simeon	22,200
Gad	40,500	Judah	76,500

Issachar	64,300	Zebulun	60,500
Manasseh	52,700	Ephraim	32,500
Benjamin	45,600	Dan	64,400
Asher	53,400	Naphtali	45,400

The total number of men was 601,730. The Levites, a month old or more, was 23,000. Not one of them was among those counted in the first census except Joshua and Caleb (Ch 26).

Daughter's Inheritance

If a father dies, leaving no sons, his daughter will inherit. After them, his brothers, fathers' brothers or nearest relative.

Joshua to Succeed Moses

The Lord said to Moses, 'Go up on this mountain and see the land I have given the Israelites. Take Joshua and lay your hands on him. Have him stand before Eleazar the priest and commission him. Eleazar will obtain decisions for him by inquiring of the Urim' (Ex. 28:30).

Offerings

Moses reminded the Israelites of their offerings: daily, Sabbath, monthly, Passover, Pentecost, Feast of Trumpets, Day of Atonement and the Feast of the Tabernacles.

Vows

When a man makes a vow, he must not break his word. If a young woman still living in her father's house makes a vow, she is obligated unless her father forbids it. A wife may make a vow, if her husband says nothing to the contrary (Ch 30:3-5, 7, 8).

Moses' Last Battle

The Lord said to Moses, 'Take vengence on the Midianites and after that, you will be gathered to your people'.

12,000 men were sent into battle with the trumpets for signaling. They killed every man, 5 Kings and Balaam. They captured their women and children, took their herds, flocks and goods as plunder. Moses was angry because they hadn't killed the women. He told them to kill all the boys and every woman who had slept with a man, but save the girls (virgins). After the battle, they had to purify themselves for 7 days.

They had to divide the spoils. There were 375,000 sheep, 72,000 cattle, 61,000 donkeys and 32,000 women. The gold articles went to the Tent of meeting for the Lord (Chapter 31).

East of the Jordan

The Reubenites and Gadites had large herds and flocks. The land east of the Jordan was suitable for this. They came to Moses with this proposal: Let this land be given to us as our possession. We can build pens for our cattle, cities for our women and children. They will remain here, but the men will cross over to fight with you. When Moses understood they would fulfill their duty, he agreed to give that land to Rueben, Gad and half the tribe of Manasseh. They rebuilt the cities and renamed them.

Stages in Israel's Journey

At the Lord's command, Moses recorded the stages in the Israelites journey. They left from Rameses on the 14th day of the first month and moved 41 times (Chapter 33).

On the plains of Moab by the Jordan River across from Jericho, the Lord said to Moses, 'Tell them to drive out all the inhabitants, destroy their carved images and idols and demolish their high places' (Chapter 33).

Distribute the land by lot to the nine and a half tribes that were left. Appoint a leader from each tribe to help assign the land. Give the Levites towns and pastureland, 48 towns in all.

Six of the towns you give the Levites will be cities of refuge to which a person may flee who has killed someone accidently. He must stay there until the death of the high priest.

No one is to be put to death on the testimony of only one witness.

No inheritance of land was to pass from tribe to tribe, but to keep what they inherited. The daughter who inherits must marry someone in her tribe.

Cities of Refuse

(All could be reached in one day).

East of Jordan	*West of Jordan*
Bezer (Reuben)	Kedesh (Naphtali)
Ramath-Gilead (Gad)	Shechem (Ephraim)
Galan (Manasseh)	Hebron (Judah)

These were all Levitical cities. They were not to save the criminal, but to protect him until he could get a fair trial (35:22-24)

.

Deuteronomy

A Review

Moses reviews the 40 years spent with the Israelites on their journey. It ordinarily would have taken 11 days.

He starts his review the third month after they left Egypt (Ex. 19:1). He had appointed capable men to help him serve as judges, following his father-in-law, Jethro's, suggestion.

They had reached Kadesh Barnea, the hill country of the Amonites (land the Lord was giving them). Moses told them to go up and take possession of it, but first they wanted to send some men ahead to explore the land. They sent 12, one from each tribe. Ten of the men brought back a discouraging report.

Moses says he told them 'Do not be afraid, the Lord is going before you and will fight for you'. They did not trust in the one who was guiding them by fire at night and a cloud by day.

The Lord was angry with them and said, 'Not a man of this evil generation shall see the good land I swore to give your forefathers except Caleb. He will see it and I will give him the land he set his feet on'. This was Hebron where Abraham had lived (Genesis 15:16 and 48:21, 22).

Moses said, 'Because of you the Lord became angry with me also (when he struck the rock in Numbers Chapter 20) and said, "You shall not enter it either. Your assistant Joshua will lead Israel in." Turn around and go back'.

They went around the hill country of Seir, the land that had been given to Esau, the twin brother of Jacob (Heb. 32:3), and Moab, the land that had been given to the descendants of Lot (Deut. 2:9).

Thirty eight years had passed. The entire generation of fighting men (aged 20-50) had died. The Lord told Moses, 'Set out now and cross the Armon Gorge. I will begin to put the terror and fear of you on all the nations'.

East of the Jordan, while Moses was still leading, two kings of the Amorites, Sihon and Og, a giant, came out against the Israelites with their whole army and were totally destroyed. No town was too strong for them. Og's bed was made of iron. It was 13 feet long and 6 feet wide.

This country, east of the Jordan, was given to Reuben, Gad and the half tribe of Manasseh upon their request but they had to cross over and help their brothers fight for their land. Their wives, children and livestock could remain there (Chapter 3).

Moses pleaded with the Lord to let him go beyond the Jordan but he would not. He said, 'That is enough, do not speak to me anymore about this matter. Joshua will lead the people across (3:23-28).

He reminded the people of the laws and decrees he had taught them and told them to teach their children after them. He said from the time God created man no other nation has heard the voice of God as they had standing at the feet of Mt. Sinai (Ex. 19:17).

He said do not become corrupt and make for yourselves an idol. I call heaven and earth as witness against you that you will quickly perish from the land that you are going in to possess.

Chapters 4:26 through 31 is a prophesy of their falling away, hundreds of years later.

Moses told this new generation how God had made a covenant with them at Horeb (Sinai) and how he had stood between them and the Lord because they were afraid.

The Ten Commandments

(See end of commandment for similar thing in the N. T.)

1. You shall have no other gods before me. {1 Cor. 8:14}

2. You shall not make a graven image or any likeness of anything in heaven, earth or waters. You shall not bow down to worship them for I am a jealous God, punishing the children for the sin of the father to the third generation of those who hate me, but showing love to a thousand generations of those who love me and keep my commandments.{1 Cor. 10:7}

3. You shall not take the name of the Lord thy God in vain. {Matt. 5:34, 37}

4. Observe the Sabbath day by keeping it holy. Six days you shall work, but the seventh is a Sabbath to the Lord. You shall do no work, neither your family, servants nor animals. Remember you were slaves in Egypt and the Lord brought you out... {Acts 20:7}

5. Honor your father and your mother that your days may be long on the earth. {Eph. 6:2}

6. You shall not murder. {Matt. 5:22}

7. You shall not commit adultery. {Matt. 5:27, 28}

8. You shall not steal. {Rom. 13:9}

9. You shall not give false testimony against your neighbor. {Eph. 4:25}

10. You shall not covet your neighbor's wife, house, land, servants or animals or anything that belongs to your neighbor. {Col. 3:5}

The Lord spoke these things from the mountain, then wrote them on stone tablets. The people returned to their tents but Moses remained to receive to the commands, decrees and laws he was to teach the Israelites (Chapter 6).

Why the Laws Were Given

Hear o Israel: The Lord our God , the Lord is one. Love the Lord your God with all your heart, soul and strength. Talk about the commandments at home, walking along the road, at night and morning. Write them on the doorframes of your houses and on your gates. When God brings you into the land with cities you did not build, houses filled with all kinds of good things, wells, vine-yards... do not forget the Lord who brought you out of Egypt and slavery.

Driving Out the Nations

They would be driving out 7 nations, all larger and stronger than they were. Destroy them totally. Make no treaty, do not intermarry. Break down their altars, burn their idols. If the people continued to love and obey God, he would bless them in every way. They would have children and livestock. They would be free of disease. No one will be able to stand up against you. Do not take their silver and gold for yourselves.

Do Not Forget the Law

Moses said the Lord led them all the way in the desert to humble and test them. He fed them with manna to teach them that man does not live on bread alone but by every word that comes from the mouth of the Lord. (This was quoted by Jesus when tempted by the devil, Matt. 4:4). During these 40 years their clothes did not wear out nor did their feet swell (8:4).

They are not to take the credit for their prosperity. It was not because of their righteousness but because of the *unright-eousness* of those they were to drive out (Eph. 2:8, 9). Moses reminded them how they had aroused his wrath when they made a golden calf.

Golden Calf

God was angry enough to destroy them and make a new nation from Moses. When Moses got down from the mountain, he saw why God was so angry. They had made a golden calf and were celebrating. He threw down the two tablets God had written with his own finger and broke them. He ground up the calf, scattered it on the water and made the Israelites drink it.

He then had to go back upon the mountain for God to rewrite what he had written. He put them into an ark he made before leaving. And that's where they had stayed for the 40 years of wandering (10:1-5).

Moses told them the land they were entering was not like Egypt where they had to irrigate like a vegetable garden, but had mountains and valleys and drinks rain from heaven. I will send both spring and autumn rains in this good land I am giving you, if you obey the commands of the Lord.

Destroy all their places of idol worship. The Lord will choose a place as a dwelling for his name, a place to bring your burnt offerings, sacrifices, tithes and special gifts. (These places were Gilgal, Bethel and Shiloh, before the final temple was built in Jerusalem).

Worshipping Other Gods

If your very own brother, son, daughter or the wife you love, or your closest friend says, 'Let us go and worship other gods', do not yield to him or listen to him. Show him no pity. Do not spare him or shield him, you must certainly put him to death (Chapter 13).

Moses reminds them of the kinds of food they may eat, that they should set aside 1/10 of all the fields produce, that every seventh year they must cancel debts. He says there should be no poor among you. You will lend to many nations but will borrow from none. (The Jews have always been known for lending money for interest). But to their fellow brothers, they were to be openhanded towards them.

They Were to Keep Three Annual Feasts

1. Passover (see Ex. 12) at the place God will choose.

2. Pentecost, 50 days after Passover
3. Feast of Tabernacle

These were to be held in the place the Lord would choose.

They would not accept a bribe because it blinds the eyes.

The Lord knew that one day the people would want a king. He said it must be from among them and one God chooses. He is to write for himself a copy of this law and read it all the days of his life. He is not to consider himself better than his brother.

The Levites were to live off offerings of the rest of the people.

Let no one live among you who casts spells or who is a medium, spiritist or consults the dead.

God will raise up for you a prophet.

Do not move your neighbor's boundary stone.

A matter must be established by 2 or 3 witnesses.

Anyone who did not want to go to war did not have to. If anyone was fainthearted, afraid, built a new house and had not dedicated it, planted a vineyard and had not eaten, been pledged to a woman and had not married her were to be excused.

Before attacking a city, they were to make an offer of peace. If they accepted, they were subject to forced labor. If not, all the men were to be put to the sword.

If the battle was in the land they were to inherit, they were to completely destroy them (Chapter 20).

They could marry captive women under certain rules.

If a man has 2 wives, the first son of the wife he does not love will receive a double portion which is the law of the firstborn.

A woman must not wear men's clothing, nor a man wear women's clothing.

A bastard shall not enter into the congregation of the Lord even to the tenth generation.

[Perez was an illegitimate son of Judah (Gen. 38).]

[David was the 11th generation from Perez (Ruth 4:18-22)]

If a man puts away his wife, he could not marry her again if she has married someone else.

If a man has recently married, he is free to stay home for one year and not go to war.

If a man is poor, pay him his wages each day before sunset.

If a guilty man deserves to be beaten, he must not receive more than forty lashes.

The Altar on Mount Ebal

Moses commanded the people: when you have crossed the Jordan, set up some large stones and coat them with plasters.

Write on them the words of the law. Mt. Ebal was about 20 miles past the Jordan, near Shechem. Jacob had once built an altar near here (Gen. 33:18-20).

When you have crossed the Jordan, Simeon, Levi, Judah, Issachar, Joseph and Benjamin shall stand on Mt. Gerizim to bless the people. Reuben, Gad, Asher Zebulun, Dan and Nephtali will stand on Mt. Ebal to pronounce curses (Deut. 27:12, 13). The Levites spoke in a loud voice and all the people said, 'Amen!'

If they did not obey, every bad thing you could imagine would befall them and it did happen (2 Kings 6:28).

Moses said, 'All of you standing here today in the presence of the Lord, your leaders, chief men, elders and officials, children and wives, the aliens, who chop your wood and carry your water, are standing here to enter into the covenant the Lord is making with you this day'. He was confirming the covenant he had made with Abraham, Isaac and Jacob (Chapter 29).

Moses said what he was commanding them was not too difficult or beyond their reach. I set before you today: life and prosperity or death and destruction. Now choose life.

Moses said he was now 120 years old and no more able to lead them. Joshua will cross over ahead of you. He summoned Joshua and told him to be strong and courageous. Do not be afraid or discouraged.

Moses wrote down this law and gave it to the priests who carried the Ark of the Covenant.

Every seven years (in the year for canceling debts) the law was to be read in their assembly (Chapter 31:9-13).

The Lord said to Moses, 'The day of your death is near. Call Joshua to the Tent of Meeting where I will commission him'.

After Moses finished writing in a book the words of this law from beginning to end, he told the Levites, who carried the Ark, to take the Book of the Law and place it beside the Ark of the Covenant. It was his witness; he also spoke the words of a song (Chapter 32).

Moses blessed all the tribes before his death (he had a busy last day). Moses climbed Mt. Nebo from the plains of Moab. The Lord showed him the whole land that he had promised Abraham, Isaac and Jacob.

He died there in Moab and was buried in the valley but no one knows where (see Jude verse 9).

He was 120 years old. His eyes were not weak nor his strength gone. The Israelites grieved for him 30 days.

Aaron died on Mt. Hor at the age of 123. It was the same year. Aaron was 3 years older than Moses (Num. 33:38, 39). It was in the 5th month.

Miriam died the first month of the 40th year.

All three died in the 40th year after leaving Egypt.

Since then, no prophet has arisen in Israel like Moses whom the Lord (Jesus) knew face to face.

In the New Testament, during the ministry of Jesus, Moses appeared to Peter, James and John on the Mount of Transfiguration (along with Elijah and Christ, Matt. 17:3). He lives on.

Hebrews 11:25 says Moses chose to be mistreated along with the people of God rather than to enjoy the pleasures of sin for a season.

Joshua

A Review

Joshua no doubt wrote this book. He was well taught in the things he had seen and heard. He had been Moses' aide these 40 years of wandering. He had even gone with Moses the first time he went on Mt. Sinai to get the tables of stone and the law (Ex. 24:12, 13).

His book will take us across the Jordan, through the conquest and the dividing of the land.

The Lord spoke to Joshua as he had to Moses. He said, 'Moses my servant is dead. Now then, get ready to cross the Jordan into the land I am about to give them. No one will be able to stand up against you all the days of your life. As I was with Moses, so I will be with you. Be strong and courageous. Do not let this Book of the Law depart from your mouth. Meditate on it day and night, so that you may be careful to do everything written in it'.

'Get your supplies ready', Joshua ordered the officials. Three days from now you will cross the Jordan.

The Reubenites, Gadites and the half tribe of Manassed had been given their inheritance on the east side of the Jordan. Their wives, children and animals could stay there, but their fighting men must go and help their brothers. After that they could go back. They told Joshua, 'Whatever you have commanded us we will do and wherever you send us we will go' (Chapter 1).

Rahab and the Spies

Joshua secretly sent two spies to look ever the land, especially Jericho. They entered the house of Rahab. The king of Jericho was told and sent men to get them.

She had hidden them on her roof under stalks of flax. She said, 'Yes, they did come here but left before the gate was closed'.

After the king's men left she made a bargain with the spies. She said, 'I know the Lord has given this land to you. I have shown kindness to you. Spare the lives of my father and mother, brothers and sisters. Our lives for your lives'.

They agreed so she let them down by a rope (her house was part of the city wall). She was told to tie a scarlet cord in the window and bring her family into her house.

When they returned to Joshua, they said, 'The Lord has surely given us the land; the people are melting in fear because of us' (Chapter 2).

After three days, the officers went throughout the camp giving this order: When you see the priests carrying the ark, follow them but keep a distance of about a thousand yards. Consecrate yourselves for tomorrow the Lord will do amazing things among you.

The Lord told Joshua to tell the priests who carried the Ark, 'when you reach the edge of the Jordan's waters go and stand in the river. When you set your foot in the Jordan, its water flowing downstream will be cut off and stand up in a heap'.

It was at flood stage at this time. It piled up a great distance away. The priests with the Ark stood on dry ground in the middle while the Israelites passed by (Chapter 3).

One person from each tribe took up a stone where the priests stood as a memorial. As soon as the priests carrying the Ark had placed their feet on dry ground, the waters of the Jordan returned at flood stage as before.

That night they camped at Gilgal on the border of Jericho. Joshua set up the 12 stones they had taken out of the Jordan. It was the 10th day of the first month of their year. (Chapter 4).

Circumcision

The Lord said to Joshua, 'Make flint knives and circumcise the Israelites that were born in the desert'. They remained in camp until they were healed.

On the evening of the 14th day of their month, the Israelites celebrated Passover (Ex. 12:6). The next day they ate some of the produce of the land, unleavened bread and roasted grain. After this, the manna stopped (see Ex. 16:35).

Jericho was tightly shut up. No one went out and no one went it. The Lord said to Joshua, 'Have the armed men march around the city once a day for six days'. This is the order they went:

1. The armed guard
2. The seven priests blowing their trumpets
3. The Ark of the Covenant
4. The rear guard followed the Ark

All this time they would return to camp and spend the night. They did this for six days. On the seventh day they got up at daybreak and marched around the city seven times.

When the priests sounded the trumpet blast, Joshua said, 'Shout!' The people gave a loud shout and the wall collapsed. The fighting men charged straight in and took the city.

They destroyed with the sword everything in it, men, women, young and old, cattle, sheep and donkeys. They put the silver, gold, bronze and iron into the treasury.

They brought out all of Rahab's family and put them in a place outside the camp. They were living among the Israelites at the time Joshua wrote this. She married Salmon and became the mother of Boaz (in the lineage of Christ, Matt. 1:5).

Joshua made this oath:

If anyone undertakes to rebuild the city of Jericho, it will be at the cost of his first born son.

This did happen centuries later in the time of Ahab. It was Heil of Bethel (1 Kings 16:34).

Achan's Sin

After their great victory in Jericho, Joshua sent men to Ai to spy out the region. They came back and said to only send 2 or 3 thousand fighting men. When they got there, the men of Ai chased them away and killed 36 men.

Joshua and the elders of Israel lay face down on the ground before the Ark until evening. The Lord said to Joshua, 'Stand up! What are you doing down on your face?' Israel has sinned (see 6:18, 19).

Achan, from the tribe of Judah, had seen some beautiful things in Jericho, a beautiful robe from Babylonia, some silver and gold, and had taken them and hid them in the ground under his tent.

The Israelites took Achan, his sons and daughters, his cattle, donkeys and sheep, his tent and all he had, to the valley of Achor and stoned everything, burned them and heaped a large pile of rocks over them.

Ai Destroyed

After this the Lord said to Joshua, 'Take the whole army with you and go up and attack Ai'.

He took 30,000 men and sent them out at night. They went behind the city. Those with Joshua went as before and fled from the city luring the men of Ai out of the city. The 30,000 took the city and set it on fire. The men of Ai looked back and saw the smoke but had no chance to escape.

Twelve thousand men and women fell that day; all the people of Ai. They carried off the livestock and plunder of the city.

Joshua built an altar on Mt. Ebal of uncut stones. They offered sacrifices to the Lord and he read all the words of the law that Moses had written, to the men, women, children and aliens.

The Gibeonites Deceive Israel

The people of Gibeon heard of the things that the Israelites had done to Jericho and Ai.

They sent a delegation wearing old clothes, worn out socks, old wineskins, dry, molded bread and pretended to have come from a far country. They wanted to make a treaty with the Israelites to let them live. Joshua did not inquire of the Lord before making the treaty. Later they learned they lived close by. They saved their lives by this deception but were made wood-cutters and water carriers. When asked why they did this, they said they feared for their lives.

The Sun Stands Still

The King of Jerusalem heard about Jericho, Ai and Gibeon. Gibeon was an important city. The king called on the five kings of the Amorites to help them attack Gibeon. The Israelites called on Joshua to save them. After an all night march, he caught them by surprise and defeated them. As they fled, the Lord hurled large hailstorms down on them from the sky. Joshua asked the Lord to let the sun stand still until the battle was won and it delayed going down about a full day; a miracle.

The 5 kings had hidden in a cave. Joshua had large rocks rolled to block the exit. When the battle was over he had them brought out, killed and hung on trees until evening, then they threw them back in the cave where they had been hiding and replaced the large rocks.

The Israelites went from one town to another until they had conquered the whole region, the hill country, the Negev, the Western foothills, the Arabah...all.

Only in Gaza, Gath and Ashdad did any survive. He waged war against all these people for a long time. Then the land had rest from war (Chapter 11).

Joshua took the land of 31 kings on the West side of Jordan.

Land Still to be Taken

When Joshua was old and well advanced in years, the Lord said to him, 'You are very old and there are still very large areas of land to be taken over. I myself will drive them out. Be sure to allocate this land to Israel for an inheritance. Divide it among the nine and a half tribes'.

Their inheritances were assigned by lot. The sons of Joseph, Manasseh and Ephraim were treated as Jacob's sons and took the place of Joseph. The Levites received no inheritance of land, only towns to live in and pastureland for their flocks and herds, so there were still 12 divisions.

Caleb

Caleb was the one chosen by Moses to first spy out the land of Canaan and gave a favorable report along with Joshua. Moses had told him, 'The land you walked on will be your inheritance'. Caleb went to Joshua to remind him of the Lord's promise.

He said, 'I was 40 years old when Moses sent me to explore the land, He has kept me alive for 45 years. I am today 85 years old. I am still as strong today as I was then. Now give me this hill country the Lord promised me that day'. Joshua blessed Caleb and gave him Hebron as his inheritance. Hebron was in the hill country and was also a city of refuge (Joshua 20:7). Hebron was also where Abraham and Sarah had lived (Gen. 23:1) and where the cave of Machpelah was that Abraham had bought for a burial place. Abraham, Sarah, Isaac, Rebekah and Jacob and Leah were buried there (Gen. 23:17-20, 49:29-32).

It had taken 5 years to gain the land they had so far.

Judah's allotment

Judah's allotment went from the Mediterranean Sea on the west to the Salt Sea on the east.

Caleb's inheritance was in Judah (Hebron). The giants lived in Judah. (Goliath whom David slew with his sling was from Gath in Judah).

Isaac lived in Judah (the Negev) when he met Rebekah.

Jerusalem was on the border of Judah.

A city of refuge was in Judah (Hebron).

Sons of Joseph

The two sons of Joseph, Ephraim and the half tribe of Manasseh, had a large inheritance bordering on the Jordan River.

One of the descendants of Manasseh had five daughters but no sons. Before Moses died, they had gone to him to decide their case. The Lord told him to say, 'If a man dies and leaves no son, the daughter will get the inheritance' (Num. 27:1-10). The land must be kept in the tribe by marriage. The daughter received the inheritance among the sons, as Moses had directed (17:3-6).

Ephraim and Manasseh wanted more and. Joshua told them to clear the forests and it would be theirs.

The Rest of the Land

There were still seven Israelite tribes who had not yet received their inheritance.

They had set up the Tent of Meeting at Shiloh in Ephraim. Joshua said, 'How long will you wait before beginning to take possession of the land?'

Joshua told them:

Appoint three men from each tribe; Make a survey; Write a description, turn by turn, and divide the land in to seven parts.

They were to bring the information to Joshua and he would cast lots for them in the presence of the Lord. The remaining allotments and some important cities found in there were:

Benjamin	Jericho, Bethel, Gibeon
Simeon	Beersheba
Zebulun	Bethlehem
Issachar	Jezreel
Asher	Carmel
Naphtali	Kedesh
Dan	Timnah

Joshua was given the inheritance he asked for in the hill country of Ephraim (Tinmath Serah)

Cities of Refuge

The Lord told Joshua to appoint six cities of refuge. They were:

Kedesh in Galilee
Shechem in Ephraim
Hebron in Judah
Bezer in Reuben
Ramath in Gilead
Golan in Manasseh

If any Israelite or alien living among then killed someone accidentally they could flee to any of these cities, stand in the entrance of the city gate and state their case before the elders of that city. He is to stay in that city until he has stood trial, until the death of the high priest or he may go back to his town (Ch 20). If the killing is intentional, the avenger of blood, a near kinsman, may kill the accused if he finds him outside the city of refuge (Num. 35:26-28).

Towns for the Levites

The Levites were given a total of 48 towns with their pasturelands. The six cities of refuge were located in these towns; also the fields and villages around Hebron had been given to Caleb.

Eastern Tribes Return Home

Joshua called the Reubenites, the Gadites and the half tribe of Manasseh. He said, 'You have done all that Moses commanded. You have not deserted your brothers. Now, return to your homes on the other side of the Jordan'.

Joshua blessed them and sent them away. They had great wealth; large herds of livestock, silver, gold, bronze and iron and a great quantity of clothing. They were told to divide with their brothers (see Joshua 1:12-17) that were not able to go to battle.

They left Shiloh. When they reached a place near the Jordan, they built an imposing altar. When the Israelites they had left heard about it, they were ready to go to war against them before hearing why they had built it. They did not intend it to be an altar to sacrifice on but as a witness that they would worship the Lord.

They wanted future descendants to know they shared with the rest across the river. After hearing what they said, the Israelites, who had come, were pleased and returned home.

Joshua's Farewell

After a long time, the Lord had given rest to Israel from their enemies.

Joshua summoned the leaders of Israel. He told them he was old, that they had seen everything the Lord had done for them. He said it was the Lord who fought for them. He told them to be strong, to obey everything written in the Book of the Law of Moses.

'Hold on fast as you have done until now. The Lord has driven out great and powerful nations but if you turn away, God will no longer drive them away. I am about to go the way of all the earth (die). Every promise has been fulfilled'.

The Covenant Renewed at Shechem

Joshua assembled all the tribes of Israel at Shechem. He gave his farewell message:

This is what the Lord the God of Israel says, 'Long ago your forefathers, including Terah, the father of Abraham and Nahor, lived beyond the River (Euphrates) and worshipped others gods. I took him away and led him through Canaan. I gave him Isaac, to Isaac I gave Jacob and Esau. Jacob and his sons went to Egypt.

I sent Moses and Aaron to bring them out. When they crossed the Red Sea I brought the sea over the Egyptians. You lived in the desert for a long time. I gave you the land of the Amorites.

The king of Moab sent for Balaam to put a curse on you but I delivered you.

You crossed the Jordan and came to Jericho. I gave seven nations into your hands; the Amorites, Perezzites, Canaanites, Hittites, Girgashites, Hivites and Jebusites.

I sent the hornet ahead of you. I gave you land on which you did not toil, cities you did not build, vineyards and oil groves you did not plant.

Throw away the Gods your forefathers worshipped and serve the Lord.

If this seems undesirable to you, then *choose you this day whom you will serve...but as for me and my house, we will serve the Lord'*.

The people answered, 'we too will serve the Lord because he is our God'.

That day, Joshua made a covenant for the people and drew up for them decrees and laws. Joshua recorded these things in the Book of the Law of God.

He took a large stone and set it up as a witness. Joshua sent the people away, each to his own inheritance.

He died at the age of 110 and was buried in the land of his inheritance; in the hill country of Ephraim.

Israel served the Lord throughout the lifetime of Joshua and the elders who outlived him.

Joseph's bones, which the Israelites had brought with them when they left Egypt (Gen. 50:25), were buried at Shechem in the tract of land Jacob, his father, had bought and where Joseph had lived (Gen. 37:12).

Eleazar, the priest and son of Aaron, also died and was buried in the hill country of Ephraim.

Joshua was 40 when he went to explore Canaan. They wandered 40 years. He died at the age of 110. He led Israel for 30 years. (110-80=30)

Judges

A Review

After the death of Joshua, the Israelites asked the Lord, 'Who will be the first to go up and fight for us against the Canaanites?'

The Lord answered, 'Judah'.

You might wonder, who spoke to the Lord now that Joshua was gone?

Moses had made a breastplate of judgment of fine linen, nine inches square, with four rows of precious stones which he wore. Inside the breastplate of judgment was the Urim and the Thummim. When they wanted an answer from the Lord, they would go to the high priest and he would consult the Urim and the Thummim. It was also used when they cast lots (Exodus 28:29, 30).

Eleazar had also died (Josh. 24:33) so it was Ithamar or one of their sons who was the high priest.

Judah asked the Simeonites to help them and they met their battles with success.

Caleb had gotten his inheritance (Josh. 14:6-14) but he may have gotten tired of fighting. Anyway, he said, 'I will give my daughter, Acsah, in marriage to the man who attacks and captures Kiriath Sepher'.

Othniel, the son of his younger brother, took it. They were cousins. She asked for a field and springs of water and Caleb gave them to her.

Moses' brother-in-law (Num. 10:29-33) who had joined the Israelites as their eyes in the desert was given an inheritance in the desert of Judah in the Negev.

The Israelites did not fully drive out the people that were left in the land each tribe was allotted.

The Lord told them *He* would not drive them out and they would be thorns and a snare to them.

After the death of Joshua, another generation grew up who didn't know God and the great things he had done.

They started worshipping the gods of the people around them and provoked the Lord to anger.

He handed them over to raiders and sold them to their enemies. His hand was against them and he no longer fought for them (2:21...)

They cried out to the Lord and he raised up for them a deliverer, Othniel, Caleb's nephew. The Spirit of the Lord came upon him and the Israelites had peace for 40 years, until he died.

Judges

<u>Othniel</u> was the first of the judges. They ruled Israel from the death of Joshua until Samuel (over 300 years). They were the leaders of the army and executed the will of God, but could not change the laws.

<u>Ehud</u> Once again the Israelites did evil in the eyes of the Lord and he gave them over to the Moabites for 18 years. When they cried out, God sent another deliverer, Ehud, a left-handed man, a Benjamite. The king of Moab was a very fat man. Ehud made a double-edged sword, about 18 inches long, which he strapped to his right thigh, under his clothing.

Ehud told the king he had a secret message for him, so he sent everyone out. Ehud plunged the sword through the king's belly and the fat closed in over it.

The servants came in and found the king dead. Ehud got away. Then, Moab was made subject to Israel and the land had peace for eighty years (Judges 3).

After Ehud died, the Israelites once again did evil in the eyes of the Lord. This time, the Lord sold them to Jabin, the king of Canaan. The commander of his army was Sisera who had 900 iron chariots and oppressed the Israelites for 20 years. Again they cried to the Lord for help.

Deborah, a prophetess, was leading Israel at that time. She held court under the palm of Deborah between Ramah and Bethel in the hill country of Ephraim. She sent for Barak. Their army of 10,000 went toward Mt. Tabor.

She said she would lure Sisera and his 900 chariots to the Kishon River. In her song in Judges 5, there was a sudden terrific rainstorm and they abandoned their chariots and fled on food. All their troops fell by the sword. Sierra fled and went to the tent of Jael, the wife of Moses' former brother-in-law's descendants (Judges 4:11, 17). She invited him in, gave him milk to drink and covered him. Exhausted, he fell asleep. While he was asleep, Jael took a tent peg and a hammer and drove it through his temple and he died. Under Deborah, they had peace 40 years (Judge 4-6). They sang a song about it.

Gideon Again the Israelites did evil in the sight of the Lord and were given to the Midianites for 7 years.

It was so bad, the Israelites made shelters in Mountain clefts, caves and strongholds. When they planted their crops, the Midianites camped on the land and ruined the crops. The Israelites were so impoverished they cried out to the Lord for help. This time the Lord sent a prophet who reminded them of their past and how they had been warned not to worship the gods of the Amorites.

The angel of the Lord (Jesus) came and sat down under the oak in Ophrah where Gideon was threshing wheat.

He said, 'The Lord is with you mighty warrior!'

Gideon replied, 'But sir, if the Lord is with us, why has all this happened to us?'

The Lord told him to go and save Israel. Gideon said, 'How? My clan is the weakest in Manasseh'. The Lord said, I will strike down the Midianites as if they were one man.

Gideon wanted a sign, which the Lord gave him. The Spirit of the Lord came on Gideon. He called men to arms throughout Manasseh, Asher, Zebulun and Naphtali.

The Lord said to Gideon, 'You have too many men'. Anyone who was fearful could turn back. 22,000 left and 10,000 remained. 'That's still too many', the Lord said.

To choose who would go, Gideon took them to the water. Those who filled their hands and brought the water to their mouths were chosen. There were three hundred who did this. The others went home. Gideon was told to go down to the Midianite camp and listen to what they were saying.

Just as he arrived, a man was telling his friend a dream. He said, 'A barley loaf came tumbling down into the Midianite camp and collapsed it'. His friend said, 'God has given the Midianites to Gideon'. He went back to the camp, divided the three hundred men into three groups.

They each had a trumpet and an empty jar with a torch inside. When they reached the Midianite camp, they blew the trumpets, broke the jars and shouted, 'A sword for the Lord and for Gideon!' The Midianites turned on each other with their swords.

The Israelites wanted Gideon to rule over them, but he said, 'the Lord will rule over you'. During his lifetime, Israel enjoyed peace for 40 years.

Gideon had 70 sons and many wives. He also had a concubine who lived in Shechem and had a son by her named Abimelech (6:8).

As soon as Gideon was dead, Israel turned again to the Baals (idols).

Abimelech was Gideon's son by the concubine in Shechem.

He went to the citizens in that city and asked, 'Which is better for you, to have all seventy of Gideon's sons rule over you or just one man?' He persuaded them.

He went to his father's home in Ophrah and on one stone murdered his seventy brothers. Jotham was the only one that escaped. After governing Shechem for 3 years, an evil spirit came between him and the city. He kept up his rampage until he captured it, killed its people, scattered salt over it, set fire to the stronghold of the temple and killed about a thousand more. He went to another city, Thebez, and was going to set fire to its tower but a woman dropped an upper millstone on his head and cracked his skull. He called to his armor-bearer to 'draw your sword and kill me, so they cannot say, "a woman killed him" (Judges 9)'.

Tola   After the time of Abimelech, a man of Issachar, Tola, rose up to save Israel. He lived in Shamir in the hill country of Ephraim. He led Israel 23 years.

Jair   Tola was followed by Jair of Gilead. He led Israel 22 years. He had 30 sons who rode donkeys and controlled 30 towns in Gilead.

Jephthah Again the Israelites did evil by worshipping idols, the gods of the people they displaced. They forsook the Lord.

The Lord was angry and sold them into the hands of the Philistines and Ammonites. For 18 years they oppressed the Is-raelites on the east side of the Jordan and also crossed over the Jordan to fight Judah, Benjamin and Ephraim.

They cried out to the Lord to save them, but He said they had forsaken Him and He would no longer save them. 'Go and cry out to the gods you have chosen. Let them save you'.

They got rid of the foreign gods and served the Lord. He could bear Israel's misery no longer.

Jephthah was a mighty warrior. His father was from Gilead, his mother a prostitute. His father's wife had sons who drove him away.

Later they wanted him to come back and fight the Ammon-ites. He sent a message to the king and asked him, 'What do you have against us that you have attacked our country?' The king said, 'When Israel came up out of Egypt, they took away my land. Now give it back peaceably'. Jephthah explained what really happened (by messenger). He told them Israel had asked to pass through their country, traveling along the king's highway. They would not allow it, so with the Lord's help, Israel captured all the cities of the Amorites and occupied them (Num. 21:21-31).

'Whatever the Lord has given us, we will possess. For 300 years, Israel had occupied the land along the Arnon. Let the Lord settle the dispute *this day* (Judges 11)'. The Spirit of the Lord came upon Jephthah. He made a vow to the Lord:

'If you give the Ammonites into my hands, whatever comes out of the door of my house to meet me when I return in triumph from the Ammonites, will be the Lord's and I will sacrifice it as a burnt offering'.

The Lord did give them into his hands. When he returned home, his daughter and only child came out to meet him.

When he told her about the vow, she said, 'Do to me as you promised, but give me two months to roam the hills and weep with my friends because I will never marry.' After this, she returned and he fulfilled his vow (Judges 11).

Jephthah lead Israel six years. He was buried in a town in Gilead, east of the Jordan.

Ibzan led Israel after Jephthah. He was from Bethlehem. He had 30 sons and 30 daughters. The daughters married outside the clan as well as the sons.

He led Israel for seven years.

Elon From Zebulon led Israel for ten years.

Abdon led Israel eight years. He had 40 sons and 30 grandsons who rode seventy donkeys. He was buried in the hill country of Ephraim.

Again the Israelites did evil in the eyes of the Lord and he delivered them into the hands of the Philistines for forty years.

Samson (Judges 13-16)

There was a man from the tribe of Dan named Manoah, whose wife was childless. The angel of the Lord appeared to her. He said, 'You are going to conceive and bear a son'.

'Drink no wine, eat nothing unclean, use no razor on his head. The boy will be a Nazarite and begin to deliver Israel from the Philistines' (see the Nazarite Vow, Num. 6:1-5). The woman told her husband about it and said, 'He looked like an angel of God'. Manoah prayed for him to come again and he did. The boy was born and named Samson. The Spirit of the Lord began to stir in him. He went to Timnah and saw a young Philistine woman and asked his parents to get her for him as a wife. They disapproved but went along with him. (It was from the Lord).

As he went back to see her, taking his parents, a young lion came roaring toward him. The Spirit of the Lord came upon him and he tore the lion apart with his bare hands. Some time later, when he went back to marry her, a swarm of bees had made honey in the carcass. He ate some and gave some to his parents.

Samson had made a feast, as bridegrooms did, and was with thirty companions. He said, 'Let me tell you a riddle. If you can give me an answer during these seven days of the feast, I will give you 30 sets of clothes. If you can't, you must give me the same'. This was the riddle:

> *'Out of the eater—something to eat.*
> *Out of the strong—something sweet.'*

When they couldn't figure it out, they threatened his wife, that they would burn her and her family to death if she didn't find out the answer. She begged and cried the whole seven days until he finally told her.

The men asked him, 'What is sweeter than honey? What is stronger than a lion?'

Samson said to them, 'If you had not plowed with my heifer, you would not have solved my riddle'.

He struck down 30 of their men, stripped them of their belongings and gave their clothes to those who solved the riddle. Later on, he went back to visit his wife and her father had given her to another man.

This time, he went out, caught 300 foxes and tied them tail to tail. He fastened a torch to every pair of tails and let them loose in the standing grain, burning the grain, vineyards and olive groves.

When they found out why he did it, they burned her and her father to death. The men of Judah bound Samson with new ropes and handed him over to the Philistines. When he saw the Philistines coming, the Spirit of the Lord came upon him and the ropes were as nothing. He found the jaw bone of a donkey and struck down a thousand men.

Samson led Israel for 20 years in the days of the Philistines.

Delilah

Samson later fell in love with a woman named Delilah. The Philistines went to her and said, 'See if you can find out the secret of his strength. Each one of us will give you 1100 shekels of silver'. She kept after him until he finally got tired of her prodding and told her the truth: 'No razor has ever been used on my head. I have been a Nazarite, set apart from birth. If my head were shaved my strength would leave me'.

Delilah summoned the Philistines, having put Samson to sleep on her lap. She called a man to shave off the seven braids of his hair. She then called out, 'Samson, the Philistines are upon you!'

He did not know the Lord had left him. The Philistines seized him, gauged out his eyes and took him to Gaza and put him to grinding in the prison.

His hair began to grow. The Philistines were celebrating in the temple of Dagon, a false god, and were in high spirits. They shouted, 'Bring out Samson to entertain us'.

Samson said to the servant, 'Put me by the pillars that support the temple where I can lean against them'. All the rulers were there. On the roof, there were about 3000 men and women watching Samson perform. Samson prayed, 'Oh God, please strengthen me just once more. Let me die with the Philistines!'

He reached for the 2 central pillars, pushed with all his might and the temple came down.

He killed more when he died than when he lived.

Micah's Idols

Someone had taken some silver from Micah's mother. Micah returned it to her, she took part of it and had it made into an idol to put in his house. He had made an ephod and some idols and installed one of his sons as his priest. A young Levite, looking for a place to stay, came to Micah's house. He invited the Levite to stay with him and he would pay him to be his priest.

The tribe of Dan had not yet come into their inheritance. They had sent 5 warriors to spy out the land and explore it. They also came to the house of Micah and recognized the voice of the young Levite. They asked him what he was doing there. When he told them, they asked him to inquire of God if their journey had the Lord's approval.

They went on their way and came to a place called Laish where they found a peaceful people and a prosperous land.

They returned home to Zorah and said 'let's go attack them! You will find an unsuspecting people and a spacious land that God has put into your hands'.

Six hundred men set out to go take it. The 5 who had spied out the land went to the house of the young Levite.

They went inside Micah's place and took his carved image, the ephod, the cast idol and other household goods.

The priest said, 'What are you doing?' They told him to 'be quiet, wouldn't it be better to serve a tribe rather than just one man?'

He was glad and went with them. Micah went after them, but seeing they were too strong for him, he went back home.

They attacked the unsuspecting people with the sword and burned their city. They rebuilt the city and named it Dan, after their forefather.

They continued to use the idols Micah had made, all the time the house of God was in Shiloh (Judges 17-18).

A Levite and His Concubine

A Levite who lived in a remote area of Ephraim took a concubine from Bethlehem. She left him and went back home. After 4 months, her husband went to try to persuade her to return. His father-in-law was glad to see him and kept urging him to stay longer.

At the end of the 5th day they all left, going toward Jerusalem. The man did not want to spend the night in a city whose people were not Israelites. They kept on until they reached Gilead in Benjamin. They went and sat in the city square, but no one took them in for the night.

Later on, an old man came in from his work in the field and invited them to his house. While they were enjoying themselves, there came a pounding on the door. They shouted to the old man, 'Bring out the man who came to your house so we can have sex with him'.

The man said, 'no, he is my guest. Here is my virgin daughter and his concubine. I will bring them to you'.

The man took his concubine and sent her out. They abused her throughout the night and at dawn they let her go.

She went to the house where her master was staying, fell down at the door and lay there until daylight. When the man left to go on his way, she was dead. He took her home, cut her into 12 pieces and sent a part to each Israelite tribe.

They all assembled before the Lord in Mizpah, 400,000 soldiers armed with swords.

The Levites related what had happened. All the men of Israel united as one man. They sent men throughout the tribe of Benjamin. Benjamin also brought together an army. On the first day, the Benjamites killed 22,000 Israelites.

The Israelites inquired of the Lord, 'Shall we go up again?' The Lord answered, 'Go'.

The Israelites went to Bethel (where the Ark of the Covenant was) and inquired of the Lord again. Again, he said, 'Go. Tomorrow I will give them into your hands'.

The Benjamites began to inflict casualties on the Israelites as before. When 30 men fell, they said, 'Let's retreat and draw them away from the city into the roads'. The Israelites charged from ambush and struck down 25,100 Benjamites. They went into Gibeah (where the Levite and his wife had stayed) and set the town afire. When the Benjamites realized the disaster had come upon them, they fled toward the desert. The Israelites went to Benjamin and put all the towns to the sword, including the animals and set the towns on fire. Altogether, there were 65,130 killed (Judges 19 and 20).

Wives for the Benjamites

The Israelites had taken an oath at Mizpah: Not one of us will give his daughter in marriage to a Benjamite.

They went to Bethel and wept bitterly. They cried, 'O Lord, why has this happened in Israel? Why should one tribe be missing from Israel today?'

The Israelites grieved for their brothers, the Benjamites. How can we provide wives for those that are left since we have taken this oath?

Six hundred of Benjamin's fighting men had fled into the desert to the rock of Rimmon where they stayed for four months.

There was a town in Benjamin who had not come to the assembly at Mizpah. They sent fighting men there to kill every male there and every woman who was not a virgin.

There were 400 young women who had never slept with a man.

The Israelites sent an offer of peace to the 600 men who had fled to the desert. They returned and were given the 400 women who had been spared. That left 200 without wives.

They had an idea. The annual festival was coming up at Shiloh. They instructed the Benjamites to hide in the vineyards and watch. When the girls of Shiloh came out to join the dancing, rush from the vineyards and seize a girl for your wife and go to the land of Benjamin. So this is what they did.

This must have been what the movie, *Seven Brides for Seven Brothers* was based on (21:17-23).

King Saul was from Gibeah in Benjamin (1 Sam. 10:9-26).

Paul the apostle was a Benjamite (Phil. 3:5).

P.S. Judges did not list *all* the judges. The other two, Eli and Samuel, are written about in 1 Samuel Chapters 1-8.

Ruth

A Review

There was a famine in the land of Judah during the days of the Judges.

It may have been the seven years before Gideon saved them (see Judges 6:1-6).

This family from Bethlehem (Elimelech and Naomi and their two sons) left and went into the land of Moab. This land belonged to the descendants of Lot (see Gen. 19:37).

While living there, Naomi's husband died. Her two sons married Moabite women and after about 10 years they also died. Naomi was left with her two Moabite daughters-in-law.

When she heard there was food in Judah, she decided to return. She told her two daughters-in-law (Orpah and Ruth) to go back to their mother's house. Orpah did but Ruth would not leave Naomi. She said to her, 'Don't urge me to leave you or turn back from you... Where you go I will go, where you stay I will stay. Your people will be my people and your God, my God. Where you die, I will die and there I will be buried'. (This is sometimes used in weddings).

The two women went on, arriving in Bethlehem as the barley harvest was beginning. The townspeople could hardly believe it was the same Naomi (Chapter 1).

Ruth said to Naomi, 'Let me go to the fields and pick up the leftover grain'. (The Law of Moses states, 'when you reap the harvest of your land, do not reap to the very edges of your field or gather the gleanings of your harvest. Leave them for the poor and the alien' Lev. 23:22).

Now as providence would have it, the first day Ruth went out to glean, it was in the field of a relative of Ebimelech's (Naomi's dead husband). His name was Boaz. He had been told about Naomi's return and the young woman who had come back with her.

When he saw an unknown woman gleaning in his field and found out from his foreman who it was, he told her not to go anywhere else. He told the men not to touch her, offered her water to drink and bread and roasted grain to eat at mealtime.

At the end of the workday, she carried to Naomi about 3/5 bushel of threshed barley and the rest of the lunch she had left. Naomi was very excited when she found out what had happened. She said Boaz was a close relative, a *kinsman-redeemer* of her husband, Ebimelech (Chapter 2).

Naomi wanted to find a good home for Ruth. She told her, 'Tonight, Boaz will be winnowing barley on the threshing floor. Wash and perfume yourself, put on your best clothes and go down to the threshing floor. Wait until he has finished eating and drinking and has lain down (asleep). Uncover his feet and lie down',

She did this. Boaz was startled to discover a woman lying at his feet. It was dark so he said, 'Who are you?'

She said, 'I am your servant, Ruth, spread the corner of your garment over me, since you are a kinsmen-redeemer'.

Boaz was very pleased and agreed to do as she asked but said, 'I am near of kin, but there is a kinsmen redeemer closer than I. If he is not willing, I will do it'.

Ruth left while it was still dark and returned to Naomi, telling her what happened.

Boaz Marries Ruth

Boaz went to the town gate to wait for the kinsman and got together ten of the elders of the town (to transact the business).

He said to the kinsman, 'Naomi has come back from Moab and is selling the land that belonged to our brother, Ebimelech. If you will redeem it, tell me as I am next in line'.

'I will redeem it', he said.

Then Boaz said, 'On the day you buy the land, you acquire the dead man's widow'.

At this, the kinsman said, 'Then I cannot redeem it, because I might endanger my own estate. You redeem it, I cannot do it'.

He then removed his sandal. (This was the way a transaction was finalized in Israel). Then Boaz said, 'You are my witnesses that I have bought from Naomi all the property of her family and have acquired Ruth, Mahlon's widow, as my wife so that his name will not disappear. The elders offered him their blessing.

Ruth became Boaz's wife and bore him a son, Obed, the father of Jessee, the father of David and in the lineage of Christ.

The women told Naomi that her daughter-in-law was better to her than seven sons.

Naomi took the child, laid him in her lap and cared for him (Chapter 4).

Scripture explaining some of these laws are:
Deut. 25:5-10
Ezek. 16:8-14
Gen 23:10-18

Ruth was the *great* grandmother of King David.

Boaz was the name of the left pillar of the Temple of Solomon (1 Kings 7:21).

1 Samuel

A Review

There was a man from Ramah of the tribe of Levi. He had two wives, Peninnah and Hannah. Peninnah had children but Hannah had none.

Every year when they would go to Shiloh (where the Tabernacle was, since the time of conquest, Joshua 18:1) the wives would go also. The wife who had children was always provoking Hannah.

While they were in Shiloh, Hannah was praying silently and Eli the priest saw her lips moving. He thought she was drunk and scolded her. She explained her situation and he said, 'Go in peace and may the God of Israel grant you what you have asked of him'.

She felt much better and her prayer was granted. In her prayer, she had made a vow that she would give him to the Lord all the days of his life and he would be a Nazarite (see Judges 13:4, 5).

Silent prayers are heard (verse 13).

Samuel

Hannah gave birth to Samuel but did not go back to the annual sacrifice until he was weaned.

She took the boy, a three year old bull, an ephod of flour and a skin of wine for her sacrifice (see Num. 15:8, 9).

She brought the boy to Eli and said, 'I am the woman who stood here beside you praying to the Lord. He has granted me what I asked of him, so now I give him to the Lord' (Chapter 1).

Hannah prayed again (whether it was heard by the man is not stated). In the prayer, she stated this: 'The Lord brings death and makes alive; he brings down to the grave and raises up (Old Testament believers understood there was life after death)'.

They went home to Ramah and Samuel stayed there with Eli. He ministered before the Lord and wore a linen ephod (the clothing of priests).

Each year, his mother made him a little robe and took it to him when they went to Shiloh for the annual sacrifice.

Eli would bless Elkanah and Hannah and say, 'May the Lord give you children to take the place of the one she prayed for and gave to the Lord' (2:20).

Hannah gave birth to three more sons and two daughters.

Eli's Wicked Sons

Eli's sons, Haphni and Phinehas were priests, but had no regard for the Lord. They took meat while it was raw (before the fat was burned) and slept with women who served at the Tent of Meeting. Eli heard reports of what his sons were doing but when he tried to rebuke them, they would not listen.

A man of God came to Eli and said, 'Why do you honor your sons more than me? I will cut short your strength. In your family line, there will never be an old man. Your two sons will both die on the same day' (4:11).

The Lord Calls Samuel

Both Eli and Samuel were asleep in the Tabernacle of the Lord where the Ark of God was. A voice called out, 'Samuel'. He thought it was Eli calling him and went to him. This happened three times before Eli realized the Lord was calling Samuel. He told Samuel if He called again say, 'Speak Lord, for your servant is listening'.

This time, the Lord himself stood there. He told Samuel, 'I am about to do something in Israel that will make the ears of everyone who hears it tingle'.

Eli knew about his son's sins and failed to restrain them. The guilt will never be atoned for by sacrifice and offering.

Samuel was afraid to tell Eli, but he insisted so he told him everything. Eli said, 'He is the Lord, let him do what is good in His own eyes'.

All Israel recognized that Samuel was a prophet of God' (Chapter 3).

The Ark Captured

The Israelites went out to fight against the Philistines and were defeated. They lost 4,000 men. They said, 'Let us bring the Ark from Shiloh so it can go with us and save us'. (The Ark symbolized God's presence and protection to them).

They sent men to Shiloh to get the Ark. Eli's two sons were there with the Ark of the Covenant. When it arrived in the camp, there was a great shout. The Philistines were afraid but went to battle.

A DAY TO REMEMBER!

Israel lost 30,000 foot soldiers, the Ark was captured and Eli's two sons died (4:1-11).

Eli was sitting in his chair by the side of the road, watching.

A man came from the battle line to report the news. When Eli heard the outcry he said, 'What is the meaning of this uproar?'

The man said, 'The army had suffered heavy losses, your sons are dead and the Ark has been captured'.

When Eli heard these things, he fell backward and broke his neck and died. He was an old man, 98 and heavy. He had led Israel 40 years.

His daughter-in-law was pregnant and went into labor after hearing all this tragedy. She died but the baby survived (Ch 4).

The Ark in Philistine Territory

The Philistines took the Ark from Ebenezer where the Israelites were camping, to Ashdod. They put it in their temple of Dagon and set it beside him. The next day, he had fallen on his face on the ground. His head and hands were broken off and were lying on the threshold. The Lord afflicted the people of Ashdod with tumors. They said, 'The Ark of the god of Israel must not stay here with us'.

They moved it to Gath. Tumors broke out on them too. Then they sent it to Ekron. Ekron called the rulers together and told them to send it back to Israel. They didn't want to send it away empty. They made models of the tumors and rats (5) and sent them as a guilt offering.

They got a new cart, two cows that had never been yoked and hitched them to the cart. The cows went straight toward Beth Shemesh keeping on the road and lowing all the way. When they got to the field of Joshua of Beth Shemesh they stopped beside a large rock.

The people chopped the wood of the cart and sacrificed the cows as a burnt offering and set the Ark on the large rock.

God struck down seventy men (Israelites) because they looked into the Ark. There were afraid and took it to Abinadab's house with his son to guard it. It stayed there for 20 years.

It was taken to Jerusalem when David built a Tabernacle for it (2 Sam. 6:12, 2 Chron. 1:4). Then it was placed in Solomon's Temple (1 Kings 8:4). After the destruction of Jerusalem by Nebuchadnezzar, nothing is known of it.

The Israelites got rid of their foreign gods and served the Lord. The Philistines came out to fight once again, but the Lord thundered with loud thunder, confusing them, while Israel slaughtered them. Throughout Samuel's lifetime, there was peace. Samuel was a judge in Israel all the days of his life. His home was in Ramah, where his parents lived, but he would go on a circuit from Bethlehem to Gilgal to Mizpah back to Ramah.

Israel Asks for a King

When Samuel grew old, he appointed his sons as judges. They served at Beersheba but did not walk in His ways.

The elders of Israel came to Samuel at Ramah. They said, 'Appoint a king to lead us, like other nations have'. This displeased Samuel.

The Lord told him, 'It is not *you* they have rejected, but me'.

Samuel told them all the things a king would make them do but they refused to listen.

Samuel Anoints Saul

The providence of God is at work here. There was a man named Kish, a Benjamite of good standing. The man sent his son, Saul, to look for some lost donkeys.

After they couldn't find them, his servant said, 'In this town, there is a man of God (prophet or seer). Let's go ask him'. He had a piece of silver to give him.

Some girls told them where to find Samuel. When they got there, he was walking to meet them. The day before Saul came, the Lord had told Samuel, 'About this time tomorrow I will send you a man from the land of Benjamin. Anoint him leader over my people, Israel'.

Saul couldn't figure out what was happening when he was invited to eat the choice piece of meat and seated at the head of the invited guests.

When Saul and his servant left the next day, Samuel asked that Saul's servant go on ahead, saying he wanted to give Saul a message from God (Chapter 9). This was a private anointing.

Samuel took a flask of oil and poured it on Saul's head saying, 'Has not the Lord anointed you leader over his inheritance?'

The Benjamites were the smallest of the tribes because all but 600 men had been killed (see Judges Chapters 20 and 21). Saul was impressive looking and a head taller than the others.

Samuel sent Saul to Gibeah. On his way, he met people his father had sent to look for him and men carrying goats, bread and wine for sacrifice. As he approached Gibeah, there were prophets coming to meet him playing musical instruments. The Spirit of the Lord came on Saul and he was changed into a different person.

Samuel told Saul to go to Gilgal to sacrifice, but to wait 7 days until he came to tell him what to do.

Samuel summoned the people of Israel at Mizpah and told them the Lord was going to give them the king they wanted. As the tribes passed by, Benjamin was chosen until finally Saul was chosen, but he had gotten cold feet and hidden among the baggage (10:22).

Samuel sent the people home. Saul also went to his home in Gibeah but found no honor at home.

Saul Takes Courage

He was still out in the fields with his oxen. He saw the people weeping and asked why.

The Ammonites were wanting to make a treaty with the Israelites on the condition that they gauge out their right eyes. When Saul heard this, the Spirit of the Lord came upon him in power.

He took a pair of oxen, cut them into pieces and sent them by messenger throughout Israel saying, 'This is what will be done to the oxen of anyone who does not follow Saul and Samuel'.

They turned out as one man, 300,000. They sent word to the Ammonites that, 'tomorrow we will surrender to you'. But during the last watch of the night (3-6 A.M) they broke into the

Ammonites camp and slaughtered them until noon. The rest scattered.

After their victory and Saul's leadership, Samuel said to the people, 'Come, let us go to Gilgal and there reaffirm the kingship'. They sacrificed and held a great celebration (Ch 11).

Samuel Bids Farewell

Samuel said to all Israel, 'Now you have a king as your leader. I have been your leader from my youth until this day'. He brought to memory the good things God has done for them (12:6-11). He told them what every man of God has from the beginning. What will happen if they obey, what will happen if they don't. He told them that asking for a king was evil, but far be it from me that I should sin against the Lord by failing to pray for you (Chapter 12).

Samuel Rebukes Saul

Saul was 30 years old when he became king and reigned over Israel 40 years (Acts 13:21).

Saul had a son named Jonathan. He attacked the Philistine outpost at Geba. The Philistines assembled to fight Israel. Israel was terrified because of the Philistine's large force. Some hid and some fled.

Samuel had told Saul to wait for him 7 days. The men began to scatter so Saul went ahead without Samuel and offered up a burnt offering. Just as he finished, Samuel arrived. (This may have been a test).

Samuel told Saul, 'You acted foolishly. Your kingdom will not endure'. (This seemed to be a small matter, but disobeying God in any matter, is not small).

The Israelites did not have any swords or spears. The Philistine blacksmiths sharpened their farm equipment (Ch 13).

Jonathan Attacks the Philistines

One day Jonathan left his post unawares and with his armor bearer went to the Philistine's camp. He said, 'Perhaps the Lord will act on our behalf. Nothing can hinder the Lord from saving, whether by many of by few'. They showed themselves and the Philistines said 'Look! The Hebrews are crawling out of the holes they were hiding in'. They shouted, 'Come up to us and we will teach you a lesson'. They climbed up and killed 20 men.

Panic struck the whole army (a panic sent by God). Saul found out Jonathan was not in camp. The word spread and they all went to come together for the battle. They found the Philistines fighting each other and the Lord rescued Israel that day (14:23).

Saul had made an oath that no one of the army could eat that day until they had avenged themselves from their enemies.

His son, Jonathan, did not know about the oath and ate some honey. The other army men started eating the plunder with its blood still in it. When Saul found out, he built an altar for the Lord for the first time.

When he found out Jonathan had eaten the honey, he was going to have him killed, but the men talked him out of it.

Saul had one wife, three sons and two daughters (14:49-50), unlike other kings. The commander of his army was Abner, his first cousin (Chapter 14).

The Lord Rejects Saul

Samuel told Saul, 'This is what the Lord almighty says: "I will punish the Amalekites for what they did to Israel when they came up from Egypt" (see Ex. 17:8-14). Attack the Amalekites and totally destroy them'.

He did, put spared the king, Agag, and the best of the animals. The Lord told Samuel, 'I am grieved that I have made Saul king. He has turned away from Me'.

Early the next morning, Samuel went to meet Saul. Saul said, 'The Lord bless you! I have carried out the Lord's instructions'.

Samuel said, 'What then is this bleating of sheep and the lowing of cattle I hear?'

Saul said, 'We saved the best to sacrifice'.

'STOP!' Samuel said, 'Let me tell you what the Lord said to me last night. You were once small in your own eyes. Why did you not obey the Lord?'

Saul said, 'I did and brought back Agag their king. The soldiers brought the plunder to sacrifice'.

Samuel said, 'To obey is better than sacrifice. Because you have rejected the word of the Lord, he has rejected you as king'.

Saul said, 'Please honor me before the elders of my people'.

Samuel put Agag to death before the Lord at Gilgal and went home to Ramah. Saul went to his home in Gibeah. They never saw each other again (Chapter 15).

Samuel Anoints David

The Lord said to Samuel, 'How long will you mourn for Saul since I have rejected him? I am sending you to Jesse of Bethlehem. I have chosen one of his sons to be king'.

Samuel went to Bethlehem on the pretext of sacrificing. He consecrated Jesse and his sons and invited them to the sacrifice.

When he saw Eliab, he thought he would be the one but the Lord said, 'The Lord does not look at the things man looks at, the Lord looks at the heart'.

Jesse's seven sons passed before Samuel. It was none of them. Samuel said, 'Is this all?'

Jesse said, 'There is still the youngest. He is tending the sheep'.

Samuel said, 'Send for him, we will not sit down until he arrives'.

He was ruddy, with a fine appearance and handsome features.

The Lord said, 'Rise and anoint him, he is the one'. The Spirit of the Lord came upon him. The Spirit of the Lord had departed from Saul and an evil spirit was tormenting him. His attendants suggested getting someone to play the harp to soothe him.

David was suggested. Saul liked him and wanted him to stay. His playing made Saul feel better (Chapter 16).

David and Goliath

The Philistines had gathered their forces for war against the Israelites.

Goliath, from Gath, a giant over 9 feet tall, stood and shouted, 'Choose a man and have him come down to me. If he kills me, we will become your subjects. If I kill him, you will become our subjects'. This went on for 40 days.

Jesse's three adult sons were with Saul but David went back and forth to tend his father's sheep at Bethlehem. Jesse sent David to see how his brothers were and to carry them some food.

While he was there, Goliath stepped out with his usual statement. David said, 'Who is this uncircumcised Philistine that he should defy the armies of the living God?'

When David's brother heard what he said, he burned with anger. He said, 'Why did you come down here? And with whom did you leave those few sheep in the desert? I know how conceited you are and how wicked your heart is…('Family talk')'.

David answered, 'Now what have I done? Can't I even speak?'

It was reported to Saul what David had said. He sent for David. David said, 'Your servant will go and fight him'. Saul said, 'You are only a boy'.

David said 'He will be like a lion or a bear that I killed while watching my father's sheep'. Saul told David to go.

He chose five smooth stones and put them into his shepherd's bag and with his sling in his hand, approached Goliath.

Goliath said, 'Am I a dog that you come at me with sticks?'

David said, 'You come against me with sword and spear but I come against you in the name of the Lord Almighty, the God of the armies of Israel'.

Reaching in his bag, he took out a stone, slung it and struck the Philistines on the forehead. He fell face down on the ground. He then took the Philistine's sword and cut off his head. He brought the head to Jerusalem but put the Philistine's weapons in his own tent.

He took the head to Saul who asked whose son he was (see 16:18-21). He must have forgotten (Chapter 17).

After killing the giant, Saul did not let him return to his father's house.

Jonathan, Saul's son, loved David as himself.

The women of the towns came out singing, 'Saul has slain his thousands and David his tens of thousands'.

Saul was angry upon hearing this and from that time on, kept a jealous eye on David. He was afraid of David because the Lord was with David but had left him. He sent him away, giving him command over a thousand men.

Saul's daughter, Michal, loved David. Saul said he could marry her for 100 Philistines foreskins.

David and his men killed 200 Philistines and brought their foreskins to him.

Saul gave him his daughter but remained his enemy the rest of his days (Chapter 18).

Saul Tries to Kill David

Saul still wanted to kill David (you can be hated for doing good). His son, Jonathan, talked with his father, telling him all the good things David had done and changed his mind. After a while, his old feelings returned. He sent men to David's house but his wife protected him. He finally went to Samuel at Ramah.

David and Jonathan

David left Ramah and went to see Jonathan. Jonathan did not know of these attempts on David's life. Even though Saul confided in Jonathan, he did not tell him this because he knew Jonathan loved David.

Saul said to David, 'As long as the son of Jesse lives on this earth, neither you nor your kingdom will be established'.

Then Jonathan knew that his father intended to kill David. He left in fierce anger because he was grieved at his father's shameful treatment of David.

David at Nob

David went to Nob to Ahimelech the priest and asked for bread. He said he only had the consecrated bread. He gave it to David. He also took Goliath's sword that had been stored there.

One of Saul's servants, Doeg, saw David there and told Saul. The king sent for Abimelech and his family. He told them, 'You knew David was fleeing and did not tell me'. He told his officials to kill the priests but they were not willing so Doeg, the one who saw David, killed 85 men who wore the linen ephod and all the town of Nob. Only one escaped.

He joined David's men. David had about 400 men with him as followers: those in distress, debt or discontented as well as his brothers and father's household.

Psalms 52 was written about Doeg going to Saul to tell him, 'David has gone to the house of Ahimelech'. The one that escaped was Abiathar, the priest's son. He brought the ephod with him.

David would consult the ephod as to what to do and where to go. He was on the run from Saul. Once, Saul and his men were on one side of a mountain and David on the other (Ch 23).

David Spares Saul's Life

Saul took 3,000 men and set out to look for David. He went into a cave but far back.

David crept up unnoticed and cut off a corner of Saul's robe. After Saul left, David called out to him and said, 'Look at this piece of your robe in my hand. I have not wronged you. May the Lord avenge the wrongs you have done o me, but my hand will not touch you'.

Saul said, 'I know that you will surely be king. Swear to me that you will not wipe out my family name'. He then went home (Chapter 24).

David, Nabal and Abigail

Samuel died and was buried at his home in Ramah. Israel mourned him. Josephus says Samuel died 18 years into Saul's reign.

David and his men were staying in the desert near Carmel. There was a wealthy man who lived nearby named Nabal. David sent some men to him to ask for food, but he refused.

When his wife, Abigail, heard about it, she hastily got some together and personally delivered it, asking for forgiveness.

David told her, 'If you had not come quickly, not one male belonging to him would have been alive by daybreak'.

About 10 days later, the Lord struck Nabal and he died.

David sent word to Abigail asking her to become his wife, which she did.

David had also married Abinoam of Jezreel. Saul had given his first wife, Michal, to somebody else.

Again David Spares Saul

Again Saul was looking for David. David went to the place Saul had camped and found them all asleep inside the camp.

Saul's spear was stuck in the ground near his head. David took the spear and a water jug and left. (The Lord had put them into a deep sleep).

David crossed over and stood on a hill. He called out, 'You did not guard your master. Where are the king's spear and water jug?'

Saul said, 'I have acted like a fool. I will not try to harm you again'.

David said, 'Here is the king's spear, let one of your young men come over and get it'. David went on his way and Saul returned home (Chapter 26).

Among the Philistines

David decided to escape to Philistine territory so Saul would give up his search for him. David, his 600 men and their families went to Gath. HE asked for a country town to live in and was given Ziklag. They lived in Philistine territory a year and four months. They went on raiding parties, destroying each place and taking their animals. His host thought he was fighting the Israelites because David had misinformed him (Chapter 27).

Saul and the Witch of Endor

The Philistines gathered their forces to fight against the Israelites.

Samuel was dead (about 22 years) and Saul had expelled the mediums (see Deut. 18:10-12).

When Saul saw the Philistine army, he was afraid. He inquired of the Lord, but got no answer.

He told his attendants 'Find me a woman who is a medium'. They said, 'There is one in Endor'.

He disguised himself and went by night. He told her she would not be punished.

He said, 'Bring up Samuel'.

Samuel said, 'Why have you disturbed me by bringing me up (from the grave)?'

Saul said, 'God no longer answers me so I have called on you to tell me what to do'. (It must have been God's will to tell Saul what would be).

She said, 'The Lord will hand over both you and Israel to the Philistines and tomorrow you and your sons will be with me (dead)'.

Saul's strength was gone, so she insisted they eat before leaving (Chapter 28).

David Sent Back

When the Philistines gathered to fight Israel, David was still living in Philistine territory and was marching in the rear. When the commanders saw them they were angry and sent them back. They said, 'He must not go up with us into battle (God provided a way of escape for David)'.

David Destroys the Amalekites

When David and his men reached Ziklag on the third day, the Amalekites had raided, burned and taken the women captive. They wept aloud.

David found strength in the Lord. He inquired of the ephod. It said: pursue them.

Of the 600 men, 200 stayed behind, too exhausted to go.

They found an Egyptian who gave them food and water and told them where the raiders were. He had not eaten for 3 days and nights.

When David found them, they were eating and drinking because of the great amount of plunder they had taken from the Philistines and Judah.

David recovered everything and shared with the 200 men who were left behind and a lot of towns in Judah, including Hebron, later his capital (see Josh. 22:8). *Share and share alike.*

Saul Takes His Life

The Philistines pressed hard against Saul and his sons. They killed Jonathan, Abinadab and Malki-Shua and wounded Saul critically.

He wanted his armor bearer to finish him off. When he would not, Saul fell on his own sword and died. Saul, his 3 sons and armor bearer all died the same day on Mt. Gilboa.

They put his armor in the temple of their god and fastened his body to the wall. Brave men of Israel came and took down their bodies, burned them and buried them under a tamarisk tree at Jabesh. Saul had rescued Jabesh Gilead when he was first made king (see 1 Sam. 11).

Later, David buried Saul and Jonathan in the tomb of Saul's father, Kish, in Benjamin. Saul had had a fourth son, Ish-Bosheth (2 Sam. 2:8) and a concubine (2 Sam. 3:7)

2 Samuel

A Review

David Hears of Saul's Death

Three days after the death of Saul, a man came to David and told him about Saul and Jonathan's death. He said *he* had killed him, and brought his crown and arm band to David.

This story was different from the one related in 1 Samuel 31:1-5).

Evidently David recognized this as someone wanting his favor. He called one of his men to strike him down for destroying the Lord's anointed (according to what he said he did in verse 16).

David wrote a lament for Saul and Jonathan. He said nothing against Saul, rather, he praised him. He said, 'Saul and Jonathan: in life they were loved and gracious. And in death they were not parted… I grieve for you Jonathan my brother. You were very dear to me. Your love for me was wonderful, more wonderful than that of a woman'.

David Anointed King Over Judah

David inquired of the Lord, 'Shall I go up to one of the towns of Judah?' (He still had Abiathar the priest and the ephod with him, 1 Sam. 30:7, 8).

The Lord said, 'Go up'.

David said, 'Where?'

The Lord answered, 'Hebron'. (This was the city of refuge).

David took his two wives and the men who were with him and their families.

The men of Judah came to Hebron and anointed David king over the house of Judah.

This was his second anointing (see 1 Sam. 16:1-13).

Abner, the commander of Saul's army, made the remaining son of Saul, king over all Israel. He was 40 years old and reigned two years.

The house of Judah followed David for seven and a half years.

There was war between the two. David grew stronger and Saul grew weaker.

During the seven and a half years David was in Hebron, 6 sons were born to him, each from a different wife (3:2-5).

Abner Goes Over to David

Abner got angry with Saul's son because he accused him of sleeping with his father's concubine.

He sent word to David, 'Make an agreement with me, and I will help you bring all Israel over to you'.

David said he would, but he wanted his first wife (daughter of Saul, Michal, see 1 Sam 18:27). She had been given to another man, Paltiel, whose heart was broken when she was taken away. This made her wife number 7.

Abner conferred with the elders of Israel and said, 'For some time, you have wanted to make David your king. Now do it!'

Abner went to David at Hebron with 20 men. David prepared a feast for him, then sent him away in peace. (Abner was Saul's commander and Joab was David's commander).

After Abner left in peace, Joab returned to Hebron and found out what had happened. He told David Abner had come there to deceive him. He sent messengers and had him brought back (David knew nothing of this).

Joab took Abner aside as if to talk to him privately, stabbed him in the stomach and he died. (It was because Abner had killed his brother, Asahel, 2:18-23). The king David wept aloud.

The people of Israel knew the king had no part in the murder of Abner (Chapter 3).

Saul's Son Ish-Bosheth Murdered

Again, men try to get in David's good graces by violence. The slipped into Israel's king's house and stabbed him in the stomach while he was taking his noonday rest. They brought his head to David.

He told them, 'When a man came to me and said, "Saul is dead", he thought he was bringing me good news. I put him to death'. He then gave an order to kill these men (Chapter 4).

David Becomes King Over Israel

All the tribes of Israel came to David anointing him king over them. He was 30 years old when he started reigning over Judah. He reigned seven and a half years over Judah and 33 years over Israel and Judah in Jerusalem.

Hiram, king of Tyre, sent carpenters and supplies to build a palace for David. After David left Hebron, he took more concubines and wives and at this time he had a total of 17 sons.

The Philistines came out against David but the Lord fought for him. David brought together 30,000 men to go get the Ark of God at Abinadab's house. It had been there 20 years (1 Sam. 7:1, 2).

They set it on a new cart, celebrating with harps, lyre, etc. The oxen carrying the cart stumbled and Abinadab's son, Uzzah, reached out and took hold of the Ark. God struck him down and he died. Why? They were supposed to use poles to carry it (see Ex. 25:10-15).

David was afraid that day, not willing to take the Ark to Jerusalem. It stayed there three months. Then it was brought to Jerusalem, according to God's instructions, amid much celebration. David's wife, Michal (Saul's daughter), was embarrassed by his undignified actions. This caused her to be childless.

David was settled in his palace and had rest from his enemies. He didn't feel right for the Ark to be housed in a tent while he lived in a house of cedar.

His prophet at that time was Nathan. The Lord told Nathan, 'Go tell my servant David "Did I ever say, why have you not built me a house of cedar?" Tell my servant David "I took you from the pasture and from following the flock to be ruler over my people, Israel. I have been with you wherever you have gone and I have cut off all your enemies. I will make your name great like the names of the greatest men of the earth. The Lord himself with establish a house for you. Your offspring is the one who will build a house for my name".

David replied, 'Who am I, O Sovereign Lord, and what is my family that you have brought me this far? For the sake of your word and according to your will, you have done this great thing and made it known to your servant... (7:18-29)'.

David's Victories

In the course of time, David defeated the Philistines, Moabites, Hadadezer and the Arameans. The Lord gave David victory wherever he went. The gold, silver and bronze articles were dedicated to the Lord.

In his cabinet, he had a commander of the army, recorder, priests, secretary and advisors (Chapter 8).

David and Mephibosheth

David asked, 'Is there anyone still left of the house of Saul to whom I can show kindness, for Jonathan's sake?' There was a servant named Ziba who told him Jonathan had a son that was crippled in both feet. When he was five years old, the news about Saul and Jonathan came. His nurse picked him up and fled but as she hurried to leave, he fell and became crippled.

His name was Mephibosheth. David told him he would restore to him the land that belonged to his grandfather, Saul, and he would always eat at his table. Saul's servant Ziba and his sons and servants were to farm the land.

David and Bathsheba

In the spring when kings go off to war, David sent Joab out, but *he* stayed in Jerusalem.

One evening he got up from his bed and walked around on the roof of his palace. He saw a woman bathing and she was very beautiful. He sent someone to find out about her then sent for her and slept with her. She returned home.

Later, she sent word to David that she was pregnant. He sent for her husband who was fighting in the war. After talking to him a while, he sent him home but he did not go home. (David was seeking a way to hide what he had done).

David then asked the man, 'Uriah, why didn't you go home?'

He said, 'The Ark, Israel and Judah are staying in tents. My master, Joab and his men are camped in the open fields. How could I go to my house to eat and drink and lie with my wife?'

Even when David made him drunk, he would not go home. In the morning, David wrote a letter to Joab and sent it with Uriah.

It said, 'Put Uriah in the front line where the fighting is the fiercest…'

Joab sent David an account of the battle by messenger. Some of the king's men died. Your servant Uriah the Hittite is dead. Uriah was one of David's mighty men (24:39).

David told the messenger to tell Joab, 'Don't let this upset you, the sword devours one as well as the other'.

After a period of mourning, David had Bathsheba brought to his house and she became his wife (Chapter 11).

Nathan Rebukes David

The Lord sent Nathan to David who told him the story about the poor man who had one little ewe lamb and the rich man who had many. David did not realize the story was about him. Nathan said, 'The Lord has taken away your sin, but your son will die'.

David fasted and prayed for seven days while lying on the ground. After the child died, he arose, cleansed himself, worshiped and ate. He said, 'Can I bring him back again? I will go to him but he will not return to me'.

David comforted his wife and they had another son, Solomon. The Lord loved him (12:24, 25). Joab sent messengers to David to come and help in the fighting, which he did.

One of David's sons, Amnon, fell in love with his half sister Tamar. He went to bed and pretended to be sick so Tamar would come and give him something to eat. She made him some bread. He sent everyone out and when she brought the bread, he grabbed her and raped her. Then he hated her more than he had loved her (he was ashamed of himself). He threw her out and she went to her brother Absalom's house.

Absalom hated Amnon for disgracing his sister and two years later had him killed. He fled Geshur and stayed there three years. David longed to go to Absalom. Finally Joab devised a way to bring him back by sending a woman to David with a parable. David told Joab to bring Absalom back but not to him, to his own house.

Absalom was very handsome, no blemish in him, with long hair. He had three sons and a daughter. He lived in Jerusalem two more years before seeing his father, David (Chapter 14).

Absalom's Conspiracy

Absalom provided for himself a chariot and horses and fifty men to run ahead of him. He would get up early and stand by the side of the road leading to the city gate. When someone came with a complaint he said, 'If only I were appointed judge in the land! Then everyone who has a complaint would come to me'. He would reach out his hand, take hold of him and kiss him so he stole the hearts of the men of Israel.

His following kept increasing. A messenger came and told David, 'The hearts of the men of Israel are with Absalom'.

David said to all his officials in Jerusalem, 'Come! We must flee or none of us will escape from Absalom'.

The king set out with his entire household and many many other people following, some foreigners. The whole countryside wept aloud as the people passed by.

Zadok and the priests were carrying the Ark of the Covenant but David sent them back with the Ark saying, 'If I find favor in the Lord's eyes, He will bring me back'. David's head was covered and he was barefoot.

He sent some of his close friends and counselors back to pretend to be on Absalom's side but to keep David informed about what was going on.

Ziba, the steward of Mephibosheth, met David and brought donkeys, food and wine. When asked where Saul's grandson, Mephibosheth, was, Ziba said, 'He is staying in Jerusalem because he thinks his grandfather's kingdom will be given back to him (not true)'.

David believed him and gave him all that belonged to Mephibosheth (see 2 Sam. 19:24-30).

Shimei, a man from the clan of Saul came out when they passed that way, cursed David and threw stones at them. One of his men wanted David to let him kill Shimei but David said, 'My son, who is of my own flesh, is trying to take my life. Leave him alone'.

Ahithophel and Hushai were with Absalom to give advice. Hushai was there to frustrate whatever advice Ahithophel gave him.

Ahithophel advised Absalom the advice was not good. He said David and his men were fighters, as fierce as a wild bear robbed of her cubs. He said, 'Even now your father is hiding in a cave. *You* lead Israel into battle and destroy them'. They thought this better.

When David got the message, they all crossed the Jordan.

Ahithophel went home, put his house in order and hanged himself because his advice had not been followed.

Barzillai from Gilead brought bedding and all kinds of food for David and his people to eat (Chapter 17).

Absalom's Death

David divided his troops under three commanders. He wanted to march out with them but they said, 'You must not go out. They don't care about us. You are worth ten thousand of us'. He said, 'I will do what seems best to you'. The king told his three commanders, 'Be gentle with the young man Absalom, for my sake'.

The battle took place in the forest of Ephraim. The forest claimed more lives than the sword.

Absalom was riding his mule. As the mule went under the thick branches of a big oak tree, Absalom's head got caught in the tree. He was left hanging in mid-air while the mule kept going. One of Joab's men told him, 'I just saw Absalom hanging in the oak tree'. Joab said, 'Why didn't you strike him to the ground?' He took three javelins and plunged them into Absalom's heart. They threw him into a big pit and piled a large heap of rocks over him.

Two men ran to tell David the news, but couldn't come out and say he was dead. David went in an upper room to weep and mourn saying, 'O Absalom, my son, my son'.

Joab told David, 'Today you have humiliated your men who saved your life and the lives of your sons, daughters and concubines…If you don't go out, not a man will be left with you by nightfall'. David put aside his grief.

He replaced Joab with Amasa (Absalom's commander).

David Returns to Jerusalem

Judah sent word to the king to return. He went as far as the Jordan. The men of Judah came to meet the king and bring him across the Jordan.

Shimei, the one who had cursed him and thrown stones (16:5-13), fell before the king and confessed his sin. The king told Shimei, 'You shall not die'.

Ziba, the steward of Saul's household, was found to have betrayed Mephibosheth. Mephibosheth had been mourning all the while David was gone. He told them to divide the fields but Mephibosheth said, 'Let him have everything, now that you have arrived home safely'.

Barzillai, the one who brought the bedding and food to David (17:27-29) was 80 years old. David invited him to stay with him in Jerusalem but he didn't want to be a burden to David and wanted to die in his own town near the tomb of his father and mother.

Have you noticed how people are living shorter lives now? Moses had written in the 90th Psalm: The length of our days is seventy years or eighty if we have the strength…'

When David returned to his palace, where he had left the concubines to take care of the palace, he put them in a house under guard. They lived as widows until their death. This was because Absalom had slept with them (2 Sam. 16: 21, 22).

There was some rebellion to be put down, Sheba and Amasa were two. Joab killed the new commander David had appointed, Amasa, and was restored to his old position. David named a new cabinet, keeping Joab, Jehoshaphat and Zadok. The rest were new.

The Gibeonites Avenged

During the reign of David, there was a three year famine. The Lord said it was because Saul had put the Gibeonites to death. (Joshua had made a treaty with them to let them live when they were taking over Canaan, Joshua 9:22).

David asked how he could make amends. They said to give them seven male descendants of Saul. They killed them and exposed them on a hill. Rizpah, Saul's concubine (2 Sam. 3:7) stayed with the bodies to keep away the birds and wild animals until it rained. This moved David to rebury the bones of Saul and Jonathan in the tomb of Saul's father, Kish of Benjamin.

The Philistine Giants Eradicated

The Philistine giants were in battle with Israel. David went with his men and became exhausted. His men said, 'Never again will you go out with us to battle!' One of the giants had a spearhead that weighed seven and a half ponds. One had a spear with a shaft like a weaver's rod and one was a huge man who had 6 fingers on each hand and 6 toes on each foot. They were descendants of Rapha. They lived in Gob and Gath.

David's Song of Praise

David sang to the Lord the words to this song when the Lord delivered him from the hand of all his enemies.

2 Samuel 22:1-5, repeated in Psalm 18:1-50

The Last Words of David, Israel's Singer of Songs (Part 1)
The Spirit of the Lord spoke through me;
His word was on my tongue.
The God of Israel spoke,
The Rock of Israel said to me:

"When one rules over men in righteousness,
When he rules in the fear of the God,
He is like the light of morning, at sunrise.
On a cloudless morning
Like the brightness after rain
That brings the grass from the earth'".

David had men he called, 'mighty'. The three mightiest were Ish-Bosheth who killed 800 men in one encounter. Eleazar struck down Philistines until his hand grew tired and froze to the sword. Shammah, after Israel's troops fled, stood in the middle of a field of lintels, struck down Philistines and brought about a great victory.

Once, while the Philistines were camped nearby, David said, 'Oh that someone would get me a drink of water from the well near the gate of Bethlehem!'

The three mighty men broke through the Philistine lines and got him the water. He refused to drink it and poured it out. He said, 'Far be it from me to do this. Is it not the blood of men who went at the risk of their lives?' (I guess he was just wishing out loud for a cold drink).

David had 30 others he called mighty men, one was Uriah the Hittite (23:39)

David Counts the Fighting Men

On his own, David decided to take a census of the fighting men. Joab asked, 'Why does my lord want to do such a thing?'

It took nine months and twenty days. Israel had 800,000 and Judah had 500,000.

After the census was taken, David realized he had sinned. God told Gad the prophet to give David three options:

1. Three years of famine
2. Three months fleeing from their enemies
3. Three days of plague

The Lord sent a plague and 70,000 died. When the Angel of the Lord (Jesus) was at the threshing floor of Araunah the Jebusite, the Lord God said, 'Enough'. David said to the Lord, 'I am the one who has sinned. Let your hand fall upon me and my family'.

David Builds an Altar

The prophet Gad told David to build an altar to the Lord on the threshing floor of Araunah.

When Araunah saw David, he asked why he had come. David said, 'To buy your threshing floor so I can build an altar to the Lord, that the plague may be stopped'.

Araunah wanted to give it to David, but he said, 'I will not sacrifice to the Lord my God burnt offerings that cost me nothing'. He bought the threshing floor and the oxen for burnt offerings and fellowship offerings and the plague stopped.

The Temple of the Lord was built on the threshing floor of Araunah (2 Chron. 3:1) on Mt. Moriah, where the Lord had appeared to David. The details of this were recorded in 1 Chronicles Chapters 22 through 29.

1 Kings

A Review

First and Second Kings were originally one book, but was later made into two.

The total time the kings reigned was 465 years, from Saul to Zedekiah. It ended in 586 BC when Judah was taken into Babylonian captivity.

The kingdom of Judah lasted 136 years longer than Israel, due to some righteous kings. The kingdom of Israel had none.

David reigned seven and a half years in Judah and 33 years over all Israel (2 Sam. 5:4, 1 Kings 2:10, 11). He was 70 years old, probably worn out from all that fighting and grief. He could not keep warm. They found a beautiful girl, Abishag, to attend to his needs and lie beside him for warmth.

Adonijah, David's fourth son, wanted to be king. He was supported by Joab, David's commander, and Abiathar his priest. The other priest, Zadok, Nathan the prophet, and David's special guards did not.

Nathan went to Bathsheba and told her what Adonijah was trying to do. David had promised that her son, Solomon, would be king after him.

Bathsheba went to see David and told him what was happening. She told him if it came to pass, she and Solomon would be treated as criminals (killed).

At that time, Nathan arrived and told him that Adonijah was sacrificing a great number of cattle, had invited great numbers of people and they were saying, 'Long live King Adonijah!'

David Makes Solomon King

David called in Bathsheba. He said, 'I will surely carry out today what I swore to you. Solomon, your son, shall be king after me'.

He then called Zadok the priest, Nathan the prophet and Benaiah. He said, 'Put Solomon on my mule. Have Zadok anoint him king at Gihon. Blow the trumpet and shout, 'Long live King Solomon!' This they did. (David still had the strength and memory to make decisions, even from his 'sick bed'. When necessary, man can do extra-ordinary things!).

Adonijah and his guests heard the noise. Abiathar told him King David had made Solomon king, that they had put him on the king's mule and that Zadok and Nathan had anointed him King of Gihon. Adonijah's guests dispersed.

He went and took hold of the 'horns' of the altar, a place of refuge. Solomon was told Adonijah was afraid. He sent men to bring him down and sent him to his home (Chapter 1).

David's Charge to Solomon

David said to Solomon, 'I am about to go the way of all the earth. Be strong show yourself a man, observe what the Lord requires… so that the Lord may keep his promise to me: "If your descendants walk faithfully, you will never fail to have a man on the throne of Israel"'.

Solomon Gets Rid of People Who Did Evil to David

1. *Joab* killed David's commanders, Abner and Amasa. He told Solomon, do not let his grey head go down to the grave in peace.
2. *Shimei* called down curses on David and threw rocks at him. He promised not to put him to death, but now he did

not consider him innocent. Bring his grey head down to the grave in blood.

3. *Adonijah,* the son who would be king, asked Bathsheba to ask Solomon for the young woman, Abishag, as his wife. (David never had relations with her). He refused and had him put to death that day.

4. *Abiathar*, the priest, had been David's priest but was with Adonijah. He was not killed but was removed from the priesthood. He was replaced by Zadok.

David asked Solomon to show kindness to the sons of Barzillai and to let them eat at his table because they helped him when he was fleeing from Absalom (2 Sam. 17:27-29 & 19:31-38).

David slept with his fathers and was buried in Jerusalem.

Solomon Asks for Wisdom

Solomon married the daughter of Pharaoh, King of Egypt. The king went to Gibeon to offer sacrifices. They were still sacrificing on high places (hills). He offered 1000 burnt offerings there.

The Lord appeared to Solomon in a dream and told him to ask for whatever he wanted.

He said, 'I am only a little child and do not know how to carry out my duties. Give your servant a discerning heart to govern your people and to distinguish between right and wrong'
The Lord was pleased. He said, 'I will give you a wise and discerning heart; also riches and honor. In your lifetime you will have no equal among kings'.

A Wise Ruling

Two prostitutes came to Solomon, each claiming a live baby. They had babies three days apart but one of the women had killed her baby by laying on him accidentally. She swapped the dead baby for the live one.

Solomon called for a sword to cut the baby in half. The real mother said, 'Give the baby to her'. Solomon told them to give the baby to that woman. Israel could see Solomon had wisdom from God (Chapter 3).

Solomon's Officials

Solomon appointed 12 district governors. Each district was supposed to provide for one month in the year. He appointed a cabinet of nine, some kin, and some from David's cabinet.

Daily Provision
About 185 bushels of flour
About 375 bushels of meal
10 head of stall-fed cattle
100 sheep and goats
Deer, gazelles, roebucks and choice of fowl

He had 4,000 stalls for chariot horses and 12,000 horses (2 Chron. 9:25). During Solomon's lifetime there was peace. They ate, drank and were happy. He was wiser than any other man. His fame spread to all the surrounding nations. Men of all nations came to listen to Solomon's wisdom.

He spoke 3,000 proverbs and 1,005 songs.

Preparation for Building the Temple

Solomon sent a message to Hiram, King of Tyre, that he would be building a temple for the Lord. He told him to have cedars of Lebanon cut for him and he would pay whatever he said.

Hiram was pleased. He said he would provide the cedar and pine logs and float them in rafts by sea to them. Solomon was to provide food for Hiram's household.

King Solomon sent laborers from Israel. There were 30,000. They worked in shifts of 10,000 a month. They would work in Lebanon one month and have two months at home. This was *forced labor* (see 1 Sam. 8:11-17).

Solomon also had 70,000 carriers, 80,000 stonecutters and 3,300 foremen to provide dressed stone for the temple (Chapter 5). They were dressed at the quarry (6:7).

Solomon Builds the Temple

480 years after the Israelites left Egypt, in the 4th year of Solomon's reign, he began to build the temple. It was 90 feet long, 30 feet wide and 45 feet high. There was a porch across the front that extended out 15 feet. It had 2 pillars. The one on the left was named Boaz (2 Chron. 3:17). The inside walls and floors were made of cedar or pine covered with gold. The building of the temple had taken seven years.

Solomon Builds His Palace

The building of the palace took 13 years. It was larger and had more rooms. Also, Pharaoh's daughter had a separate palace. He judged from his palace (7:7).

The Temple's Furnishings

Solomon sent to Tyre for Huram (Hiram), from an Israelite tribe, Naphtali. He was highly skilled in bronze work. He came to Solomon and did all the work assigned to him.

He made all this:

The two pillars with capitals on top

400 pomegranates, for decoration

10 stands with 10 basins

The Sea and the 12 bulls under it

The pots, shovels and sprinkling bowls

These things were all made of burnished bronze (Ex. 27 for instructions God gave Moses on the Mt. for the tabernacle).

The Ark Brought In

The altar, table, lamp stands, floral work, basins and sockets for the door were made of gold.

When the temple was finished, Solomon brought in the things his father had dedicated: the silver, gold and furnishings (Chapter 7).

The priests brought the Ark of the Covenant and placed it in the Most Holy Place, beneath the wings of the cherubim.

There was nothing in the Ark except the two stone tablets that Moses had placed in it a Horeb (8:9).

When the priests withdrew, the cloud filled the Temple (the glory of the Lord).

Solomon Speaks

'The Lord has fulfilled his promise to my father David... My father had it in his heart to build a temple for the name of the Lord, but he said, "Your son will build it"...'

Solomon's Prayer of Dedication

He said, 'You have kept your promise to your servant David, my father...But will God really dwell on earth? The heavens, even the highest heavens, cannot contain you... When a man wrongs his neighbors and comes before your altar in this temple...then hear from heaven and forgive the sin of your people Israel.

When the heavens are shut up and there is no rain, because your people have sinned, when famine or plague, blight, mildew, locusts, grasshoppers or an enemy or whatever may come, hear and forgive...

Do whatever the foreigners asks of you, as do your own people Israel...When your people go to war, then turn back to you, hear their prayer and plea...'

When Solomon had finished his prayer and supplication from before the altar where he had been kneeling with his hands spread out toward heaven, he stood and blessed the whole assembly.

To The People

Not one word has failed... May the Lord be with us as He was with our fathers... so that all the peoples of the earth may know that the Lord is God and that there is no other. But your hearts must be fully committed.

Dedication of the Temple

Then the king and the people offered sacrifices: 22,000 cattle and 120,000 sheep and goats, burnt offerings, grain offerings and the fat of the fellowship offerings. This was over a period of 14 days.

After all this celebration, he sent the people away. They went home joyful and glad in their hearts for all the good things God had done (Chapter 8).

The Lord Appears to Solomon

When Solomon finished building everything (after 20 years) the Lord appeared to him a second time (in 3:5, it was in a dream).

God Speaks

I have heard the prayer and plea you made. If you walk before me in integrity...I will establish your royal throne forever...but if you, or your sons turn away, I will reject this temple and Israel will become an object of ridicule...

Solomon's Other Activities

Solomon gave Hiram, King of Tyre, 20 towns in Galilee for the supplies he had given them. Hiram was not pleased with them. Solomon built the temple, his palace and terraces, the wall of Jerusalem and the towns of Hazor, Megiddo and Gezer, also towns in the desert and store cities for his chariots and horses.

The laborers were the people in Canaan. They did not drive out, the Amorites, Hittites, Perizzites, Hivites and Jebusites. The Israelites were fighting men, government officials, charioteers, etc. They also supervised the men who did the work.

Three times a year, Solomon made the sacrifices (Passover, Pentecost and Tabernacle). He also had ships built. Hiram sent men to help in this endeavor also (Chapter 9).

The Queen of Sheba Visits Solomon

The Queen of Sheba heard about the wisdom of Solomon and came to see for herself. She came with a great caravan of gifts for him: spices, gold, precious stones...No question was too hard for him. When she saw the palace, the food on his tables, the servants, temple and burnt offerings she was overwhelmed.

She said, 'Not even half was told me'.

Jesus himself spoke of her to the Pharisees. He said, 'The Queen of the South will rise at the judgment with this generation and condemn it, for she came from the ends of the earth to listen to Solomon's wisdom and now, one greater than Solomon is here (Mt. 12:42).

Solomon's Splendor

The weight of gold that Solomon received yearly was about 25 tons. His goblets and household articles were pure gold. He had a fleet of trading ships that returned every 3 years with gold, silver, ivory, apes and baboons. The whole world sought an audience with Solomon and anyone who came brought gifts.

Solomon's Wives

King Solomon loved many foreign women. Women the Israelites were told not to marry because they would turn their hearts away from God. He had 700 wives of royal birth and 300 concubines. Solomon did not follow the Lord completely as the Lord told him to. He built 'high places' for his foreign wives to worship their gods.

The Lord became angry with him. He told him, 'Since this is your attitude and you have not kept my Covenant and my decrees, I will tear the kingdom away from you…but for the sake of David, your father, I will not do it during your lifetime. I will do it during the days of your son.'

Solomon's Adversaries

God raised up some adversaries against Solomon. David's commander Joab had struck down all the men of Edom (2 Sam. 8:13) but Hadad, while still a boy, fled to Egypt with some Edomite officials. Rezon was another adversary.

Jeroboam did his job well and Solomon put him in charge of all his labor force. Ahijah, a prophet, met him, wearing a new cloak. He took the cloak off and tore it into 12 pieces. He told Jeroboam, 'This is what the Lord says: "I am going to tear the kingdom out of Solomon's hands and give *you* 10 tribes. I will always have a lamp before me in Jerusalem, the city where I chose to put my name"'.

Solomon tried to kill Jeroboam, but he fled to Egypt.

Solomon's Death

Solomon reigned in Jerusalem over all Israel 40 years. He was buried with his father in the city of David. His son, Rehoboam, succeeded him (Chapter 11).

Israel Rebels Against Rehoboam

Rehoboam went to Shechem where the Israelites had gone to make him king. Jeroboam was still in Egypt, but when he heard about this, he returned. He, along, with the assembly of Israel, went to Rehoboam to try to get him to lighten the yolk of Solomon had put on them. He told them to come back in three days for his decision.

He consulted the older men and they advised him to be a servant to the people, then he consulted the younger men and they told him to make the yoke even heavier. He followed the advice of the younger men. The Israelites called Jeroboam to their assembly and made him king.

Only the house of Judah and Benjamin remained loyal. Rehoboam was going to fight but was told to go home. This was the Lord's doing.

Golden Calves at Bethel and Dan

Jeroboam went to live in Shechem but he thought: if the people go to the temple in Jerusalem to offer sacrifices, they will kill me and return to Rehoboam.

He told the people, 'It's too much for you to go to Jerusalem'. He made two golden calves and put one in Bethel and one in Dan. He built shrines and appointed priests that were not Levites and made sacrificial offerings (Chapter 12).

The Man of God From Judah

A man of God came from Judah to Bethel while Jeroboam was standing by his altar. He cried out to the altar and said, 'A man named Josiah will be born to the house of David and will sacrifice the priests of the high places here'.

Jeroboam stretched out his hand and said, 'Seize him!' His hand shriveled up. He said, 'Pray for me that my hand by restored' and he did.

The king said, 'Come home with me and have something to eat'. The man of God answered, 'Even if you were to give me half of your possessions, I would not go and I would not eat or drink'.

There was an old prophet living in Bethel. His sons told him what had happened. He rode after him and found him sitting under an oak tree. The old prophet said, 'Come home with me and eat'. The young prophet said he couldn't. The old prophet said an angel had told him to bring him back (but he was lying). The young prophet believed him and went.

While they were still sitting at the table, the word of the Lord came to the old prophet and he cried out to the man from Judah, 'This is what the Lord says: "You have defied the word of the Lord and have not kept the command I gave you. You came back and ate and drank. Your body will not be buried in the tomb of you fathers".

As he left there and went on his way, a lion met him on the road and killed him. When the old prophet heard about it, he went out and found the body with the donkey and the lion standing beside it. The lion had not eaten the body or mauled the donkey. The old man brought his body back and buried it in his own tomb.

He said, 'When I die, bury me beside him'. (He was filled with regret. A person may leave the truth but he'll never forget it, Capter 13.)

The Divided Kingdom

Ahijah's Prophecy Against Jeroboam

Jeroboam's son was ill. He told his wife to go to Shiloh to the prophet Ahijah, in disguise, to see what would happen to the boy. The Lord had forewarned Ahijah she was coming and what to tell her.

The boy would die, his kingship would be destroyed. The Lord told his wife (through the prophet) that he had done more evil than all who lived before him. He reigned 22 years. His son, Nadab, succeeded him.

Rehoboam, King of Judah

Rehoboam was 41 years old when he became king and reigned 17 years in Jerusalem. Judah also did evil. They set up high places and engaged in the practices of the nations the Lord had driven out. In the fifth year of his reign, the King of Egypt attacked Jerusalem and carried off the treasures of the temple and the palace.

His son, Abijah succeeded him. He reigned three years. There was war between Abijah and Jeroboam. His son, Asa, succeeded him. Asa reigned in Jerusalem 41 years. He did what was right, even deposing his grandmother.

He did not remove the high places but his heart was fully committed to the Lord all his life. In his old age his feet became diseased. Nadab, son of Jeroboam, became king of Israel in the second year of Asa. He reigned 2 years walking in the ways of his father. As soon as he began o reign, he killed Jeroboam's whole family (see 1 Kings 14:10). It was because of the sins of Jeroboam.

Baasha reigned 24 years in Israel and continued the evil ways (Chapter 15). Elah reigned in Israel two years and was killed by his chariot commander, Zimri.

Zimri succeeded him and killed off Baasha's whole family. He only reigned 7 days.

1 Kings says these events were written in the book of the Annals of the King of Israel.

Josephus says the holy prophets wrote them.

Peter says, 'No prophecy of scripture came about by the prophet's own interpretation, but men of God spoke from God as they were carried along by the Holy Spirit (2 Peter 1:20, 21).

Omri was the next King of Israel. He reigned 12 years. He built a city on the hill of Samaria. It became the capital of Israel until its fall in 722 B.C. He sinned more than those before him. Ahab, his son, succeeded him. He reigned in Samaria 22 years. He did more evil tan *any* of those before him, assisted by his wife Jezebel. They set up an altar for Baal (an idol) and started worshipping it.

During Ahab's time, Hiel of Bethel rebuilt Jericho (continues later) at the cost of his oldest and youngest sons (see Josh. 6:26).

Elijah was the prophet to Israel during the time of Ahab. There was a three and a half year famine. At first Elijah was sent to the Kerith Ravine east of the Jordan and was fed by ravens. When the water dried up, he was sent to a widow in Zarephath.

Jesus said in Luke 4:24, 'There were many widows in Israel in Elijah's time, when the sky was shut up for three and a half years...but Elijah was sent to a widow in Zarephath'.   In Revelation 11:6 it says, 'These men have power to shut up the sky so that it will not rain during the time they are prophesying'.

This widow had one last meal when Elijah arrived and asked for bread. This flour and oil was not used up while she fed Elijah.

This drought was punishment for Israel's idolatry. The drought was severe in Samaria.

The Lord told Elijah to go to Ahab for the drought was about to end. There was a faithful man, Obadiah, who was in charge of Ahab's palace. Elijah met him and told him to tell

Ahab he was there. He was afraid to tell him but did so. He had hidden 100 of the Lord's prophets in two caves and fed them.

Elijah told Ahab to bring him the 450 prophets of Baal and two bulls. Each one was to call on his god. The prophets of Baal went first. They prepared their bull and called on Baal from morning until noon. Elijah began to taunt them saying, 'Shout louder!' They continued this until evening and nothing happened.

Elijah prepared the altar with twelve stones and dug a trench around it. They poured twelve large jars of water on the meat and wood and into the trench. Elijah prayed, 'O Lord, let it be known today that *you* are God in Israel…' Fire came down and burned up the sacrifice, wood, stones, soil and water. The people were convinced. Elijah had the false prophets slaughtered.

He told Ahab to eat and drink, for there is the sound of heavy rain. He went up on Mt. Carmel. He sent his servants to go and look toward the sea. After the seventh time, the servant said, 'A cloud as small as a man's hand is rising from the sea'.

Then Elijah sent him to tell Ahab, 'Hitch up your chariot and go down, before the rain stops you'. The power of the Lord came on Elijah and he ran ahead of Ahab (Chapter 18).

Elijah Flees to Horeb (Sinai)

Ahab told his wife, Jezebel, about all her prophets being killed. She threatened to kill Elijah. He was afraid and ran for his life. He sat down under a broom tree and prayed that he might die. He said, 'I have had enough, Lord'. He fell asleep. An angel touched him and said, 'Get up and eat'. There was bread baked over hot coals and water. This happened twice. This food lasted 40 days until he reached the mountain of the Lord, Horeb. Elijah told the Lord, 'I am the only one left and now they are trying to kill me too'.

The Lord said, 'Go back. Anoint Elisha to succeed you as prophet. I reserve 7,000 in Israel whose knees have not bowed down to Baal…'

When Elijah found Elisha, he was plowing with 12 yokes of oxen. Elijah threw his cloak around him. Elisha knew this meant he would take Elijah's place. He requested that he kiss his father and mother goodbye.

He killed the oxen, cooked them with the plowing equipment, fed the people and followed Elijah.

Ahab Defeats Ben-Hadad

Ben-Hadad's entire army and 32 other kings attacked Samaria. He sent word to Ahab that he wanted what Ahab had and he agreed. Then, Ben-Hadad wanted what his officials had. This they refused. A prophet came and told Ahab the Lord would give him that vast army. They won that day and the next spring they tried it again in the valley. They won again.

Ben-Hadad went to Ahab. He said, 'I will return the cities my father took from your father'. He wanted to live.

Ahab made a treaty with him and let him go. This displeased the Lord. He sent a prophet to tell him, 'You have set free a man I had determined should die'.

Naboth's Vineyard

Ahab lived in Samaria, but there was a man who lived in Jezreel who had a vineyard close to his palace. Ahab wanted it to use it for a vegetable garden. Naboth wouldn't sell or trade it because it was his father's inheritance under the Law of Moses (Lev. 25:23). Ahab was angry. His wife, Jezebel, said, 'I'll get it for you'. She wrote letters (in Ahab's name) accusing Naboth of cursing both God and the king. (It was untrue). He was stoned and Ahab took possession of the vineyard.

Elijah found him there and told him in the same spot where dog's licked up Naboth's blood, they would lick up his and his descendants would be cut off in Israel. Also, Jezebel would be devoured by dogs. Ahab humbled himself and God said he would not bring disaster in his day but in the days of his son, Ahaziah (see 2 Kings 9:30-36, 10:1-17).

Micaiah Prophesies Against Ahab

Ahab and Jehoshaphat agreed to go to war against Ramoth Gilead, but wanted to be sure of victory. Ahab's 400 prophets were predicting success, but they sent for Micaiah, a prophet of the Lord. Ahab hated him because he never said anything good about him.

Micaiah at last told him, 'The Lord has put a lying spirit in the mouths of these prophets of yours. The Lord has decreed disaster for you'.

Ahab Killed

Ahab and Jehoshaphat (King of Judah) went into battle together. Ahab wore a disguise. The King of Aram had given orders not to fight anyone except the King of Israel. Someone at random drew his bow and hit the King of Israel between the sections of armor. (The Lord never missed his mark).

The battle raged with the king propped up in his chariot. That evening he died. He was brought back to Samaria for burial but they washed the chariot and dogs licked up the blood that flowed from the chariot to fulfill the scripture (21:19). He reigned 22 years.

Jehoshaphat King of Judah

Jehoshaphat was the son of Asa. He was 35 years old when he became king and reigned 24 years. He did what was right.

He was also peaceful with Ahab, the King of Israel. After Ahab died and his son, Ahaziah, was king, he was not partners with him because he walked in the ways of his father and mother (Ch 22).

Kings of Israel: Saul, David and Solomon (40 years each).

Divided Kingdoms

Judah

Rehoboam	17 years
Abijah	3 years
Asa	41 years
Jehoshaphat	25 years

Israel

Jeroboam	22 years
Nadab	2 years
Baasha	24 years
Elah	2 years
Zimri	7 days
Omri	12 years
Ahab	22 years
Ahaziah	2 years

(This is only through the end of 1 Kings)

2 Kings

A Review

This book contains the history of the rest of the kings of both Israel and Judah and their conquests by Assyria and Babylon. It shows how God directs the affairs of nations.

Elijah, then Elisha, were both prophets to Israel, the northern kingdom.

After Ahab's death, his son Ahaziah reigned over Israel 2 years. He fell and injured himself. He sent messengers to Baal to find out if he would recover.

The Angel of the Lord sent Elijah to intercept the messengers and ask them, 'Is it because there is no God in Israel that you are going to consult Baal? Tell him, you will not leave your bed, you will die'.

When they told the king he asked, 'What kind of man was it?' They said, 'He was a man with a garment of hair and a leather belt around his waist (see also Matt. 3:4)'. The king said, 'That was Elijah'.

Ahaziah sent a captain with 50 men to Elijah to tell him to come down. They said, 'Man of God, the king says to come down!' Elijah said, 'If I am a man of God, may fire come down from heaven and consume you and your 50 men'. It did. This happened twice, but the third time, the captain fell on his knees and begged Elijah for their lives.

The Lord told Elijah to go down. He told the king the same thing he had already been told and he died.

Elijah Taken up to Heaven

Elijah and many prophets knew he was to be taken up to heaven that day. He was sent by the Lord to three places before he was taken up: Bethel, Jericho and the Jordan River. Elisha would not leave him. When they got to the Jordan, Elijah took his cloak, rolled it up and struck the water. It divided and they crossed on dry ground. Elisha asked to inherit a double portion of his spirit. Elijah said, 'If you see me when I am taken up, it will be yours'.

Suddenly, as they were walking along, a chariot and horses of fire appeared, separating the two of them. Elijah went up to heaven in a whirlwind.

Elisha took the fallen cloak, struck the water and it divided for him. He crossed over. The prophets from Jericho searched for Elijah but did not find him (see Gen. 5:24).

The first thing Elisha did (after dividing the Jordan) was to heal bad water by adding salt.

Elisha is Jeered

Elisha left Jericho and went to Bethel. Some youths came out saying, 'Go on up, you baldhead, go on up you baldhead!'

He called a curse down on them in the name of the Lord. Two she-bears came out of the woods and mauled 42 of the youths. He went on from there to Mt. Carmel and to Samaria.

Moab Revolts

Joram, a son of Ahab, became King of Israel and reigned 12 years. He did evil but not as much as his parents. He got rid of Baal. The King of Moab had to supply Ahab with 100,000 lambs and the wool of 100,000 rams. After he, Ahab, died, the king rebelled.

The King of Israel asked Jehoshaphat, the King of Judah, and the King of Edom to go with him to fight Moab. They agreed but after a seven day march through the desert, they had no more water. They went to Elisha. Because of his respect for Jehoshaphat, he went to the Lord.

He told them to make the valley full of ditches. The next morning they were full of water and the sun made it look like blood to the Moabites. The Lord gave the Moabites over to them. They destroyed the towns, fields and good trees.

When the King of Moab saw they were beaten, he sacrificed his first born son who was to succeed him (Chapter 3).

The Widow's Oil

The wife of a man who had been a prophet cried out to Elisha for help to pay her creditors. He asked if she had anything of value. 'Only a little oil' she said. He said, 'Go ask all your neighbors for jars. Pour oil into them and go sell it and pay your debts'.

The Shunammite Woman

One day, Elisha went to Shunem. A woman invited him to her house for a meal. After that, whenever he came by, he would stop to eat. She asked her husband if they could make a small room for him on the roof and furnish it with a bed, table, chair and lamp. He had a servant named Gehazi.

Elisha asked her what he could do for her. His servant, Gehazi said, 'She has no son and her husband is old'.

Elisha told her, 'About this time next year, you will hold a son in your arms'.

When the child got older, he went to the field where his father was reaping, complaining of his head. A servant carried him to his mother. She held him until noon and he died.

She immediately set out to find Elisha at Mt. Carmel. They could see something was terribly wrong. Elisha sent Gehazi ahead to lay his staff on the boy's face but nothing happened. Elisha stretched himself out on the boy and he grew warm. He did this once more, the boy sneezed seven times and opened his eyes (Heb. 11:35).

Death in the Pot

There was a famine in the region of Gilgal. Elisha was meeting with a company of prophets and told his servant to cook a large pot of stew for them.

One of them gathered some wild gourds and cut them up in the stew. As they began to eat, they cried out, 'O Man of God, there is death in the pot'. He put some flour in the pot and it was okay.

Feeding a Hundred Men

A man brought Elisha 20 loaves of bread to feed 100 men. They all ate and had some left over (as the Lord did, Luke 9:13).

Naaman Healed of Leprosy

Naaman was the commander of the King of Aram. He was highly regarded but he had leprosy. His wife had a young servant girl that had been a captive of Israel. She told Naaman's wife there was a prophet in Samaria who could cure him.

Naaman got permission to go, taking a letter to the King of Israel, money and clothing. When the King of Israel read the letter he said, 'Am I God? Can I kill and bring back to life?'

Elisha heard about it and sent a message: 'Have the man come to me and he will know there is a prophet in Israel'. When he got to Elisha's door, a messenger told him to go and wash seven times in the Jordan. This angered Naaman, but his servant reasoned with him and he obeyed. His flesh was as clean as a young boy's. He went back to Elisha and tried to give him the gifts he had brought, but Elisha refused.

He asked for some earth to take home.

Gehazi, Elisha's servant, ran after Naaman and asked for some money and clothing. Because of this, he and his were made leprous and he went from Elisha's presence.

An Axhead Floats

Elisha and a company of prophets went to the Jordan to cut down trees and make a bigger place to meet. As one of the men was cutting down a tree, the axhead fell into the water. Elisha cut a stick, threw it into the water and made the iron float.

Elisha Traps Blinded Arameans

The King of Aram was at war with Israel, but Elisha would warn the king of Israel as to their whereabouts. They set out to find Elisha and capture him.

When he got up the next morning, they were surrounded by an army with horses and chariots.

Elisha told his servant, 'Don't be afraid. Those who are with us are more than those who are with them'. The Lord opened the servant's eyes. He looked and saw the hills full of horses and chariots of fire.

Elisha prayed for God to strike the men with blindness and led them to Samaria. After setting a great feast before them, he sent them home. Aram stopped raiding Israel after that.

Famine is Samaria

There was a great famine in Samaria. Everything was very expensive. The King, Joram, was passing by on the wall. A woman asked him for help. He said, 'If the Lord won't help you how can I?'

She and another woman agreed to eat their babies. They ate hers but when it came time to eat the other woman's, she had hidden it. The king blamed Elisha and sent a messenger ahead to kill him, but they held the door. Elisha told them, 'This time tomorrow, food will sell cheap'.

The Siege Lifted

There were 4 men with leprosy. They said, 'If we stay here we will die, if we go into the city, we will die. Let's go over to the camp of the Arameans and surrender'. When they arrived, no one was there. The Lord had caused the Aramean army to hear the sounds of a great army (they thought Israel had hired the Hittites and Egyptians to attack them). In fear, they left their tents, horses, money, clothes and food and ran for their lives.

These men felt guilty and went back and reported it to the gatekeepers. The Israelites went out and gathered up the bounty and ended the famine for a while (Chapter 7).

The Shunammite's Land

Elisha had sent the Shunammite's family to the land of the Philistines during a seven year famine. She came back home and went to the king to beg for her house and land. *The providence of God was at work*. At this *exact time*, Gehazi was talking to the king about some things Elisha had done, especially about the Shunammite woman and the raising of her son from the dead (Chapter 4:8-36). Just then, the woman and her son walked in.

Gehazi said, 'This is the woman and her son!'

The King assigned an official to return everything that belonged to her, plus the income it had brought (8:1-6).

Ben-Hadad, King of Aram, was ill and sent Hazael to Elisha to see if he would recover. He answer was yes, but he would die.

The next day, after finding out he would recover, Hazael took a thick cloth, soaked it in water and spread it over the king's face so that he died. He then became king (8:7-15).

Jehoram, King of Judah

Good king Jehoshaphat's son, Jehoram, became King of Judah. He was 32 years old and reigned 8 years. He married a daughter of Ahab and walked in the ways of Israel.

Ahaziah, King of Judah

Ahaziah became king at age 22 and he reigned 1 year. He was also related to Ahab's family by marriage. Ahaziah went to visit King Joram who had gotten injured in battle.

During the meantime, Elisha had sent one of his prophets to anoint Jehu, son of Jehoshaphat, King over Israel.

While King Hazael of Judah was visiting King Joram in Jezreel they heard troops approaching and rode out in separate chariots to meet them. (The lookout had reported, 'The driving is like that of Jehu, he drives like a madman).

When Jehu was anointed, he was told to destroy the house of Ahab, so that day Jehu shot King Joram with his bow and wounded King Hazael of Judah. He was carried back to Jerusalem for burial.

Jezebel painted her eyes, arranged her hair and was looking out of a window. Jehu told some eunuchs to throw her down and she was trampled underfoot of horses. When they went to bury her, they found nothing but skull, feet and hands. The words of Elijah's prophesy's were fulfilled (see 1 Kings 21:19-23), that dogs would devour Jezebel's flesh at Naboth's vineyard.

Ahab's Family Killed

Elisha had told Jehu to destroy the whole house of Ahab, slave or free (9:7, 8). First, he had 70 sons of Ahab killed (10:1-11), then 42 relatives of Ahaziah, the King of Judah.

Next, he called an assembly of the ministers of Baal under the pretext of offering sacrifices to Baal. He had posted 80 men to kill everyone inside.

Jehu destroyed Baal worship in Israel but not the golden calves in Bethel and Dan. He obeyed the destruction of Ahab but did not return to the Lord.

He reigned for 28 years and his descendants sat on the Israeli throne for four generations. He was buried in Samaria and Jehoahaz, his son succeeded him.

Athaliah and Joash

The King of Judah was killed on the same day Ahab's son was killed (9:21-27). King Ahaziah's mother proceeded to destroy the whole royal family so she could rule. She ruled for six years but Ahaziah had a young son.

His half sister, Jehosheba, was marred to a high priest, Jehoiada (2 Chron. 22:11). Jehosheba stole the baby away and hid him and his nurse in a bedroom in the temple for 6 years. In the seventh year, Jehoiada, the high priest, brought out the king's son, put the crown on him and proclaimed him king.

As the people were rejoicing, blowing trumpets, clapping and shouting 'Long live the king', Athaliah came out to see what all the noise was about. The high priest ordered her killed outside the temple area.

Joash was seven years old when he began to reign and reigned 40 years. He did what was right in the eyes of the Lord all the years. Jehoiada, the priest, instructed him. Joash wanted to repair the temple, but by his 23rd year, it still had not been repaired. Jehoiada made a chest for offerings. They were used to hire workmen to repair it.

When Jerusalem was threatened by attack, Joash gave the sacred objects and gold to the King of Aram so he would withdraw. After Jehoiada's death, Joash turned away from God and even killed Jehoiada's son.

Joash was murdered by two of his officials. Amaziah, his son, succeeded him.

Elisha Dies

Jehoash was king of Israel when Elisha was suffering from the illness that killed him. He went to see Elisha and wept over him. He said, 'My father! My father! The chariots and horsemen of Israel'. This is the same thing Elisha said when Elijah went up to heaven in a whirlwind (2 Kings 2:12). It seemed to be a high tribute.

Once, some Israelites were burying a man when they saw a band of Moabite raiders. They threw the man in Elisha's tomb. When the body touched Elisha's bones, he came to life (13:21).

Israel Attacks Judah

Amaziah, son of Joash, became King of Judah and reigned 29 years. He executed the officials who murdered his father.

Jehoash attacked Judah, took the king, broke down a 600 foot section of the Jerusalem wall and took the gold and silver from the temple.

Amaziah lived 15 years after the death of Jehoash. His 16 year old son, Azariah (or Uzziah), was made king. He ruled 52 years, partly in isolation. He ruled through his son, Jotham. The Lord afflicted him with leprosy and until the day he did, he lived in a separate house (see why he had leprosy in 2 Chron. 26, also reviewed later).

The next three kings only served short terms and were assassinated: Zechariah–six months, Shallum–one month, Pekahiah–two years (Chapter 15). Pekah served 22 years but he too was assassinated.

Jotham and Ahaz, Kings of Judah

Jotham, who had ruled while his father Azariah had leprosy, ruled on his own sixteen more years. He rebuilt the Upper Gate of the temple.

Ahaz, King of Judah

He was 20 years old and reigned 16 years. He walked in the ways of the Kings of Israel and even sacrificed his own son in the fire. He built a large new alter and redid a lot of other things in the temple (2 Chron. 28 for more details).

Hoshea, Israel's Last King

Israel disobeyed God from the beginning of their kingdom until the end. All the kings did evil, some worse than others.

God brought the curses on them he had promised in Deuteronomy 28:47-68. He did this through Assyria. They laid siege to it for 3 years, then deported the Israelites to Assyria.

The Exile of Israel

They were exiled because they worshipped other gods and followed the practices of the nations the Lord had driven out. The Lord warned them through his prophets but they would not listen. They followed worthless idols and as a result they became worthless. They made calves, Asherah poles, Baal, sacrificed their sons and daughters and practiced divination and sorcery. They were taken from their homeland into exile in Assyria.

Samaria Resettled

Samaria was also built on a hill, like Jerusalem, about 880 BC by Omri, the 6th King of Israel (1 Kings 16:24). It is about 42 miles north of Jerusalem.

After the Israelites were deported, the King of Assyria brought in other people to replace them. When lions were killing some of the people, the king sent one of the captive priests back to teach the people how to worship the Lord.

They worshipped the Lord but also continued to serve their own gods. The religion was further corrupted. There were some people left behind who intermarried with these people that were brought in. They were mixed Jews, eventually called Samaritans, despised by true Jews (see John 4:4-9).

Hezekiah, King of Judah

Six years before the fall of Israel, Hezekiah began to reign in Judah. He was 25 years old and reigned 29 years. He did what was right. He removed the high places, smashed the sacred stones and cut down the Asherah poles. The bronze snake Moses had made in the wilderness was still being worshipped. Hezekiah broke it into pieces. It was called Nebushtan. It was hundreds of years old.

He kept the commands God had given Moses. The King of Assyria attacked some of the cities of Judah but Hezekiah gave him gold to withdraw. It was taken from the temple. 2 Kings 17-20 and Isaiah 36-39 are the same (3 Chapters).

The King of Assyria continues to harass Hezekiah. He wanted to know what Hezekiah was basing his confidence on. Isaiah had sent word for Hezekiah not to be afraid. Assyria's commander called out, 'Do not listen to Hezekiah. He is misleading you when he says the Lord will deliver you'.

The people remained silent because the king commanded them to.

Again, the Assyrian King sent messengers to Hezekiah saying, 'Surely you have heard what the Kings of Assyria have done to all the countries, destroying them completely'.   He didn't want to destroy Judah, it seems.

Hezekiah prayed for help against all odds. He prayed, 'It is true, O Lord, that the Assyrians have laid waste these nations. Now, O Lord, deliver us from his hands, so that all kingdoms on earth may know that you alone, O Lord, are God' (Chapter 19).

The King of Assyria thought it was his great might that conquered these lands, but it was ordained of God (19:25).

Isaiah sent this message from God, 'He will not enter this city or shoot an arrow here. I will defend this city and save it, for my sake and the sake of David my servant'.

That night, the angel of the Lord (the Lord himself) went out and put to death 185,000 men in the Assyrian camp. King Sennacherib withdrew and returned to Nineveh and stayed there.

Hezekiah's Illness

Hezekiah became ill. The prophet Isaiah went to him and said, 'Put your house in order for you will not recover'.

Hezekiah wept bitterly. He prayed, 'O Lord, I have walked before you faithfully and with wholehearted devotion'.

Before Isaiah had left the court, the word of the Lord came to him. 'Go back, tell Hezekiah, "I have heard your prayers and seen your tears. I will heal you and add 15 years to your life. Prepare a poultice of figs and apply it to the boil'.

He died at age 54. He would only have been 39 years old if the 15 years were not added (see 18:2). [25 + 29 = 54 -15 = 39].

Hezekiah brought water into Jerusalem by means of a tunnel. Isaiah prophesied that the time would come when everything in Hezekiah's palace and all that his father's had stored up would be carried to Babylon and that some of his descendant's would become eunuchs in the palace of the King of Babylon (more information in 2 Chron. 29-32).

Manasseh

Manasseh was 12 years old when he became king and reigned 55 years. A son of Hezekiah but evil. He rebuilt the high places, altars to Baal and made Asherah poles. He sacrificed his own son in the fire. His father was the best of the Kings of Judah and his son, Manasseh was the worst and led the people astray.

The Lord said through his prophets, 'I am going to bring such disaster on Jerusalem and Judah that the ears of everyone who hears of it will tingle. I will wipe out Jerusalem'.

Amon

Amon, son of Manasseh, was 22 when he became king and reigned 2 years. He continued in the evil his father had done and was assassinated by his own officials.

Josiah

Josiah was 8 years old when he became king and reigned 31 years. If he was the first son of Amon, he was a father at age 16. [22 + 2 = 24 – 8 = 16] He did what was right, not turning to the right or the left as Moses has instructed in Deuteronomy 5:32. In his eighteenth year, he started repairs on the temple. Hilkiah, the high priest, found the Book of the Law in the temple. When King Josiah heard the words, he knew it had not been obeyed.

They went to consult with a prophetess named Huldah. She told them the Lord was going to bring disaster on Judah, but because they had humbled themselves, they would not see it. (It was not because of Josiah).

The king read the words of the book and all the people pledged to obey them. He then proceeded to destroy every high place and every idol in the whole country, every false god and place of worship.

He even went to Samaria and did the same. They observed the Passover for the first time since the days of the Judges (2 Chron. 35:1-19).

He served the Lord with all his soul, heart and strength. He was killed in battle by the pharaoh of Egypt, Neco.

The stages of Josiah's spiritual growth:
1. At age 16, he began to seek the God of David (2 Chr. 34:3)
2. At age 20, he began to get rid of all the idols (2 Chr. 34:3-7)
3. At age 26, he started repairing the temple (2 Chr. 34:8)

Jehoahaz and Jehoiakim

After Josiah's death, his son Jehoahaz was made king. He reigned 3 months and was carried off to Egypt by pharaoh Neco (who had killed Josiah). His half brother, Eliakim, was made king in Jehoahaz's place and his name changed to Jehoiakim. He reigned 11 years.

During Jehoiakim's reign, Nebuchadnezzar invaded Judah and he was his servant for 3 years, and then rebelled. When he died, his son, Jehoiachin became king. He reigned 3 months. Nebuchadnezzar laid siege to Jerusalem and King Jehoiachin (who was 18 years old) surrendered to him along with his family, fighting men, craftsmen and artisans, a total of 10,000. Only the poorest people were left.

Nebuchadnezzar made Jehoiachin's uncle king and changed his name to Zedekiah. He reigned eleven years. In Zedekiah's ninth year, Nebuchadnezzar marched against Jerusalem with his whole army. It was under siege for two years. He burned the temple, the royal palace and all the houses of Jerusalem; every important building. They broke down the Jerusalem walls and carried into exile the people that remained. They left behind some of the poorest people to work the vineyards and fields. They took all the gold and silver items from the temple (bronze pillar, bronze sea, pots, shovels, dishes, censers and sprinkling bowls). In his 37th year of exile, Jehoiachin was released and ate at the king's table and given an allowance. By then, he was about 55 years old. (This was after Nebuchadnezzar's death).

The Rest of the Kings of Israel and Judah

Israel		Judah	
Joram	12 years	Jehoram	8 years
Jehu	28 years	Ahaziah	1 year
Jehoahaz	17 years	Joash	40 years
Jeroboam	41 years	Amaziah	29 years
Zechariah	6 months	Azariah	52 years
Shallum	1 month	Jotham	16 years
Menahem	10 years	Ahaz	16 years
Pekahiah	2 years	Hezekiah	29 years
Hoshea	9 years	Manasseh	55 years
(went into Assyrian captivity)		Amon	2 years
		Josiah	31 years
		Jehoahaz	3 months
		Jehoiakim	11 years
		Jehoiachin	3 months
		Zedekiah	11 years
		(went into Babylonian captivity)	

1 Chronicles

A Review

The books of Chronicles could be called the books of history. Chapters 1-9 list the genealogy from Adam to King Saul. The rest of the book retells the life of David.

Altogether there were 62 generations from Adam to Christ.

1. Adam
2. Seth
3. Enosh
4. Kenan
5. Mahalalel
6. Jared
7. Enoch
8. Methuselah
9. Lamech
10. Noah

10 generations, Adam to flood. 1 generation at that time was 155 years. See Genesis 5 for ages.

11. Shem
12. Arphaxad
13. Shelah
14. Eber
15. Peleg
16. Reu
17. Serug
18. Nahor
19. Terah
20. Abraham

10 generations, from flood to Abraham.

21. Isaac
22. Jacob
23. Judah
24. Perez
25. Hezron
26. Ram
27. Amminadab
28. Nahshon
29. Salmon
30. Boaz
31. Obed
32. Jesse
33. David
34. Solomon

Divided Kingdom

35. Rehoboam
36. Abizah
37. Asa
38. Jehoshaphat
39. Jehoram
40. Azariah (Uzziah)
41. Jotham
42. Ahaz   The Kings of Judah
43. Hezekiah   until the exile.
44. Manasseh
45. Amon
46. Josiah
47. Jehoiakim
48. Jehoiachin
    Zedekiah (uncle)

49. Jeconiah
50. Shealtiel
51. Zerubbabel
52. Abuid   Royal line from the captured
53. Eliakim   Jehoiachin; born after the
                 exile to Babylon.
54. Azar
55. Zadok
56. Akim
57. Eliud   Note: No man cold have
58. Eleazar   known all these names,
59. Matthan   but God does.
60. Jacob
61. Joseph
62. Jesus

These were not always the oldest sons. Example, Adam's son, Seth, was his third as Abel was killed and Cain banished. Noah's son, Shem, was the second son (Gen. 10:21) and Jacob's son, Judah, was his fourth (in the line of Jesus).

Things of note the Bible mentions about some are:

Nimrod was a mighty warrior (Gen. 10:8-12)

Peleg, in his time the earth was divided. That is, they were scattered and given new languages.

Ishmael, as well as Jacob, had 12 sons (1:29).

Boaz was the great-grandfather of David (2:11, 12)

David was the baby of the family (2:15). He had six sons born in Hebron, nine in Jerusalem (besides those born by his concubines, 3:19).

Solomon was Bathsheba's 4th son (3:5)

Jabez was more honorable then his brothers. He cried out to God, 'O that you would bless me and enlarge my territory! Let your hand be with me and keep me from harm so that I will be free from pain'. (This request was granted and a book written about it).

Reuben, Jacob's first born slept with his father's concubine, Bilhah (Gen. 35:22) and his rights as firstborn were given to the sons of Joseph (5:1, 2).

Levi, Jacob's third son, was the great-grandfather of Moses and Aaron. The temple musicians were also Levites. Asaph wrote songs.

Joshua descended from Joseph (7:20). Joseph's son was Ephraim.

After the Babylonian captivity, the first to resettle on their property were some priests, Levites and temple servants.

Saul Takes His Life

The Philistines were fighting against Israel on Mt. Gilboa. Saul and his three sons were all involved. The sons all got killed and Saul wounded. He wanted his armor-bearer to finish him off. He wouldn't, so Saul fell on his own sword. The Philistines put his armor in the temple of their gods and his head in the temple of Dagon. It all happened because of his unfaithfulness and because he did not inquire of the Lord.

David Becomes King

All Israel came together to make David king (see 1 Sam. 16:1-13). They marched to Jerusalem. The Jebusites were living there and David said, 'Whoever leads the attack against them will be my commander'. Joab did.

David led a group he called his 'mighty men'. The three mightiest were Jashobeam (who killed 300 men in one encounter), Eleazar (when the troops fled from a field of barley, he stayed and fought and won a victory), Abishai (the brother of Joab, was chief of the three. He also killed 300 men).

Uriah the Hittite was among the mighty men. Many mighty men joined David's army, some from Saul, some Gadites,

Benjaminites, and Manasseh. Day after day men came until he had a tremendous army, all volunteers.

All the tribes sent men, armed for battle, to make David king over all Israel. They spent three days there, eating and drinking food they had brought from home. There was joy in the land.

David said to the assembly after conferring with his officers, 'Let's go bring the Ark back'. It was at Kiriath Jearim.

Uzzah and Ahio, sons of Abinadab, were guiding it on a new cart. The people were singing and playing musical instruments. The oxen pulling the cart stumbled and Uzzah reached out his hand to steady the Ark. The Lord struck him dead because he had touched the Ark.

David was afraid to take it any further and left it at the house of Obed Edom for three months.

David's Family

Hiram, King of Tyre, sent cedar logs, stonemasons and carpenters to build a palace for David. In Jerusalem, David took more wives and had more sons and daughters (13).

Philistine's Defeated

The Philistines came out against David, but he inquired of God what to do and God was with him. The Lord made the nations fear him.

The Ark Brought to Jerusalem

After David built himself buildings, he made a place to put the Ark, a tent. He told them only the Levites could carry the Ark. They were supposed to carry it with poles on their shoulders, as Moses commanded. There was much rejoicing and excitement over its return, but one of his wives, Michal, was embarrassed to see David dancing and celebrating. After it was in place, they offered sacrifices.

David gave a loaf of bread, a cake of dates and a cake of raisins to each Israelite man and woman there. On that day, David wrote a psalm of thanks to the Lord (16:8-36).

Even though the Ark had been brought to Jerusalem, the tabernacle Moses had made in the wilderness and where the offerings were still made was in Gibeon.

David felt bad because he was living in a new house of cedar and the Ark of the Covenant was under a tent. He wanted to build a house for God. God sent word by Nathan the prophet that David was not the one who would build it. When his days were over, his son would build it (Chapter 17:1-4).

God said he had never asked anyone to build him a house. He says He took David from the pasture and from following the flock to make him ruler and he would make his name like the names of the greatest men of the earth. David went in and prayed, thanking the Lord for all he had done.

David's Victories

The Lord gave David victory after victory: the Philistines, Gath, Moabites, Zobah, the Arameans, Hadadezer, and Edom.

He stored up the articles of gold, silver and bronze taken from these nations to be used in building the temple.

His officials were:
Joab (over the army)
Jehoshaphat (recorder)
Zadok ⎤
Abimelech ⎦ (priests)
Shavsha (secretary)
Benaiah (over the Kerethites and Pelethities)
His sons (officials at the king's side)

The Ammonites

David thought he was being nice by sending a delegation to Ammon when their king died. They thought he was using this to spy out the country and seized the men he had sent, shaved them and cut off their garments in the middle and at the buttocks. He then sent them away. David told them to stay in Jericho until their beards had grown before coming home.

The Ammonites realized they were in trouble and hired trooped to go against Israel. Eventually they lost 7,000 charioteers and 40,000 foot soldiers, all because of a misunderstanding.

Kings went off to war in the spring. Joab led the Israelites against Rabbah and other Ammonite towns and made laborers of them. Then they went to Gezer. They killed the brother of Goliath, then Gath where David's brother killed a man with 24 fingers and toes.

David Takes a Census

David insisted on taking a census of the fighting men. In all Israel, there were one million one hundred thousand men who could handle a sword. Joab realized this was wrong and it was also evil in God's sight. David realized he had sinned and God was going to punish him for it. He gave him three things from which to choose: three years of famine, three months of being defeated by their enemies or three days of plague.

David chose the plague and 70,000 men in Israel died. Even the Lord was grieved and said, 'Enough'.

David asked the Lord to let the plague fall on him and his family. It's hard to see others suffer for something you did. It does not say why this was wrong, but it seems that numbers mean nothing, if the Lord is with you in battle. He did not win by might.

David was told to build an altar on the threshing floor of Araunah. He went to Araunah and asked to buy the threshing floor to build an altar for burnt offerings, so the plague would stop.

Araunah offered to give it to him, but David insisted on paying for it. After David had sacrificed there he said, 'The House of the Lord is to be here (the temple)'.

Preparations for the Temple

David starts making preparations for building the temple. He said his son, Solomon, was young and inexperienced and the house to be built was to be magnificent in the sight of all nations. He appointed stonecutters, provided iron for the nails, bronze, cedar logs, gold, silver, workmen, masons, carpenters and skilled craftsmen.

He talked to his son, Solomon, and told him he had wanted to build, but the Lord told him he had fought too many wars and shed much blood. He told Solomon he would be granted peace and quiet so he could build the house (temple).

He made Solomon king before he died.

The Levites, 30 years old or more, were counted. There were 38,000. They were to supervise the work, some to be officials and judges, some gatekeepers and some to praise the Lord with musical instruments.

The sons of Moses, Gershom and Eliezer were counted as part of the tribe of Levi (1 Chron. 23:14, 15). The sons of Aaron, Eleazar and Ithamar's descendants were the priests Zadok, a descendant of Eleazar, and Abimelech, a descendant of Ithamar.

Since the Israelites were not moving about anymore and there was no need for them to move the tabernacle and items of worship, they were assigned to other duties. They took care of the courtyards, side rooms and other work in the temple. The priests were divided into 24 groups. They had regular times to serve at the worship services (one or two weeks at a time). The rest of the Levites were appointed by the casting of lots (Ch 24).

The Musicians

There seemed to be 288 leaders involved in the ministry of music, from the sons of Asaph, Heman and Jeduthun. Chapter 23:5 says there were 4,000 in all. These were also chosen by lot, all Levites.

Other Duties

Other duties decided by lot were gatekeepers, treasury guards and civil duties. There were four gates to be guarded and a storehouse for the treasuries, where the valuable plunder was stored; things dedicated by David, Samuel, Saul, Abner and Joab.

The Army

Back then, the only military was the army, broken up by divisions. There were 24,000 men in a division. They served on active duty one month at a time (27:1). This would amount to 288,000. Each division was under a different leader, one from each of the 12 tribes.

Other Overseers

Other things David needed overseers and their helpers for were: royal storehouses, storehouses in the towns and villages throughout the land, field workers, vineyards, the produce of the vineyards, olive and sycamore trees, the supplies of olive oil, herds grazing in Sharon, herds in the valleys, the camels, the donkeys, the flocks. All these were in charge of David's property. Also, David's uncle, Jonathan, was a counselor and scribe, Jehiel took care of the king's sons; Ahithophel was the king's counselor, Hushai was the king's friend and Joab the commander of the Royal Army (Chapter 27).

David's Plans for the Temple

David assembled all his officials and mighty men. He made this speech (paraphrased):

'I had it in my heart to build a house for a place of rest for the Ark of the Covenant of the Lord. I made plans to build it. God said, I was not to build it because I was a warrior, but my house would be king over Israel. He chose my son, Solomon, to build it. Now, I charge you to follow all the commands of the Lord so that you may pass on this good land to your descendants forever.

Then he said to Solomon: Serve the God of your father. If you seek him, he will be found by you, but if you forsake him, he will reject you forever (28:9, 10)'.

David gave Solomon all the plans for the temple that the Spirit had put in his mind: the temple, it's buildings, storerooms, upper and inner rooms, place of atonement, treasuries for the dedicated things, divisions of the priests and Levites, the weights of the gold and silver to be used in making various articles to be used in the temple. David said he had all this in writing. He told Solomon to do the work and not to be afraid or discouraged, for the Lord would be with him.

Gifts for Building

Still speaking to the whole assembly, David said, 'The task is great and my son, that God has chosen, is young and inexperienced. With all my resources, I have provided supplies: gold, silver and bronze, wood, precious stones and marble. I now give my personal treasures (besides the rest): 3,000 talents of gold (about 110 tons) and 7,000 talents of refined silver (about 260 tons).

The people assembled were given an opportunity to give, which they did freely and wholeheartedly.

David Prayed Before Them All

...Everything in earth and heaven is yours. Wealth and honor come from you...All this abundance that we have provided comes from your hand...I have given willingly...I have seen with joy how willingly your people, who are here, have given to you...They bowed and fell prostrate before David.

Solomon Acknowledged

The next day, they made sacrifices of burnt offerings to the Lord. They ate and drank with great joy and acknowledged Solomon as king. Everyone there pledged submission to Solomon.

David ruled 40 years, seven in Hebron and 33 in Jerusalem. The records of his reign were written by Samuel, Nathan and Gad (29:29).

God loved David because he nearly always honored Him. He was a very loving and penitent person. He died at age 70 (2 Sam. 5:4).

2 Chronicles
A Review

The books of Chronicles give us additional information to things written in Kings. 2 Chronicles goes from the time of Solomon to the fall of Jerusalem in 586 BC, and the kingdom of Judah.

Solomon

When Solomon's kingdom was firmly established, he, along with the commanders, judges, leader and heads of families went to Gibeon to offer sacrifices.

After all this time, the tabernacle Moses made one year after leaving Egypt was still in use after close to 480 years (1 Kings 6:1).

The Ark had been brought to Jerusalem. The Lord appeared to Solomon and told him to ask for whatever he wanted. Solomon asked for wisdom and knowledge to lead the people.

Because of this, he was given more wisdom than any other man and also more wealth, riches and honor than any other man (1:7-12).

Silver and gold became common in Jerusalem.

Solomon started making preparations for building the temple. He had 70,000 carriers, 80,000 stone cutters and 3,600 foremen. These were aliens.

He sent a message to Hiram, King of Tyre, to send him cedar, pine and Algum logs from Lebanon. He also asked for someone skilled to work in gold and silver, bronze and iron, engraving and yarn. His payment for this was:

About 125,000 bushels of ground wheat

About 125,000 bushels of barley

About 115,000 gallons of wine

About 115,000 gallons of olive oil

King Hiram replied, 'The Lord has given King David a wise son. I am sending you Huram-Abi, a man of great skill. He is trained in the work you need and will work with your craftsmen. Send the wheat, barley, wine and oil and we will cut the logs and float them by rafts to Joppa'.

The temple was to be used for:
  Burning incense
  Setting out the consecrated bread
  Making burnt offerings morning and evening, Sabbaths,
  New moons and appointed feasts (2:4)

Solomon began to build the temple in the 4th year of his reign on Mt. Moriah. It was built on the threshing floor of Araunah where David had built an altar (see 1 Chron. 21:18).
  The foundation was 30 feet by 90 feet.
  The Most Holy Place was 30 feet by 30 feet.
  The curtains were of blue, purple and crimson yarn and fine linen.
  The two pillars were named Jakin and Boaz.

Huram-Abi, the skilled workman from Tyre, made many of the things for the temple.
  The two pillars and their decorations (400 pomegranates, 4:13).
  The stands with their basins (4:6)
  The Sea and twelve bulls under it (4:14)
  The pots, shovels and meat forks (4:11), these things were of polished bronze.

These things were made of pure gold:
The tables of the bread of the presence
The lamp stands
The floral work
The wick trimmers, sprinkling bowls and dishes and censers, the doors of the Most Holy Place, temple and main hall.

When the work was finished they carried the Ark to the Most Holy Place. There was nothing in it except the two tablets Moses had placed in it a Horeb. The Tent of Meeting was brought up with its furnishings.

When everything was completed, the temple was filled with a cloud (the glory of the Lord). The whole assembly of Israel was there. Solomon blessed them and explained why he was chosen to build the temple.

He offered a <u>prayer of dedication</u>. Some of the things he said were:

1. Lord, you have kept your promise
2. Will God really dwell on earth with men?
3. When your servants pray toward this place, hear from heaven and forgive.
4. When Israel is defeated by an enemy because they have sinned, when they confess, forgive.
5. When the heavens are shut up and there is no rain because of sin, when they pray toward this place and turn from sin, forgive.
6. When famine and plague comes and a plea is made, forgive.
7. When foreigners come and pray toward this temple, do whatever he asks so the peoples of earth may know your name and fear you (Chapter 6).

When Solomon finished praying, fire came down from heaven and consumed the burnt offering and sacrifices. He sacrificed 22,000 head of cattle and 20,000 sheep and goats.

At the end of 20 years, Solomon had built the temple and his own palace. He brought Pharaoh's daughter, his wife, to the palace he had built for her.

The Queen of Sheba heard of Solomon's fame and came to Jerusalem to see him and ask him hard questions. She brought a large caravan of gifts; spices, gold and precious stones. When she saw his wisdom, his palace, the food on his table, the offering at the temple, she said, not even half was told to me. King Solomon gave her more than she had brought him.

Solomon lived amid an abundance of gold. The weight he received yearly was 25 tons.

Solomon had a great throne of ivory and gold, sailing ships that brought in all kinds of goods and thousands of horses and chariots.

After ruling for 40 years he too died and his son, Rehoboam succeeded him.

Rehoboam

All this luxury of Solomon's had put a heavy yoke on the people. Rehoboam consulted both the old and young as to how to serve the people.

The older ones said to lighten the load, while the younger ones said to make it even heavier.

He followed the advice of the younger men he had grown up with. (This turn of events was from God).

Israel rebelled against this and Rehoboam was only able to keep Judah and Benjamin. He lived in Jerusalem. The priests and Levites who trusted in the Lord went to Jerusalem, even abandoning their property to do so (Chapter 11).

Rehoboam had 18 wives and 88 children. He reigned 17 years. He and Judah abandoned the Lord. The Lord brought Shishak, King of Egypt, against Jerusalem and Rehoboam humbled himself. After his death, his son Abijah became king and reigned three years. He was a good king. The armies of Judah and Israel came together to fight. Abijah tried to dissuade Jeroboam, King of Israel, by telling him God was on their side but to no avail. Israel lost many men and three towns. Abijah married 14 wives and had 38 children.

After him was Asa. He also did right in the sight of the Lord. He won a great battle over the Cushites and got a large amount of plunder and cattle. Asa removed the idols from the whole land of Judah and Benjamin and from the towns they had captured.

A lot of people from Manasseh, Simeon and Ephraim had come back from Israel, when they saw that the Lord was with Asa. They vowed to be faithful to the Lord.

For 35 years the land was at peace. When Asa saw trouble brewing, he took silver and gold out of the treasuries of the temple and gave it to Ben-Hadad, the King of Aram, to get them to withdraw. The Lord was not pleased that Asa asked someone other than him to help him.

The Lord told him:

'For the eyes of the Lord range throughout the earth to strengthen those whose hearts are fully committed to him. You have done a foolish thing'.

In his thirty-ninth year, Asa was afflicted with a disease in his feet and even then, did not seek help from the Lord.

In his forty first year, he died.

Jehoshaphat

Asa's son, Jehoshaphat, succeeded him. In his early years, he walked in the ways of his father and amassed great wealth and honor. He sent priests to the towns of Judah to teach them the Law. He became more and more powerful and built up a great army of fighting men (1,160,000).

He married one of Ahab's daughters. Ahab and Jehoshaphat went to war together to attack Ramoth-Gilead. Ahab wore a disguise so no one would know who he was, but someone drew his bow at random and hit the King of Israel. While the battle raged, he sat propped up in his chariot, then at sunset he died. Ahab ruled 22 years.

When Jehoshaphat returned to his palace in Jerusalem, Jehu the seer went out to meet him. He said to him, 'Should you help the wicked and love those who hate the Lord?'

Jehoshaphat appointed judges to help him. He warned them to serve faithfully in the spirit of the Lord. Some men came and told Jehoshaphat, 'A vast army from Ammnon, Moab and Mt. Seir are coming against you'.

He prayed because he did not know what to do. The spirit of the Lord came upon a Levite, a descendant of Asaph. He said, 'Do not be afraid, the battle is not yours, but Gods'.

Early the next morning, Jehoshaphat told the people to sing. When the men of Judah came to the overlook, all they saw were dead bodies and so much plunder it took 3 days to collect it. They returned joyfully to Jerusalem and went to the temple.

The kingdoms were fearful and Jehoshaphat's kingdom had rest on every side (Chapter 20).

He was 35 years old when he became king and reigned 25 years. He made an agreement with the king of Israel to build a fleet of trading ships, but the Lord destroyed them (Ch. 20).

Jehoram

Jehoshaphat's first son, Jehoram, became King over Judah. He was 32 years old and reigned eight years. He killed all his brothers, married a daughter of Ahab and did evil, as Ahab had done. He led Judah astray. The Lord caused Judah to be attacked and his goods, sons and their wives to be carried off. Jehoram was given a disease of the bowels and died in great pain.

Ahaziah

All Jehoram's sons had been killed except the youngest, Ahaziah. He was king at age 22 and reigned one year. He went to Israel to visit King Joram. While there, he met his death. There was no one able to take the place of the king so his mother, Athaliah, destroyed the whole royal family of Judah and made herself ruler.

Ahaziah had a young son named Joash. His aunt hid him and his nurse in the temple for 6 years. His aunt's husband was a priest. In the seventh year, the priest Jehoiada revealed the child and made a covenant with the people. He said, 'The king's son shall reign, as God has promised the descendants of David'.

Jehoiada guided Joash as long as he lived. When Athaliah heard all the noise the people were making over having a king again, she tore her robes and shouted, 'Treason!'

Joash was 7 years old when he became king and reigned 40 years. Joash repaired the temple with the temple tax, brought by free will offerings placed in a chest outside the gate. As long as Jehoiada lived, burnt offerings were made continually in the temple. He lived to be 130 years old, much older than the promised age. God's providence?

After Jehoiada's death, Joash turned away from God. He even had Jehoiada's son stoned to death. His officials killed him in his bed (Chapter 24).

Amaziah

Amaziah was 25 years old when he became king and reigned 29 years. He executed the officials who murdered his father, but not their families (Deut. 24:16).

He had 300,000 men, 20 years old or more, but that wasn't enough to suit him so he hired 100,000 more from Israel. A man of God came and told him he was not to hire unfaithful men to fight with him, so he sent them home. Amaziah went to battle with the Edomites with his own army and won but brought back their gods and sacrificed to them.

God brought Israel against him. They broke down a 600 foot long section of the Jerusalem wall and took the treasures of the temple. He turned away from the Lord, even leaving Jerusalem. He was killed in Lachish (Chapter 25).

Uzziah (Azariah)

He was 16 years old when he became king and ruled for 52 years. He did what was right, having been instructed by Zechariah, the son of the good priest Jehoiada (24:20).

He was a restorer, a builder, a lover of the soil and a protector of his people, having a well trained army of 300,000. His fame spread and he became powerful. His pride led to his downfall. He went into the temple to burn incense, which only the Levites were supposed to do.

Leprosy broke out on him. He had to live outside the palace the rest of his life and his son, Jotham, had charge of the palace and governed in his place (Chapter 26).

Jotham

Jotham was 25 years old when he became king and reigned 16 years. He did what was right. He rebuilt the upper gate, repaired the wall and built towns, forts and towers (Ch 27).

Ahaz

Ahaz was 20 years old when he became king and reigned 16 years. He did not do what was right. He cast idols for worshipping and offered sacrifices to them. Israel came and fought them. In one day, they killed 120,000 soldiers in Judah and took 200,000 wives, sons and daughters captive.

A prophet went out to meet the army as it returned. He told them they did not win because God was for them, but because he was angry with Judah and to return the captives. They returned them to Jericho with food and clothing.

King Ahaz became more and more unfaithful to the Lord and became a total idol worshipper. He closed the doors of the temple and put up altars on the street corners.

Hezekiah

Hezekiah was 25 years old when he became king and reigned 29 years. In his first month, he opened the doors of the temple and brought in the priests and Levites. Hezekiah realized why Judah was being punished.

He purified the temple and offered sin offerings for the kingdom. The people brought animals for burnt offerings. The King sent letters to Ephraim and Manasseh (in Israel) inviting them to come and join in the celebration of the Passover. Some came. A very large crowd assembled in Jerusalem on the 14th day of the second month. Not since the days of Solomon had there been such a gathering of people for the Passover and with great rejoicing.

The morning and evening burnt offerings were resumed as well as on the Sabbath, New Moons and appointed feasts as written in the Law of Moses.The land prospered so much Hezekiah had to build store rooms.

The King of Assyria invaded Judah. Hezekiah told the people God would help them fight. The King of Assyria wrote a letter saying, 'On what are you basing your confidence? Hezekiah is misleading you'.

King Hezekiah and the prophet Isaiah prayed for help and the Lord sent his angel who destroyed all the fighting men of the Assyrians (see 2 Kings 20). He was given great riches and honor. He made treasuries, storage buildings for food supplies, villages and channels of water into the city (Ch 29-32).

Manasseh

Manasseh was 12 years old when he became king and reigned 55 years. He did evil. He rebuilt the high places and erected altars to the idols his father had destroyed. He practiced sorcery, divination and witchcraft. He put carved images in God's temple. The Lord brought the army of Assyria against

Judah and they took Manasseh prisoner with a hook in his nose and shackles. This brought him to repentance. He was brought back and tried to make amends. He got rid of the foreign gods and the altars he had built and restored temple worship (Ch 33).

Amon

Amon was 22 years old when he became king and reigned only 2 years. He did evil, but did not repent as his father had done. He was assassinated by his officials in his palace (Ch. 33).

Josiah

Josiah was eight years old when he became king and reigned 31 years. He did what was right, not turning aside to the right or to the left. In the 8th year of his reign, when he was 16 years old, he began to seek God, destroying all the altars of the idols, even to towns in Israel.

In his 18th year he began repairs on the temple, entrusting the work to supervisors. While repairing the temple the book of the Law of Moses was found. Josiah knew it had not been kept.

God spoke through a prophetess, Huldah. She said the Lord was going to bring disaster on Judah, but Josiah would not see it. Josiah and the people celebrated the Passover.

Josiah provided from his own possessions 30,000 sheep and goats, 3,000 cattle as well as offerings from others. It was the greatest celebration since the prophet Samuel.

Josiah disguised himself in battle and was shot by an archer in his chariot.

Jehoahaz

Jehoahaz was 23 years old and reigned three months. The King of Egypt carried him off to Egypt and made his brother king. He changed his name from Eliakim to Jehoiakim.

Jehoiakim

Jehoiakim was 25 years old when he became king and reigned 11 years. He did evil. Nebuchadnezzar, King of Babylon, attacked him and took him to Babylon in bronze shackles. He also took articles from the temple (2 Kings 24:1).

Jehoiachin

He was made king at age 18, reigned three months and ten days. He was taken to Babylon and his uncle, Zedekiah, took his place.

Zedekiah

Zedekiah was 21 years old when he became king and reigned 11 years. He did evil and would not turn to the Lord, neither the rest of the people.

The Lord brought against them the Babylonians, who spared not young or old. They carried away the articles from the temple, set it afire as well as the palaces and anything of value.

Those who escaped the sword were carried away as servants until 70 years were completed. This happened in the first year of Cyrus, king of Persia.

Cyrus made a proclamation in writing which said, 'The Lord, the God of Heaven, has given me all the kingdoms of the earth and he has appointed me to build a temple for him at Jerusalem in Judah. Anyone of his people among you – may the Lord his God be with him, and let him go up (return)'. (Ezra 1).

Ezra

A Review

Written by Ezra (7:28, 8:1)

Because of the sinfulness of Judah in turning away their hearts from God and worshipping idols, they were sent into captivity for 70 years under King Nebuchadnezzar in Babylon.

Now the time is drawing to a close and the Lord moved the heart of Cyrus, King of Persia, to let them return.

This fulfilled what the prophetess Huldah had told Josiah in 2 Chronicles 34:22-28.

This did not all happen in one day. The exile was spread out over a period of about 19 years. The first was in the third year of Jehoiakim's reign and ended at the end of Zedekiah's reign in 586 BC (2 Chron. 36:11…).

Dates of departure:	Dates of return:
605, 597 and 586 BC	538, 455 and 444 BC

Cyrus's Proclamation

'The Lord, the God of Heaven, has given me all the kingdoms of the earth and He has appointed me to build a temple for him at Jerusalem in Judah. Anyone of his people among you – may his God be with him and let him go up to Jerusalem in Judah and build the temple of the Lord, the God of Israel, the God who is in Jerusalem. The people of any place where survivors may now be living are to provide him with silver and gold, goods and livestock and freewill offerings for the temple of God in Jerusalem'(1:2-4).

The family heads of Judah and Benjamin, priests and Levites, all who wanted to, prepared to leave with their neighbors assisting them. King Cyrus brought out the articles belonging to the temple that Nebuchadnezzar had carried away. There were 5400 articles (Chapter 1).

The people were in the company of Zerubbabel, a descendant of King Jehoiachin, and in the lineage of Christ (Matt. 1:13). The number returning with Zerubbabel was 49,897 men. This included the priests, Levites, singers, gatekeepers and temple servants.

Each went to his own town, but some could not prove their ancestry. The journey from Babylon to Palestine would have taken about four months.

They gave to the treasury for the rebuilding of the temple according to their ability.

Although the foundation had not been laid, on the first day of the seventh month they started offering burnt offerings.

Levites 20 years or older were to supervise the building. It began one year and one month after their return.

When enemies offered to help in the building, Zerubbabel said, 'we alone will build it'. The people around them tried to discourage the building. They wrote a letter to King Artaxerxes trying to get the work stopped. They wrote him, 'The Jews are rebuilding that rebellious and wicked city. If it is built, there will be no more taxes, tribute or duty paid to you. Issue an order for the men to stop work'. He stopped the work temporarily until about 15years later. (During the second year after the reign of Daruis, Chapter 4)

When Zerubbabel started back building, men came to him and said, 'Who authorized you to rebuild this temple?' (5:3).

A letter was sent to King Darius. It said, 'The people are building with large stones and the work is being carried on with diligence. They say King Cyrus issued a decree to rebuild the temple. Let a search be made to see if this is true (5:17)'.

In fact, it was true. It was to be 90 feet high and 90 feet wide. The costs were to be paid by the royal treasury and the gold and silver articles (taken from Solomon's temple) returned. Do not interfere with this work on the temple of God (6:15).

It was dedicated and the Passover celebrated for seven days (see Ex. 12).

Ezra

Ezra, a descendant of Aaron, through his son Eleazar, came up from Babylon next.

He was well taught in the Law of Moses. He brought a letter written by King Artaxerxes. It said, 'To Ezra, the priest, a teacher of the Law of the God of Heaven: Any of the Israelites in my kingdom who wish to go to Jerusalem may go'.

He was to take the silver and gold from the king as well as free-will offerings.

With part of this money, he was to buy animals to sacrifice at the temple in Jerusalem.

Ezra thanked God that he had put it into the king's heart to bring honor to the house of the Lord in Jerusalem.

He took courage and gathered leading men from Israel to go up with him.

1754 more men returned with Ezra. They fasted in order to humble themselves for the journey (Chapter 8).

He said he was ashamed to ask for soldiers and horsemen for protection (because he had told the king, 'the gracious hand of our God is on everyone who looks to him').

Everyone arrived safely, after a 4 month trip. They weighed out the silver and gold, recorded it and sacrificed burnt offerings (Chapter 8).

Intermarriage

Leaders came to Ezra and told him the people, including the priests and Levites, had intermarried with the neighboring peoples.

Ezra said when he heard this, he pulled hair from his head and beard and lay down appalled (9:1-3).

He prayed, 'O my God, I am too ashamed and disgraced to lift up my face to you... You have been gracious in leaving us a remnant, you have not deserted us in our bondage, and you have granted us new life... We have disregarded the commands you gave us when you said, "Do not give your daughters in marriage to their sons or take their daughters for your sons". You have punished us less than we deserved (Chapter 9).

While Ezra was praying and confessing, weeping and throwing himself down, a large crowd gathered around him.

One of the men, Shecaniah, said, 'Let us make a covenant before our God to send away all these women and their children (see Deut. 7:3).

A proclamation was sent out for all the exiles to assemble. Ezra stood up and said to them, 'You have been unfaithful, you have married foreign women. Separate yourselves from the peoples around you and from your foreign wives'.

Those guilty of intermarriage were:

17 priests
10 Levites
84 others
111 men had married foreign women.

They agreed to send their wives and children back from whence they came, to make Israel pure again spiritually (Ch. 10).

Their seventy years in exile showed the Jews that they were not chosen eternally no matter what they did. It was conditional on the fact they had to be faithful.

Daniel was taken in the first exile (Dan. 1:1-7).

Esther and Mordecai were taken about eight years later in the reign of Jehoiachin (Esther 2:6).

Nehemiah

A Review

Nehemiah was the cupbearer of King Artaxerxes of Persia. He was serving in the winter residence of the citadel of Susa when some men came there from Judah. Nehemiah inquired of them how things were going for the exiles who had returned to Jerusalem. He found out the wall was still broken down and the province was in disgrace.

When he heard these things, he was very dejected. For some days he wept and mourned, fasted and prayed. He remembered the warning of Moses that they would be scattered if they were unfaithful, but God would bring them back.

When they brought wine before the king, he could see that Nehemiah was sad. When asked why, even though he was fearful, he told the king, 'The city where my fathers are buried lies in ruins and its gates have been destroyed by fire'.

The king said, 'What is it you want?' Nehemiah answered, 'If your servant has found favor in your sight, let me go and rebuild it'. The king consented.

He asked for letters for safe travel and timber to build with. When he arrived at Jerusalem, after three days he started examining the walls at night before deciding what to do. He said nothing about why he was there.

When he told them what he wanted to do and had the king's blessing they said, 'Let us start rebuilding'. Despite ridicule, the work progressed, section by section.

44 sections were repaired by different people or families. The people worked with all their hearts. They worked from the first light of dawn until the stars came out, with materials in one hand and a weapon in the other. They stayed inside Jerusalem at

night, none taking off his clothes or shedding his weapon even when they went for water (Ch. 4). The Jews were charging interest to their poor countrymen (see Ex. 22:25). Nehemiah told them to stop. For the 12 years Nehemiah was governor, neither he nor his brothers ate the food allotted to the governor. Each day 150 Jews ate at his table. Each day, one ox, six sheep and poultry were pre-pared and every ten days an abundant supply of wine was used.

The Wall Completed

The wall was completed in 52 days. After this, the nations were afraid because they knew the work had been done with God's help. Gatekeepers, singers and Levites were appointed. The gates were not to be opened until the sun was hot.

The city of Jerusalem was large but few people were in it because the houses had not been rebuilt. Nehemiah got a listing of people who had returned with Zerubbabel (see Ezra 2). Altogether 49,943 (7:66, 67). Some of the heads of families contributed to the work.

Ezra Reads the Law

Ezra, the priest and scribe of the Law of Moses, was told to bring out the Book of the Law of Moses. He stood on a high wooden platform and read from day-break until noon. He made it clear so the people could understand what was bring read.

Nehemiah the governor, Ezra the priest and the Levites said, 'This day is sacred to the Lord. Do not mourn or weep. Go, enjoy choice food and sweet drinks'.

They found written in the Law that the Israelites were to live in booths during the feast of the seventh month (Lev. 23:37-40). So they went out and gathered branches and made booths to live in for a week. Each day Ezra would read from the Law (Ch. 8).

The tenth day of the seventh month was the Day of Atonement. The 15th through 22nd was the feast of Tabernacles, which they had just celebrated. A review of the history of Israel was recited. An agreement was made to follow the Law of Moses. 83 men signed the agreement to give tithes as directed by him. A priest, descended from Aaron, was to accompany the Levites when they received the tithes (Ch 10). The leaders of the people settled in Jerusalem. The casting of lots was used to allow one out of every ten (of the rest of the people) to settle in Jerusalem.

3,044 men lived in Jerusalem, the rest in their ancestral towns (Chapter 11, 12). There were 32 towns in Judah and Benjamin. The family heads of the Levites were recorded in the reign of Darius the Persian.

Dedication of the Wall

The Levites were brought to Jerusalem. The singers were brought together. The leaders went on top of the wall. Two large choirs, one going to the right, the other to the left, proceeded. Great sacrifices were offered. Great rejoicing was heard far away.

Nehemiah's Reform

Nehemiah had returned to Babylon and while he was gone they were doing some things that were against the law.

They let foreigners use a storeroom in the temple. The Levites and singers had not received the portions due them.

Nehemiah prayed and brought to God's remembrance some of the things he had done: he warned men about working on the Sabbath, selling grain, bringing in fish and other merchandise and selling it in Jerusalem on the Sabbath, spending the night outside. He tried to keep the people straight. Some had married foreign women and he chastised them. He prayed that God would remember him with favor.

Esther

A Review

Background:
1. In the first year of Cyrus, King of Persia, he let all the exiles (who wanted to) return to Jerusalem in Judah with Zerubbabel. They started rebuilding the temple (Ezra 1:2-4).
2. They met opposition and a letter was written to Xerxes (Ahasuerus) to stop the work. It was stopped until the second year of King Darius (about 15 years).
3. A letter was written to him for a search to be made to see if Cyrus had authorized the work. He had authorized it, so it was resumed with diligence and completed in the sixth year of King Darius.

Queen Vashti Deposed

Esther's story happened during the reign of King Xerxes in the citadel of Susa, Nehemiah and Daniel also lived there (Dan. 8:2 and Neh. 1:1).

King Xerxes had given a banquet that lasted a week. His Queen, Vashti, had also given a banquet for the women in the royal palace. He sent for Queen Vashti in order to display her beauty, but she refused to come. He consulted his wise men about what should be done. This was their advice:

Issue a royal decree that Vashti is never again to enter the presence of King Xerxes. Give her position to someone else. Then all the women will respect their husbands.

This pleased the king. Later, a search was made for beautiful young virgins to be queen instead of Vashti.

In the citadel of Susa, there was a Jew from the tribe of Benjamin named Mordecai. He had been taken captive with Jehoiachin (see 2 Kings 24:10-16).

He had a cousin named Esther that he had raised because her father and mother had died. Esther was taken as a candidate for queen and given special food and beauty treatments. Mordecai had told her not to reveal her nationality.

Before a girl was allowed to go in to King Xerxes she had to complete 12 months of beauty treatments, 6 months with oil of myrrh and 6 months of perfumes.

It had now been four years after Vashti, when Esther was taken to the king. He was attracted to her and made her queen.

She continued to follow Mordecai's instructions. He heard two of the king's men plotting an assassination and told Esther who in turn told the king. The men were hanged (Chapter 2).

King Xerxes gave a man named Haman a seat of honor, but Mordecai would not kneel down or pay him honor. This enraged Haman. He knew Mordecai was a Jew and looked for a way to destroy all the Jews there.

He said to the king, 'There is a certain people scattered among your provinces whose customs are different and do not obey the king's laws. If it pleases the king, let a decree be issued to destroy them'.

This was done. It was to be carried out the thirteenth day of the twelfth month. This was the day before the Passover. The city of Susa was bewildered (Chapter 3).

There was great mourning among the Jews. Esther sent one of the eunuchs to find out what was troubling Mordecai. He gave him a copy of the decree and urged her to go before the king and plead for her people.

No one was to appear before the king without being asked. She said it had been 30 days since she had been called to go to the king.

Mordecai told her, 'Don't think because you are in the king's house you will escape. Who knows that you have come to royal position for such a time as this?'

She said, 'I will go. If I perish, I perish'.

Esther's Request

Esther put on her royal robes. When the king saw the queen, he held out his scepter. He said, 'What is it Queen Esther?' She said, 'If it pleases the king, let him and Haman come to a banquet I have prepared for him'.

After they had eaten, the king asked again, 'What is your petition?' Esther answered, 'Let the King and Haman come tomorrow to another banquet and I will answer the question'.

Haman was in high spirits and boasted to his friends and wife, 'I'm the only person Queen Esther invited to accompany the king to her banquet'. His hate for Mordecai kept him from enjoying himself.

His wife and friends suggested he build a gallows 75 feet high and ask the king to have Mordecai hanged on it.

Mordecai Honored

That night, the king could not sleep and called for the records to be brought in. He noticed Mordecai had exposed an assassination plot against him and had received no honor for it.

The next morning he asked Haman, 'What should be done for the man the king delights to honor?' Thinking he was talking about himself, Haman said, 'Bring a royal robe the king has worn and a horse the king has ridden on and lead him through the city streets'.

The king said, 'Go at once, do this for Mordecai the Jew who sits at the king's gate'.

Haman knew he couldn't talk against Mordecai now.

Haman Hanged

The king and Haman went to Esther's banquet. When the king again asked her for her request she said, 'Grant me my life and spare my people. We have been sold for destruction'.

King Xerxes said, 'Who is he? Where is the man who dared do such a thing?'

Esther said it was Haman. Then he was terrified. The king went out to the palace garden and Haman stayed behind to beg Queen Esther for his life.

When told Haman had built a gallows to hang Mordecai on, the king had Haman hung on it instead (Chapter 7).

Esther told the king who she was and of her relation to Mordecai. He gave his signet ring to Mordecai.

An order was written overruling the one Haman had sent. He gave the Jews the right to assemble and protect themselves and to avenge themselves on their enemies.

The thirteenth day of the month came, the day the Jews were to be put to death. The Jews killed those who were against them and, at the request of Esther, hanged the ten sons of Haman on gallows.

Purim Celebrated

The fourteenth day they rested and made it a day of feasting and joy and giving presents to each other. They made this an annual celebration and called it Purim. It was for two days.

Mordecai became great in the king's house and his fame went out throughout all the providences. He was second in rank to the king himself and worked for the good of his people.

Job
A Review

We don't know the exact time Job lived in but it was after Noah and Daniel (Ezeiel. 14:14). The land of Uz was in the East and seemed to be near Edom (Lamentations. 4:21). He was a believer in God and made burnt offerings for his children as the head of his house (1:5). He also was wealthy, respected, blameless, upright and shunned evil.

Job Tested

God allows us to be tested and he allowed Job to be tested by Satan.

> 1st Test: In one day, he lost his wealth.
> 2nd Test: In one day, he lost his sons and daughters.
> 3rd Test: He lost his health.

Painful sores covered his entire body. His wife advised him to curse God and die. He told her, 'Shall we accept good from God and not trouble?'

Three Friends Come to Comfort Job

His three friends, Eliphaz, Bildad and Zophar came to comfort him. When they saw him, they wept and sat on the ground for seven days and seven nights without speaking.

Job broke the silence and cursed the day of his birth. He said, 'I have no peace, quietness or rest, only turmoil'.

Based on his experience, Eliphaz thought Job's suffering must have been caused by sin. He said, 'Where were the upright ever destroyed? Those who sow trouble will reap it (4:7, 8). If it were I, I would appeal to God. I would lay my causes before him'.

Job Replies

'Oh that I might have my request, that God would grant what I hope for (6:8). A despairing friend should have the devotion of his friends (6:14). You have proved to be of no help (6:21). Would I lie to your face? (6:28) My night drags on and I toss until dawn (7:4). I despise my life…(7:16)'.

Bildad Speaks

'How long will you say such things? (8:2) If you look to God and plead with the Almighty, even now He will restore you to your rightful place (8:5, 6). Surely God does not reject a blameless man'.

Job Replies

'I know that this is true (9:1). He (God) moves mountains, shakes the earth, speaks to the sun and it does not shine, when He passes me I cannot see Him…

He destroys both the blameless and the wicked (9:22). He is not a man like me that I might answer Him…

If only there were someone to arbitrate between us, then I would speak without fear. I would say, "Tell me what charges you have against me" (10:12)'.

Zophar Speaks

He condemns Job. He says, 'If you put away the sin that is in your hand and allow no evil to dwell in your tent, then you will lift up your face without shame… life will be brighter… you will be secure… (Chapter 11)'

Job Replies

'I have become a laughingstock to my friends. Is not wisdom found among the aged? God makes nations great and destroys them (Chapter 12). What you know, I also know. You smear me with your lies. If only you would be silent! Would it turn out well if He (God) examined you? Though He slays me, yet will I hope in Him (Chapter 13).

Man born of woman is of few days and full of trouble. Man's days are determined… If a tree is cut down, it will sprout again, but when man dies, he breathes his last and is no more. Until the heavens are no more, men will not awake or be roused from their sleep. If a man dies, will he live again? I will wait for my renewal to come (Chapter 14)'.

Eliphaz Speaks

'Your own mouth condemns you. Do you limit wisdom to yourself?' He talks about the judgment that befalls wicked men, implying Job to be among them (Chapter 15).

Job Replies

'Will your long-winded speeches never end? My face is red with weeping. Deep shadows ring my eyes. My prayer is pure (Chapter 16). My spirit is broken, my days are cut short, the grave awaits me'.

Bildad Speaks

'When will you end these speeches? Be sensible and then we can talk. Why are we regarded as cattle and stupid in your sight? The lamp of the wicked is snuffed but…the memory of him perishes from the earth (Chapter 18)'.

Job Replies

'Ten times now you have reproached me. My kinsmen have gone away, my friends have forgotten me...My breath is offensive to my wife...those I love have turned against me, I am nothing but skin and bones.

I know that my Redeemer lives and in the end He will stand upon the earth (Ch 19)'.

Zophar Speaks

'I am greatly disturbed. Surely you know how it has been from old, ever since man was placed on the earth. The joy of the godless lasts but a moment and his doom is sure (Chapter 20)'.

Job Replies

'Why do the wicked live on, growing old and increasing in power? They see their children established, their homes safe, they spend their years in prosperity... (Chapter 21)'.

Eliphaz Replies

'Is it for your piety that God rebukes you? Though you were a powerful man, owning land, an honored man... will you keep to the old path that evil men have trod? They were carried off before their time, their foundations washed away by a flood'.

Job Replies

'If only I knew where to find Him, I would state my case before Him. When He has trusted me, I will come forth as gold. I have treasured the words of His mouth more than my daily bread (Chapter 23).

Why does the Almighty not set times for judgment?

He (God) spreads out the northern skies over empty space;
He suspends the earth over nothing.
He wraps up the water in his clouds.
Yet the clouds do not burst under their weight.

I will never admit you are in the right; until I die, I will not deny my integrity (Chapter 27).

Where does wisdom come from? God alone knows where it dwells. The fear of the Lord is wisdom (Chapter 28)'.

The Good Things Job Did

'How I long for the days gone by, when God watched over me. My children were around me, young men saw me and stepped aside, old men rose to their feet. Whoever heard me spoke well of me.

I rescued the poor; I made the widow's heart sing. I was eyes to the blind, feet to the lame, a father to the needy.

Men listened to me; after I had spoken, they spoke no more.

When I smiled at them, they scarcely believed it. I was like one who comforts mourners (Chapter 29).

Now they mock me; men whose fathers I would have disdained to put with my sheepdogs. They detest me and keep their distance.

Now my life ebbs away. Days of suffering grip me. My gnawing pains never rest.

I cry out to you, O God, but you do not answer. My skin grows black and peels, my body burns with fever (Chapter 30).

I made a covenant with my eyes not to look lustfully at a girl'. Job claims to have been pure morally, to have been honest, treated his servants fairly... He says he kept himself pure because he dreaded destruction from God.

He said no stranger had to spend the night in the street because his door was always open to the traveler (Chapter 31).

Elihu

A fourth person speaks up named Elihu. He was angry at Job for justifying himself and also angry with the three friends because they had failed to convince Job.

He said he was young and Job was old but it is not only the old who are wise and understand what is right.

'The spirit within me compels me. I must open my lips and reply (Chapter 32). You have said, "I am pure and without sin yet God has found fault with me". Far be it from God to do evil. He repays man for what he has done. He brings on man what his conduct deserves. He shows no partiality'.

Should God reward you on your terms? When you refuse to repent? Elihu says God does not have to answer to man, he reveals himself through dreams, panic and suffering. When a man responds favorably to his suffering, God restores him.

The Lord Speaks

The Lord answered Job out of the storm. He said, 'Brace yourself like a man; I will question you and you shall answer me.

Where were you when I laid the earth's foundation?

Who shut up the sea when I fixed limits for it and said, 'This far you may come and no further'?

Have you seen the gates of the shadow of death?

Where does the darkness reside?

Have you entered the storehouses of the snow, hail or lightning, rain, dew, ice and frost?

Can you bring forth the constellations?

Who endowed the heart with wisdom?

Who provides food for the raven?

What about the mountain goat, the wild donkey, the wild ox, the ostrich, the horse, the hawk and the eagle?'(Chapter 39)

The Lord said to Job, 'Will the one who contends with the Almighty correct him?'

Job Answers

'I am unworthy… I have no answer…'

The Lord Speaks

'Would you condemn me to justify yourself? Look at the behemoth and leviathan'; the mighty animals God had made.

Job Answers

'I know that You can do all things; no plan of yours can be thwarted. I spoke of things I did not understand; things too wonderful for me to know'.

Job said, 'My ears had heard of You but now my eyes have seen You. I despise myself and repent in dust and ashes' (Ch 42).

The Lord Speaks to Job's Friends

The Lord said, 'I am angry with you because you have not spoken what is right.

Take 7 bulls and 7 rams and go to Job and sacrifice a burnt offering for yourselves. Job will pray for you'.

The Lord made Job prosperous again by giving him twice as much as he had before. His family and friends came to comfort him and brought gifts. He had 7 sons and 3 daughters, 14,000 sheep, 6,000 camels and 1,000 donkeys.

After all this, Job lived 140 more years and saw his children to the 4th generation. He is known for patience.

Psalms

A Review

Writers:

David	75	Solomon	2
Unknown	47	Moses	1
Asaph	12	Ethan	1
Sons of Korah	11	Heman	1
			150

In reviewing a Psalm, I will give the author, if known, and one or more verses of the thoughts contained therein. The Psalms were written over a long period of time.

Psalm 1 Unknown

Blessed is the man who does not walk in the council of the wicked, or stand in the way of sinners or sit in the seat of mockers. But his delight is in the Law of the Lord and on His law he meditates day and night (verse 12).

Psalm 2 David (Acts 4:25)

You are my son, today I have become your Father (verse 7).

Psalm 3 David (2 Sam. 15)

I will not fear the tens of thousands drawn up against me on every side (verse 6).

Psalm 4 David

I will lie down and sleep in peace for You alone, O Lord, make me dwell in safety (verse 8).

Psalm 5 David

In the morning, O Lord, you hear my voice; in the morning I lay my requests before you and wait in expectation (vs 3).

Psalm 6 David

Be merciful to me, Lord, for I am faint. Heal me for my bones are in agony (verse 2).

Psalm 7 David

O Lord my God, I take refuge in You. Save and deliver me from all who pursue me (verse 11).

Psalm 8 David

O Lord, our Lord, how majestic is your name in all the earth! (verse 1) You made him a little lower than the angels and crowned with glory and honor (verse 5).

Psalm 9 David

You, Lord, have never forsaken those who seek you (verse 9)…the needy will not always be forgotten nor the hopes of the afflicted ever perish (verse 18).

Psalm 10 David

Break the arm of the wicked and evil man. Call him to account for his wickedness that would not be found out (vs 15).

Psalm 11 David

The Lord examines the righteous, but the wicked and those who love violence, His soul hates (verse 5).

Psalm 12 David

May the Lord cut off all flattering lips and every boastful tongue (verse 3)

Psalm 13 David

How long must I wrestle with my thoughts and every day have sorrow in my heart? (verse 2)

Psalm 14 David

The fool hath said in his heart, there is no God (verse 1)

Psalm 15 David

Lord, who may dwell in your sanctuary? Who may live on your holy hill? Those who do what is right, speak the truth, who do not slander, do no wrong to their neighbor, cast no slur, those who despise a vile man and honors those who fear the Lord (verse 24).

Psalm 16 David

I have set the Lord always before me. Because He is at my right hand, I will not be shaken (verse 8).You will not abandon me to the grave nor will you let you holy one (Jesus) see decay (verse 10).

Psalm 17 David

Keep me as the apple of your eye (verse 8).
And I, in righteousness, will see your face (verse 15).

Psalm 18 David (2 Sam. 22)

The Lord is my rock, fortress and deliverer. I will call upon the Lord... From His temple He heard my voice.

Psalm 19 David

The heavens declare the glory of God. There is no speech or language where their voice is not heard (verse 4).

Psalm 20 David

Some trust in chariots and horses but we trust in the Lord, our God (verse 7).

Psalm 21 David

The King (David) trusts in the Lord; through the unfailing love of the most high, he will not be shaken (verse 7).

Psalm 22 David

My God, my God, why have you forsaken me? (See Matt. 27:46). They divide my garments among them and cast lots for my clothing (John 19:24). (In Psalms verse 1 and 18).

Psalm 23 David

The Lord is my shepherd, I shall not want.
He maketh me lie down in green pastures.
He leadeth me beside the still waters.
He restoreth my soul:
He leadeth me in the paths of righteousness for his name's sake.
Yea though I walk through the valley of the shadow of death, I will fear no evil, for thou art with me;
Thy rod and staff they comfort me.
Thou preparest a table before me in the presence of my enemies;
Thou anointest my head with oil;
My cup runneth over.
Surely goodness and mercy shall follow me all the days of my life
And I will dwell in the house of the Lord forever.
(I used the King James Version here because it is so familiar).

Psalm 24 David

The earth is the Lord's and everything in it (verse 1)

Psalm 25 David

To You, O Lord, I lift up my soul (verse 1). No one whose hope is in You will ever be put to shame (verse 3). Remember not the sins of my youth (verse 7).

Psalm 26 David
> Test me, O Lord, and try me, examine my heart and my mind (verse 2).

Psalm 27 David
> The Lord is my light and my salvation – whom shall I fear? (verse 1).This is what I seek: that I may dwell in the house of the Lord all the days of my life (verse 4).

Psalm 28 David
> The Lord is my strength and my shield, my heart trusts in him (verse 7).

Psalm 29 David
> The voice of the Lord is upon the waters (verse 3). It is powerful, majestic…It shakes the desert and twists the oaks…

Psalm 30 David
> Weeping may remain for a night, but rejoicing comes in the morning (verse 5).

Psalm 31
> I trusted in thee, O Lord, You are my God. Let Your face shine on your servant (verse 16).

Psalm 32 David
> Blessed is he whose transgressions are forgiven, whose sins are covered. You forgave the guilt of my sins (verse 5).

Psalm 33
> By the word of the Lord were heavens made (verse 6). He spoke and it came to be (verse 9). Blessed is the nation whose God is the Lord. No king is saved by the size of his army (verse 16).

Psalm 34 David

I sought the Lord and he answered me; he delivered me from all my fears (verse 4). The angel of the Lord encamps around those who fear him and delivers them. Whoever loves life and desires to see good days, keep your tongue from evil and your lips from speaking lies (vs 13). The eyes of the Lord are on the righteous and his ears are attentive to their cry (vs 15). A righteous man may have many troubles but the Lord delivers him from them all (vs 19).

Psalm 35 David

May those who seek my life be disgraced and put to shame (verse 4).

Psalm 36 David

How priceless is your unfailing love! Both high and low among men find refuge in the shadow of your wings (verse 7).

Psalm 37 David

Do not fret because of evil men or be envious of those who do wrong; for like the grass, they will soon wither (verses 1 and 2). Better the little that the righteous have than the wealth of many wicked (vs 16). I was young and now I am old yet I have never seen the righteous forsaken or their children begging for bread. They are always generous and lend freely (vss 25 and 26). There is a future for the man of peace (vs 37).

Psalm 38

(Psalm 38 through 41 sound as if David sinned and was brought down with a disease because of it). Because of your wrath there is no health in my body (verse 3). My wounds fester and are loathsome because of my sinful folly (verse

5). I wait for you Lord…Do not let them gloat…when my foot slips (verses 15 and 16).

Psalm 39 David

You are the one who has done this (verse 9). Hear my prayer, O Lord, listen to my cry for help (verse 12)…before I depart and am no more (verse 13).

Psalm 40 David

I waited patiently for the Lord; he turned to me and heard my cry (verse 1). He put a new song in my mouth (verse 2).

Psalm 41 David

I said, 'O Lord have mercy on me; heal me for I have sinned against you' (verse 4). My enemies whisper, 'A vile disease has beset him; he will never get up from the place where he lies'. Even my close friend, whom I trusted, he, who shared my bread, has lifted up his heel against me (verses 8 and 9). I know that you are pleased with me for my enemy does not triumph over me (verse 11).

Psalm 42 Korah

As the deer pants for the water so my souls pants for you, O God (verse 1).

Psalm 43

Judge me, O God, and plead my cause against an ungodly nation; rescue me from the deceitful and wicked men (vs 1).

Psalm 44 Korah

…Our fathers have told us what you did in their days, in days long ago (verse 1). You gave us victory over our enemies; you put our adversaries to shame (verse 7). For your sake we face death all day long… (verse 22).

Psalm 45 Korah

All your robes are fragrant with myrrh and aloes and cassia (vs 8). All glorious is the princess within her chambers; her gown is interwoven with gold (vs 13) (a wedding song).

Psalm 46 Korah

God is our refuge and strength, an ever present help in trouble. Therefore we will not fear (verses 1 and 2). Be still and know that I am God (verse 10).

Psalm 47 Korah

He subdued nations under us, peoples under our feet. He chose our inheritance for us (verses 3 and 4).God reigns over the nations; He is seated on His holy throne (verse 8).

Psalm 48 Korah

Great is the Lord and most worthy to be praised (verse 1). God is our God forever and ever; He will be our guide even to the end (verse 14).

Psalm 49 Korah

Why should I fear when evil days come? No man can redeem the life of another or give to God a ransom for him (verses 5 through 7). God will redeem my life from the grave; He will surely take me to Himself (verse 15). Do not be overawed when a man grows rich for he can take nothing with him when he dies (verses 16 and 17).

Psalm 50 Asaph (God speaks)

I have no need of a bull from your stall or of goats from your pens, for every animal from the forest is mine, and the cattle on a thousand hills. I know every bird in the mountains; the creatures of the field are mine. If I were hungry I would not tell you for the world is mine and all that is in it (verses 9 through 12).

Psalm 51 David

(This is when the prophet, Nathan, came to David after he had committed adultery with Bathsheba, 2 Sam. 11). I know my transgressions; my sin is always before me (vs 3). Create in me a pure heart, O God; do not cast me from your presence or take your holy spirit from me (verse 10 and 11).

Psalm 52 David

(This was when Doeg told Saul, 'David has gone to the house of Abimelech', 1 Sam. 22:9-22).Why do you boast... you who are a disgrace in the eyes of God? (verse 1). You love evil rather than good, falsehood rather than speaking the truth (verse 3).

Psalm 53 David

The fool says in his heart, there is no God (verse 1). God looks down from heaven on the sons of men to see if there are any who understand, any who seek God (verse 2).

Psalm 54 David

(This was when the Ziphites went to Saul and said, 'Is not David hiding among us?'1 Sam. 23:19). Strangers are attacking me; ruthless men seek my life, men without regard for God. The Lord has delivered me from all my troubles (vs 7).

Psalm 55 David

If an enemy were insulting me I could endure it... But it is you, a man like myself, my companion, my close friend, with whom I once enjoyed sweet fellowship. His speech is smooth as butter, yet war is in his heart (verse 21).

Psalm 56 David

(This was when the Philistines had seized David in Gath, 1 Sam. 21:10-15) What can mortal man do to me? (verse 4).

Psalm 57 David

(This was when he fled from Saul into the cave 1 Sam. 24). I will take refuge in the shadow of your wings, until the disaster has passed (vs 1). (Song: When the storm passes by)

Psalm 58 David

Even from birth the wicked go astray from the womb, they are wayward and speak lies (verse 3).

Psalm 59 David

(When Saul had sent men to watch David's house, 1 Sam. 19-1-17). For no offense or sin of mine, O Lord. I have done no wrong, yet they are ready to kill me (vss 3 and 4). You are my fortress, my refuge in times of trouble (vs 16).

Psalm 60 Daniel

(When Joab struck down 12,000 Edomites, 2 Sam. 8). Who will bring me into the fortified city? Who will lead me to Edom? (vs 9). With God we will gain the victory (vs 12).

Psalm 61 David

Lead me to the rock that is higher than I (verse 2).

Psalm 62 David

My soul finds rest in God alone; my salvation comes from Him (verse 1).

Psalm 63 David (When he was in the desert of Judah)

My soul thirsts for you, my body longs for you, in a dry and weary land where there is no water (verse 1).

Psalm 64 David

Hide me from the conspiracy of the wicked, from the noisy crowds of evildoers (verse 2).

Psalm 65 David

You care for the land and water it (verse 9)…you soften it with showers and bless its crops (verse 10).

Psalm 66

He turned the sea into dry land; they passed through the waters on foot (verse 6). How awesome are your deeds! So great is your power (verse 3).

Psalm 67 (Herald of Truth song)

May God be gracious to us and bless us and make His face shine upon us (verse 1).

Psalm 68 David

As smoke is blown by the wind, as wax melts before the fire (vs 2). The mountains of Bashan are majestic… (vs 15). There is the little tribe of Benjamin, leading them (vs 27).

Psalm 69 David

Those who hate me without reason outnumber the hairs of my head (verse 4). I am a stranger to my brothers, an alien to my own mother's sons (verse 8).

Psalm 70 David

Hasten O God, to save me; O Lord come quickly to help me

Psalm 71

Do not cast me away when I am old; do not forsake me when my strength is gone (verse 9).

Psalm 72 Solomon? (for him)

Endow the king with your justice, O God. He will judge your people in righteousness (verse 1 and 2). He will defend the afflicted...(verse 4). The kings of Tarshish and of distant shores will bring tribute to him (verse 10). All kings will bow down to him (verse 11).

Psalm 73 Asaph

But as for me, my feet had almost slipped; I had nearly lost my foothold (verse 2). This is what the wicked are like; always carefree...(vs 12)....until I entered the sanctuary of God; then I understood their final destiny (vs 17).

Psalm 74 Asaph

Why have you rejected us forever, O God? (verse 1). They burned your sanctuary (verse 7). No prophets are left and none of us knows how long this will be (verse 9). Do not forget the lives of your afflicted people forever (verse 19).

Psalm 75 Asaph

It is God who judges: he brings one down; he exalts another (verse 7).

Psalm 76 Asaph

In Judah God is known; his name is great in Israel (verse 1). His tent is in Salem. His dwelling place is Zion (verse 2).

Psalm 77 Asaph

I thought about the former days, the years of long ago (verse 5). With your mighty arm you redeemed your people, the descendants of Jacob and Joseph (verse 15).

Psalm 78

(Asaph reviews the story of Israel from the exodus to David)What our fathers have told us, we will tell the next generation (verse 3 and 4). He did miracles in Egypt, made the water stand firm like a wall, and guided them by cloud and fire. He rained down manna. They also had meat. God's anger rose against them. They turned to him again. He drove out nations before them. They angered God with their high places. He chose the tribe of Judah. He chose David to be the shepherd of his people.

Psalm 79 Asaph

The nations have invaded your inheritance. They have defiled your holy temple. They have reduced Jerusalem to rubble (vs 1). Deliver us and forgive our sins, for your name's sake (vs 9). Why should the nations say, 'Where is their God?' (vs 10).

Psalm 80 Asaph

You brought wine out of Egypt (verse 8). You cleared the ground for it, and it took root and filled the land (verse 9). Restore us, O Lord God (verse 19).

Psalm 81 Asaph

We heard a language we did not understand. You shall not bow down to an alien god. I am the Lord your God (vs 10).

Psalm 82 Asaph

…All the nations are your inheritance (verse 8).

Psalm 83 Asaph

They plot against those you cherish. They say, 'let us destroy them as a nation that the name of Israel be remembered no more' (verse 4).

Psalm 84 Korah

I would rather be a doorkeeper in the house of my God, then dwell in the tents of the wicked (verse 10).

Psalm 85 Korah

You restored the fortunes of Jacob. You forgave the iniquity of your people – You turned from your fierce anger (verses 2 and 3). Our land will yield its harvest (verse 12).

Psalm 86 David

You are forgiving and good, O Lord, abounding in love to all who call on you (verse 5).

Psalm 87 Korah

He has set his foundation on the Holy Mountain (Zion) (vs 1). And the Most High Himself will establish her (vs 5).

Psalm 88 Korah

For my soul is full of trouble and my life draws near the grave (verse 3). Do you show your wonders to the dead? Do those who are dead rise up and praise thee? (verse 10).

Psalm 89 Ethan

I have sworn to David my servant I will establish your line forever (verse 4). I will appoint him my firstborn, the most exalted of the kings of the earth (verse 27). My covenant will I not break (verse 34).

Psalm 90 Moses (probably the oldest psalm)

A thousand years in God's sight are like a day that has just gone by (vs 4). The length of our days is seventy years; or eighty if we have the strength; yet their span is but trouble and sorrow, for they quickly pass and we fly away (vs 10).

Psalm 91

For He will command His angels concerning you, to guard you in all your ways (verse 11).

Psalm 92

It is good to praise the Lord and to sing praises unto thy name (verse 1). The righteous will flourish (verse 12). They will still bear fruit in old age (verse 14).

Psalm 93

The world is firmly established; it cannot be moved (vs 1).

Psalm 94

The Lord knows the thoughts of man (verse 11).

Psalm 95

Today, if you hear His voice, do not harden your hearts (verse 8). For forty years I was angry with that generation (verse 10). I declared an oath in my anger, 'They shall never enter my rest' (verse 11).

Psalm 96

Great is the Lord and most worthy of praise (verse 4).

Psalm 97

He guards the lives of his faithful ones (verse 10).

Psalm 98

All the ends of the earth have seen the salvation of our God (verse 3).

Psalm 99

Moses and Aaron called on the Lord and He answered them. He spoke to them from the pillar of cloud (vss 6-7).

Psalm 100

Worship the Lord with gladness.

Psalm 101 David

No one who practices deceit will dwell in my house.

Psalm 102

Let this be written for a future generation, that a people, not yet created, may praise the Lord (verse 18). You remain the same and your years will never end (verse 27).

Psalm 103 David

The Lord is compassionate and gracious, slow to anger and abounding in love (vs 8). As far as the east is from the west, so far has He removed our transgressions from us (vs 12).

Psalm 104

Never again will the waters cover the earth (verse 9). The moon marks off the seasons (verse 19). The sun knows when to go down.

Psalm 105 and 106 (Tells the story of Israel)

Joseph was sold as a slave. They bruised his feet with shackles; his neck was put in irons (verse 18). Jacob lived as an alien in the land of Ham (Egypt) (vs 23). Moses and Aaron performed miraculous signs among them (vss 26 & 27). They brought out Israel. God gave them the lands of the nations (verses 43 and 44). He led them through the Red Sea (106:9). At Horab they made a calf (106:19). At the waters of Meribah, Moses got into trouble by striking the rock. They mingled with the nations and adopted their customs (106:35).

Psalm 107

Those who were merchants of the sea saw his wonderful deeds in the deep (verse 24). He turned rivers into a desert, flowing springs into thirsty ground and fruitful land into a salt waste (verses 33 and 34) Sodom?

Psalm 108 David

Give us aid against the enemy, for the help of man is worthless (verse 12).

Psalm 109 David

Wicked and deceitful men have opened their mouths against me (verse 2).

Psalm 110 David (A prophesy of Jesus)

The Lord (God) says to my Lord (Jesus), 'Sit at my right hand until I make your enemies a footstool for your feet (verse 1). The Lord (God) has sworn and will not change his mind: "You are a priest forever, in the order of Melchizedek" (verse 4)'.

Psalm 111

The fear of the Lord is the beginning of wisdom (verse 10).

Psalm 112

A righteous man will be remembered forever (verse 6).

Psalm 113

He settles the barren woman in her home as a happy mother of children (verse 9).

Psalm 114

When Israel came out of Egypt, the sea looked and fled, the Jordan turned back (verses 1 through 3).

Psalm 115

Idols, made by man, have mouths but cannot speak, ears but cannot hear, noses, but cannot smell, hands but cannot feel, feet but cannot walk…(verses 5 through 7).

Psalm 116

Precious in the sight of the Lord is the death of His saints

Psalm 117

The Lord's faithfulness endures forever (verse 2).

Psalm 118

The stone the builders rejected has become the capstone (see Acts 4:11). This is the day the Lord has made. Let us rejoice and be glad in it (verse 24).

Psalm 119

(The longest psalm, 176 verses)

How can a young man keep his way pure? By living according to your word (verse 9). Your statutes are my delight; they are my counselors (verse 24). It was good for me to be afflicted so that I might learn your decrees (verse 71). Your word is a lamp to my feet and a light for my path (verse 105). The statutes you have laid down are righteous (verse 138). I have put my hope in your word (verse 147).

Psalm 120

I am a man of peace; but when I speak, they are for war (vs 7).

Psalms 121

I lift up my eyes to the hills from whence cometh my strength (verse 1).

Psalm 122 David

I rejoice with those who said to me, Let us go to the house of the Lord (verse 1).

Psalm 123

I lift up my eyes to you (verse 1).

Psalm 124 David

> If the Lord had not been on our side… (verse 1).

Psalm 125

> As the mountains surround Jerusalem, so the Lord surrounds his people (verse 2).

Psalm 126

> Those who sow in tears will reap with songs of joy (vs 5).

Psalm 127 Solomon

> Unless the Lord builds the house, its builders labor in vain (verse 1). Sons are a heritage from the Lord, children a reward from him (verse 3).

Psalm 128

> May you live to see your children's children (verse 6).

Psalm 129

> The Lord has cut me free from the cords of the wicked (vs4).

Psalm130

> In His word, I put my hope (verse 5).

Psalm 131 David

> I do not concern myself with great matters (verse 1).

Psalm 132

> The Lord has chosen Zion (Jerusalem) for his dwelling place (verse 13, see 1 Chron. 28:2).

Psalm 133

> How good and pleasant it is when brothers live together in unity (verse 1).

Psalm 134

Praise the Lord for his servants, who minister in the sanctuary (verses 1 and 2).

Psalm 135

The Lord does whatever pleases Him; in the heavens and on the earth (verse 6).

Psalm 136

Give thanks to the Lord, for He is good. His love endures forever (verse 1).

Psalm 137 (Written after the Babylonian captivity)

Remember, O Lord, what the Edomites did on the day Jerusalem fell. 'Tear it down' they cried. 'Tear it down to its foundation!' (verse 7).

Psalm 138 David

I will bow down toward your holy temple (verse 2).

Psalm 139 David

You have searched me and know me; you know when I sit and when I rise, you perceive my thoughts (vss 1-2). Where can I flee from your presence? (vs 7) If I go to the heavens, you are there. If I make my bed in the depths, you are there (vss 8-11). I am fearfully and wonderfully made (vs 14). All the days ordained for me were written in your book be-fore one of them came to be (vs 16). (Are our days numbered?)

Psalm 140 David

Keep me from the hands of the wicked men of violence (vs 4).

Psalm 141 David

Let not my heart be drawn to what is evil (verse 4).

Psalm 142 David (When he was in the cave, 1 Sam. 22:1, 2)

> Set me free from my prison (verse 7).

Psalm 143 David

> Show me the way I should go, for to you, I lift up my soul (verse 8).

Psalm 144 David

> What is man that you care for him, the son of man that you think of him? (verse 3)

Psalm 145 David

> The Lord is gracious and compassionate, slow to anger and rich in love (verse 8).

Psalm 146

> Do not put your trust in mortal men who cannot save (vs 3).

Psalm 147

> He determines the number of stars and calls them each by name (verse 4). He supplies the earth with rain and food for the cattle (verses 8 and 9).

Psalms 148, 149 and 150 (Praise the Lord; Psalms 148 to 150)

> Let everything that has breath praise the Lord (150:6). Angels, heavenly hosts, sun, moon and stars; sea creatures, hail, snow and clouds, mountains and hills and trees, all creatures, kings and rulers, young men and maidens (148:1-12). Praise Him in his sanctuary, in His heavens, for His acts of power, for his surpassing greatness...

Proverbs

A Review

When Solomon was king, the Lord appeared to him in a dream. He said, 'Ask for whatever you want me to give you'.
Solomon asked for a discerning heart to govern the people and to distinguish between right and wrong.
The Lord said, 'I will give you a wise and discerning heart so that there will never have been anyone like you, nor will there ever be (1 Kings 3:5-12)'.
Even though Solomon wrote most of these proverbs, it was God who gave him this wisdom. He didn't go to school to learn it, nor did he learn it in the school of hard knocks. This wisdom was inspired by God.

Purpose

To attain wisdom and discipline in order to live a successful life, being able to distinguish between good and bad behavior, doing what is just and fair, advice to the young, how to lead life wisely and skillfully.
Solomon says the fear of the Lord is the beginning of knowledge. This fear He wants is that we will be submissive to Him (1:1-6).

Choose Wisdom

We would be wise to listen to the teaching of our fathers and mothers (in most cases). If sinners entice you, do not give in to them. Their feet rush to sin and ill-gotten gain. They will eat the fruit of their ways.

Wisdom's Benefits

Search for wisdom as if it were hidden treasure. Wisdom will
save you from the ways of wicked men who leave the straight-
est paths.

It will save you from the adulteress who has ignored the
covenant of God (Chapter 2).

Keeping the commands of God will prolong your life and bring
prosperity. It will bring health to your body and nourish-
ment to your bones.

When you honor the Lord with your wealth, you barns will overflow.

Wisdom is precious; by wisdom the Lord made the world.

Do not withhold good from those who deserve it. Do not say,
'Come back later' when you have it now (Chapter 3).

A Father's Wisdom

When I was a boy in my father's house (David's), still tender
and an only child of my mother, he taught me wisdom was
supreme and not to swerve to the right or to the left (Ch 4).

Warning Against Adultery

The lips of an adulteress drip honey, but in the end she is bitter
as gall. Keep a path far from her; do not go near the door to
her house. May you rejoice in the wife of your youth. May
you ever be captivated by her love (Chapter 5).

Folly

If you have put up security for your neighbor, free yourself.

Go to the ant, you sluggard. Consider its ways and be wise.

A little sleep, a little slumber, a little folding of the hands to rest;
Poverty will come on you like a bandit.

Things God Hates

1. Haughty eyes
2. A lying tongue
3. Hands that shed innocent blood
4. A heart that devises wicked schemes
5. Feet that are quick to rush into evil
6. A false witness who pours out lies
7. A man who sits up dissention among brothers (Ch 6)

Men do not despise a thief it he steals to satisfy his hunger when he is starving.

Jealousy arouses a husband's fury and he will show no mercy when he takes revenge (Chapter 6).

Do not rebuke a mocker or he will hate you. Instruct a wise man and he will be wiser still (9:8).

A wise son brings joy to his father but a foolish son grief to his mother.

Lazy hands make a man poor.

He who sleeps during harvest is a disgraceful son.

Love covers all wrongs.

He who holds his tongue is wise. (Chapter 10)

Chapter 11

The Lord abhors dishonest scales.

A kindhearted woman gains respect.

Be sure of this: the wicked will not go unpunished.

He who wins souls is wise.

Chapter 12

A wife of noble character is her husband's crown but a disgraceful wife is like decay in his bones.

A righteous man cares for the needs of his animals.

Chapter 13

He who guards his lips guards his life.
He who gathers money little by little makes it grow.
A good man leaves an inheritance for his children's children.
He who spares the rod hates his son.

Chapter 14

The wise woman builds her house.
There is way that seems right to a man, but in the end it leads to
  death.
A quick-tempered man does foolish things.
The rich have many friends.
A heart at peace gives life to the body.
Whoever is kind to the needy honors God.
Righteousness exalts a nation but sin is a disgrace to any people.

Chapter 15

A gentle answer turns away wrath, but a harsh word stirs up anger.
A happy heart makes the face cheerful, but heartache crushes the
  spirit.
Better a meal of vegetables where there is love, than a fatted calf
  with hatred.
A cheerful look brings joy to the heart.

Chapter 16

In his heart a man plans his course, but the Lord determines his steps.
Kings value a man who speaks the truth.
Pride goes before destruction, a haughty spirit before a fall.
There is a way that seems right to man, but in the end it leads to death.
Gray hair is a crown of splendor.

Chapter 17

He who mocks the poor shows contempt for their maker.
Acquitting the guilty and condemning the innocent; the Lord
   detests them both.
A friend loves at all times.
A man of knowledge uses words with restraint.
Even a fool is thought wise if he keeps silent.

Chapter 18

A gift opens the way for the giver.
The first to present his case seems right, until another comes for-
   ward and questions him.
The tongue has the power of life and death.
He who finds a wife finds a good thing.
There is a friend who sticks closer than a brother.

Chapter 19

It is not good to have zeal without knowledge.
It is not fitting for a fool to live in luxury.
How much worse for a slave to rule over princes.
Many are the plans in a man's heart, but it is the Lord's purpose
   that prevails.
He who robs his father and drives out his mother is a son who
   brings shame and disgrace.

Chapter 20

Wine is a mocker and beer a brawler.
Every fool is quick to guard.
Even a child is known by his actions.
It's no good, it's no good! Says the buyer; then off he goes and
   boasts about his purchase.

Avoid a man who talks too much.

The glory of young men is their strength.

Chapter 21

Better to live on a corner of the roof than share a house with a quarrelsome wife.

In the house of the wise are stores of choice food and oil, but a foolish man devours all he has.

There is no wisdom, no insight, no plan that can succeed against the Lord.

Chapter 22

A good name is more desirable than great riches.

Train a child in the way he should go and when he is old he will not turn from it.

Folly is bound up in the heart of a child, but the rod of discipline will drive it far from him.

Have I not written thirty sayings for you, sayings of counsel and knowledge?

Do not move an ancient landmark set up by your forefathers.

Chapter 23

Do not wear yourselves out to get rich.

Do not eat the food of a stingy man (he is the kind of man who is always thinking about the costs).

Do not let your heart envy sinners.

Do not despise your mother when she is old.

Those who linger over wine…in the end it bites like a snake.

Chapter 24

Eat honey for it is good.

Though a righteous man falls seven times, he rises again.

Finish your outdoor work and get you fields ready; after that, build your house (get your priorities straight)

A little sleep, a little slumber, a little folding of the hands to rest; poverty will come on you like a bandit.

Chapter 25

These proverbs were copied by the men of Hezekiah, King of Judah.

A word, aptly spoken is like apples of gold in settings of silver.

If you find honey, eat just enough. Too much and you will vomit.

Seldom set foot in your neighbor's house; too much of you and he will hate you. (Don't overstay your welcome).

If your enemy is hungry, give him food to eat; if he is thirsty, give him water to drink.

In doing this you will heap burning coals upon his head.

A north wind brings rain.

It is not honorable to seek one's own honor.

Chapter 26

Like one who seizes a dog by the ears is a passer-by who muddles in a quarrel not his own.

Don't deceive your neighbor, then say, 'I was only joking'.

Without wood a fire goes out, without gossip a quarrel dies down.

Chapter 27

Do not boast about tomorrow, for you do not know what a day may bring forth.

Do not go to your brother's house when disaster strikes you; better a neighbor than a brother far away.

Riches do not endure forever.

Chapter 28

The wicked man flees though no one pursues.

He who conceals his sin does not prosper, but whoever confesses
and renounces them finds mercy.

A man tormented by the guilt of murder will be a fugitive until death.

Chapter 29

By justice a king gives a country stability, but one who is greedy
for bribes tears it down.

A wise man keeps himself under control.

A child, left to himself, disgraces his mother.

An angry man stirs up dissension and a hot tempered one
commits many sins.

Chapter 30

These are some sayings of Agur.

Who has gone to heaven and come down?

Do not add to his words or he will rebuke you and prove you a liar.

Keep falsehood and lies far from me.

Give me neither poverty nor riches.

Do not slander a servant to his master.

Things That are Never Satisfied

1. The grave
2. The barren womb
3. Land, which is never satisfied with water
4. Fire, which never says, enough!

Small Things That are Wise

1. Ants, they store up food in the summer.
2. Coneys, they make their home in the crags.
3. Locusts, they have no king, but advance in ranks.
4. Lizard, they can be caught with the hand, yet they are found in King's houses.

Chapter 31

The sayings of King Lemuel that his mother taught him:
O son of my womb, do not spend your strength on women.
It is not for kings to drink wine or beer, lest they drink and deprive the oppressed of their rights.
Speak up for those who cannot speak for themselves.

The Wife of Noble Character

A wife of noble character is of great value. Her husband trusts in her, she is willing to work hard, she contributes financially to the family and is always on call day or night. She is aware of the poor and needy. She looks ahead and stores up food for hard times and also clothing. Her husband and children are blessed, because she fears the Lord and guides them in the right way.

Ecclesiastes

A Review

These are the words of Solomon, son of David and King of Jerusalem. When Solomon was made King, the Lord appeared to him and said, 'Ask for whatever you want me to give you'.

Solomon asked for wisdom and knowledge to lead the people. God said, 'Wisdom and knowledge will be given to you, also wealth, riches and honor, such as no king has ever had or will ever have (2 Chron. 1:7-12).

Solomon reigned 40 years in Jerusalem, then rested with his fathers and was buried in the city of David (2 Chron. 30, 31). He writes about this in Ecclesiastes; how it is the destiny of man to die (7:2).

Things Solomon Accomplished

Solomon said he wanted to see what was worthwhile for men to do under heaven during the few days of their lives.

He said he undertook great projects:

He built houses, the temple, planted vineyards, made gardens, parks, planted all kinds of fruit trees, made reservoirs to water groves of trees, bought male and female slaves, owned numerous herds and flocks, amassed large amounts of silver and gold, acquired men and women singers and a harem. (This is putting it mildly).

He said he denied himself nothing his eyes desired but when he surveyed all his hands had done, everything was meaningless.

He wrote that he imparted knowledge to the people; pondered, searched out and set in order many proverbs.

He searched to find just the right words and what he wrote was upright and true (12:9, 10).

Wisdom

Solomon asked, 'What does man gain from all his labor?' Generations come and go but the earth remains forever.

The wind blows to the south and turns to the north.

All streams flow into the sea, yet the sea is never full.

What has been will be again. There is nothing new under the sun.

There is no remembrance of men of old, nor will there be of those that follow (past the third generation).

The wise man, like the fool, will not be long remembered by man (God remembers).

When he looked at all the things he had toiled for, he hated them because they would be left to others; to those who had not worked for them. To those who would have control over all the work he had poured effort into.

What does a man get for all the toil and anxious striving?

Even at night, his mind does not rest. A man can do nothing better than to eat and drink and find satisfaction in his work (Chapter 2).

(The Lord may have done a good thing when he told Adam, 'By the sweat of your brow you will eat your food until you return to the ground, Gen. 3:19).

A Time for Everything

Solomon said there was a time for everything; a season for every activity.

1. A time to be born and a time to die
2. A time to plant and a time to uproot
3. A time to kill and a time to heal
4. A time to tear down and a time to build

5. A time to weep and a time to laugh
6. A time to mourn and a time to dance
7. A time to scatter stones and a time to gather
8. A time to embrace and a time to refrain
9. A time to search and a time to give up
10. A time to keep and a time to throw away
11. A time to tear and a time to mend
12. A time to be silent and a time to speak
13. A time to love and a time to hate
14. A time for war and a time for peace

God has made everything beautiful in its time. He has set eternity in the hearts of men. He says everything God does will endure forever. Nothing can be added to it and nothing taken from it.

God will bring to judgment both the righteous and the wicked.

There is nothing better for man than to be happy and to do good while they live (Chapter 3). That is his lot.

Oppression

He said he saw the tears of the oppressed. There was a man alone, he had neither son nor brother.

'For whom am I toiling?' he asked, 'Why am I depriving myself of enjoyment?'

Two are better than one because they have a good return for their work.

If one falls, his friend can help him up. Pity the man who falls and has no one to help him up! If two lie down together, they will keep warm. How can one keep warm alone?

Though one can be overpowered, two can defend themselves. A cord of three strands is not easily broken. (Ch 4)

Stand in awe of God; let your words be few. (Contentment comes from being thankful). Whoever loves money never has enough. Whoever loves wealth is never satisfied.

The sleep of a laborer is sweet but the abundance of a rich man permits him no sleep.

Naked a man comes from his mother's womb.   As he comes, so he departs (Chapter 5).

A Common Destiny

The day of death is better than the day of birth. Death is the destiny of every man. Do not say, 'Why were the old days better than these?'

When times are good, be happy; when times are bad consider: God made the one as well as the other. There is not a righteous man on earth who does what is right and never sins.

God has made man upright, but men have gone in search of many schemes (Chapter 7).

A bribe corrupts the heart. Wisdom brightens a man's face and changes his hard appearance.

Obey the King

A king's word is supreme, who can say to him, 'What are you doing?' No one has power over the day of his death.

Anyone who is among the living has hope. The dead know nothing of what is happening under the sun (on earth). Never again will they have a part in anything that happens.

The race is not to the swift or the battle to the strong. Time and chance happens to them all (Chapter 9).

If a man is lazy, the rafters sag; if his hands are idle, the house leaks.

Do not revile the king even in your thoughts, or curse the rich in your bedroom, because a bird of the air may carry your words (Chapter 10). (A little bird told me).

Bread Upon the Waters

Cast your bread upon the waters, for after many days, you will find it again (your kindness will be repaid).

However many years a man may live, let him enjoy them all, but let him remember the days of darkness for there will be many. We must take the bad along with the good. Banish anxiety from your heart.

Sow your seed in the morning and at evening let your hands be idle.

Remember Your Creator

Remember your creator in the days of your youth before the evil days come and you grow old.

Start living for God early before the grinders (teeth) cease, because they are few.

And those looking (eyes) through the windows grow dim. And the sound (ears) of grinding fades; when men are afraid of heights and dangers of the street, and desire is no longer stirred.

Then man goes to his eternal home and mourners go about the streets.

The dust returns to the ground it came from, and the spirit returns to God who gave it. (The old man crosses over).

The Conclusion of the Matter

Fear God and keep his commandments, for this is the whole duty of man.

God will bring every deed into judgment, including every hidden thing, whether it is good or evil (Chapter 12)

Song of Solomon

A Review

1 Kings 4:32 says Solomon spoke three thousand proverbs and his songs numbered a thousand and five.

He described plant life, from the cedar of Lebanon to hyssop that grows out of walls.

He also taught about animals like birds, reptiles and fish. It is no wonder he would use the beauties of nature and of animals to describe the beauty of a maiden.

The song seems to have been written by a young Solomon about a young Shulammite maiden he had met and fallen in love with (Chapter 6:13).

The Girl Speaks

Dark am I, yet lovely, like the tent curtains of Solomon.

She said she was darkened by the sun, while taking care of vineyards. She was a country girl (maybe his only true love).

She wanted to know where Solomon grazed his flock and was told to follow the tracks of the sheep.

The Courtship

Solomon told her he likened her to a mare harnessed to one of the chariots of Pharaoh and her eyes were like doves. That she was like a lily among thorns. She told him he was like an apple tree among trees of the forest.

She charged the daughter of Jerusalem:

Do not arouse or awaken love until it so desires (let it mature).

Spring Has Come (2:11-13)

The winter is past;
The rains are over and gone,
Flowers appear on the earth;
The season of singing has come,
The cooing of doves is heard in our land.
The fig tree forms its early fruit;
The blossoming vines spread their fragrance.
Arise, come my darling; my beautiful one, come with me.

Now they are feeling confident. She says, 'My beloved is mine and I am his'. Chapter 3:1-5 *may* have been a dream in which she feared she might lose Solomon.

The Marriage Procession

Who is this coming up from the desert, perfumed with myrrh and incense? It is Solomon's carriage, made of wood from Lebanon. With posts of silver, its base of gold, seat upholstered with purple.

Look at King Solomon wearing the crown, the crown with which his mother (Bathsheba) crowned him on the day of his wedding (3:6-11).

He Meets His Bride

How beautiful you are.
Your eyes behind your veil are doves
Your hair like a flock of goats
You teeth like a flock of sheep
Your lips like a scarlet ribbon
You breasts like two fawns
There is no flaw in you.

Married Love

You have stolen my heart, how delightful is your love.
Your lips drop sweetness as the honeycomb.
You are a garden, locked up...
A well of flowing water.
(Everything he needs, Chapter 4).

The Invitation

Let my love come into his garden, and taste its choice fruits.

Solomon's Absence Felt

I slept, but my heart was awake. My lover is knocking at
my door. I have taken off my robe; I have washed my feet.

My heart began to pound, but when I opened the door, he
left. I looked for him but did not find him.

Friends asked, 'How is your beloved better than others?'

He is outstanding among ten thousand. His head is purest
gold; his hair is wavy and black as a raven. His arms are rods of
gold. His appearance like the cedar of Lebanon. His mouth is
sweetness of itself.

Solomon Speaks

You are beautiful, my darling, lovely as Jerusalem.
Sixty queens there may be, and eighty concubines, and virgins
beyond number; but my dove, my perfect one, is unique, the
only daughter of her mother, the favorite of the one who bore
her.

Wife Speaks

I belong to my lover and his desire is for me.

Let us go early to the vineyards; if the pomegranates are in bloom; then I will give you my love.

Under the apple tree I roused you; there your mother conceived you, there she, who was in labor, gave you birth.

Love is as strong as death.

It burns like a blazing fire.

Many waters cannot quench love.

The Joy of Married Love

I have become in his eyes like one bringing contentment.

A lack of self-consciousness during intimacy is a pure love.

Love transcends beauty and physical attraction.

Isaiah

A Review

A major prophet to Judah during the reigns of four kings: Uzziah (Azariah) 52 years, Jotham 16 years, Ahaz 16 years and Hezekiah 29 years.

He was born during the reign of Uzziah but Uzziah reigned 52 years, so most probably Isaiah prophesied longer than any other man. He saw the destruction of Judah by Babylon.

The writer of 2 Chronicles says Isaiah wrote Isaiah (2 Chron. 26:22).

Isaiah was quoted in several New Testament books (Matt. 3:3 in Isaiah 40:3, John 12:38 in Isaiah 6:10, Acts 8:26-44 in Isaiah 53:7, 8, 1 Peter 2:6 in Isaiah 18:16 and many more).

He prophesied the coming of the Messiah in 7:14, 9:6, 7, 11:1-9, 42:1-9 and other places.

The oldest manuscripts we have, by him, were in the Dead Sea Scrolls.

The first vision Isaiah recorded was of Judah and Jerusalem. The Lord told him to tell them he had no pleasure in their sacrificial offerings because they were meaningless. They were just going through the motions and were vain.

He told them to repent and learn to do right. Though their sins were like scarlet, they would be as white as snow, but if they resisted, they would be devoured by the sword.

His First Prophesy (2:2, 3)

In the last days, the mountain of the Lord's temple will be established as chief among the mountains; it will be raised above the hills, and all nations will stream to it.

Many people will come and say, 'Come, let us go up to the mountain of the Lord, to the house of the God of Jacob. He will teach us His ways, so that we may walk in His paths'.

The Law will go out from Zion, the word of the Lord from Jerusalem.

Menakin Begin

Menakin Begin quoted this passage after his meeting with President Carter at Camp David:

They shall beat their swords into plowshares,
And their spears into pruning hooks,
Nation will not take up sword against nation
Nor will they train for war anymore (2:4).

The Lord is going to bring about judgment on Judah and Jerusalem. Some of the things they were doing were: practicing divination, clasping hands with pagans, their land is full of silver and gold, their land is full of horses and chariots, they bow down to idols.

The Lord is about to take away supply (food and water) and support, but it will be well with the righteous (3:10).

The Women of Zion

The women of Zion are haughty, walking along with outstretched necks, flirting with their eyes, tripping along with mincing steps, with ornaments jingling on their ankles.

The Lord will snatch away their finery: bangles, headbands, necklaces, earrings, bracelets, veils, headdresses, ankle chains, perfumes, charms, signet and nose rings, fine robes, capes, cloaks, purses, mirrors, linen garments, tiaras and shawls.

In that day, seven women will take hold of one man and say, 'We will eat our own food and provide our own clothes.

Only let us be called by your name. Take away our disgrace'.
(Few men?)

The people have no regard for the deeds of the Lord, no
respect for the work of his hands. Therefore my people will go
into exile (6:1-8).

Isaiah's Commission (6:1-8)

In the year King Uzziah died (740 BC), Isaiah saw the Lord
seated on his throne (in heaven). The voice of the Lord said,
'Whom shall I send? And who will go for us?'

Isaiah said, 'Here am I, send me!'
The Lord said, 'Go and tell this people:
Be ever hearing, but never understanding.
Be ever seeing, but never perceiving.
Make the heart of this people calloused...'
Isaiah said, 'For how long, O Lord?'
Until the Lord has sent everyone far away (Chapter 6).

When Ahaz was king, Isaiah was sent to him. He told him
the King of Aram had allied himself with Ephraim (Israel) but to
not be afraid. Within 65 years, Ephraim would be too shattered
to be a people (by Assyria). Assyria was the Lord's instrument
to punish Ephraim (Israel).

A Prophesy of Jesus (9:1-6)

In the past, he humbled Zebulun and Naphtali but in the
future he will honor Galilee of the Gentiles by the way of the
sea, along the Jordan (where Jesus lived).
The people walking in darkness have seen a great light;
On these living in the land of the shadow of death, a
light has dawned (Matt. 4:14, 15)

Also...

For to me a child is born, to us a son is given,
And the government will be on his shoulders.
And He will be called wonderful counselor, Mighty God,
Everlasting Father, Prince of Peace… (Chapter 9).

God's Judgment

I will send Assyria against the godless nation, a people who anger me.

When the Lord has finished his work, He will punish the King of Assyria because they thought it was by their strength and wisdom they had done this.

Only a remnant will ever return. The people of Zion (Jerusalem) need not be afraid (at this time, Ch 10).

Another Prophesy of Jesus

A shoot will come up from the stump of Jesse. From his roots a branch will bear fruit. The Spirit of the Lord will rest on him… (Chapter 11).

God is bringing down other nations, one at a time; Assyria, Babylon, the Philistines, Moab, Damascus, Cush (Ethiopia), Egypt, Edom, Tyre and the earth.

When the judgments come upon the earth, the people will learn righteousness.

In days to come Jacob will take root,
Israel will bud and blossom
And fill the world with fruit.

Those who were exiled in Assyria and Egypt will come and worship the Lord on the holy mountain in Jerusalem (Ch 27).

Another Prophesy of Jesus (28:16)
See, I lay a stone in Zion, a tested stone, a precious cornerstone for a sure foundation; the one who trusts will never be dismayed (1 Peter 2:6, Rom. 9:33).

The Lord Says (29:13)

These people come near to me with their mouth and honor me with their lips, but their hearts are far from me.

Their worship of me is made up only of rules taught by men. (This was quoted by Jesus in Matthew 15:8, 9).

Woes

Woe to those who carry out plans that are not mine; who go down to Egypt for help without consulting me.

This brings neither help nor advantage.

Repentance and rest is your salvation; in quietness and trust is your strength.

The Lord is a God of justice.

When you cry for help, as soon as He hears, he will answer you.

The Egyptians are men and not God.

Assyria will fall by a sword that is not of man. (The angel of God put to death 185,000 Assyrians).

Isaiah 36-39 / 2 Kings 18:17- Ch. 20 say the same thing!

The King of Assyria has taken Israel and now wants Judah. He poses this question to King Hezekiah, 'On what are you basing your confidence?'

The commander stood and called out in Hebrew, 'Do not let Hezekiah deceive you. He cannot deliver you. Who of all the gods of these countries (he had taken) as been able to save his land from me? How can the Lord deliver Jerusalem from my hand?'

The people remained silent because the king had commanded them, 'Do not answer him'.

Hezekiah sent a group to Isaiah and told him what had happened. Isaiah said, 'tell your master this is what the Lord says: "Do not be afraid of what you have heard. I am going to put a spirit in him so that when he hears a certain report, he will return to his own country".

Hezekiah Prays

Hezekiah received a letter from Sennacherib, King of Assyria. In it he said, surely you have heard what the kings of Assyria have done to all the countries (destroying them completely). Hezekiah went to the temple and spread out the letter before the Lord. He said, 'It is true, O Lord, that the Assyrian kings have laid waste all these peoples and their lands. Now, O Lord, deliver us from his hand so that all kingdoms on earth may know that you alone, O Lord, are God'.

Isaiah's Message to Hezekiah (37:21-29)

This is the message the Lord has spoken against Sennacherib, King of Assyria.

> Against whom have you raised your voice
> And lifted your eyes in pride?
> I will defend this city and save it,
> For my sake and for the sake of David, my servant.

Then the angel of the Lord (the Lord himself) went out and put to death 185,000 men in the Assyrian camp (38:36).

The king returned to Nineveh and stayed there. Later on, his own sons killed him (story also told in 2 Kings 18:13-19:37).

Other times, the Lord himself came to rescue people (Gen. 18:1-33, Joshua 5:13-6:17 and Judges 6:11-7:22).

Note: Assyria did not take Judah, but Babylon did (about 136 years later).

Hezekiah's Illness (Chapter 38)

Hezekiah became ill, Isaiah was sent to him. He told him, 'This is what the Lord says: Put your house in order, because you are going to die'.

Hezekiah turned his face to the wall and prayed, saying, 'O Lord, I have walked before you faithfully and with wholehearted devotion'. He wept bitterly.

The Lord changed his mind and added 15 years to his life. After his recovery, Hezekiah wrote a poem (38:9-20).

He wrote: surely it was for my benefit that I suffered such anguish. (He had a boil. A poultice of figs was applied to it and he recovered. He was only 39 years old at the time, as he died at age 54, 2 Kings 18:1, 2).

Babylon Visits (Chapter 39)

The King of Babylon heard Hezekiah had been ill and sent a gift by an envoy. Hezekiah showed the men everything in his palace.

Isaiah told Hezekiah the Lord said, 'The time will come when everything in your palace and all that your fathers have stored up will be carried off to Babylon.' (This is where the men had come from). Some of your descendants will be taken away and will become eunuchs in the palace of the King of Babylon. (End of story also told in 2 Kings Chapters 18-20).

Comfort for God's People (Chapter 40)

Isaiah is told to cry out to his people.
Some things he said:
Speak tenderly to Jerusalem; her sin has been paid for.
'All men are like grass, the grass withers and the flowers
    fall, but the word of our God stands forever'.

Whom did the Lord consult, who taught him?
To whom will you compare to God?
He sits enthroned above the earth and its people are like
    grasshoppers.
Lift up your eyes and look to the heavens: He brings out
    the starry host one by one and calls them each by
    name.
The Creator of the ends of the earth will not grow tired
    or weary.
Those who hope in the Lord will renew their strength.
They will soar on wings like eagles; they will run and
    not grow weary, walk and not be faint.

Israel's Helper

You, O Israel, my servant Jacob, whom I have chosen; you, descendants of Abraham my friend.

I said, 'You are my servant; do not fear, for I am with you; so that people may see and know, that the hand of the Lord has done this. Present your case. Bring in your idols to tell us what is going to happen. I have stirred up one from the North. One who treads on rulers as if they were mortar'.

Another Prophesy of the Lord Jesus (Ch 42:1-7)

My chosen one in whom I delight;
I will put my spirit on him.
He will not shout or cry out,
Or raise his voice in the streets.
I will make you to be a covenant
For the people and a light for you Gentiles,
To open eyes that are blind,
To free captives from prison.
New things I declare; before they spring into being I announce them to you (42:9).

Israel, Blind and Deaf

You have seen many things, but have paid no attention. Your ears appear open, but you hear nothing.

Who handed Jacob over to become lost? And Israel to be plunderers? Was it not the Lord?

They would not follow his ways, nor obey His laws. Before me no god was formed, nor will there be one after me. *I, even I, am the Lord* and apart from me, there is no Savior.

You have not brought me sheep for burnt offerings, nor honored me with your sacrifices, grain offerings, incense, Calamus or the fat of your sacrifices, but you have burdened me with your sins (Chapter 43).

Your first father sinned (Adam); your spokesmen rebelled (Moses and Aaron).

Idols (Chapter 44)

All who make idols are nothing.
The things they treasure are worthless.
The blacksmith takes a tool – He shapes an idol with hammers; he cuts down trees of Cedars, Cypress or Oak.
With some of it he warms himself.
With some of it he bakes bread.
With some of it, he fashions a god and worships it.
They know nothing, they understand nothing.
I am the Lord, who has made all things. Apart from me there is no God.

Cyrus

God will raise up King Cyrus of Persia to deliver them (Ezra 1). He will rebuild my city (Jerusalem) and set my exiles free. God said He did not create the world to be empty, but to be inhabited. Before me every knee will bow; by me every tongue will swear (Rom. 14:11).

Gods of Babylon (Chapter 46)

Bel and Nebo were two of Babylon's gods. Their idols were large and had to be borne by beasts of burden (Dan. Ch 3). They cannot move, they cannot answer, they cannot save anyone.

The Fall of Babylon

Daughter of the Babylonians – No more will you be called tender or delicate. I was angry with my people and gave them into your hand.

You showed no mercy; even on the aged you laid a heavy yoke. Disaster will come upon you.

Stubborn Israel (Chapter 48)

You, who are called by the name of Israel and come from the line of Judah, I told you these things long ago; before they happened, I announced them to you.

From now on I will tell you of new things.

Israel Freed

The Lord's chosen ally will carry out His purpose against Babylon.

If only you had paid attention to my commands, your descendants would have been like the sand. Their name would never be cut off.

Leave Babylon, flee the Babylonians!

They will come from afar; some from the north, some from the west.

Can a mother forget the baby at her breast and have no compassion on the child she has borne?

Your sons hasten back and those who laid you waste depart from you. I will beckon to the Gentiles.

Another Prophesy of the Lord

Isaiah says the Lord wakens him each morning to listen like one being taught. Revelation to Isaiah (about Jesus):

I offered my back to those who beat me, my cheeks to those who pulled out my beard; I did not hide my face from mocking and spitting (Matt. 26 and 27).

Salvation

My salvation is on the way. The heavens will vanish like smoke, the earth will wear out like a garment and its inhabitants die like flies, but my salvation will last forever, through all generations (a prophesy).

A Prophesy of the Life and Death of Jesus (Ch. 52)

My servant (Jesus) will be raised, lifted up and highly exalted. His appearance was disfigured, his form marred. He had no beauty or majesty to attract us to him; He was despised and rejected by men.

A man of sorrows and familiar with suffering, we esteemed Him not.

He was pierced for our transgressions – by His wounds we are healed. He was oppressed and afflicted yet He did not open His mouth.

Phillip and the Eunuch

In Acts 8:26-39 Phillip was sent by an angel to go meet an Ethiopian eunuch who had been to Jerusalem to worship. He was reading this passage in Isaiah Chapter 53.

He was led like a sheep to the slaughter
And as a lamb before the shearer is silent,
So He did not open His mouth.
In His humiliation He was deprived of Justice
Who can speak of his descendants?
For His life was taken from the earth.

Phillip, the evangelist, asked if he understood the scripture. He didn't, so Phillip explained to him it was a prophesy of the savior, Jesus, that had recently been crucified.
Jesus poured out his life for all of us.

Salvation is Free

The invitation is to *all* who are thirsty. It is to be an everlasting covenant. Let him turn to the Lord and he will find mercy and God will freely pardon.
Those who walk uprightly will enter into peace and find rest as they lie in death. The Lord said He would not accuse forever nor will I always be angry, for then the spirit of man would grow faint. I will guide him and restore comfort to him (Ch 57)

Fasting (Chapter 58)

Is it not to share your food with the hungry?
If you spend yourselves in behalf of the hungry and satisfy the needs of the oppressed, then your light will shine in the darkness and your night will become like the noonday.
It was also used for discipline, sincerity and spiritual revival; devoting oneself to fasting and praying.

Redemption

Surely the arm of the Lord is not too short to save, nor his ear too dull to hear. But your iniquities have separated you from your God; your sins have hidden his face from you so that He will not hear.

The Redeemer will come to those who repent of their sins. Though in anger I struck you, in favor I will show you compasssion. No longer will violence be heard in your land, nor ruin or destruction within your borders. Isaiah foresees a time in the future when Israel will shine again.

The Year of the Lord (Chapter 61:1)

The Spirit of the Lord is on me,
Because he has anointed me
To preach good news to the poor.
He has sent me to proclaim freedom for the prisoners
And recovery of sight for the blind,
To release the oppressed,
To proclaim the year of the Lord's favor.

Jesus went to Nazareth, where he grew up. The scroll of the prophet Isaiah was handed to him in the synagogue. He read this passage, rolled up the scroll, handed it back to the attendant and sat down. He said, 'Today this scripture is fulfilled in your hearing'(Luke 4:14-21).

Isaiah Prophesies (Chapter 62)

For Jerusalem's sake I will not remain quiet; until her righteousness shines out like the dawn, her salvation like a blazing torch. You will be called by a new name that the Lord will bestow. Never again will I give your grain as food for your enemies, never again will foreigners drink the new wine for which you have toiled.

The People Remember (Chapter 63 and 64)

His people recalled the days of old, the days of Moses and his people; your tenderness and compassion are withheld from us.

You, O Lord, are our Father, our Redeemer from of old is you name. Since ancient times no one has heard, no ear has perceived, no eye has seen any God besides you.

How then can we be saved? All our righteous acts are like filthy rags. Do not be angry beyond measure, O Lord. Do not remember our sin forever.

Our holy and glorious temple has been burned with fire and all that we treasured lies in ruins.

Will you keep silent and punish us beyond measure?

The Lord's Judgment and Salvation (Chapter 65)

The Lord speaks through Isaiah:

All day long I have held out my hands to an obstinate people. A people who continually provoke me…Who eat the flesh of pigs and whose pots hold the broth of unclean meat. Such people are smoke in my nostrils…

As when juice is still found in a cluster of grapes and men say, 'Don't destroy it, there is yet some good in it'; so will I do – On behalf of my servants, I will not destroy them all.

I will bring forth descendants from Jacob and from Judah; those who will possess my mountains. But as for you who forsake the Lord, I will destine you for the sword.

New Heavens and a New Earth (Chapter 65:17…)

'Behold, I will create new heavens and a new earth. The former things will not be remembered, nor will they come to mind.

The sound of weeping and crying will be heard in it no more. Never again will there be in it an infant who lives but a few days, or an old man who does not live out his years; he who dies at a hundred will be thought a mere youth...

Before they call, I will answer; while they are still speaking I will hear'.

Judgment and Hope

'Heaven is my throne, and the earth is my footstool'.

This is the one I esteem (Chapter 66):

He who is humble and contrite in spirit but...

The Lord will repay those that do evil with what they deserve.

Can a country be born in a day or a nation be brought forth in a moment?

As a mother comforts a child, so will I comfort you; and you will be comforted over Jerusalem.

I will send some of those who survive to the other nations – to Tarshish, to the Libyans and Lydians, Tubal, Greece and to the distant lands that have not heard of my fame or seen my glory. (They will proclaim my glory among the nations, 66:19).

They will bring all your brothers, from all the nations, to my holy mountain in Jerusalem; on horses, in chariots and wagons, and on mules and camels. I will select some of them also to be priests and Levites (66:20).

Note: Isaiah writes about the captivities of both Israel and Judah by Assyria and Babylon. He was alive when Israel was taken, but did not see Judah taken. The Lord revealed many future happenings to him as if they had already taken place.

Jeremiah

A Review

Jeremiah was a prophet to Judah its last 40 years, lasting until their Babylonian captivity in 586 BC.

He was the son of a priest in Benjamin. His call came in the thirteenth year of the reign of Josiah, a good king.

The Lord told him, 'Before I formed you in the womb, I knew you. Before you were born, I set you apart; I appointed you as a prophet to the nations' (1:5).

Jeremiah also felt inadequate saying, 'I am only a little child'. This meant he was inexperienced. The Lord told him to go to everyone I send you to and say whatever I command you. The Lord then reached out and touched his mouth.

You are to stand against the whole land – against the kings of Judah. They will fight against you, but will not overcome you, for I am with you and will rescue you (Chapter 1).

Israel Touches God

Speaking of earlier days, the Lord told Jeremiah to proclaim: I remember how as a bride you loved me and followed me through the desert. Why did you follow worthless idols and become worthless yourselves?

You did not ask where is the Lord who brought us up out of Egypt through a barren wilderness – where no one travels and no one lives. Has a nation ever changed its gods?

I had planted you like a choice vine. Although you wash yourself with soda and use an abundance of soap, the stain of your guilt is still before me. As a thief is disgraced when he is caught, so the house of Israel is disgraced; yet when you are in trouble you say, come and save us.

If a man divorces his wife and she marries another man, should he return to her again? Would not the land be completely defiled? (See Deut. 24:1-4).

Even when Judah saw what happened to Israel (Assyrian captivity) they had no fear. They did not repent and return to me.

The house of Judah will join the house of Israel. Like a woman unfaithful to her husband, so you have been unfaithful to me. I am bringing disaster from the north (Babylon), even terrible destruction.

Not One is Upright

Go up and down the streets of Jerusalem. If you can find one person who deals honestly and seeks the truth, I will forgive this city.

I thought, (says Jeremiah), these are only the poor. They do not know the way of the Lord. I will go to the leaders and speak to them; but with one accord, they too had broken off the yoke.

The Lord said, 'Should I not avenge myself on such a nation as this?'

I am bringing a distant nation against you – a people whose language you do not know, whose speech you do not understand.

They will devour your harvests and food, your sons and daughters, your flocks and herds, your vines and fig trees and destroy your fortified cities. I will destroy you completely. When the people ask why tell them: As you have forsaken me (the Lord) and served foreign gods in your own land, now you will serve foreigners in a land not your own.

A horrible and shocking thing has happened in the land:
The prophets prophesy lies,
The priests rule by their own authority,
And my people love it this way.
But what will you do in the end?

Jeremiah Speaks

'To whom can I speak and give warning? Who will listen to me? Their ears are closed so they cannot hear. The Word of the Lord is offensive to them; they find no pleasure in it, but I am full of the wrath of the Lord and I cannot hold it in'.

The Lord says:

'From the least to the greatest, all are greedy for gain; prophets and priests alike, all practice deceit.

They dress the wound of my people as though it were not serious (lightly).

'Peace, Peace', they say, when there is no peace.

Are they ashamed of their loathsome conduct? No, they have no shame at all. They don't even know how to blush (6:10-15).

This is what the Lord says:

'Stand at the crossroads and look;

Ask for the ancient paths,

Ask where the good way is,

And walk in it and you will find rest for your souls (6:16)'.

This is the word that came to Jeremiah from the Lord: 'Stand at the gate of the Lord's house and proclaim this message:

Reform your ways and your actions and I will let you live in this place. If you do not oppress the alien, the fatherless or the widow, do not shed innocent blood and do not follow other gods, I will let you live in this place, in the land I gave your forefathers.

What I did to Shiloh I will now do to the house that bears my name (see 1 Sam. 4:1-11)'.

This did not happen (to Judah).

Jeremiah Laments

'The harvest is past. The summer has ended and we are not saved' (8:20). Is there no balm in Gilead? Oh, that I had in the desert a lodging place for travelers, so that I might leave my people and go away from them (9:2).

Jeremiah's Prayer

I know, O Lord, that a man's life is not his own; it is not for man to direct his steps. Pout out your wrath on the nations who do not acknowledge you. They have devoured Jacob.

The Lord told Jeremiah both the house of Israel and the house of Judah had broken the covenant he made with their forefathers.

The Covenant

Genesis 17, Exodus 19:1-8, Deuteronomy 29 and 30, Joshua 8:30-34, Joshua 24, 2 Kings 23:1-3...

Love the Lord, walk in His ways, keep his laws, decrees. God will bless them. If they turn away, they will be destroyed (Deut. 30:16-19).

At times, Jeremiah's life was threatened. All servants of the Lord, at times, must suffer for his sake. Jeremiah, like many others, wondered why the wicked prosper.

The Lord told Jeremiah to buy a linen belt and put it around his waist, but do not let it touch water. Take the belt and hide it in a crevice in the rocks.

Days later, he was told to dig it up. It was ruined and useless. The Lord said, 'These wicked people will be like this belt, completely useless!'

Can the Ethiopian change his skin? Or the leopard its spots? Neither can you do good who are accustomed to doing evil (Chapter 13).

Jeremiah told the Lord, 'the prophets keep telling the people, you will not see the sword or suffer famine'.

The Lord said, 'the prophets are prophesying lies in my name (Chapter 14). Even if Moses and Samuel were to stand before me, my heart would not go out to this people'.

If they ask you, 'Where shall we go?'

Tell them:
Those destined to death, to death;
Those for the sword, to the sword;
Those for starvation, to starvation;
Those for captivity, to captivity.

Day of Disaster

The Lord told Jeremiah: 'You must not marry or have sons or daughters in this place. Do not enter a house where there is a funeral meal; do not go to mourn or show sympathy. Do not enter a house where there is feasting and sit down to eat and drink'.

The Blessed Man

Blessed is the man who trusts in the Lord,
Whose confidence is in Him.
He will be like a tree planted by the water
That sends out its roots by the stream.
It does not fear when heat comes;
Its leaves are always green.
It has no worries in a year of drought
And never fails to bear fruit (17:7-8).

The Lord told Jeremiah to go to the potter's house and buy a jar and proclaim the words he tells him. 'I am going to bring a disaster on this place that will make the ears of everyone who hears of it tingle. I will make them eat the flesh of their sons and daughters, and they will eat one another's flesh during the stress of the siege'.

Then break the jar. I will smash this nation just as this potter's jar is smashed and cannot be repaired.

When the priest, Pashhur, heard this prophesy, he had Jeremiah beaten and put in the stocks at the temple for a while.

Jeremiah complains to the Lord:

The work of the Lord has brought me insult and reproach all day long. But if I say, I will not mention Him or speak anymore in His name, His word is in my heart like a fire, a fire shut up in my bones. I am weary of holding it in; indeed I cannot.

King Zedekiah Makes a Request

Nebuchadnezzar, King of Babylon, is attacking us. Inquire of the Lord for us. Perhaps the Lord will perform wonders for us as in times past and he will withdraw from us.

Jeremiah answered, 'This is what the Lord says: I myself will fight against you. Whoever stays in the city will die by the sword, famine or plague. Whoever goes out and surrenders to the Babylonians will live; he will escape with his life'.

People from many nations will pass by this city and ask, 'Why has the Lord done this?' The answer will be, 'Because they have forsaken the covenant of the Lord and have worshipped and served other gods' (Chapter 22).

Do not weep for the dead, but weep for the ones who are exiled, because they will never return or see their native land again.

Jehoahaz will never return (captured).

Jehoiakim died but not mourned.

Jehoiachin taken captive to Babylon and lived out his life there. None of their offspring will sit on the throne.

King Jehoiachin, his officials, the craftsmen and artisans were carried into exile by Nebuchadnezzar, King of Babylon. He was only 18 years old and had reigned three months. Ten thousand surrendered. (See 2 Kings 24:8-16).

Two Baskets of Figs

The Lord showed Jeremiah two baskets of figs. One basket was good, the other not fit to eat. He said the good basket represented the exiles. He would watch over them and bring them back, but the bad basket would be destroyed (Chapter 24).

At this time, Jeremiah had been prophesying 23 years (25:3).

Death Threat

During the reign of Jehoiakim, Jeremiah was sent to the temple to warn them of what was to come. He was seized and in danger of death. Some of the elders stepped forward and said another man, Micah, had prophesied the same thing in the days of Hezekiah. Uriah was another man who had prophesied the same thing but was put to death by King Jehoiakim. Through the intercession of friends, Jeremiah was spared (Chapter 26).

In the days of Zedekiah (the last king) the Lord told Jeremiah to make a yoke and wear it around his neck.

He gave this message to Zedekiah: 'Bow your neck under the yoke of the King of Babylon; serve him and his people, and you will live. Why should you die? Why should this city become a ruin?

The Lord told me the pillars, sea and all other furnishings left (that were not taken when Jehoiachin went into exile) will be taken to Babylon and remain there until I bring them back to this place' (see Ezra 1:7-11).

Hananish, a false prophet, spoke to the people and told them that within two years, God would break the yoke of Nebuchadnezzar and bring the exiles back. He convinced the people but it didn't happen and two months later, this false prophet was dead.

Jeremiah Writes to the Exiles

He wrote:

Build houses and settle down; plant gardens and eat what they produce.

Marry and have sons and daughters; find wives for your sons and give you daughters in marriage – increase there...

When the seventy years are completed, I will bring you back to this place.

For I know the plans I have for you, plans to give you hope and a future. Then you will call upon me and come and pray to me, and I will listen to you.

You will seek me and find me. When you seek me with all your heart, I will be found by you (29:11-13).

Even among the exiles, there were false prophets (29:24-32).

This word came to Jeremiah from the Lord: 'Write in a book all the words I have spoken to you'.

A New Covenant Revealed

'The time is coming,' declares the Lord, 'where I will make a new covenant with the house of Israel and the house of Judah (not like the first one). I will put my law in their minds and write it on their hearts. I will be their God, and they will be my people...

They will all know me, from the least to the greatest. I will forgive their wickedness and remember their sins no more' (Chapter 31:31-34; New Testament: Hebrews 8:7-13, Luke 22:17-20, Ephesians. 1:5-10).

Jeremiah Buys a Field

This is now the tenth year of Zedekiah. The Babylonians are already besieging Jerusalem. There is one year left. Jeremiah is confined to the courtyard where he is imprisoned.

His cousin, Hanamel, came to Jeremiah and said, 'buy my field at Anathoth' (evidently Jeremiah was a near kinsman; see

Lev. 25:15-28, Ruth 3:1-10). The documents were sealed and placed in a clay jar for safekeeping. This showed Jeremiah believed what he was saying, that they would be returned to their land. The exiles needed to have taken their records with them because they needed proof when they returned (Nehemiah 7).

The Lord told Jeremiah to go to the king, Zedekiah, and tell him he would not die by the sword, but would be captured (2 Kings 25:2-7).

They did kill his sons and blind him.

The Lord told Jeremiah to write on a scroll all the words he had spoken to him. Jeremiah dictated them to his scribe, Baruch, then sent him to the temple to read it. They looked at each other in fear and asked him if Jeremiah had dictated it. When he said yes, they said to go and hide.

They went and told the king about it. He was sitting in his winter apartment in front of a fire and sent for the scroll. After hearing three or four columns, he cut them off and threw them into the fire. Jeremiah had Baruch to rewrite another scroll. This king was Jehoiakim.

Zedekiah, the next king, paid no attention to Jeremiah either. He did send a priest to ask Jeremiah to 'pray to the Lord our God for us'. He had called on Pharaoh's army to help them and while that was going on, the Babylonians had withdrawn.

When Jeremiah left the city to see about his property, the guard at the Benjamin gate thought he was deserting to the Babylonians. He had him beaten and imprisoned. The king had him placed in the courtyard and given bread from the street bakers (until it was gone, Chapter 37).

Jeremiah kept on telling the people if they stayed they would die, but if they went over to the Babylonians they would live. Some officials told the king he was discouraging the soldiers and suggested they put him in a cistern.

Another official told the king he would die if left there, so he was set free and put in the courtyard again. King Zedekiah sent for Jeremiah (in private). He promised not to harm him and wanted the truth. Jeremiah told him, 'If you surrender, your life will be spared'.

The Fall of Jerusalem

In the eleventh year of Zedekiah, the Jerusalem wall was broken through. The king and soldiers fled by night toward the Jordan valley.

The Babylonian army overtook Zedekiah in the plains of Jericho. They captured him, killed his sons and the nobles and put out Zedekiah's eyes. They set fire to the royal palace, broke down the walls of Jerusalem and carried into exile those that remained.

They left some of the poor people who owned nothing and gave them vineyards and fields.

Nebuchadnezzar had given orders not to harm Jeremiah. He was sent to his home and remained among his own people. He was given provisions. He went to Gedaliah, who had been appointed over the towns of Judah, and stayed with him at Mizpah.

When the Jews who had scattered heard who had been put in charge, they came back. Gedaliah told them not to be afraid of the Babylonians.

For a little while all was well, then Gedaliah was assassinnated and all with him at Mizpah. The bodies were thrown into a cistern that King Asa had made.

The army officers and what few people there were left went to ask Jeremiah saying, 'Tell us where we should go and what we should do. Whether it is favorable or unfavorable, we will obey the Lord'.

Ten days later, the word of the Lord came to Jeremiah.

The Lord said, 'If you stay in this land, I will build you up and not tear you down. Do not be afraid of the King of Babylon. If you say, no, we will go and live in Egypt, the sword and famine will overtake you there. Do not go to Egypt'.

They said to Jeremiah, 'we will not listen'.

The Lord said, 'I am going to hand Pharaoh over to his enemies just as I handed Zedekiah over to Nebuchadnezzar'.

Message to Baruch

Jeremiah's scribe, Baruch, was worn out. The Lord told him wherever he went, he would escape with his life (45:1-4).

Messages About the Nations

Egypt: There is no balm in Gilead…your warriors will be laid low. They will fall over each other. I will hand them over to Nebuchadnezzar. Later Egypt will be inhabited as in times past.

Philistines: See how the waters are rising in the North (Babylon). They will become an overflowing torrent. Fathers will not turn to help their children. The Lord is about to destroy the Philistines.

Moab (Lot): Moab will be praised no more. Moab will be destroyed and her towns invaded. The fall is at hand. Moab will be destroyed as a nation because she has defied the Lord. Whoever flees from the terror will fall into a pit. Whoever climbs out of the pit will be caught in a snare. (Yet I will restore the fortunes of Moab in days to come, Chapter 48).

Ammon (Lot): Israel will drive out those who drove her out. You trust in your riches and say 'who will attack me?' (Afterward, I will restore the fortunes of the Ammonites).

Edom (Esau): I will bring disaster on Esau. Leave your orphans; I will protect their lives. Your widows too can trust in me. As Sodom and Gomorrah were overthrown, along with their neighboring towns, no one will live there, no man will dwell in it.

Damascus: Damascus has become feeble, she has turned to flee and panic has gripper her. I will set fire to the walls of Damascus. It will consume the fortresses of Ben-Hadad.

Elam: There will not be a nation where Elam's exiles do not go. I will restore the fortune of Elam in days to come.

Babylon: Babylon will be captured. A nation from the north will attack her. In those days, the people of Israel and Judah will go in tears to seek the Lord. They will ask the way to Zion and turn their faces toward it. I will punish Babylon as I punished Assyria.

I set a trap for you, O Babylon, and you were caught before you knew it. The Lord has stirred up the kings of the Medes because his purpose is to destroy Babylon. I will bring them down like lambs to the slaughter. Babylon must fall because of Israel's slain. For the Lord is a God of retribution; He will repay in full.

Babylon's History

Babylon was located about 60 miles south of Bagdad, Iraq. The Euphrates River flowed through the city. It was built in a square with two sets of walls 10 and 12 feet thick. The Hanging Gardens (one of the ancient wonders of the world) was there. It was destroyed by the Assyrians but later rebuilt. The Persians took the city in 539 BC, 47 years after the fall of Jerusalem. It lies in ruins today (*Worldbook Encyclopedia* page 9, 10).

The Fall of Jerusalem

Zedekiah was 21 years old when he became king and reigned 11 years.

In his ninth year, Nebuchadnezzar marched against Jerusalem and built siege-works all around it. This went on for two years.

By the fourth month, famine had set in. The wall was broken through and the army fled at night. They were overtaken in the plains of Jericho and King Zedekiah was captured. His sons were slaughtered before his eyes, and then his eyes put out. He was taken to Babylon and imprisoned until he died.

The commander of Nebuchadnezzar's imperial guard came to Jerusalem. He burned every important building and broke down the walls.

The Babylonians took all the precious items in the temple, even the 18 cubit pillars, back to Babylon. He took prisoner important people associated with the running of the temple and had them executed at Riblah.

4,600 people were taken to Babylon as exiles plus the 10,000 already there (2 Kings 24:14).

After 37 years, Jehoiachin was freed from prison. He was 18 when imprisoned so that would make him 55.

He put aside his prison clothes and ate at the king's table. He was given an allowance as long as he lived. He never returned to his native land.

Dates

Dates of departure: 605, 597, 586 BC
Dates of return: 538, 455, 444 BC

The Last Kings and Their Reigns

Josiah	31 years	2 Kings 22:1
Jehoahaz	3 months	2 Kings 23:31
Jehoiakim	11 years	2 Kings 23:36
Jehoiachin	3 months	2 Kings 24:6
Zedekiah	11 years	2 Kings 24:17, 18

No more kings after Zedekiah (Jeremiah 1:3).

The first exile started in the 3rd year of Jehoiakim's reign and ended at the end of Zedekiah's reign (19 ½ years).

Daniel was taken in the first exile during Jehoiakim's reign (Daniel 1:1-7).

Esther and Mordecai were taken about 8 years later during Jehoiachin's reign (Esther 2:6).

Returned

Zerubbabel first, Ezra second, and Nehemiah third. Zerubbabel was the grandson of Jehoiachin and in the lineage of Christ (Matt. 1:12).

Darius was the son of Xerxes/Ahasuerus (ruled 485 – 465 BC, 9:1).

Lamentations

A Review

Jeremiah was a prophet to Judah for 40 years, starting in the thirteenth year of Josiah and continuing on after the destruction of Jerusalem in 586 BC. He was an eye-witness.

Over and over he warned them to repent but they didn't believe it would happen to them, even though it happened to the northern kingdom, Israel.

Jeremiah is so sad and laments over the loss.

Jerusalem Deserted

How deserted lays the city (Jerusalem), once so full of people! Judah has gone into exile. She dwells among the nations; no one comes to her appointed feasts. All the splendor has departed from the daughter of Zion.

No Treasures

The enemy laid hands on all her treasures; she saw pagan nations enter her sanctuary – those you had forbidden to enter.

The Lord has sapped my strength. My eyes overflow with tears. No one is near to comfort me. My enemies have heard of my distress and rejoice.

The Lord is like an enemy; in His fierce anger He has spurned both king and priest.

The law is no more, her prophets no longer find visions from the Lord.

My eyes fail from weeping. I am in torment within because my people are destroyed, because children and infants faint in the streets of the city. They say to their mothers, 'Where is bread and wine?' Their lives ebb away in their mother's arms.

The Lord has done what He planned; He has fulfilled His word which He decreed long ago.

No Peace

I have been deprived of peace; I have forgotten what prosperity is.

Hope

Because of the Lord's great love we are not consumed, for His compassions never fail. They are new every morning; great is your faithfulness. I say to myself, 'The Lord is my portion; therefore I will wait for Him'. The Lord is good to those whose hope is in Him. He does not *willingly* bring affliction.

His Persecution

When Jeremiah tried to warn the people, they became his enemies. They hunted him like a bird, tried to end his life in a pit (Jer. 28:6-13).

I called on your name O Lord, from the depths of the pit and you heard my plea. You redeemed my life.

The punishment of my people is greater than Sodom, which was overthrown in a moment.

Those killed by the sword are better off than those who die of famine, racked with hunger, they waste away for lack of food from the field.

Disbelief

The kings of the earth did not believe, nor did any of the world's people, that enemies and foes could enter the gates of Jerusalem.

It happened because of the sins of her prophets and the iniquities of her priests. The Lord himself has scattered them.

Gone

The elders are gone from the city gate; the young men have stopped their music. Joy is gone from our hearts.

Restore us to you, O Lord, that we may return; renew our days of old.

Note: Jeremiah probably suffered over Judah more than any other man, but he did not blame God. He knew first-hand the people would not listen or take warning as he had warned them for 40 years without success. The Lord has to keep his word.

Ezekiel
A Review

A prophet of God to the Babylonian exiles called 'Son of Man'. He was a captive of the second campaign of Nebuchadnezzar in 597 when 10,000 were taken (2 Kings 24).

Ezekiel dates his prophesies (1:2, 8:1, 20:1, 24:1).

His ministry started in the fifth year of King Jehoiachin's exile. He was 30 years old at this time. This was the age that priests started serving (Num. 4:3).

He dwelt among the other captives, by the Kebar River. The elders sometimes met in his home (8:1, 14:1 and 20:1).

Ezekiel had heavenly visions. In it were four living creatures whose faces were like a man, a lion, an ox and an eagle. Beside each creature were wheels. When the creatures moved, the wheels moved. They also had wings. Above the creatures was an expanse like the appearance of a rainbow; above this, the figure of a man of the likeness of the glory of the Lord (Ch. 1).

These creatures were called Cherubim in Ezekiel Ch 10.

References to Cherubim

1. They were placed by the Garden of Eden (after Adam and Eve were put out) to guard the tree of life (Gen. 3:24).

2. A cherubim made of gold was placed on each end of the Ark of the Testimony (on the mercy seat) with outstretched wings, as if to protect it. This was placed in the Most Holy Place. It was where the commandments were stored (Exodus 25:10-22, Hebrews 9:4, 5).

3. The inner sanctuary of the temple had two large carved cherubim, each ten cubits wide with arms outspread from one wall to the other. They were overlaid with gold (1 Kings 6:23-35).

4. The curtains of the tabernacle also had cherubim worked into them (Exodus 26:1).

Their work seems to be to *guard*.

Ezekiel's Call

The man Ezekiel saw, who had the likeness of the glory of the Lord (1:28) spoke to him and said, 'Son of man, stand up on your feet and I will speak to you' (Ezekiel had fallen face down).

He said, 'I am sending you to the Israelites, a rebellious people. Whether they listen of not, they will know that a prophet has been among them. Do not be afraid and do not rebel'.

In an outstretched hand was a scroll with words of lament, mourning and woe. Ezekiel was told to eat it. It tasted as sweet as honey.

He said, 'I will make you as hardened as they are. I will make your forehead like the hardest stone. Go to your countrymen in exile'.

The Spirit lifted him and took him to the exiles who lived near the Kebar River. He sat there for 7 days until the word of the Lord came to him again. It said, 'Son of man, I have made you a watchman for the house of Israel. A watchman would watch out for his fellow Israelites. (Maybe that is why he was shown the vision of the cherubim). If you do not warn them, you will be held responsible'.

He could only speak when the Lord wanted him to speak, otherwise he was silent. He was told to take a clay tablet and draw the city of Jerusalem, with siege works, ramp, camps and battering rams around it.

'Put an iron pan between you and the city and turn your face toward it. Lie on your left side 390 days for Israel and on your right 40 days for Judah'.

The days represented years. He was also to be tied so he could not turn. He was to make bread of wheat, barley, beans, lentils, millet and bake it over cow dung. The bread and water would be rationed so he would realize what the people in Jerusalem were going through (Chapter 4).

He was told to shave his head and beard and divide the hair into thirds; burn a third, strike a third with a sword and scatter a third to the wind but save a few strands. This represented what would happen to Judah. A third would die of plague of famine, a third would die by the sword and a third would be scattered (Chapter 5).

'Son of man, set your face against the mountains. Your high places and altars will be demolished (places of idol worship). Why? So you will know that I am the Lord. The end has come. Their silver and gold will not be able to save them in the day of the Lord's wrath. Their beautiful jewelry will be plunder to foreigners (Chapter 7).

Idolatry in the Temple

One year and two months later, Ezekiel was sitting in his house with the elders when he had another vision. He was taken in the Spirit to the temple in Jerusalem and saw them wor-shipping detestable things; idols of animals, crawling things, Tammuz (an Assyrian deity) and the sun. The Lord told a man clothed in linen to put a mark on the forehead of those who grieved over this. The rest were to be slaughtered.

Ezekiel saw the vision of the cherubim again that he saw in Chapter 1. The glory of the Lord departed from the temple and stopped about the cherubim. While he watched, the cherubim spread their wings and rose from the ground; and so the Lord's glory left the temple (Chapter 10). When the temple was destroyed, the Lord was not there (1 Kings 8:10, 11).

Promised Return

Ezekiel cried out, 'Oh Sovereign Lord! Will you completely destroy the remnant of Israel?'

The Lord replied, 'I will gather you from the nations and bring you back from the countries where you have been scattered and I will give you back the land of Israel'.

The cherubim lifted the glory of the Lord up and stopped above the mountains east of Jerusalem (the Mount of Olives is east of Jerusalem). After this, the Spirit lifted Ezekiel up and brought him back to the exiles in Babylon and he told them what he had seen.

Again, the word of the Lord came to him saying, 'Pack your belongings for exile, during the day while they watch. Dig through the wall. Cover your face so that you cannot see. When they ask, 'What are you doing?' say, 'I am a sign to you''.

This was an enactment of what was going to happen to Zedekiah, the last king of Judah. He and his army fled by night, but were captured. He was blinded and taken to Babylon (2 Kings 25:1-7).

No Delay

There is a proverb in the land of Israel: 'The days go by and every vision comes to nothing'. I, the Lord, will speak what I will and it shall be fulfilled without delay. Israel also says, 'The vision he sees is for many years from now'. The Lord says, 'None of my words will be delayed any longer'.

False Prophets

'Son of man, prophesy against the prophets of Israel. Their prophesies are false. I have not sent them. They lead my people astray, saying 'peace' when there is no peace. Also the women ensnare people by their magic charms'.

Some of the elders of Israel that were in exile came to Ezekiel and sat down. The word of the Lord came to him and said, 'These men have set up idols in their hearts'.

A prophet was not to intercede for an idolatrous man if he does not renounce his practices. If he should do so, he will be as guilty as they are (Chapter 14).

Judgment Inescapable

'Son of man, if a country sins against me by being unfaithful and I stretch out my hand against it to cut off its food supply and send famine upon it and kill its men and their animals, even if these three men–Noah, Daniel and Job–were in it, they could save only themselves by their righteousness' (14:12-14).

Unfaithful Jerusalem

Paraphrasing:

I took you when things were hopeless. I cared for you, gave you the best of everything and you turned away from me.

You once had beautiful clothes, plenty of food. You made yourself idols, sacrifices your sons and daughters, gave yourselves to the nations around you as a prostitute would.

Now, the nations will all see your nakedness when I take away your glory. You became more depraved than the nations around you. Sodom never did what you have done.

Sodom's Sins

Arrogant overfed and unconcerned, did not help the poor and needy. They were haughty and did detestable things. (Ch 16:48-50)

At one time, you would not even mention your sister Sodom (before *your* wickedness was uncovered) (Ch. 16: 56, 57). Your sins were more than theirs.

When I make atonement for you, for all you have done, you will remember and be ashamed.

Parable of a Vine

The Lord tells a parable of a great eagle breaking off the top of a cedar tree and planting it by water. Then another great eagle came along and the vine looked to it for growth.

This story is a prophesy of Zedekiah's attempt to get military assistance from Egypt before Nebuchadnezzar destroyed Jerusalem. The Lord never wanted Israel to turn to other nations for help instead of to Him.

Prophesy of the Church?

The Lord said He would take a shoot and plant it on the mountain heights of Israel. It will produce branches and bear fruit… (17:22-24, also see Isaiah 11:1-5).

The Soul Who Sins

This proverb was quoted about Israel:

'The fathers eat sour grapes, and the children's teeth are set on edge' (see Ex. 20:5). You will no longer quote this proverb in Israel. The soul who sins is the one who will die.

If a man does what is just and right: Does not eat at the mountain shrines or look to the idols.

Does not defile his neighbor's wife or lie with a woman during her period.

Does not oppress anyone. Returns what he took in pledge.

Does not rob, gives food to the hungry and clothing to the naked. Does not take excessive interest, judges fairly, follows my decrees and keeps my laws. That man is righteous. He will surely live.

If this man has a son, who does the opposite of these things, his blood will be on his own head. If a son has a father who does detestable things, yet the son does not, he will not die for his father's sins. The son will not share the guilt of the father, nor will the father share the guilt of the son.

If a righteous man turns from his righteousness, none of the righteous things he has done will be remembered. But, if a wicked man turns away from his wickedness and does what is just and right, he will surely save his life (Chapter 18).

Note: The world says: we are weighed in the balances. If the good outweighs the bad, we will be saved. *Not so* (18:24-27). It's the condition we are found in, at the end of our life that determines it.

Israel's Princes (Chapter 19)

Ezekiel laments the princes of Judah. They were young sons of Josiah (this shows the good father and wicked sons spoken about in Chapter 18).

[Age shown is when they started to reign]

1. *Jehoahaz* (age 23) reigned three months and was carried away to Egypt (2 Kings 23:31-33).
2. Jehoiakim (age 25) reigned 11 years, appointed by Egypt, taken to Babylon by Nebuchadnezzar (2 Kings 24:1-6).

3. *Jehoiachin* (age 18) reigned three months, taken to Babylon by Nebuchadnezzar along with a lot of other people. Imprisoned but later released.
4. *Zedekiah* (age 21) (Jehoiachin's uncle, 2 Kings 24:17) Blinded and imprisoned in Babylon until his death (Jeremiah 52:1-11).

Rebellious Israel

After Ezekiel had been prophesying 2 years, the elders came to inquire of the Lord, from Ezekiel. The Lord told him, 'I will not let you inquire of me'.

Then he began to tell them how they had been chosen. God brought them out of Egypt to the most beautiful of lands; gave them the law. From the very beginning, they had not totally ridden themselves of idol worship. They had desecrated the Sabbath and had not followed his decrees. He did not destroy them in the desert for the sake of his name. Now, when this exile is finished, He will bring them back from where they have been scattered and show himself holy in the sight of the nations. When Ezekiel used trees and animals to illustrate what they did, they thought he was just telling parables (Chapter 20).

The Sword is Coming

The Lord told Ezekiel to groan before the people because he was sending the sharpened sword of the Babylonians against them. The time of punishment had reached its climax. In the place where they were created, their blood would be shed (Ch 21).

Jerusalem's Sins

Son of man, confront Jerusalem with all her detestable prac-tices: they had shed blood, treated their parents with contempt, oppressed the alien, mistreated the fatherless and widows, des-pised God's holy things, desecrated the Sabbath, were immoral with even their family members. They charged excessive inter-est, accepted bribes, used extortion and forgotten God (22:6-12).

All have sinned: prophets, princes, priests and people. The people have become dross (worthless residue left over when metals have been purified).

Two Adulterous Sisters

Israel and Judah (Samaria and Jerusalem). They were daughters of the same mother (Israel). They are likened to adulterous women going after everyone they lusted after.

Samaria was punished first and this should have been a warning to Jerusalem but it was not. The Bible looks on going after other religions as spiritual adultery (Chapter 23).

Ezekiel's Wife Dies

Son of man, record this date because the King of Babylon has laid siege to Jerusalem this very date: January 15th, 588 BC. (2 Kings 25:1, 2, Jeremiah 52:4).

The word of the Lord came to Ezekiel: Son of man, I am about to take away from you the delight of your eyes. Do not lament or weep or shed any tears. Groan quietly; do not moan for the dead. Keep your turban fastened and your sandals on your feet; do not cover the lower part of your face or eat the customary food of mourners.

Ezekiel spoke to the people in the morning, and in the evening his wife died. This was to be an example to the people. The temple was to be destroyed (the delight of their eyes) and also their loved ones there but they were to go on with their lives.

The vision he saw was of Jerusalem, 400 miles from Babylon. When a fugitive came to tell him the news of Jerusalem's fall, his mouth would be opened. He would no longer be silent. After Jerusalem fell, the warnings stopped.

Ezekiel starts prophesying against their enemies.

Ammonites – They were descended from Lot and his younger daughter (Gen. 19:38). They were old enemies. Some who fought against them were Jephthah, Saul and David. They rejoiced when Jerusalem was destroyed. They were destroyed.

Moabites – They were also descended from Lot and his older daughter (Gen. 19:37). They also had contempt for Judah. They said, 'the house of Judah has become like all the other nations'. There were punished.

Philistines – Once mighty and long-lasting foes. Many kings fought against them, also Judges. The most notable was Samson (Judges 13-16). They wanted to destroy the Israelites. When Nebuchadnezzar attacked Judah, he also defeated the Philistines. The Philistines are no more.

Edomites – They were old enemies of the Israelites. They refused to let Moses and the children of Israel cross their land after they left Egypt (Num. 20:14-21). They continued to be against them and sided with Babylon when they invaded Judah. Its land was made desolate.

Tyre – They rejoiced at the fall of Jerusalem because they thought it would mean more trade for them. It was a seaport city. It received heavy flow, but was in use in the New Testament times (Matt. 11:21, Acts 21:17). They had grown proud because of their wealth but they were also dishonest. They were destroyed but rebuilt during the Roman Period.

Some of the things handled at Tyre before their fall.
(The ships of Tarshish carried these things) (Ezek. 27:25).
Hermon – pine trees
Lebanon – cedars
Bashan – Oaks
Cyprus – cedar wood
Egypt – linen

Elishah – awnings of blue and purple
Gebal – craftsmen
Tarshish – silver, iron, tin and lead
Greece – bronze
Beth Togarmah – horses and mules
Aram – turquoise, purple fabrics, linen, rubies, embroidery
Israel and Judah – wheat
Minnith – confections, honey, oil and balm
Damascus – wine and wool
Dan – wrought iron, cassia, calamus
Dedan – saddle blankets
Arabia – lambs, rams and goats
Sheba and Rasmah – spices precious stones, gold
Haran, Canneh, Eden – garments of blue fabric
Sheba, Assher and Kilmad – embroidered work, rugs
Ophir – gold and algrum wood
Land of Havilah – gold and onyx (Gen. 2:11, 12)

Sidon – No longer will the people of Israel have malicious neighbors who are painful briers and sharp thorns. They will be punished.

Egypt – Four Chapters are directed against Egypt. It is to be a lesser power. Because their pharaoh had said, 'The Nile is mine, I made it for myself', the Lord is going to make Egypt a wasteland and scatter them for 40 years. After that, he will bring them back.

It will never again exalt itself above other nations. Because the campaign against Tyre had lasted so long, the army got no reward from them. He gave Egypt to Nebuchadnezzar to plunder and carry off its wealth. The sword of Babylon will come against you and shatter your pride. Just as other nations have enjoyed their brief glory in human history, Egypt will fall. Babylon also destroyed Nineveh of Assyria.

Ezekiel a Watchman

Ezekiel was made a watchman for the house of Israel. God told him to tell the nations He was coming against, to choose one of their men to be a watchman to warn them.

In the twelfth year of Ezekiel's exile, a man who had escaped came and told him, 'The city has fallen!'.

The evening before the news came, Ezekiel's mouth was opened and he was free to speak. He was faithful watchman, but they did not heed his words. When they came true, they knew he was a prophet.

The Lord is My Shepherd

The word of the Lord came to Ezekiel and said to prophesy against the shepherds of Israel. They had not taken care of their sheep. They had not strengthened the weak or searched for the lost. God said, 'I myself will look after them. I will rescue them from all the places they were scattered and bring them out from the nations and back to their own land. I will send showers of blessings' (Chapter 34).

It is not for the people's sake that the Lord is going to bring them back, but for the sake of His holy name and so the nations will know that he is the Lord.

I will resettle your towns, rebuild the ruins. The land will be cultivated. The people who pass by will say, 'This land that was laid waste has become like the garden of Eden'. (Salvation is not deserved or earned).

The Valley of Dry Bones

The Lord took Ezekiel by the Spirit and sat him in the middle of a valley, full of dry bones. The Lord told Ezekiel to say to these bones, 'I will make breath enter you and you will come to life. I will attach tendons, flesh and skin'.

There was a rattling sound and the bones came together but had no breath. Then he said to say to the four winds–O breath, breathe into these slain that they might live. They came to life and stood on their feet.

He said to me, 'Son of man, these bones are the whole house of Israel. They say 'our bones are dried up–our hope is gone'. This is an allegory (using one thing to explain another to make it clearer).

The Lord was showing Ezekiel that Israel would come back and be profitable again. As they were, they were as dross (worthless), the same as dead (Ezek. 22:18-19).

Example:
1. Today we're the same way. Those who live in sin are dead but are made alive in Christ (Eph. 2:1-5, Col. 2:13, 14).
2. The widow who lives for pleasure is dead even while she lives (1 Tim. 5:6).
3. To the church in Sardis: you have a reputation of being alive but you are dead (Rev. 3:1).
4. The Lord would gather the Israelites from wherever they were and bring them back to their land (those who wanted to).
5. This happened in the first year of Cyrus, King of Persia (Ezra 1:1-3).
6. It says the Lord moved the heart of Cyrus to make this proclamation throughout his realm.
7. 'The Lord, the God of heaven, has given me all the kingdoms of the earth. He has appointed me to build a temple for him at Jerusalem in Judah. Anyone of his people among you – may his god be with him and let him go up to Jerusalem in Judah and build the temple of the Lord, the God of Israel, the God who is in Jerusalem'.

One Nation

The word of the Lord came to Ezekiel. He told him to take two sticks of wood. Write on one 'Judah' and the other 'Israel'.

Then he was told to join them as one stick. The two peoples had been separated since the death of Solomon with ten tribes known as Israel and the other two known as Judah.

Never again will they be divided into two kingdoms.

God is bringing everything together in preparation for sending His son. He has preserved the lineage from David. He sent His angel, Gabriel, to Mary (later) to tell her she would conceive and bring forth a son and was to call his name Jesus:

He shall be great and shall be called the Son of the Highest; and the Lord God shall give unto him the throne of his father, David. He shall reign over the house of Jacob forever; and of His kingdom there shall be no end (Luke 1:31-33).

All earthly kingdoms end, but the kingdom of Christ (the church) is a spiritual kingdom that will be everlasting. Every nation will be a part of it and every person (who believes) will be His chosen people.

A New Temple

Chapters 40-48 give a very detailed description of a magnifiicent temple, similar to Solomon's but much larger. This temple was never built. There have been three temples built and destroyed in Jerusalem: Solomon's, the one built after the exile, and Herod's temple.

In a vision Ezekiel was taken to Israel to a very high mountain and told to tell Israel what he had seen. He saw a man who looked like bronze. He had a measuring rod in his hand and started measuring the wall around the temple area, the outer court, north gate, south gate and inner court.

There were rooms for preparing sacrifices, rooms for the priests and the temple. He continues to measure everything... It was very large (three stories). Then he measured the area around the temple. It was 750 feet each way – to separate the holy from the common.

He saw the glory of God coming from the east (it looked like his vision by the Kebar River in Ezekiel Chapter 1). His glory entered the temple. Ezekiel heard someone speaking from inside the temple. He said, 'Son of man, this is the place of my throne. I will live among the Israelites forever' (Luke 1:31-33).

Describe this temple to the people of Israel. The top of the mountain will be holy. The Levites, from the family of Zadok, were to make offerings. One gate was to remain shut, because the glory of the Lord had entered there. The glory of the Lord filled the temple. The priests were to wear the same linen clothes, eat the same food and given the same land for their houses as Moses had told them.

All measurements must be accurate.

They were to continue to celebrate the Holy Days and the Passover and its sacrifices. The people were to worship at the entrance to the east gate and Sabbaths and new moons. The prince was to go in and out of the same gate, but the people were to go in one way and out another.

A lamb, grain and oil offering should be made each morning. None of the people were to be separated from their property. The temple faced east. Water was flowing from under it and became a river that he could not cross. It had all kinds of fish, fruit trees on the banks that bore fruit every month. Their leaves were for healing (see Rev. 22:1, 2).

Divide the land equally but give Joseph two portions. The land is also for the aliens who have settled among you. Consider them as native born Israelites. The Levites should have the best of the land. Zadok was faithful and did not go astray as some Levites did. The city will be in the center of the land, with pastureland all around. The rest of the land will be for the workers from the city.

Exit Gates

There will be three gates on each side, named after the twelve tribes of Israel. The distance around will be 18,000 cubits (nearly 5 miles).

Explanation

Could this beautiful and perfect place, that was never built, be another allegory like the valley of dry bones (Chapter 37:1-4)?

Other Allegories

1. Ezekiel lying on his side, to bear the sins of Judah; Ch 4:1-6
2. Bringing out his belongings packed for exile, digging through a wall and covering his face, to show Zedekiah would be blinded.
3. God likened Israel to a prostitute, a once beautiful woman who played the harlot; Chapter 16.
4. Two eagles and a vine, to show they should not have depended on foreign powers; Chapter 17.
5. Two adulterous sisters (Israel and Judah), Chapter 23.

Could these Chapters (40-48), be the perfect place God used to describe heaven to them?

Isaiah 2:2-4—In the last days the mountain of the Lord's temple will be established as chief among the mountains; it will be raised above the hills, and all nations will stream to it. Many people will come and say, 'Come, let us go up to the mountain of the Lord, to the house of the God of Jacob. He will teach us His ways, so that we many walk in His paths'. The law will go out from Zion, the word of the Lord from Jerusalem.

Revelation 22:1-2—The angel showed John the river of the water of life, as clear as crystal, flowing from the throne of God and of the Lamb down the middle of the great street of the city. On each side of the river stood the Tree of Life, bearing 12 crops of fruit, yielding its fruit every month. And the leaves of the tree are for the healing of the nations.

Revelation 21:10-14—And he carried me away in the Spirit to a mountain, great and high, and showed me the Holy City, Jerusalem, coming down out of heaven from God. It shone with the glory of God... It had a great high wall with twelve gates... On the gates were written the names of the twelve tribes of Israel.

These descriptions are so similar to the ones in Ezekiel 47:1-12 and 48:31. Also, the passage of 47:1-12 could not be real. That's why I believe it to be an allegory of the church or the heavenly Jerusalem.

Ephesians 5:27—That he might present it to himself a glorious church, not having spot or wrinkle, or any such thing; but that it should be holy and without blemish.

Note: The Lord wanted the *temple* to be without flaw and he wants his *church* to be that way.

Daniel
A Review

When Hezekiah was sick an envoy from Babylon visited him and brought a gift. He showed them all his treasures.

Isaiah the prophet went to see him. He said, 'Hear the word of the Lord: all that is in your house and all that your fathers have laid up will be carried to Babylon and your sons will be made eunuchs in the palace of the King of Babylon' (Is. 39:1-7).

In the third year of the reign of Jehoiakim, Nebuchadnezzar came to Jerusalem and besieged it. He carried off the king, some articles from the temple and some young men from the royal family. He had them trained for three years in the language and literature of the Babylonians. After that, they were to enter the king's service.

Some from Judah were Daniel, Shadrach, Meshach and Abednego (new names).

The length of Nebuchadnezzar's reign was 43 years and Daniel served under him. Belshazzar and Cyrus, about 66 years, 605 – 539 BC.

Daniel and his three friends asked to eat vegetables and water, rather than the royal food and wine.

Even though living in a foreign land, they were determined to live by God's law. (God is with us no matter where we are).

King Nebuchadnezzar had a dream, but couldn't remember what it was about. He sent for all his wise men. He wanted them to tell him what the dream was and its interpretation. They said, 'There is not a man on earth who can do this'. He was going to have them all executed.

Daniel went to the king and asked for some time. He might be able to interpret it.

That night, the dream and its interpretation were revealed to Daniel. Daniel told the king, 'There is a God in heaven who reveals mysteries and he has shown King Nebuchadnezzar what will happen in days to come'.

The Dream (Chapter 2)

O King, before you stood a large statue...
Its head was made of pure gold;
Its chest and arms of silver;
Its belly and thighs of bronze;
Its legs of iron and its feet of iron and clay.

The Interpretation

1. You are that head of Gold (Babylon)
2. After you, another kingdom will arise (Medes and Persians)
3. The third kingdom will be Greece
4. The fourth kingdom (iron and clay) will be Rome

In the time of the fourth kingdom, the God of heaven will set up a kingdom that will never be destroyed (2:36-44). King Nebuchadnezzar placed Daniel in a high position, and in charge of all his wise men. His friends were appointed administrators.

The king made an image of gold ninety feet tall and nine feet wide. He summoned all his officials. The herald proclaimed, 'As soon as you hear all kinds of music, you must fall down and worship this image. Whoever does not fall down and worship will be thrown into a blazing furnace'.

Some astrologers went to the king and told him there were some Jews who did not worship the image he had set up (Shadrach, Meshach and Abednego). He was furious. He had the furnace heated seven times hotter than usual and had them thrown in fully clothed and tied up. The fire killed the men who threw them in. The king was amazed to see *four* men walking around in the fire. He shouted for them to come out and saw that the fire had not harmed them. He said God had sent his angel to rescue them. He said they were willing to give up their lives rather than worship any god other than their own.

Nebuchadnezzar Has Another Dream

He saw a tree whose top reached to the sky, its leaves beautiful, its fruit abundant, where beasts found shelter and birds lived in its branches.

A messenger said in a loud voice, 'cut down that tree and trim off its branches but leave the stump. Let his mind be changed from that of a man and let him be given the mind of an animal until seven times pass him by' (seven years).

Daniel interpreted the dream. He hated to tell him what it meant. He said, 'You, O King, are that tree... You will be driven away from people and live with the wild animals. You will eat grass like cattle... until you acknowledge the Most High is Sovereign over the kingdoms of men'.

This came true twelve months later, after he was giving himself the glory for his accomplishments (4:1-33). His hair grew like feathers of an eagle and his nails like the claws of a bird. King Nebuchadnezzar wrote verses (4:34-37). He accepted and acknowledged God.

Belshazzar—The Writing on the Wall

King Belshazzar gave a great banquet for one thousand of his nobles. They brought in the gold and silver goblets, his father had taken from the temple in Jerusalem to drink out of and praised the gods of gold and silver.

Suddenly, the fingers of a human hand appeared and wrote on the wall.

The King watched the hand as it wrote. He was very frightened. His mother, hearing the noise, came in and told them to send for Daniel.

The King said, 'Are you one of the exiles my father brought from Judah?'

Daniel told him the story of what had happened to his father, Nebuchadnezzar, and how he had acknowledged the Most High God.

'But you, his son, have not humbled yourself, though you knew all this'.

This is what the Lord's hand wrote:

Mene, Mene, Tekel, Parsin

Mene – God has numbered the days of your reign and brought it to an end.

Tekel – God has numbered the days of your reign and found it wanting.

Parsin – Your kingdom is divided and given to the Medes and Persians (Chapter 5).

That very night, Belshazzar was slain and Darius the Meade took over the kingdom (Chapter 5).

Daniel in the Lion's Den

Darius appointed 120 satraps (princes) to rule throughout the kingdom. They tried to find grounds to get rid of Daniel (he was one of three administrators over them). They couldn't find anything against him, so they made a decree that anyone who prayed to any god or man other than the king over the next thirty days would be thrown into a den of lions.

When Daniel learned of the decree, he went to his upstairs room, as he always did, got down on his knees and gave thanks.

Of course, they went straight to the king and told him. The king was greatly distressed because of Daniel, but couldn't change his order. Daniel was thrown into the lion's den. The king could not eat or sleep that night.

He got up at the first light of dawn and hurried to the lion's den. He called to Daniel and he answered. He said, 'My God has sent His angel and shut the mouths of the lions'. The king was overjoyed. The men who had falsely accused Daniel were thrown in, along with their wives and children. Darius also accepted God. He wrote in every language throughout the land:

I issue a decree that in every part of my kingdom, people must fear and revere the God of Daniel. For He is the living God and He endures forever; His kingdom will not be destroyed, His dominion will never end. He rescues and He saves; He performs signs and wonders in the heavens and on earth. He has rescued Daniel from the power of the lions.

Daniel's Vision

The writing goes back to the first year of Belshazzar. Daniel himself had a dream while lying on his bed at night.

He couldn't understand his own visions. It was similar to the dream Daniel had interpreted for Nebuchadnezzar in 2:27-45.

The four beasts stood for the four kingdoms.
1. Babylon (the present one)
2. Medes and Persia
3. Greeks
4. Romans (in the time of those kings, the God of haven will set up a kingdom that will never be destroyed... It will endure forever, Dan. 2:44).

This kingdom had to be the one the prophets spoke about:
Jeremiah 31:31-34
'The time is coming' declares the Lord, 'where I will make a new covenant with the house of Israel and the house of Judah.

(Not like the one made with their forefathers). I will put my law in their minds and write it in their hearts... I will forgive their wickedness and remember their sins no more'.

The Most High does not live in houses made by man.

Joel 2:26-32, Acts 2:17-21

In the last days God says, 'I will pour out my spirit on all people... I will show wonders in the heaven above signs on the earth below... and everyone who calls on the name of the Lord will be saved'.

Isaiah 53:7... Also Acts 8:26-39

'He was led like a sheep to the slaughter and as a lamb before the shearer is silent, so he did not open his mouth. In his humiliation he was deprived of justice. Who can speak of his descendants? For his life was taken from the earth'. (This was a description of Jesus before his crucifixion).

As Daniel saw in his vision, this kingdom was to be different, based on the belief that Jesus Christ is the son of God. It was hard for everyone to understand this was not an earthly kingdom, but a spiritual kingdom.

Even Herod, when he heard about the birth of the baby Jesus, gave orders to kill all the boy babies in the Bethlehem area two years old and under. (He wanted to preserve his kingdom).

Most of the Jews did not believe this to be the New Kingdom prophesied about and put the Lord to death! They did not realize this was the plan from the beginning; that Jesus would shed His blood as a sacrifice for us (Isaiah 53).

After 37 years (33 – 70 AD) of oppressing the saints and the disbelief of most of the Jews, God is once again going to destroy Jerusalem and the temple worship.

He warns the people who are believers to leave Jerusalem (Rev.18:4, Mark 13:14-20, Matt. 24:15-18, Luke 21:20-24).

Please compare Daniel 7:24 to Revelation 17:12.   There was a three and a half year war between the Romans and the Jews (66-70 AD). This is the fulfillment of the verse in Daniel 7:25 of a time, times and a half (3 ½ years).

Jesus also described these happenings in Matthew Chapter 24 and Luke Chapter 21. This was about 500 years before it happened. How could Daniel understand it? (Chapter 7)

Another Vision

Two years later Daniel had another vision, in the third year of Belshazzar, in the citadel of Susa, the Persian Royal City.

He saw a ram with two horns, charging toward the west, north and south. No one could stand against him. Suddenly a goat with one horn came in mid-air and attacked the ram furiously, knocking him powerless. His horn was broken off but 4 more came in its place. Out of one of these horns, another horn started growing until it reached the heavens, threw some of the starry host down to earth and trampled them.

It set itself up to be great and took away the daily sacrifice and sanctuary.

Daniel heard two holy ones speaking. One said, 'How long will this take?' He said 2,300 evenings and mornings (1,150 days). The angel, Gabriel, told Daniel the wisdom concerned the time of the end.

It seemed to be a contribution of the other vision:
Two-horned ram – The Medes and Persians
Goat – Greece
4 horns – Rome
A stern-faced king will arise. Nero? He persecuted Christians, the war started under him, he killed many of his own family (Josephus). He took a stand against the Prince of princes (8:25), Jesus and Christianity. He committed suicide in 68 AD, while the war was in progress.

This vision made Daniel exhausted and ill for several days. He said the vision was beyond understanding (Chapter 8).

Daniel's Prayer

About seven or eight years later (Belshazzar reigned 10 years) in the first year of Darius the Meade, Daniel was reminded (from the passage from Jeremiah 25:11, 12) that the exile would last 70 years. It was nearing an end.

He prayed unto the Lord:

He confessed the wrongs of Judah, Israel and the people of Jerusalem had done in not obeying his laws. (Even though Daniel did no wrong, he says 'we').

They had been fore-warned about what would happen to them, but still had not turned to God.

Daniel asked God to turn away from His anger, that the nation was an object of scorn to those around them. (Ezekiel had written, 'if a country sins against me by being unfaithful, even if these three men – Noah, Daniel and Job – were in it, they could only save themselves, Ezek. 14:13, 14).

Daniel told God his request was not because they were righteous, but because of His great mercy. While he was praying and confessing sins, Gabriel the arch angel, came to him in swift flight at the time of the evening sacrifice.

They did not offer sacrifices while in exile, but Daniel probably prayed at that hour, remembering what had been.

Gabriel had come to give him incite to his vision. He said 70 weeks had been decreed for the people to finish their transgression. These 70 weeks was 70 years (Jeremiah 25:11).

He also said from the commandments to restore Jerusalem (in the 20th year of King Artaxerxes, Num. 2:1-5). 444 BC until Christ, would be seven 'sevens' and sixty-two sevens (69 years).

After 62 sevens (62 years) the anointed one will be cut off. The people of the ruler (Romans) will destroy the city and sanctuary. War will continue until the end. In the middle of the 'seven' (3 ½ years) there will be an end to sacrifice and offering and he will set up and abomination that causes desolation on the temple. This prophesy was fulfilled in AD 70 when Titus, the Roman general, destroyed the temple and Jerusalem and more than a million people died (Chapter 9).

Another Vision

In the third year of Cyrus, about 535 BC, Daniel had another vision. This time, he mourned for three weeks.

He was on the bank of the Tigris River with some other men. They didn't see the vision as they fled and hid.

A hand touched him and said he was highly esteemed and to not be afraid. He was there to explain what would happen in a time yet to come.

Daniel was so overcome, he lost strength but the man touched him and reassured him (Chapter 10).

Chapter 11 gives a forecast of the politics to come, starting with Darius the Meade and continuing through the Persians, Greeks and Romans. A lot of wars went on during this time, seeking power. Many countries will fall. Even Egypt will not escape. He says the King of the North will extend his power over many countries. This was probably the Romans.

He said Michael, the great prince, would protect his people during the time of distress that had not happened from the beginning of nations until then. (At that time, Daniel is told his people, those found written in the book, will be delivered, see Revelation 20:12).

Two others were seen by Daniel on opposite banks of the river. One of them asked, 'How long will it be until these astonishing things happen?' The man (angel) lifted both hands toward heaven and swore by God: It will be for a time, times and half a time (3 ½ years, the length of the Roman/Jewish war that ended in 70 AD). At that time the daily sacrifice will be abolished. (The daily sacrifice was over before then).

The larger part of the Jewish population did not believe in the New Kingdom of Jesus Christ. The Lord had to destroy the temple and the people because of their unbelief.

The man (angel) who spoke to Daniel said, 'As for you, go your way until the end. You will rest and then at the end of your days you will rise to receive your allotted inheritance'.

Work of Angels

1. Bear the souls of the departed dead (Luke 16:22).
2. Watch over little children (Matt. 18:11).
3. Serve those who will inherit salvation (Heb. 1:14).
4. Aid to bring sinners in contact with the gospel (Acts 8:26).
5. Have charge of maintaining 'the little book' in Rev. 10
6. They stood by the apostles (Acts 27:23).
7. They influence human affairs through government (Daniel 10:14).

Both of the named angels, Michael (Daniel. 10:13) and Gabriel (8:16, 9:21) appeared to Daniel.

Note: All these visions seem to be about the Kingdom of Christ and the destruction of Herod's temple and the animal sacrifices. (The temple of Solomon had already been destroyed).

Hosea

A Review

Hosea prophesied during the reigns of four kings: Uzziah (Azariah), Jotham, Ahaz and Hezekiah of Judah and Jeroboam of Israel (770–725 BC). He did not see Israel go into exile, which happened in 722 BC.

His life was an example to the Israelites of how you could still love someone who was unfaithful to you. The Lord told him to marry an adulterous wife, because the land was adulterous in leaving the Lord and worshipping idols. In fact, not one king from the northern kingdom was faithful.

He married Gomer. She conceived and bore him a son name Jezreel. The Lord said he would soon punish the house of Jehu because of the massacre at Jezreel (see 2 Kings 9 and 10, especially 10:30-31).

Gomer then bore a daughter name Leruhamah, because the Lord said He would no longer show love to the house of Israel, only Judah.

The third child was named LoAmmi (for you are not my people and I am not your God). The Lord said, 'I will not show my love to her children, because they are the children of adultery (the Israelites)'.

She said, 'I will go after my lovers who give me my food and water (Israel)'.

She will chase after her lovers but not find them. Then she will say, 'I will go back to my husband as at first', not realizing I was the one who gave her grain, new wine and oil.

I will show my love to the one I called 'not my loved one'. I will say to these called, 'not my people' you are my people; and they will say, 'you are my God' (Hosea 2:23 and Romans 9:25).

The Lord told Hosea to go show his love to his wife again, though she is loved by another and is adulterous. He bought her for 15 shekels of silver (½ the price of a common slave) and some barley (eaten by the poorest people).

He told her, 'you are to live with me many days, but you must not be a prostitute or be intimate with any man and I will live with you'.

The Israelites displayed no faithfulness, love, or acknowledgement of God. One reason was because there was no one to guide them. Their kings were bad, the priests were sinful. The Lord said the Israelites were stubborn, like a stubborn heifer. How could he pasture them like lambs in a meadow? (Ch 4)

He starts calling Israel, Ephraim, and says they will be laid to waste. They said, 'He has torn us to pieces but he will heal us. He will come to us like the winter rains, like the spring rains that water the earth'.

The Lord says, 'I desire mercy, not sacrifice, acknowledgment rather then burnt offerings. Like Adam, you have broken the covenant' (Chapter 6). Ephraim is like a dove, easily deceived and senseless – calling on Egypt, then Assyria.

They have rejected what is good. They set up kings without my consent. They sow the wind and reap the whirlwind. Ephraim will return to Egypt and eat unclean food in Assyria. What will you do on the day of you appointed feasts and festivals? The prophets were supposed to be watchmen, but they were corrupted also.

When I found Israel, it was like finding a grape in the desert; when I saw your fathers, it was like seeing the early fruit on the fig tree, but when they came to Baal Beor, they consecrated themselves to that shameful idol (see Num. 25:1-9).

Now, they will be wanderers among the nations. Ephraim will be disgraced and ashamed of its wooden idols. Thorns and thistles will grow up and cover their altars.

Since the days of Gibeah, you have sinned (Judges 20 and 21). The roar of battle will rise against your people, your king will be destroyed.

Israel's Last King

Hoshea was the last King of Israel. He reigned nine years. Shalmaneser, King of Assyria, came up to attack him. He had been paying tribute but had stopped.

Shalmaneser put Hoshea in prison and laid siege to Samaria for three years, deporting the Israelites to Assyria.

Samaria was also built on a hill about 880 BC by Omri, the sixth King of Israel (1 Kings 16:24). It is about 25 miles north of Jerusalem.

All this happened because the Israelites had sinned against the Lord, who brought them up out of Egypt. They worshipped other gods and followed the practices of the nations the Lord had driven out for them.

They built high places where they worshipped idols, set up sacred stones and Asherah poles and burned incense.

The Lord kept warning them through prophets to repent, but they refused to listen and became worthless. They even sacrificed their sons and daughters.

He gave them over to plunderers. They disobeyed God from the beginning of their kingdom until the end. *All* the kings did evil so God brought the curses on them He had promised in Deuteronomy 28:47-68.

God Loved Israel

God remembered when Israel was good. He said in Chapter 11, 'When Israel was a child, I loved him. Out of Egypt I called my son. How can I give you up? How can I hand you over? My compassion is aroused'.

Jacob (Judah)

In the womb he grasped his brother's heel (Gen. 25:26).
As a man, he struggled with God (Gen. 32:24-29).
He struggled with the angel and overcame him; he wept and begged for his favor.
He found him at Bethel and talked with him there – the Lord God Almighty, the Lord is His name (Ex. 3:15).
Jacob fled to the land of Aram where he served to get a wife. To pay for her, he tended sheep (Gen. 29:18).
The Lord used a prophet to bring Israel up from Egypt (Moses).
I cared for you in the desert, in the land of burning heat.
I will destroy you, O Israel, because you are against me, against your helper.
The people of Samaria must bear their guilt.
Return, O Israel, to the Lord your God.

Note: We can never get so low that if we truly repent and return to God, he will forgive us (Rev. 2:5).

Joel

A Review

Joel is a small book: only three Chapters. Its most famous passage is the one quoted by Peter in his Pentecost sermon (Acts
2:17-21 and Joel 2:28-32). You might be surprised to know the
first two Chapters in Joel deal with a plague of locusts in Judah.
We don't know when this happened but it was one of the curses
for disobedience that Moses warned the Israelites about before
his death.

Deuteronomy 28:38-42

> You will sow much seed in the field, but you will harvest
> little because locusts will devour it. You will plant vine-
> yards and cultivate them but you will not drink the wine of
> gather the grapes, because worms will eat them. You will
> have olive trees throughout your country, but you will not
> use the oil because the olives will drop off. Swarms of
> <u>locusts</u> will take over all your trees and the crops of your
> land.

1 Kings 8:37 – 39

> (Solomon's prayer of dedication of the temple) When
> famine of plague comes to the land, or blight or mildew,
> <u>locusts</u> or grasshoppers…Whatever disaster or disease may
> come; when a prayer of plea is made, forgive.

Proverbs 30:27

> <u>Locusts</u> have no king, yet they advance together in ranks.
> Since ancient time, locusts have been known for their habit
> of destroying crops. They have long hind legs for jumping
> and four wings. They make a noise by rubbing their hind

legs and front wings. They travel in swarms and settle on green fields like a blanket. Swarms of locusts are sometimes so large they shut out the light of the sun. (*Worldbook Encyclopedia 12*, page 374).

Joel realized this was brought on them by God for their sins. This happened many times throughout time. The word of the Lord came to Joel. He said, 'Has anything like this ever happened in the days of you forefathers?' The priests are in mourning, the fields are ruined, the harvests are destroyed, the grain and drink offerings are withheld from the house of your God. The flood has been cut off before our very eyes. The cattle moan, the herds mill about because they have no pasture. Even the wild animals pant for you (Ch 1). (We've all seen flocks of birds come in and strip berries off bushes in a moment).

A large and mighty army has come (locusts) before them; the land was like the Garden of Eden, now like a desert wasteland. They charge like warriors, they scale walls like soldiers. They all march in line, not swerving from their course. Each march straight ahead…they run along the wall…climb into the houses through the windows. (When a wall of a house lies in their path, they keep going straight, even over the roof. When they come to water, they still continue on straight and are drowned. Those behind use their bodies for a bridge or drown themselves; never turning to the right or to the left).

The Lord speaks

'Even now, return to the Lord for He is gracious and compassionate, slow to anger and abounding in love, He relents from sending calamity.

Who knows? He may turn and have pity and leave behind a blessing…'Blow the trumpet in Zion (to call a sacred assembly). Everyone was to come. Evidently they showed remorse because the Lord caused the locusts to go into the sea and blessed them again (2:20).

The Day of the Lord
(Peter's sermon on Pentecost, Acts 2:17-21)

I will pour out my spirit on all people. Your sons and daughters will prophesy, your old men will dream dreams, your young men will see visions.

Even on my servants, both men and women, I will pour out of my spirit in those days. I will show wonders in the heavens and on earth, blood and fire and billows of smoke. The sun will be turned to darkness and the moon to blood before the coming of the great and dreadful day of the Lord.

And everyone who calls on the name of the Lord will be saved; for on Mt. Zion and in Jerusalem there will be deliverance, as the Lord has said, among the survivors whom the Lord calls.

Some of the things that happened when Jesus was crucified:
1. Darkness from the 6th to the 9th hour
2. The curtain of the temple was torn in two from top to bottom
3. The earth shook and rocks split
4. Tombs broke open and many holy people were raised to life. After Jesus' resurrection they went into Jerusalem and appeared to many
5. Blood, fire and vapor of smoke represented the thousands of animals that were sacrificed as it was the time of the Passover

This was the fulfillment of the prophesy of Joel (Acts 2:16). Jesus said to go and make disciples of all nations. We are all children of Abraham and of the promise that we would be blessed through his seed (Jesus). No matter where we are, we are with Him in spirit. Old things have passed away, all things are made new. (Jeremiah 31:31-34 and Hebrews 8:8-13.

Amos

A Review

Amos prophesied when Uzziah (Azariah) was King of Judah and Jeroboam II was King of Israel in the mid 700's BC. This book is not placed in order as it happened. Isaiah follows Amos' ministry.

Amos refers to rural life and said he was not a prophet nor a prophet's son (before being called) but was a herdsman and a gatherer of sycamore fruit (Amos 7:14). He lived in Tekoa, about six miles south of Bethlehem. He said his prophesy took place two years before 'the' earthquake. This must have been an earthquake of huge pro-portions; similar to the one that happened in Haiti in 2010. Zachariah also mentions it in Zachariah 14:5.

Josephus, writer of the history of the Jews, also mentions the earthquake that happened when he went into the temple and offered incense on the altar. This earthquake killed 30,000 men (page 611 of Josephus' writings). When Jesus died on the cross the earth shook and the rocks split. The tombs broke open and the bodies of many holy people who had died were raised to life.

The two most dangerous faults in this country are the New Madrid Fault (in New Madrid, MO) and the San Andreas Fault in California. The most loss of life ever recorded from an earthquake was in 1556 AD; when 830,000 died in Shenski, China.

Over and over Amos starts out by saying 'Thus saith the Lord'. No matter how humble our beginnings are, the Lord is the one speaking through us by his words.

Judgments

Amos said the Lord will roar from Zion. (When we hear the roar of a lion, it brings forth fear). He warns the Lord is going to bring judgments on 8 nations: Damascus (1:3-5), Gaza (1:6-8), Tyre (1:9, 10), Edom (1:11, 12), Ammon (1:13-15), Moab (2:1-3), Judah (2:4, 5) and Israel (2:6-16).

Their Sins

Damascus (Syria)–She thrashed Gilead with sledges having iron teeth.

Gaza (Philistines)–She took captive whole communities and sold them to Edom.

Tyre–She sold whole communities of Israelites to Edom, disregarding a treaty of brotherhood (see 1 Kings 5:1-12).

Edom–Descendants of Esau, blood relatives, going back to the time when Jacob took Esau's birthright, he forgave Jacob but his descendants never did.

Ammon–Descendants of Lot and his daughter, aiding aggressors against Israel and attempting to extend their borders at the expense of Israel

Moab–They burned as if to lime the bones of Edom's king.

Judah–They have rejected the law of the Lord and have been led astray by the worship of false idol gods, the gods their ancestors followed.

Israel–They sell the righteous and needy, trample the poor, deny justice, profane my name, lie on garments taken in pledge in the house of their god, commanded the prophets not to prophesy.

Against Israel

The Lord speaks through Amos, 'I brought you up out of Israel, you only have I chosen from all the families on the earth'.

Do two work together unless they have agreed to do so?

An enemy will overrun the land; he will bring down your strongholds... I will destroy the altars of Bael.

I gave you empty stomachs, withheld rain (drought) when the harvest was 3 months away, locusts drowned your fig and olive trees, I sent plagues, I killed your young men – yet you have not returned to me.

Now – prepare to meet your God, O Israel.

Lament and Call to Repentance

Fallen is virgin Israel, never to rise again. There will be only 1/10 left. Do not seek Bethel; do not journey to Gilgal or Beersheba.

You despise him who tells the truth. Though you have built stone mansions you will not live in them. Though you have planted lush vineyards, you will not drink their wine.

There will be wailing in the streets, the public square and the vineyards. It will be as a man fled from a lion only to meet a bear.

I hate your religious feasts and assemblies – away with the noise of your songs. I will not listen to the music of your harps.

You lie on your beds inlaid with ivory, dine on choice lambs and fattened calves. You drink wine by the bowlful but you do not grieve over the ruin of Joseph (Ephraim and Manasseh).

Your feasting and lounging will end. The Lord detests the pride of Jacob (the ancestor of Judah).

Visions

The Lord showed Amos a vision. He was preparing swarms of locusts to strip the land clean. Amos cried out, 'Sovereign Lord, forgive! How can Jacob survive?' The Lord relented.

The Lord showed Amos another vision. He was calling for judgment by fire. It was to dry up the great deep and devour the land. Again Amos cried out, 'Sovereign Lord, I beg you stop! How can Jacob survive?' The Lord relented.

He showed Amos another vision. He was standing by a wall that had been built true to plumb. He asked Amos, 'What do you see?' Amos replied, 'A plumb line'.

The Lord said He would spare them no longer.

Then Amos prophesied,

'Jeroboam will die by the sword,

Israel will go into exile,

Away from their native land'.

Amaziah the priest told Amos to get out, to go to Judah and prophesy there. Amos told him he was sent to Israel and this is what he was told to say:

Your wife will become a prostitute;

Your sons and daughters will fall by the sword.

Your land will be divided up.

You will die in a foreign country.

Israel will go into exile,

Away from their native land.

The Lord showed Amos a basket of ripe fruit and said, 'the time is ripe for my people Israel; I will spare them no longer... The days are coming when I will send a famine through the land; not for food or water, but a famine of hearing the words of the Lord. Israel will be destroyed and there is no place they can hide! I will not totally destroy it'.

Restoration

In that day I will restore David's fallen tent...

I will repair the broken places and restore its ruins, and build it as it used to be...

I will bring back my exiled...

God still intends to rebuild the house of David (in whose line Christ was to come).

Sometime after the church was established, the Gentiles were being taught. Some Jews thought they should be circumcised like Moses had taught. They held a conference at Jerusalem to consider the matter and decided it was not necessary under the law of Christ.

James, the Lord's brother, quoted this passage in Amos 9:11, 12: After this, I will return and rebuild David's fallen tent. Its ruins I will rebuild and I will restore it; that the remnant of men may seek the Lord.

'And all the Gentiles who hear my name', says the Lord, 'who do these things that have been known for ages'.

Obadiah

A Review

This is what the Sovereign Lord says about Edom: Edom (Seir), was the land where Esau (Jacob's twin brother) lived.

Background

Isaac, the son of Abraham, was 40 years old when he married Rebekah. It was 20 more years before he was blessed with children, Esau and Jacob.

Even before Rebekah gave birth, the boys struggled within her. The Lord told her there were two nations in her womb and the elder would serve the younger.

Isaac favored Esau and Rebekah favored Jacob. One day, Esau was out hunting and came home famished. Jacob had made some porridge and Esau wanted some badly. Jacob told him he could have some if he would sell him his birthright. He agreed.

Later

Esau loved to hunt and his father loved the savory dish he made from venison. One day, his father asked him to make the dish, bring it to him and he would bless him before he died (he was old and nearly blind). This blessing was the blessing of the first-born (see Gen. 27:28, 29).

Rebekah had heard this request. She told Jacob to get 2 goats from the flock and she would make the dish. She had

Jacob put some of the goat-skins on his hands and neck and take the dish she had made to his father.

Isaac had a little doubt but gave Jacob his blessing. When Esau arrived with his savory meat and found out what had happened, he tried to get his father to take away the blessing, but he could not (Gen. 27:38-40).

Jacob Leaves

Rebekah, in fear of what Esau might do, sent Jacob to her brother's house in Haran. Jacob went there and stayed 20 years. By then, he had fathered twelve sons and had become wealthy.

He was on his way home with his entire family when they came near the land of Seir, or Edom. (This is where Esau had settled). They saw each other after 20 years and reconciled. Jacob told Esau that seeing his face was like seeing the face of God (Gen. 35:28, 29).

Jacob also had a favorite son, Joseph. He was the son of his beloved wife, Rachel. His brothers were jealous of him and when opportunity arouse, sold him to a caravan of Ishmaelites who carried him to Egypt. He was sold to Potipher, an official of Pharaoh. While in Egypt, Joseph interpreted some dreams.

One was of seven years of plenty and seven years of drought. Joseph was put in charge of storing up grain for the famine. His family came to Egypt for grain. (Jacob and his entire family eventually moved to Egypt).

They all stayed a total of 430 years in Egypt. The Egyptians made slaves of them and the Lord heard their cry. He sent Moses to deliver them out of their bondage and back to the land he had promised to Abraham, Isaac and Jacob (Gen. 15:12-16). By this time the nation had grown large and was called the Israelites.

On the Way

On their way back, they were nearing the land of Moab. Moses sent messengers to the king saying, 'This is what your brother, Israel, says: you know about all the hardships that have come upon us. We are now here at Kadesh, a town on the edge of your territory. Please let us pass through your country (Joshua 24:4). We will travel along the king's highway. We will not go through any field or drink any water'.

Edom Refused

They said, 'if you pass through we will attack you with the sword'. They came out with a large army to show them they meant it (Num. 21:14-21).

They continued to harass and oppose Israel and at the last, sided with Babylon when Nebuchadnezzar invaded Judah in 586 BC (when they were carried into exile).

Even though Esau forgave Jacob, his descendants never did.

Obadiah's Vision

Here are some of the things the Lord said about Edom:

The pride of your heart has deceived you. You say to yourself, 'who can bring me down to the ground?'

Though you soar like the eagle and make your nest among the stars, from there I will bring you down.

Your friends will deceive you – those who eat your bread will set a trap for you.

Because of the violence against your brother Jacob, you will be covered with shame and destroyed.

You stood aloof while strangers carried off his wealth. You were like one of them.

You should not look down on your brothers in the day of his misfortune, nor rejoice in the day of their destruction, nor boast in the day of their trouble.

As you have done, it will be done to you. Your deeds will return upon your own head.

The house of Jacob will possess its inheritance but the house of Esau will be stubble. There will be no survivors from the house of Esau.

The Lord has spoken.

Jonah

A Review

Nineveh was the capital city of Assyria, the great power before the Babylonians. It was a Gentile city. God loved them too.

Nimrod is credited with founding Nineveh. He was the grandson of Ham, son of Noah. The beginning of his kingdom was Babel (Gen. 10:10). It was during his generation that the Lord scattered the people of the earth (Gen. 11:1-9).

The story of Jonah in the scriptures is very plain but I'd like to write Josephus' words because the language is colorful.

Josephus' Words

Jonah had been commanded by God to go to the kingdom of Nineveh and when he was there, to publish it in that city; how it should lose the dominion it had over the nations. But he went not, out of fear; nay he ran away from God to the city of Joppa, and, finding a ship there, he went into it and sailed to Tarsus in Cilicia.

Upon the rise of a most terrible storm which was so great that the ship was in danger of sinking, the mariners, the master and the pilot himself, made prayers and vows in case they escaped the sea; but Jonah lay still and covered in the ship without imitating anything that the others did.

As the waves grew great and the sea became more violent by the winds, they suspected, as is usual in such cases, that someone of the persons that sailed with them was the occasion of this storm. They agreed to discover, by lot, which of them it was.

When they cast the lots, the lot fell upon the prophet. When they asked him whence he came and what he had done, he replied that he was a Hebrew by nation and a prophet of Almighty God. He persuaded them to cast him into the sea if they would escape the danger they were in, for that he was the occasion for the storm which was upon them.

Now, at the first, they durst not do so, as esteeming it a wicked thing to cast a man who was a stranger and who had committed his life to them, into such a manifest perdition. But at last, when their misfortune overbore them and the ship was just going to be drowned and when they were animated to do it by the prophet himself, and by the fear concerning their own safety, they cast him into the sea; upon which the sea became calm.

It is also reported that Jonah was swallowed down by a whale and that when he had been there three days, and as many nights, he was vomited out upon the Euxine Sea, and this alive, and without any hurt upon his body. There, on his prayer to God, he obtained pardon for his sins and went to the city Nineveh, where he stood so as to b heard, and preached that in a very little time they should lose their dominion of Asia. When he had published this, he returned. Now I have given this account about him as I found it written in our books (Josephus).

Now Jonah proclaimed only these eight words:
'Forty more days and Nineveh will be overturned!'

They believed Jonah and fasted (both man and beast). They put on sackcloth. They said, 'God may relent'. He did. This made Jonah angry. He even wanted to die.

He went and sat down east of the city to see what would happen. He made a shelter for himself. (I guess he was waiting out the 40 days).

God made a vine to grow over Jonah for a shade, and then had a worm chew it off. God asked Jonah if he had a right to be angry and he said he did.

God said there were more than 120,000 people who could not tell their right hand from their left (young). Should I not be concerned about that great city? Jonah wasn't as forgiving as God was. This story had six miracles performed in it:

1. The storm (1:4)
2. The storm stopped (grew calm, 1:15)
3. The fish swallowed Jonah (1:17)
4. The fish vomited Jonah out (2:10)
5. God provided a full-grown vine to give Jonah shade (4:6)
6. God provided a worm to chew it down (4:7)

This prophesy was given sometime around 740 BC. Israel was taken into captivity by Assyria in 722 BC and the Assyrian Empire fell in 612 BC by the Medes and Babylonians.

Nineveh

One might wonder, how could such a large city be destroyed by man alone?' By many, many soldiers.

Example: Look at the large ant hills made by tiny ants, look at the pyramids of Egypt, look at the Great Wall of China – all made by thousands of hand-laborers.

Nineveh was built on the east bank of the Tigress River (what is now Iraq). A lot of the city has been excavated. In the 1800's, a library was discovered with many tablets on literature, history, religion, medicine... the writing was in Aramaic.

They had many gods, but evidently knew there was a God in heaven. (The whole world had probably heard of the children of Israel's exploits) (*Worldbook Encyclopedia 1*, pages 778 – 781).

Note: We know for sure these things happened because in Matt. 12:38-41 Jesus uses Jonah's story. The Pharisees wanted to see a miraculous sign. He said, 'A wicked and adulterous generation asks for a miraculous sign! But none will be given except the sign of the prophet, Jonah. For as Jonah was three days and three nights in the belly of a huge fish, so the Son of Man will be three days and three nights in the heart of the earth. The men of Nineveh will stand up at the judgment with this generation and condemn it; for they repented at the preaching of Jonah'.

Micah

A Review

Micah prophesied during the reign of Jotham, Ahaz and Hezekiah (Kings of Judah), 752 – 697 BC. Of those three kings, Ahaz was one of the worst kings Judah had and Hezekiah one of the best. It was during Micah's time that Israel fell to the Assyrians (722 BC). Micah prophesied these words from the Lord, 'I will make Samaria a heap of rubble. Her wound is incurable. Disaster has come from the Lord. Your children will go from you into exile' (Chapter 1)

False Prophets

Their prophets say, 'Do not prophesy about these things; disgrace will not overtake us. They will cover their faces in shame, because there is not an answer from God.

Her leaders judge for a bribe, her priests teach for a price and her prophets tell fortunes for money' (Chapter 3)

Prophesy of the Church (Chapters 4:1, 2)

In the last days, the mountain of the Lord's temple will be established as a chief among the mountains; it will be raised about the hills and peoples will stream to it.

Many nations will come and say, 'Come, let us go up to the mountain of the Lord, to the house of the God of Jacob. He will teach us His ways, so that we may walk in his paths'.

The Law will go out from Zion, the word of the Lord from Jerusalem. (This is not the law of Moses but the law of Christ).

Judah Also Warned

Judah is not faultless either. They didn't fall until 136 years after Israel. (Israel 722, Judah 586) The Lord knew it was going to happen.

Their prophesy was this:

'I will gather the lame, assemble the exiles and those I have brought to grief. I will make the remnant a strong nation. The former dominion will be restored to you. But now, you must leave the city. You will go to Babylon. There you will be rescued, out of the hand of your enemies'.

They do not know the thoughts of the Lord; they do not understand his plans (Chapter 4).

Bethlehem (Another Prophesy)

But you, Bethlehem (Ephrathah) though you are small among the clans of Judah, out of you will come one who will be ruler over Israel (Micah 5:2 and Matthew 2:5, 6).

This is a prophesy of the birth of Christ in Bethlehem of Judah. Isaiah had foretold Jesus' virgin birth (7:14). Micah told us where it would be (5:2). There are many prophesies of Jesus Christ in the Old Testament.

Deliverance and Destruction

Micah writes, 'when the Assyrians invade our land, the Lord will deliver us'.

After the Assyrians took Samaria, they wanted Judah also. It was during Hezekiah's rule. He sent his commanders to find out why Hezekiah was so confident; since Assyria had defeated so many lands.

Hezekiah prayed to the Lord for help against great odds. God heard his prayers and sent Isaiah to tell him the King of Assyria would not enter the city nor shoot an arrow there.

The Lord said *He* would defend the city (Isaiah 37). That night the Angel of the Lord went out and put to death that great army of 185,000 Assyrians that had assembled for battle.

Sennacherib, the Assyrian King, returned home to Nineveh and stayed there (Isaiah 36 and 37). Assyria was defeated by the Babylonians in 605 BC.

What Does the Lord Require of Us?

He has shown you, O man, what is good. And what does the Lord require of you? To act justly, and to love mercy and to walk humbly with your God.

Israel's Guilt

Am I to forget your ill-gotten treasures and your dishonest scales? Do not trust a neighbor; put no confidence in a friend. Even with her who lies within your embrace, be careful of your words–a man's enemies are the member of his own house-hold (this was in those troubled times), but may still be true (see Matt. 10:34-39).

Micah Gives Hope

He writes, 'As for me, I watch in hope for the Lord.
I wait for God, my Savior.
Though I have fallen, I will rise.

I will see His righteousness.

The day for building your walls will come.

They will turn in fear of the Lord – (to the Lord) you do not stay angry forever.

You will again have compassion on us.

You will be true to Jacob and show mercy to Abraham as you pledged on oath to our fathers in days long ago (Deuteronomy 7:8)

Note: The remnant of people we keep reading about are the ones who wanted to return and keep the laws (Ezra 1:1-5). Christ was to come through them when the time was right. They had to be cleansed and prepared.

Nahum

A Review

Lets review a little of Nineveh. It was a very great Gentile city, located on the east back of the Tigress River. It was the capital of Assyria.

Jonah was sent there by the Lord to preach to them. He ran away at first and was swallowed by a great fish for 3 days. After that, he went and proclaimed, 'Forty more days and Nineveh will be overturned'.

The whole town put on sackcloth and fasted. When God saw their repentance, He had compassion and did not destroy them.

Their repentance did not last. God is again angry with Nineveh and is letting them know by the prophet Nahum, what He intends to do, but this time it will happen.

Nahum writes:

'The Lord is slow to anger and great in power; the Lord will not leave the guilty unpunished. His way is in the whirlwind and the storm. He rebukes the sea, makes the rivers run dry, the mountains quake, the hills melt away and the earth tremble. *Who can withstand His indignation?*

He cares for those who trust in Him, but with an overwhelming flood He will make an end of Nineveh.

Trouble will not come a second time. They will be entangled among thorns and drunk from their wine; they will be consumed like dry stubble'.

Nineveh was such a strong and large city that it was thought to be impossible to destroy, but nothing is too hard for the Lord.

God's Wrath

God is a God of love, but also of wrath. What causes His wrath is sin.

Paul wrote in Romans 1:18, 'For the wrath of God is revealed from Heaven against all ungodliness and unrighteousness of men who hold the truth in unrighteousness'.

John wrote in Revelation 6:16, 17, 'For the great day of his wrath has come; and who shall be able to stand?'

Jesus said in Matthew 23:7, 'O generation of vipers, who hath warned you to flee from the wrath to come?'

Examples of God's Wrath

1. The flood
2. Sodom and Gomorrah
3. Nineveh
4. Jerusalem (twice)
5. Earthquakes, floods, etc.
6. Cursing the ground (because of Adam's sin)
7. Destroying many cities and powerful nations

We have to go to history to find out how that great city could be destroyed.

Babylon had been attacking Assyria for over 2 years but the King of Assyria, thinking that he was victorious, gave a big feast; with lots of wine being served. While all this was going on, the Koher River (a tributary of the Tigris) which was swollen by rain overflowed, giving the enemy full access to the city. When the king realized what had happened, he gathered his concubines, eunuchs and himself and set fire to the buildings and palaces. No doubt, God caused this natural disturbance (the unexpected flood) to help the enemy. God planned it years before it happened.

These verses in Chapter 1 are easier to understand now: (verse 8) 'With an overwhelming flood, (verse 10) drunk from the wine, consumed like dry stubble'.

The Battle

God destroyed Nineveh by the armies of Babylon.

The shields of Babylon were red (2:3). Their chariots were rushing to and fro in the streets (2:4). The nobles (of Assyria) were stumbling in their march (half drunken). The gates of the rivers are opened (2:6) (because of the sudden flood). The people fled away from the city (2:8). Nineveh had much treasure from the wars they had won. Now it was being looted by others (2:9).

Why?

The city brought the destruction on themselves. God gave them plenty of warning and He gives us plenty of warning.

It was because of their wickedness. They were very harsh in battle and to prisoners. They were always fighting and wanting more lands to conquer. They had many gods and pagan worship, though they should have known there was a God in heaven (Romans 1:18-26).

Nahum writes:

'Nothing can heal your wound; your injury is fatal. Who has not felt your endless cruelty?

Habakkuk

A Review

This prophesy was made sometime in the 600's. The northern kingdom had already been taken by Assyria in 722 BC, then Assyria (Nineveh) was taken in 612 BC. Judah was in the process, in this prophesy, of being taken next. It was taken in three periods: 606, 597 and finally burned in 586 BC. (Over a period of 20 years) The purpose of the prophesy is to warn Judah of the coming destruction by Babylon which would also be destroyed later. It is presented in a question and answer method.

Q: Habakkuk asks God, 'O Lord, how long must I call for help? Why do you tolerate wrong?'

> **A**: The Lord answers, 'I am going to do something (in your days) that you would not believe, even if you were told. I am raising up the Babylonians, that ruthless people, who sweep across the whole earth to sieze dwelling places not their own. They laugh at the fortified cities; they build earthen ramps and capture them. They sweep past, like the wind, and go on – their strength is their god'.

Q: Habakkuk asks another question, 'Your eyes are too pure to look on evil; how can a holy and good God let the wicked swallow up a people that are better than the destroyer? You have made men like fish in the sea. (Solomon says in Ecclesiastes 9:12 'As fish are caught in a cruel net, or birds are taken in a snare, so men are trapped by evil times that fall unexpectedly upon them'). The righteous must suffer along with the good. Habakkuk said he would stand at his station and see what God would say to him.

A: The Lord answers (Chapter 2), 'Write down this revelation and make it plain, on tablets, so that a herald may run with it. The revelation awaits an appointed time. It will certainly come and will not delay. (This prophesy is about Babylon the destroyer). He is puffed up; wine betrays him' (Daniel 5). Belshazzar was having a banquet and drinking when he saw the hand-writing on the wall and was destroyed that very night. He is greedy–never satisfied; he gathers to himself all the nations and takes captives all the people. Because they had plundered many nations, they would be plundered (after the conquest).

Babylon may have been the oldest nation built soon after the flood. They probably thought it could not be destroyed, but the only kingdom that cannot be destroyed is the Lord's kingdom (Heb. 12:28)

Habakkuk's Prayer (Chapter 3)

'Lord, I have heard of your fame and stand in awe of your deeds'.

He called on God to once again let the world see them.

He brings to mind the exodus of his people, the glory on the mountain, the plagues, the destruction of the people of Canaan, the rivers that opened up for them (Red Sea, Jordan River).

His Submission

'Yet I will wait patiently for the day of calamity to come on the nation invading us.

Though the fig tree does not bud and there are no grapes on the vine, though the olive crop fails and the fields produce no food, though there are no sheep in the pen and no cattle in the stalls, yet I will rejoice in the Lord, I will be joyful in God my Savior'.

Starvation would be their lot, along with being carried away from their land (Judah) never to see it again (2 Kings 25:1-11).

Others have kept the faith –

Job said, 'though He slays me, yet will I hope in Him' (Job 13:15).

Samuel was told not to grieve over Saul (1 Sam. 16:1).

Jesus prayed, if it was possible, to let this cup (his death on the cross) pass from him, yet not what I will, but what you will. Even Jesus and God had to do things they did not want to do (Chapter 3).

Zephaniah

A Review

The end is getting closer. This prophesy is in the days of Josiah. Josiah was only eight years old when he began to reign. He reigned 31 years but it was in the 18th year of his reign when the Book of the Law was found while repairing the temple.

He began his reform after that, so this prophesy seemed to be in the first years of his reign. Even though Josiah was a good king, the ones before him were very evil (Manasseh and Amon).

Zephaniah traces his own ancestry back four generations (son of Cushi, son of Gedaliah, the son of Amariah, the son of Hezekiah). He was either proud of his ancestry or, if his mother, being Jewish, had married a foreigner (Cushi) he would have to show a pure Jewish line for three generations (see Deut. 23:8).

The Prophesy

I will stretch out my hand against Judah and Jerusalem. I will cut off every remnant of Baal and Molech.

The Lord has prepared a sacrifice. The great day of the Lord is near. That day will be a day of wrath, distress, anguish, trouble and ruin.

This day of the Lord would be the day the Babylonians destroyed Jerusalem. They killed the last king's (Zedekiah's) sons before his eyes, then put Zedekiah's eyes out and took him to Babylon in shackles. They burned the temple Solomon had built and all important buildings there. They took the remainder, who were still alive, into exile in Babylon except for a few poor (2 Kings 25).

This destruction did not happen in a day, but over a period of years starting in 605 BC and ending in this final day, 586 BC.

Our Final Day

We should see this as a lesson for us also. We don't know what day or hour the Lord will return. It will be as in the days of Noah. People were eating and drinking, marrying and giving in marriage up until the day Noah entered the Ark. We must also be ready (see Matt. 24:36-44).

To the Faithful

Seek the Lord, all you humble of the land, you who do what He commands. Seek righteousness and humility. Perhaps you will be sheltered on the day of the Lord's anger.

Nations Babylon Will Conquer

The Philistines: Gaza, Ashkelon, Ashdod and Ekron (the remnant of the Lord's people will find pasture there).

Moab and Ammon will become like Sodom and Gomorrah, a place of weeds and salt pits. (They were descendants of Lot, but always enemies of Israel).

The Cushites, Assyria and Nineveh.

(Nineveh will be as dry as a desert. Flocks and herds will lie down there. Creatures of every kind will roost on her columns). Nineveh was destroyed in 612 BC. It eventually disappeared completely until the nineteenth century when it was discovered by archeologists.

Reason for Judgment

She obeys no one, accepts no correction.
She does not trust in the Lord,
Her officials are roaring lions,
Her rulers are evening wolves,

Her prophets are arrogant
Her priests profane the sanctuary
The unrighteous know no shame.

The Remnant

My worshippers, my scattered people, will bring me offerings. I will remove from this city those who rejoice in their pride.

Never again will you be haughty on my holy hill. I will leave within you the meek and humble, who trust in the name of the Lord (see 2 Kings 25:12).

The remnant of Israel will do no wrong; they will speak no lies; nor will deceit be found in their mouths.

They will eat and lie down and no one will make them afraid. I will give you honor and praise when I restore your fortunes.

Haggai
A Review

This prophesy came in the second year of Darius, 520 BC. The kingdoms of both Israel and Judah had no kings to date it from. The prophesy was to Zerubbabel, the governor of Judah and Joshua, the high priest. In the first year of Cyrus, the Lord moved his heart to let the exiles return and to build the temple of the Lord in Jerusalem. The family heads of Judah and Benjamin, the priests and Levites and any who wanted to, could leave.

This first return was in 538 BC., 49,897 returned. They also brought back the articles belonging to the temple that Nebuchadnezzar had carried away. Zerubbabel led this group. He was of royal blood (though there were no more kings) and in the lineage of Christ (Matt. 1:13 on Joseph's side and Luke 3:27 on Mary's side). They built an altar and began to offer burnt offerings, but had not yet laid the foundation of the Lord's temple.

In the second year, they laid the foundation. The people around them began to discourage the building and wrote a letter to King Artaxerxes. He wrote back for the work to be stopped. The work did stop until Darius started to reign, about fifteen years later.

A letter was written asking him to search the royal archives to see if King Cyrus had issued a decree for them to rebuild the temple. It was found. It stated the size and that the costs were to be paid out of the royal treasury. And, for them to stay away and not interfere with the work (Ezra Chapter 1-6).

A Call to Build

The word of the Lord came through the prophet, Haggai:

'Is it a time for you to be living in your paneled houses, while this house remains a ruin? Go up into the mountains and bring down timber and build the house, so that I may take pleasure in it and be honored'.

The Lord had been withholding a good harvest by drought and they didn't seem to know why. After this message of the Lord, their spirit was stirred and they began to work on the house of the Lord (Chapter 1).

The word of the lord came again to Haggai. He said to ask them, 'Who of you is left who saw this house in its former glory? Does it not seem to you like nothing?' (It seems some were there who had seen it).

The Lord told them to be strong and work for He was with them. 'The glory of this present house will be greater than the glory of the former house. In this place, I will grant peace' (the size of the building is not important to God). The temple was completed in the sixth year of the reign of King Darius (516 BC).

The Passover was celebrated (Ezra 6:15-19) on the 14th day of the first month as the Lord commanded Moses (see Exodus 12). The people, at first, didn't seem to have their whole heart into the return and seemed ceremonially unclean to the Lord.

After they got busy building and thinking of spiritual things, the Lord told them, 'From this day I will bless you'. (Their fields will produce). He told Zerubbabel He would make him like his signet ring (give him trust and authority, Chapter 3).
Ex. Pharaoh gave Joseph his signet ring (Gen. 41:41)
King Xerxes gave Mordecai his signet ring (Esther 8:2).

Zechariah

A Review

Zachariah and Haggai were prophets at the same time.

Zachariah's first prophesy was in the eighth month of the second year of Darius and Haggai's last was in the ninth month of the second year of Darius.

His First Message

The Lord was angry with your forefathers. He said, 'Return to me and I will return to you. Do not be like your forefathers. They would not listen or pay attention to me. Where are your forefathers now?'

When they repented they said, 'The Lord has done to us what we deserve'.

Three months later, he had another vision during the night. The angel of the Lord was standing among the myrtle trees. He asked the Lord Almighty (God), 'How long will you withhold mercy from Jerusalem and the towns of Judah, which you have been angry with these 70 years?'

This is what the Lord says, 'I will return to Jerusalem with mercy and then my house will be rebuilt'.

Before me stood a man with a measuring line to measure Jerusalem (the walls had not been rebuilt as yet). He said the Lord would be a wall of fire around it. Whoever touches it would touch the apple of His eye.

A Prophesy of the Church

'Shout and be glad, O daughter of Zion. For I am coming and I will live among you,' declares the Lord. Many nations will be joined with the Lord in that day and will become My people. I will live among you and you will know that the Lord Almighty has sent me to you. The Lord will again choose Jerusalem... He has roused himself from His holy dwelling'.

(This has to be when Jesus came to earth to establish his church, Acts 2).

God's Cleansing

Joshua (the high priest, Haggai 1:1) was standing before the angel of the Lord. The angel said, 'Take off his filthy clothes. I have taken away your sin and will put rich garments on you. I will remove the sin of this land in a single day' (3:9).

The angel awoke Zechariah and told him (in person): 'the bonds of Zerubbabel have laid the foundation of this temple; his hands will also complete it. Then you will know that the Lord Almighty has sent me to you'. (The Angel of the Lord seems to be Jesus himself).

Two years later, some men from Bethel came to ask the priests if they should mourn and fast in the fifth month as they had been doing. (This date, the tenth day of the fifth month, was when Nebuchadnezzar had burned the temple and destroyed Jerusalem, Jeremiah 52:12 – 14). This was never commanded by God. The only day in the year they were told to fast was on the Day of Atonement (Lev. 16: 29-31). What he wanted them to do was hear his word.

The Lord Almighty said, 'Once again, men and women of ripe old age will sit in the streets of Jerusalem; each with cane in hand because of his age. Boys and girls will play there (no fear).

The seed will grow, the vine will yield its fruit, the ground will produce its crops and the heavens drop their dew'.

Things to do: speak truth, render sound judgments, don't plot evil or swear falsely. Your fasts will become joyful occasions.

Many people will yet come to Jerusalem, to seek the Lord Almighty; men from all languages and nations. They will say, 'Let us go with you, because we have heard that God is with you'.

Another Prophesy of Jesus

See, your king comes to you, righteous and having salvation, gentle and riding on a donkey, on a colt, the foal of a donkey... (Matt. 21:5, John 12:15). *His rule will extend from sea to sea, to the ends of the earth.*

I will bend to Judah as I bend my bow and fill it with Ephraim. Though I scatter them among the peoples, yet in distant lands they will remember me. They and their children will survive, and they will return.

Assyria's pride will be brought down and Egypt's scepter will pass away. The Lord will strike all the nations that fought against Jerusalem.

Babylon and Assyria are already gone. Tyre, Damascus, the Philistines... will be next.

The survivors from all the nations that have attacked Jerusalem will go up year after year to worship and celebrate the Feast of Tabernacles.

Malachi

A Review

Malachi was a prophet about a hundred years after the exile's return from their Babylonian exile. He was the last of twelve prophets before the coming of John the Baptist and the Christian age (about 400 years later). Haggai and Zerubbabel had stirred up the people to rebuild the temple that had been destroyed by Nebuchadnezzar's armies. Ezra, a priest and scribe, had tried to make Israel pure again by sending back the foreign women some 111 men had married. (This number included priests and Levites). He also read the Law of Moses to the people. They had all stood from daybreak until noon to hear it read (Nehe. 8:1-3).

Nehemiah rebuilt the wall of Jerusalem against much opposition (Nehemiah 6). In the beginning there was much hope, but now, after about 100 years, their love is growing cold again. The Lord speaks to them through His prophet Malachi. He asks questions and answers them.

I have loved you', says the Lord, 'But you ask, 'how have you loved us?' 'Was not Esau Jacob's brother? I have loved Jacob but Esau I have hated. His mountain, Edom, was turned into a wasteland'.

They said, 'We will rebuild. The Lord said He would demolish. (Psalm 127:1 says, 'except the Lord builds the house, its builder labors in vain').

'The priests show contempt for my name. You ask, "how have we shown contempt?" You place defiled food on my table. You bring blind animals for sacrifice; also crippled or diseased animals. Is that wrong?

'Oh that one of you would shut the temple doors, so that you would not light useless fires on my altar. I am not pleased with you, and will not accept the offering. Cursed is the cheat, who has an acceptable male in his flock, and vows to give it, but instead sacrifices a blemished animal'.

All offerings were to be made without defect. (Leviticus Chapters 1-7 to see what kind of offerings they were supposed to make. The priests were unfaithful. The Lord said He had sent this admonition so that his covenant with Levi may continue (the Levites were the priests). The Lord said the lips of a priest should preserve knowledge. People should seek instruction from him because he is the messenger of the Lord Almighty (Haggai 1:1).

He said they had not followed His ways and had caused many to stumble. The same thing is going on today. Another thing some of the people were again doing was marrying foreign women. God never wanted this (see Ex. 34:16, Deut 7:3, 4); because he was seeking godly offspring. He said, 'do not break faith with the wife of your youth. I hate divorce'.

A Prophesy Concerning Jesus

'I will send my messenger, who will prepare the way before me'. Before the Lord came, He sent John the Baptist to announce His coming and make the people ready to receive Him. Jesus himself said, 'Elijah has already come and they did not recognize him, but have done to him everything they wished. In the same way, the Son of man is going to suffer at their hands'. The disciples understood that He was talking about John the Baptist (Mt. 17:11-13).

Robbing God

'Will a man rob God? Yet you rob me'. You ask, 'How do we rob you?' 'In tithes and offerings. Bring the whole tithe into the storehouse. Test me and see if I will not throw open the flood gates of heaven and pour out so much blessing that you will not have room enough for it'.

The Day of the Lord

The day is coming when every evildoer will be stubble. But for you who revere my name, the sun of righteousness will rise with healing in its wings.

You will go out and leap like calves released from the stall. Remember the law of my servant Moses, the decrees and the laws I gave him at Horeb.

Since then, no prophet has risen in Israel like Moses, whom the Lord knew face to face (Deut. 34:10).

New
Testament

Matthew

A Review

Matthew, one of the apostles, was previously a tax collector. When Jesus called him, he was sitting at the tax collectors booth. He got up immediately and followed Jesus. He may have been a man of means as many tax collectors and 'sinners' came to eat at his house. When Jesus was asked why he ate with them he said, 'I have not come to call the righteous, but sinners' (9:9-13).

His gospel may have been put first because of the genealogy of Jesus; tying the Old Testament to the New Testament. It is one of four books called 'the gospels'. It is about the life on earth of Jesus. He is written of as the Messiah, the Son of God and the Savior of the world.

Matthew's genealogy is through Joseph, Jesus' legal father. It connects him to his royal heritage (the kings). Joseph is not mentioned past Jesus' childhood. Normally women are not listed in a genealogy, but this one names four, none of which were a normal circumstance.

Tamar—the mother of two illegitimate sons by her father-in-law, Judah (Gen. 38:27-30)

Rahab—the prostitute/innkeeper who hid the men who went to spy out Jericho. She later married an Israelite, Salmon, and gave birth to Boaz (Josh. 2:2, 6:25, Ruth 4:21).

Ruth—was from Moab, the land settled by Lot's oldest daughter (Gen. 19:36, 37). She was David's great-grand-mother.

Bathsheba—who had been the wife of Uriah and later married David. She gave birth to Solomon (2 Sam. 12:24).

There were 14 generations from Abraham to David, 14 generations from David to the exile and 14 generations from the exile to Christ; 42 generations in all.

The Birth of Jesus

Joseph and Mary were pledged to be married but were not as yet. Mary was a virgin at this time. When Joseph realized Mary was with child, he wanted to 'put her away' privately. An Angel of the Lord appeared to him in a dream and told him it was of the Holy Spirit.

They lived outwardly as husband and wife, but had no union until after Jesus was born. This fulfilled what was prophesied by Isaiah in Isaiah 7:14. He was born of a virgin.

Matthew made no mention of the shepherd's visiting Mary but related the story of the wise men. Jesus was born in Bethlehem during the time of King Herod.

The wise men had seen His star in the east and went to worship Him. King Herod was disturbed. He told them to search for the child and report to him so he could worship Him also. They brought gifts of gold, incense and myrrh. They were warned in a dream not to go back to Herod. Joseph was also warned to not return home, but to go to Egypt until the death of Herod. When Herod realized he had been outwitted by the wise men, he gave orders to kill all the boy babies in the Bethlehem area two years old and under. After Herod died, Joseph was told in a dream to return to Israel. They went to live in Nazareth.

Matthew now went to about 29 years later. John the Baptist came, preaching in the desert of Judah, saying 'Repent, for the kingdom of heaven is near' (see Isaiah 40:3). He wore clothes made of camel's hair with a leather belt around his waist. People went to him from all Judea, confessing their sins and were baptized in the Jordan River.

Jesus also came to him. John tried to deter him saying, 'I need to be baptized by you'. Jesus told him to 'let it be so now, it is proper for us to do this to fulfill all righteousness'.

After Jesus' baptism, the Spirit of God descended like a dove and lit on him. A voice said, 'This is my Son, whom I love; with Him I am well pleased'.

After this, Jesus was led by the Spirit to the desert to be tempted by the devil after fasting 40 days and 40 nights. He did not give in to the temptation.

After this, Jesus started His ministry. He walked along the Sea of Galilee and saw two brothers, Peter and Andrew, fishing. He said to them, 'follow me and I will make you fishers of men'. Going on a little further, He saw two other brothers, James and John. All four left their nets and followed Him.

Jesus went throughout Galilee preaching the Good News of the kingdom and healing people. Large crowds followed Him. He went up on a mountainside and sat down. He began to teach. This sermon is called 'The Sermon on the Mount' and is covered in Chapters 5 through 7. It covered the Beatitudes, salt and light, the Law, murder, adultery, divorce, oaths, love for enemies, giving, prayer, fasting, laying up treasure, worrying, judging, asking, bearing fruit, the wise and the foolish builders...

Jesus healed many people, completed his naming of the apostles and sent them out on the 'limited commission' (to Jews only). He gave them power to work miracles like He had.

John the Baptist had been put in prison. He sent his disciples to ask Jesus, 'Are you the One who was to come or should we expect someone else?' Jesus told them to go back and report what they had heard and seen.

He told the people around Him John was the One Malachi had written about in Malachi 3:1. 'I will send my messenger ahead of you, who will prepare your way before you'.

Everywhere Jesus went, crowds followed Him and He healed them, teaching everywhere he went. He taught in parables. Some of them were:

- The sower of seed
- The wheat and the tares
- The mustard seed
- The parable of the hidden treasure
- The pearl of great price
- The parable of the net

Jesus arrived at his hometown, Nazareth. They said, 'where did this man get this wisdom and these miraculous powers? Isn't this the carpenter's son? Isn't his mother's name Mary and aren't his brothers James, Joseph, Simon and Judas? Aren't all his sisters with us?'

Jesus said, 'Only in his hometown and in his own house is a prophet without honor' (13:54-57).

Herod Antipas had arrested John the Baptist because he told him it was not lawful for him to have his brother Philip's wife.

On his birthday, his wife's daughter danced. She pleased Herod so much he promised to give her whatever she asked for. Her mother told her to ask for John the Baptist's head on a platter. Herod was distressed but granted the request. When Herod heard these reports about Jesus' miraculous powers he thought it was John risen from the dead!

Jesus withdrew to a solitary place, but crowds followed him on foot. There was no place to find food. A person was found who had five loaves and two fish. Jesus had the people to sit down on the grass, gave thanks and broke the loaves. With this, He fed 5,000 men plus women and children and had 12 basketfuls left over.

Jesus bade His disciples to get into a boat and cross over to the other side. During the night (3-6 AM), Jesus went to them, walking on the lake. When they realized it was Him, Peter wanted to walk to Him and started to sink.

They went to the Tyre and Sidon region and a Canaanite woman who had heard of Jesus begged him to heal her daughter. Jesus said He was only sent to the lost sheep of Israel but He had compassion and healed her. Jesus spent 3 days there, healing and teaching. This time he fed 4,000. They were not Israelites (15:31).

There were two sects of Jews, the Pharisees and the Sadducees. They wanted to see a sign. He said, 'if the sky is red at night, it will be fair weather, if it is red in the morning, it will be stormy'.

Peter's Confession

Jesus asked His apostles, 'who do people say the Son of Man is?'

They said, 'some say John the Baptist, others Elijah, still others Jeremiah or one of the prophets'.

'What about you? Who do *you* say I am?

Simon Peter answered, 'You are the Christ, the Son of the Living God'.

Jesus said this had been revealed to him by His Father in heaven. He said, 'On this rock I will build my church and the gates of Hades will not overcome it (his death). I will give you the keys of the kingdom of heaven; whatever you bind on earth will be bound in heaven and whatever you loose on earth will be loosed in heaven'. This happened on the Pentecost after Jesus' death, burial and resurrection (Acts 2).

Beginning of the End

From that time on, Jesus started preparing His apostles for His death, at the hands of the elders, chief priests and teachers of the law. He said He must be killed and on the third day raised to life.

The Transfiguration

Six days later, Jesus took Peter, James and John to a high mountain by themselves. Jesus was transformed (changed) and Moses and Elijah appeared and talked to Him. Peter wanted to build three tabernacles but a voice from heaven said, 'this is my son, whom I love; with Him I am well pleased. Listen to Him'. This is the same thing that was said after Jesus' baptism (Matt. 3:17). The three were afraid but Jesus told them not to be, but not to tell anyone until after He was raised from the dead.

When they rejoined the other disciples they had been trying to heal a man, but could not. Jesus healed him and told them they had too little faith.

Who is Greatest?

The disciples asked Jesus who was the greatest in the kingdom of heaven. He called a little child and showed them it was the humble qualities they displayed that made a person great. He told them not to look down on one of these little ones, that their angels in heaven always see the face of God.

Jesus said, 'If your brother sins against you, go to him privately and show him his fault. If his listens, you have won your brother. If he won't listen, take 2 or 3 others. If he won't listen to them, take it up before the church. If that doesn't work, treat him as a pagan' (Matt. 18:15-17).

How Many Times Should I Forgive?

Peter asked this question of Jesus. He thought seven times would be plenty but Jesus said, 'Seventy times seven' (don't keep count).

Divorce

Some Pharisees asked Jesus if it was lawful to divorce your wife for any reason. Jesus said, 'In the beginning the Creator made them male and female and said, "For this reason a man will leave his father and mother and be united to his wife and the two will become one flesh". Whatever God has joined together, let not man separate' (Matt. 19:4-6).

Jesus said Moses permitted it, but it was not this way from the beginning. He also said if anyone divorces (except for marital unfaithfulness) and marries another, commits adultery.

Earthly Treasures

A rich young man asked Jesus, 'teacher, what good thing must I do to get eternal life?' Jesus said to obey the command-ments. He said he had always done that. Jesus knowing his heart said, 'if you want to be perfect, sell your possessions, give them to the poor, and come follow me'.

The young man went away sorrowful because he had great possessions.

The disciples asked, 'Who can be saved?'

Jesus said, 'With man this is impossible, but with God all things are possible'. He said everyone who has left houses or brothers or sisters of father or mother or wife or children or fields (for my sake) will inherit eternal life...

Workers in the Vineyard

A land owner went out early in the morning and hired men to work in his vineyard for a denarius (a common day's wage). Later on he went out and found others idle, and sent them to work. Each hour the same thing happened even into the last hour of the day.

When it came time to pay, they all received the same pay. Those who worked long hours began to grumble, saying it was unfair. The landowner said, 'don't I have a right to do what I want to with my own money?'

This represents Christianity. If we have been Christians our whole life or in our older age, the reward is the same. *Obedi-ence* is what is important, not length of time.

Jesus Predicts His Death

Jesus and His disciples were going up to Jerusalem. He took 'the 12' aside and told them He would be betrayed to the chief priests and teachers of the law. They would turn Him over to the Gentiles to be mocked, flogged and crucified, but on the third day, He would be raised to life.

The mother of James and John went to Jesus to ask a favor of Him. She wanted Him to allow her sons to sit on His right and left in His kingdom. (They still did not understand that His was not an earthly kingdom).

Jesus told her it was not for Him to grant, that those places were for those the Father had prepared. (When all is finished, everything will be turned over to God).

Jesus told them, 'Whoever wants to be great among you must be your servant'.

Jesus Enters Jerusalem

On His way to Jerusalem, they went through Jericho where Jesus healed two blind men sitting by the roadside.

As they neared Jerusalem, Jesus sent two disciples to get a colt for him to ride in on (this was the way kings entered). (Also, see the prophesy in Zech. 9:9).

The city was stirred up upon seeing this and said, 'who is this?' They were told it was Jesus, the prophet from Nazareth in Galilee.

He entered the temple where buying and selling was going on (it was approaching the Passover). He overturned the tables of the money changers saying, 'my house will be called a house of prayer, but you are making it a den of robbers'.

Even while Jesus was at the temple, He healed the blind and lame. That night, He went to Bethany to spend the night. It was about a mile east of Jerusalem and was the home of His friends, Mary, Martha and Lazarus.

Early the next morning, He was on his way back to Jerusalem. He saw a fig tree, went over to get some figs but found none. He said to it, 'may you never bear fruit again!' It withered.

Jesus entered the temple and started teaching in parables:

- The two sons
- The tenants
- The wedding banquet
- Paying taxes to Caesar

Marriage at the Resurrection?

The Sadducees (who say there is no resurrection) asked Jesus a question. There were seven brothers who married a woman, none leaving any children. Whose wife will she be in the resurrection?

Jesus said, 'at the resurrection, people will neither marry, nor be given in marriage; they will be like the angels'.

The Pharisees also tested Him. They asked, 'which is the greatest commandment?'

Jesus said, 'love the Lord with all your heart, soul and mind. The second is like it: love your neighbor as yourself'.

Seven Woes

Jesus condemned the Pharisees. He said they sit in Moses' seat and they must obey them, but do not do as they do – they don't practice what they preach.

Everything they do is for man to see. They like to be honored and called 'Rabbi'. Jesus said we only have one master and we're not to call anyone on earth 'father' for we have *one father* and He is in heaven. (This is speaking of a title).

He said they had neglected the important matters of the law: justice, mercy and faithfulness. On the outside you *appear* to be righteous but on the inside you are full of hypocrisy and wickedness.

Signs of the End of the Age

As Jesus was leaving the temple with His disciples, they called His attention to it.

Jesus said, 'Do you see all these things? I tell you the truth, not one stone here will be left on another; every one will be thrown down'.

They said, 'when will this happen?' (24:15-35).

Jesus was speaking of the destruction of Jerusalem and the temple that was to have its fulfillment in AD 70.

This description was recorded in a book by the Jewish historian, Flavius Josephus. The battle for Jerusalem and the temple took five months. The whole war took 3 ½ years. Biblical references can be found in Revelation 8:16–13:10 and Daniel 12:1–11. The signs of his coming and the end of the age are described in Matthew 24:4–14 and 36–44.

Jesus told his disciples, 'the Passover is two days away. The Son of man will be handed over to be crucified'.

While He was in Bethany at the home of Simon the Leper, a woman anointed Him with expensive perfume (see John 12:3). Matthew doesn't name her, but John says it was Mary, sister of Lazarus and Martha.

Judas' Betrayal

One of the 12 apostles, Judas, went to the chief priests and agreed to betray Jesus for 30 pieces of silver.

The Last Meal (Thursday Night)

The disciples came to Jesus and asked Him where they would be eating the Passover. He told them to go into the city to a certain man's house. (The Passover was on about the 14th of our April).

When evening came, they were reclining at the table when Jesus said, 'One of you will betray me'. Upon questioning, He said, 'the one who has dipped his hand into the bowl with me'.

While they were eating, Jesus established the Lord's Supper (so called today). He first took the bread, gave thanks, broke it and gave it to His disciples; then the cup (fruit of the vine). This represented His body and blood that was poured out for the forgiveness of sins. He said He would not drink it again until He drank it with them in His father's kingdom (the church). When they had sung a hymn, they went out to the Mount of Olives.

Jesus told His disciples, 'this very night you will all fall away on account of me'. Peter said he *never* would. Jesus said, 'this very night, before the rooster crows, you will disown me three times'.

Jesus got no sleep that night. He went to Gethsemane to pray, taking Peter, James and John with Him. But while they kept falling asleep, He kept praying if it were possible to let that cup pass (not to have to go through the agony).

While Jesus was still speaking, Judas arrived with a large crowd, armed with swords and clubs. To identify Him, Judas kissed Him.

When they arrested Jesus, Peter drew his sword and cut off the ear of the high priest's servant. Jesus said, 'every day I sat in the temple courts teaching, why didn't you arrest me then?'

Before the Sanhedrin

They took Jesus to the high priest, Caiaphas. Peter followed at a distance. They tried to find some way they could put Him to death. Finally, two men came forward and said, 'this fellow said, "I am able to destroy the temple of God and rebuild it in three days!"'.

They asked Him if He was the Christ, the Son of God. He admitted He was. The priest said, 'He has spoken blasphemy!' Blasphemy was worthy of death (Lev. 24:16). They started striking Him with their fists, spitting on His face and slapping Him.

Peter was sitting in the courtyard and denied Him three times, like Jesus had said. When he heard the rooster crow, he wept bitterly. Judas also had a change of heart and returned the 30 pieces of silver. He then went away and hanged himself.

They bought a 'potter's field' as a burial place for foreigners with the money.

Jesus was sent to Pilate, the governor. He asked Jesus if He was the king of the Jews and Jesus answered yes.

His wife sent word to Pilate, 'Don't have anything to do with that innocent man'.

He tried to release Him but got nowhere so he washed his hands in front of the crowd, releasing Barabbas (a notorious prisoner), had Jesus flogged and handed Jesus over to be crucified.

Jesus Mocked

Jesus was stripped and a scarlet robe put on Him (in mockery) and a crown of thorns. He was struck on the head again and again.

They forced a man from Cyrene to carry the cross to a place called Golgotha. They cast lots for His clothes and put this sign above His head: *This is Jesus, the King of the Jews.* He was crucified between two robbers.

Mark 15:25 says, 'He was crucified the third hour (9 AM). From the sixth until the ninth (12 to 3) darkness was over the land'.

Jesus cried out in a loud voice, 'My God, my God, why have you forsaken me?'

The moment He died, the curtain of the temple was torn in two from top to bottom, the earth shook and the rocks split. Many holy people came from the tombs. After Jesus' resurrection, they went into the city and appeared to many.

Many of the women were there watching from a distance; Mary Magdalene, Jesus' mother and the mother of James and John.

Joseph of Arimathea asked for Jesus' body and placed it in his own tomb.

They remembered Jesus had said, 'after three days, I will rise again'. They made the tomb secure lest His followers should come and steal the body.

On the first day of the week (Sunday), Mary Magdalene and Jesus' mother went to look at the tomb. There was another earthquake. An angel came from heaven, rolled back the stone and sat on it. He told the women, 'He is not here. He has risen. Go tell His disciples. He is going ahead of you into Galilee'.

As they were leaving, Jesus met them and said, 'greetings. Don't be afraid. Go tell my brothers to go to Galilee'.

The guards went into the city and reported to the chief priests what had happened. They gave the soldiers a large sum of money to say during the night while they slept, His disciples stole Him away.

The Great Commission

On a mountain in Galilee, Jesus came to His apostles and said, 'All authority in heaven and on earth has been given to me. Go and make disciples of all nations, baptizing them in the name of the Father, the Son and the Holy Spirit, and teaching them to obey everything I have commanded you. And surely I am with you always, to the very end of the age'.

Note: Galilee was a few days away from Jerusalem (where He was crucified) but the apostles were told to tarry in Jerusalem where the church was established on Pentecost. He probably went to Galilee (home) to escape the confusion going on in Jerusalem. [C.W.]

Mark

A Review

Mark, whose full name was John Mark, was not one of the apostles. He was a cousin of Barnabas (Col. 4:10) and a son of another Mary (Acts 12:12). She was probably a woman of means because she had a servant named Rhoda (Acts 12:12, 13).

Mark and Barnabas went with Paul on his first missionary journey, but Mark wanted to return home (Acts 15:38).

Later, Paul said he was profitable to him and wanted Timothy to bring him to him (in prison) near the end of his life (2 Tim. 4:11).

Mark's account is also about the life of Jesus while on earth. His account is 12 Chapters less than that of Matthew's. He had no genealogy and not many references to the Old Testament.

He simplified the story but listed a lot of areas where things happened like; Galilee, Capernaum, mountainsides, Nazareth, in boats, Bethany and Jerusalem.

The first Chapter was a reference to the Old Testament (Malachi. 3:1).

It was about the coming of John the Baptist to prepare the way for Jesus, Jesus' baptism by John and the calling of his first four apostles; Peter, Andrew, James and John in the region of Galilee. They were all fishermen. They did not hesitate but left their father, Zebedee, with the boat and followed Jesus. Peter and Andrew left their nets and followed Him.

They all went to Capernaum. When the Sabbath came, Jesus went to the Jewish synagogue and began to teach. The people were amazed. There was a man there who was possessed by an evil spirit (the evil spirits knew who Jesus was). Jesus cast it out.

They left the synagogue and went to the home of Peter and Andrew. Peter's mother-in-law was in bed, sick with a fever. Jesus healed her. All this spread quickly. By sunset, the whole town had gathered at the door and Jesus healed many.

Early the next morning, while it was still dark, Jesus went to a solitary place to pray. When His companions found him he said, 'Let us go to other places also; so they traveled throughout Galilee'. Everywhere He went, people followed Him.

After a few days, they went back to Capernaum. The house was so crowded, some men carried a paralyzed man on the roof, made an opening and let him down that way.

As Jesus was again walking along by the lake, He saw Levi (Matthew) sitting at the tax collectors booth and called him.

John the Baptist and his disciples fasted, but Jesus' did not. They also picked and ate grain on the Sabbath and He healed on the Sabbath (under the Law of Moses the Sabbath was a day of rest). Once, to escape the press of the crowds, He taught them on a boat.

Jesus names his 12 apostles:
Peter, Andrew, James, John, Philip, Bartholomew, Matthew, Thomas, James (son of Alpheus), Thaddeus, Simon and Judas Escariot

Jesus' family heard about all these people crowding around Him and went to take charge. They arrived and sent someone in to call Him. They said, 'you mother and brothers are outside looking for you'.

Jesus said, 'Whoever does God's will is my brother and sister and mother'.

Again, Jesus got into a boat to teach the people on the shore. He taught in parables (the sower, the lamp on a stand, the growing seed and the mustard seed).

When evening came, Jesus said, 'let us go over to the other side of the lake'. While He was sleeping, a furious storm came upon them. When they woke Him, He quieted the wind and waves by saying, 'Peace, be still'.

This lake, or sea, is the Sea of Galilee. It is quite large (about 12 ½ by 7 ½ miles). The region where they landed was the country of Gadarenes. There was a man there with an evil spirit who lived in the tombs. He could not even be bound with a chain and would cry out and cut himself with stones. He didn't have just one evil spirit, but many. The demons begged Jesus to let them enter a large herd of pigs that were nearby. He did and they rushed into the lake and were drowned. The people in that place wanted Jesus to leave so He crossed back over and started healing once more.

There was a woman who had been subject to bleeding for 12 years. She had been to many doctors and spent all she had. She thought, 'if I could just touch His clothes I could be healed' so she was able to. Jesus realized power had gone out from Him, turned around and said, 'who touched me?' The woman was afraid and fell at His feet and told Him her story. Jesus said, 'daughter, your faith has healed you. Go in peace'.

Nazareth

Jesus and His disciples went to His hometown, Nazareth and began to teach in the synagogue. They were amazed but took offense at Him because to them, He was just the carpenter's son. Jesus said to them, 'Only in His hometown, among His relatives and in His own house is a prophet without honor'.

Jesus Sends Out the Twelve

Jesus sent the 12 apostles out without Him. They were to go two by two, carry no clothes, food or money and stay in one place. If they were not welcomed, they were to shake the dust off their feet there.

John the Baptist

When Herod heard about all Jesus was doing, he thought John the Baptist, that he had beheaded, had been raised from the dead. Mark also tells the story. Herod had given orders to have him arrested because Herod had married his brother Philip's wife and John had told him it was not lawful for him to have her. Herod gave a banquet on his birthday. His wife, Herodias' daughter, danced for them. Herod asked her what he could give her. She went to ask her mother what she should ask for. She said, 'the head of John the Baptist'. It was brought to her on a platter.

The disciples returned and told Jesus all they had done while they were gone. Jesus said, 'let's go to a quiet place', but that was not to be. It was later in the day and they were in a remote place. Jesus said, 'give them something to eat'. They said it would take eight months wages to feed everybody. They found five loaves and two fish. Jesus directed them to sit down on the grass and in groups of hundreds and fifties, gave thanks and fed 5,000 men.

Jesus Walks on the Water

Jesus told His disciples to get into the boat and go on ahead of Him to Bethsaida. He went up on a mountainside to pray.

The boat was in the middle of the lake. They saw someone walking on the water and thought it was a ghost. When He saw they were afraid, He said, 'Don't be afraid, it is I'.

The Pharisees had many traditions – even going beyond the Law of Moses. They couldn't understand why Jesus would eat with unwashed hands. He told them, 'Nothing outside a man can make him unclean. It is what comes *out* of a man that makes him unclean'. Things like evil thoughts, sexual immorality, theft, murder, envy, slander...The food we eat means nothing in Christianity.

Jesus left that place and went to the vicinity of Tyre (Gentile country). Even there, He couldn't find any rest. A Greek woman begged Jesus to drive out a demon from her daughter. Jesus had only been sent to the Jews first, but he healed her.

Another large crowd was following Jesus and had not eaten in three days. This time, there were 4,000 fed, with 7 loaves and a few small fish.

The 'Good Confession'

Jesus and His disciples moved on to some villages around Caesarea Philippi. He asked them, 'who do people say I am?' They replied, 'some say John the Baptist, others say Elijah, others one of the prophets'. 'What about you? Who do *you* say I am?' Peter answered, 'You are the Christ'. (Matthew says more, Matt. 16:13-19).

Jesus said, 'If anyone would come after me, He must deny himself. What good is it for a man to gain the whole world and lose his soul?'

Mark relates the story of the transfiguration of Jesus as does Matthew. Jesus told Peter, James and John not to mention it to anyone until after the resurrection. They didn't understand what this meant.

Mark tells about some of the same things Matthew wrote about: who is the greatest in the kingdom, causing little ones to sin, divorce (whatever God has joined together, let not man separate), the rich young ruler, the request of James and John to sit on His right and left hand.

At this time Jesus was teaching His disciples. He was on His way to Jerusalem, knowing what was to happen to Him there (9:30, 31).

They have now arrived in Jericho. Blind Bartimaeus was sitting by the roadside begging. When he heard Jesus was passing by, he started shouting. Jesus said, 'what do you want me to do for you?' He said, 'Rabbi, I want to see'. He was healed.

The Last Week

They approached Jerusalem. When they reached Bethpage and Bethany, Jesus sent two of His disciples to the village ahead where they would find a colt tied there. He rode it into Jerusalem. Many people spread their cloaks and tree branches for him to ride over. He went to the temple first, then to Bethany with the 12.

The next day (Monday) on His way back to the temple, He condemned the fig tree. When He arrived, He threw out the money changers and would not allow anyone to carry merchandise through the temple courts.

The next day (Tuesday), Jesus continued to teach in the temple courts. The chief priests, teachers and elders approached Him and asked, 'Who gave you the authority to do this?' This day, He spoke about the parable of the tenants, paying taxes to Caesar and marriage at the resurrection.

Jesus sat down across from where the offerings were being put. Many rich people put in large amounts, while a poor widow put in 2 very small copper coins. Jesus said she put in more than all the others because she gave all she had.

End of Jewish Dispensation Nears

As they were leaving the temple, they discussed its magnificence (this was the temple Herod had built that took 46 years, John 2:20).

Jesus said, 'Not one stone here will be left on another; everyone will be thrown down'.

When Peter, James, John and Andrew were alone with Jesus they asked Him when these things would happen and what would be the sign.

He said, 'When you see the abomination that causes desolation standing where it does not belong – let those in Judea flee to the mountains. Those days will be days of distress *unequaled* from the beginning until now…'(He was speaking of the destruction of Jerusalem and the temple that would happen in 37 years in AD 70, see Matt. 24:15 – 25).

In that same section, He speaks of the end of the world (13:26, 27 and 32-37). Men will see the Son of Man coming in clouds with great power and glory. He will send His angels and gather His elect from the four winds…

No one knows that day or hour, only the Father. Watch!

Jesus Anointed at Bethany

The Passover was two days away. The chief priests and teachers were trying to find some way to arrest and kill Jesus before the Passover. While He was in Bethany, reclining at the table in the home of Simon the Leper, a woman (Mary, see John 12:3) came and poured a very expensive perfume on His head made of pure nard. Some rebuked her but Jesus told them to leave her alone; that whenever the gospel is preached throughout the world, what she had done would be told in her memory.

Thursday (about April 14th) Jesus' disciples asked, 'where do you want us to go and make preparations for the Passover?'

He told 2 disciples, 'Go into the city. Follow a man carrying a jar of water. When he enters the house, say to the owner, "the teacher asks: Where is the guest room where I may eat the Passover with my disciples?" He'll show you a large upper room. Make preparations there'.

That evening while He was reclining at the table along with the 12, He said, 'One of you will betray me'.

While they were eating, Jesus took bread, gave thanks and broke it saying, 'Take it; this is my body'. Then He took the cup, gave thanks and they all drank from it. He said, 'this is my blood'.

He said He would not drink it again until He drank it anew in the kingdom of God.

Jesus instituted the Lord's Supper on that Thursday night, the night of His betrayal.

Leaving that place, He took Peter, James and John and went to Gethsemane to pray. His soul was overwhelmed to the point of death. He asked if it was possible, to take that cup from Him. It was not possible. It had been the plan from the beginning, to offer Himself as a sacrifice for mankind.

Soon Judas (who betrayed Him) arrived with a crowd, armed with swords and clubs and Jesus was arrested (see Matt. 26:52-56).

He was taken to the high priest. All the rulers came together although it was night. The high priest was Caiaphas.

They looked for something to accuse Him of that could be worthy of death. Finally, the high priest asked Him if He was the Christ, the Son of the Blessed One. When Jesus said He was, He said they didn't need any more witnesses, that He had spoken blasphemy.

Peter was in the courtyard warming himself. He was recognized by one of the servant girls but denied he knew Jesus three times.

Very early in the morning (Friday) the rulers had reached a decision to hand Him over to Pilate, the governor of Judea.

He also asked Jesus if He was the King of the Jews and He said yes. Other than that, He made no reply. Pilate was amazed. He tried to release Him, but to no avail. After having Him flogged, He was turned over to be crucified. He was taken to a place called Golgotha. They cast lots to see who would get His clothes.

It was the third hour (9 AM) when He was crucified. He hung on the cross six hours. Darkness came over the land from 12 noon until 3 PM, at which time He died.

The women were watching from a distance, those who followed Him and cared for His needs, even after His death.

His Burial

It was preparation day (the day before the Sabbath). Their day started at 6 PM. They had three hours to get Him from the cross and into a grave. Joseph of Arimathea asked for His body, wrapped it in linen cloth and put it in His own tomb, cut out of a rock. A stone was placed at the entrance.

After the Sabbath was over, two women brought spices to the tomb to anoint His body. When they got to the tomb, the stone was rolled away and Jesus was gone. A man in white was sitting there (an angel). 'Go tell Peter and the disciples. He is going ahead into Galilee'.

When Jesus arose, He appeared first to Mary Magdalene, then to two men walking in the country, then the eleven.

He told the disciples, 'Go into all the world and preach the good news to all creation. Whoever believes and is baptized will be saved, but whoever does not believe will be condemned...'

After He had spoken these things, He was taken up into heaven and sat at the right hand of God and the disciples went out and preached everywhere, the Lord confirming their word by signs.

Luke

A Review

Luke was written by Luke, a Greek and a doctor (Col. 4:14). He was not an eyewitness to the things Jesus did. He was a fellow-worker with Paul and was with him until the end of his life (2 Tim. 4:11). While Zechariah was carrying on his priestly duties, the angel Gabriel appeared to him and told him his wife, Elizabeth, would bear him a son. He would be filled with the Holy Spirit from birth.

He was to never drink wine or fermented drink. He was to be named John. Zechariah was unable to speak until the baby was born and he wrote down, 'His name is John'. In Elizabeth's sixth month, the angel came back to earth to Nazareth; to a virgin named Mary. She was pledged to be married to a man named Joseph, a descendant of David.

He told her she was highly favored with God. That she too would bear a son and he would be named Jesus. He said Jesus would reign over the house of Jacob forever, that his kingdom would never end. She said, 'I am the Lord's servant, may it be to me as you have said'.

Gabriel told Mary that her relative was also going to bear a son. Mary went to visit Elizabeth. When Elizabeth heard Mary's greeting, the baby leaped in her womb. Mary stayed with Elizabeth three months.

When John was born, the Lord showed her mercy. She was older (1:18). He was circumcised on the eighth day. When he grew up he lived in the desert.

Birth of Jesus

In the days of Caesar Augustus (27 BC – 14 AD) he wanted a census taken of the whole Roman world. Mary and Joseph went from Nazareth to Bethlehem (because Joseph belonged to the line of David). They went there to register. While there, Jesus was born and because there were so many people in the town, they had to place him in a manger.

There were some shepherds nearby watching over their flocks. An angel appeared to them to announce the birth. They said, 'today, in the city of David, a Savior has been born to you. He is Christ the Lord'. Then a great company of heavenly hosts appeared praising God. After they had left, the shepherds went to find Jesus.

On the eighth day, they took Him to be circumcised and named him Jesus. There were, in the temple, two people looking forward to this event; Simeon and Anna.

When Joseph and Mary had done everything required by the Law, they returned to Nazareth. Luke makes no mention of them going to Egypt (see Matt. 2:13-23).

History of Circumcision

When Abraham was 99 years old, God made a covenant with him. He would make a great nation of Abraham. He would give his descendants the land of Canaan. He would be their God and they would be His people. As a sign, every male born among them, whether born or bought, should be circumcised on the eighth day. If not, the covenant would be broken (Gen. 17:9-14)

1. Abraham circumcised Isaac on the eighth day as God had commanded (Gen. 21:4).
2. And it came to pass that on the eighth day, they came to circumcise the child; and they called him Zechariah, after the name of his father. His mother answered and said, 'Not so; he shall be called John' (Luke 1:19, 20).

3. And when eight days were accomplished for the circum-
    cising of the child, his name was called Jesus…the name
    the angel had given him (Luke 1:31).
4. The Sabbath day was s day of rest, but if the eighth day fell
    on the Sabbath, Jesus said a child could be circumcised so
    that the Law of Moses would not be broken (Jn. 7:22, 23).
5. Paul wrote that he was circumcised on the eighth day, of
    the stock of Israel, of the tribe of Benjamin, a Hebrew of
    the Hebrews; as touching the law, a Pharisee (Phil. 3:5).
6. And you are complete in Him; who is the head of every
    power and authority. In Him you were circumcised. Not
    with a circumcision done by hands, but by the putting off
    of the sins of the flesh by being buried with Him in
    baptism (Col. 2: 10, 11).
7. Circumcision was a part of the Law, but as other things in
    the Law, it is *not* in effect now.

The Boy Jesus

When Jesus was 12 years old, He went with His parents to
Jerusalem to celebrate the feast of the Passover, a yearly
celebration that lasted a week (Lev. 23:4-8). He stayed behind.
His parents returned to look for Him. After three days, they
found Him in the temple sitting among the teachers (both listening and asking questions).

He went home with His parents and was obedient to them.

John

In the fifteenth year of Tiberius Caesar, about 29 AD, John
began his ministry. He preached in the country around the
Jordan River saying, 'Repent–prepare the way for the Lord'.
Crowds came to him to be baptized, including Jesus. When
Jesus was baptized, God spoke to Him from heaven saying, 'you

are my son whom I love; with you I am well-pleased'. At this time, Jesus was about 30 years old (3:23).

After His baptism, He went to a desert where He fasted forty days and was tempted by the devil. Luke gave Jesus' genealogy all the way back to God (3:23-38).

Jesus Rejected at Nazareth

Jesus returned to His hometown, Nazareth and went to the synagogue on the Sabbath day. The scroll of Isaiah was handed to Him to read. He selected Chapter 61:1, 2. After reading it, He rolled up the scroll and sat down. He said, 'today this scrip-ture is fulfilled in your hearing'.

He returned to Capernaum, a town in Galilee, where He healed Peter's mother-in-law and many others.

One day, as He was standing by the lake, He got into Peter's boat and asked Him to pull away from the shore to teach. After He finished, He told them to put out into deep water and let down their nets for a catch.

Peter said, 'Master, we've worked hard all night and haven't caught anything, but because you say so, I will'. They caught such a large number, their nets began to break. They called for help and filled both boats. Jesus told them, 'from now on you will catch men'.

Jesus healed a leper and a paralytic and called Matthew (Levi). Matthew had a large house (5:29). One Sabbath, Jesus and His disciples went through a grain field and ate some grains (rubbing the grain in their hands and eating the kernels). The Pharisees thought this was unlawful. Jesus told them David and his companions had once eaten the consecrated bread when they were hungry (1 Sam. 21:1-6).

The Twelve Apostles

Before Jesus named His 12 apostles, He went to a mountainside and spent the night praying. When morning came, He chose 12: Simon Peter, Andrew, James, John, Philip, Bartholomew, Matthew, Thomas, James (son of Alphaeus), Simon, Judas (son of James) and Judas Iscariot.

Love Your Enemies

Jesus said to love your enemies, and do good to those who hate you, pray for those who mistreat you, give to everyone who asks, do to others as you would have them do to you, because even sinners love those who love them. He said we would be judged according to the way we judge others.

If a blind man leads a blind man, they will both fall into a pit.

Jesus met a centurion (an army commander) who had a servant he thought highly of. He asked Jesus to heal him. He told Jesus He did not need to go to his house, but just say the word. Jesus said He had not found such great faith in Israel.

The Widow's Son

Jesus went to a town called Nain. As He approached the town gate, a dead person was being carried out – the only son of a widow. Jesus' heart went out to her. He said, 'young man, I say to you, get up'. He gave him back to his mother alive.

John the Baptist was not yet in prison. He had heard about all these things Jesus was doing and sent two of his disciples to ask Him, 'Are you the one who was to come or should we expect someone else?' After this was confirmed, Jesus paid John this compliment: 'Among those born of women, there is no one greater than John; yet the one who is least in the kingdom is greater than he'

Anointed by a Sinful Woman

Jesus had been invited to dine at a Pharisee's house. When a woman, who had lived a sinful life in that town, heard of it, she brought an alabaster jar of perfume, stood behind Him; weeping and wetting his feet with her tears. Then wiped them with her hair, kissed them and poured perfume on them.

Some of the guests objected to this but Jesus said, 'her many sins have been forgiven – for she loved much. He who has been forgiven little, loves little'.

This woman was *not* Mary Magdalene, as some suppose (she had had seven demons cast out). She was already traveling about with other women who were helping to support Jesus and His disciples out of their own means (8:1-3).

After this, Jesus told two parables, the sower (whose seed fell on different kinds of ground), and a lamp put on a stand.

The crowd was great. His mother and brothers stood outside wanting to see Him. Jesus said, 'My mother and brothers are those who hear God's word and put it into practice'.

One day, Jesus said to His disciples, 'Let's go over to the other side of the lake'. He fell asleep and a squall came up. The disciples woke Him and said, 'Master, we're going to drown!'

He rebuked the wind and all was calm. They were amazed and said, 'even the winds and the waves obey Him' (Song: Peace Be Still).

When they reached the other side, there was a man there who lived in the tombs and had many demons. The demons knew who Jesus was and begged Him to go into a herd of pigs nearby. When they entered the pigs, they rushed down a steep bank into the lake and were drowned (8:26-36).

Jesus sent out the 12 disciples and gave them power to heal, going from village to village, carrying nothing for the journey.

Herod heard about all these things and wondered who it could be.

Jesus fed 5,000 men with five loaves and two fishes, with twelve baskets left over.

Peter confessed that Christ was the Son of God.

Jesus took Peter, James and John with Him upon the mountain to pray. His face changed and His clothes became bright. Moses and Elijah appeared and talked with Jesus. They talked about His departure.

After this, Jesus started preparing His disciples for his departure (9:44).

As the time approached for Him to be taken up to heaven, Jesus set out for Jerusalem. As they were walking along, a man said to Him, 'I will follow you wherever you go'. Jesus said, 'Foxes have holes and birds of the air have nests but the Son of Man has no place to lay His head'.

Another said, 'I will follow you, but first let me go back and say goodbye to my family'. Jesus told him, 'no one who puts his hand to the plow and looks back is fit for service in the kingdom of God'.

The Lord sent out 72 disciples ahead of Him, to every town He was about to pass through, two by two. Whatever house they stayed in, they were to eat and drink whatever they gave them, for the worker deserves his wages'. (This is where we get the authority to have paid preacher, etc.).

The 72 returned with joy. They said, 'even the demons submit to us in your name'. In private He told the disciples, 'Blessed are the eyes that see what you see. Many prophets and kings wanted to see what you see and hear what you hear, but did not'.

Jesus told them the story of the Good Samaritan as an example of what a good neighbor is like.

Mary and Martha

Jesus had some special friends – Mary and Martha. They opened their home to Him and His disciples. Martha was doing all the preparations and Mary was sitting at Jesus' feet. Martha went to Jesus and asked Him, 'Lord, don't you care that my sister has left me to do all the work?' He said Mary had chosen what was better.

Jesus was often leaving His disciples to go to a private place to pray. John taught his disciples to pray. They said to Jesus, 'Lord, teach us to pray'. He said:

Our Father, which art in heaven
Hallowed by thy name.
Thy kingdom come, thy will be done,
In earth as it is in heaven.
Give us this day our daily bread
And forgive us our debts as we forgive our debtors.
Lead us not into temptation but deliver us from evil.
For thine is the kingdom and the power and the glory,
forever. Amen (KJV)

Jesus gives us the name of the prince of demons: Beelzebub. Jesus said the people of that day were a wicked generation, always wanting miraculous signs, but none would be given expect the sign of Jonah. He said the Queen of the South came from the ends of the earth to listen to Solomon. We should be the light of the world. He said their outside appearance looked good, but inside they were full of greed and wickedness and neglected justice. They didn't receive this well. He said he did not come to bring peace, that families would be divided (religiously).

He said, 'When you see a cloud rising in the west you say, "it is going to rain" and when the south wind blows, you say "it's going to be hot"' (Chapter 12).

They mentioned eighteen Galileans who had died when the tower in Siloam fell on them. He said it was *not* because they were more guilty than the rest.

He told the parable of a fig tree that did not produce for three years. The owner wanted to cut it down. He said, 'why should it take up the soil?' The manager asked for one more year to dig around it, fertilize it – if that doesn't work, then cut it down (the Lord wants to give us every chance).

One Sabbath Jesus was teaching in a synagogue. A woman was there all bent over and could not straighten up for eighteen long years. Jesus healed her. Anytime He healed on the Sabbath, they condemned Him for it, considering it work.

Jesus is still on His way to Jerusalem, teaching all along the way. Someone asked him, 'Lord, are only a few going to be saved?' He said, 'make every effort to enter through the narrow door. Many will try to enter and will not be able to'.

Some Pharisees came to Jesus and told Him to go some place else that Herod (Antipas) wanted to kill Him. He told them to, 'Go tell that fox (not a complimentary term) that I will drive out demons and heal people today and tomorrow and on the third day, I will reach my goal'. This must have been Wednesday of the last week. (He was speaking of His death).

Jesus taught: when you are invited to a feast, do not take a place of honor. Everyone who exalts himself will be humbled and he who humbles himself will be exalted. (Let others honor you). Blessed is the man who will eat at the feast in the kingdom of God.

Jesus said (paraphrasing) we must love Him *more* than our father and mother, wife and children, brothers and sisters and our own life. He has to come first (14:26).

If we lose a possession in this life, we search until we find it. Jesus said there would be rejoicing in heaven when a sinner repents. He told the parable of the prodigal son to show what He meant.

A man had two sons. One wanted his share early. The father gave it to him. He went into a far country an soon spent it in wild living. He was in deep need. He came to his senses. He said my father's hired men have plenty. I'll go home and ask to be a hired man (he no longer felt worthy to be a son). Before he got home, his father saw him and ran to him. When the son said he was no longer worthy to be his son, the father called for a ring, the best robe and sandals for his feet. He said, 'this son of mine was lost and is found'. (When we're penitent and turn back to God, He forgives us now, even as He did in days gone by).

Jesus said no one can serve two masters. He also said, 'if your brother sins, rebuke him. If he repents, forgive him'.

Jesus said the Law and the prophets were proclaimed until John. He also said, 'anyone who divorces his wife and marries another woman commits adultery, and the man who marries a divorced woman commits adultery' (Matt. 5:31, 32).

The Rich Man and Lazarus

There was a rich man who lived a life of luxury, and at his gate a beggar named Lazarus lay–longing to eat his crumbs. In time, they both died. The angels carried the beggar to Abraham's side. The rich man was in torment. This rich man asked Abraham to let Lazarus dip his finger in water to cool his tongue. Abraham said a great gulf had been fixed so that neither one could cross over.

He wanted to warn his brother not to come to that place of torment. Abraham said if they would not listen to Moses and the prophets, they would not listen to one sent from the dead. (Everything has been said. There will be no new revelation).

Continuing on to Jerusalem, along the border between Samaria and Galilee, ten lepers met him and stood at a distance. They called out in a loud voice, 'Jesus, Master, have pity on us!'

He told them to go and show themselves to the priest. On their way, they were cleansed. One came back to thank Jesus and he was a Samaritan. Jesus asked, 'Where are the other nine?' (Only a small percentage are thankful).

Description of the Last Day

Jesus said His kingdom would not be a visible kingdom, because He reigns *within* us, but first He must suffer many things and be rejected. Once He ascended to heaven, He would not be seen again until the end.

He said His return would be like the lightning that lights up the sky from one end to the other. (Everyone will see him). He said it would be like in the days of Noah – an ordinary day, without warning.

Jesus Again Predicts His Death

We are going up to Jerusalem. Everything written by the prophets about the Son of Man will be fulfilled.

He will be handed over to the Gentiles. They will mock Him, insult Him, spit on Him, flog Him and kill Him. On the third day, He will rise again.

Near Jericho a blind man was sitting by the road begging. He heard a crowd going by and asked what was happening. When told it was Jesus of Nazareth, he started calling out to Him. Mark said his name was Bartimaeus (Mark 10:46).

Zacchaeus

A tax collector named Zacchaeus lived in Jericho. He was short, so he climbed up in a sycamore tree so he could see. When Jesus reached that spot he said, 'Zaccheaus, come down. I must stay at your house today'.

Zacchaeus said, 'Here and now I give (present tense) half of my possessions to the poor. If I have cheated anybody out of anything, I will pay back four times the amount (Ex. 22:1)'. Jesus said, 'Today salvation has come to this house. This man too, is a son of Abraham'. (As are all believers)

The Triumphal Entry

As they neared Jerusalem, Jesus sent two disciples to get a colt, tied up and having never been ridden. The owner asked, 'Why are you untying the colt?' They replied, 'The Lord needs it'.

They put cloaks on the road and on the colt. The crowd began to praise the Lord saying, 'Blessed is the King who comes in the name of the Lord'.

When He approached the city He wept over it. He said, 'the days will come when your enemies will build an embankment, circle you and hem you in on every side... because you did not recognize the time of God's coming to you'. (He was referring to the fall of Jerusalem in 70 AD).

Every day after that (Monday through Thursday) He taught in the temple. One day the rulers asked Him who gave Him authority to do what He was doing. He didn't tell them. He knew if they didn't respect the prophets, they wouldn't respect the Son.

He told them things would be different after the resurrection. We will not marry, we will not die. We will be like the angels.

Satan entered Judas before the Last Supper and he agreed to betray Jesus.

On Thursday night it was the Passover and they ate it together in a large upper room. He told them this was the last one He would eat with them. He instituted the Lord's Supper in memory of Him. He took the bread, broke it and gave it to them. He said, 'This is my body given for you; do this in remembrance of Me'.

After supper, He took the cup saying. 'this is the New Covenant in my blood'.

He told them they had stood by Him in His trials. He told Simon (Peter), Satan had asked to sift Him as wheat, but He had prayed for him.

Jesus left the upper room and went to the Mount of Olives to pray. He prayed this:

Father, if you are willing, take this cup from me;
yet not my will, but yours be done.

An angel from heaven appeared to Him and strengthened Him. His sweat was like drops of blood falling to the ground.

Jesus Arrested

A crowd arrived with Judas leading them. He approached Jesus to kiss Him, but Jesus asked him, 'Judas, are you betraying the Son of Man with a kiss?'

Peter, who had a sword, struck the servant of the high priest (Malcus) and cut off his right ear. Jesus touched the man's ear and healed him.

Peter followed at a distance. A servant girl recognized him, but he denied knowing Jesus three times as predicted.

At day break (Friday morning), Jesus was taken before the council and admitted to being the Son of God. They then carried Him to Pilate and said, 'This man claims to be Christ, a king'.

Pilate said, 'Are you?' Jesus said, 'yes'. Pilate said he found no basis for a charge against Him and sent Him to Herod who was in Jerusalem for the feast of Passover.

When Herod saw Jesus, he was pleased because he'd been wanting to see Him perform a miracle. He asked Jesus many questions, but got no answers.

That day, Herod and Pilate became friends – before this they had been enemies.

Pilate tried to dissuade the crowd three times. As they led Him away, a large number of people followed, including women who were mourning and wailing. Jesus told them not to weep for Him.

There was a written notice above Him as He hung on the cross. It read: *This is the King of the Jews.* Luke recorded three statements Jesus made on the cross (He made more).

1. Father, forgive them for they do not know what they are doing (the people).
2. I tell you the truth, today you will be with me in paradise (to the thief).
3. Father, into your hands I commit my spirit (to God the Father).

Jesus' Burial

Joseph, a member of the council, asked Pilot for the body and buried Jesus in his own tomb (before 6 PM because the Sabbath began at that time). The women went home, prepared spices but rested on the Sabbath as they were still living under the Law of Moses. Early on the first day of the week (Sunday) they took the spices they had prepared and went to the tomb. When they got there, the stone was rolled away and the tomb was empty. Two men in shiny clothes stood beside them.

They said, 'why do you look for the living among the dead? He is not here *He has risen!'*

Remember how He told you while He was still with you in Galilee: 'The Son of Man *must* be delivered into the hands of sinful men, be crucified and on the third day be raised again'.

Then they remembered. The women were Mary Magdalene, Joanna, Mary the mother of James, and others. They told the apostles, but they did not believe them. Peter got up and ran to the tomb (Luke omits John), wondering what happened.

That same day, Jesus joined Himself to some men going to Emmaus. They were talking about what had happened the past few days. When Jesus joined them, He questioned them and they told Him what had happened.

Beginning with Moses and all the prophets, He explained to them what the scriptures had said. It was nearly evening so they invited Jesus to stay with them.

While He was at the table with them, He took bread, gave thanks, broke it and began to give it to them. Then their eyes were opened and they recognized Him. He disappeared from their sight.

They got up, found the eleven and told them what had happened. While they were still talking, Jesus himself stood among them. He said, 'peace be with you'.

They were startled, but He showed them His hands and feet. He said a ghost does not have flesh and bones. Then He asked if they had anything to eat and they gave Him a piece of broiled fish.

He opened their minds so that they could understand the scriptures. He said, 'This is what is written:

The Christ will suffer and rise from the dead on the third day. Repentance and forgiveness of sins will be preached in His name to all nations, beginning in Jerusalem'.

He told them He would be sending them what His father promised, but to stay in the city until that power came (Acts1:3).

The Ascension

They went out in the vicinity of Bethany. He lifted up His hands and blessed them and was taken up into heaven.

They returned to Jerusalem, staying continually in the temple, praising God.

John

A Review

The apostle John wrote the gospel of John, 1, 2, 3 John and Revelation. John and James were brothers. Jesus called them the 'Sons of Thunder' (Mark 3:17). Their father was Zebedee. They were fisherman with him (Matt. 4:18-22). Their mother was also a follower of Jesus (Matt. 27:56). John called himself the disciple Jesus loved (19:15-57).

Herod killed his brother James early on. John referred to Jesus as the word and the light. He was with God from the beginning. Without him, nothing was made that has been made.

This word became flesh and dwelt among us. No one has seen God, except through His son.

When John the Baptist came baptizing, they were trying to find out who he was. He said, 'I am the voice of one calling in the desert. Make straight the way for the Lord'.

When John saw Jesus coming to him for baptism he said, 'Look, the Lamb of God, who takes away the sin of the world'.

Even though they were kin, John said he would not have known him except that the one who sent me to baptize with water told me, 'The man on whom you see the spirit come down and remain is he who will baptize with the Holy Spirit. I have seen and I testify that this is the Son of God'.

Andrew and John were disciples of John the Baptist, but when they heard him say, 'Look, the Lamb of God!' they started following Jesus.

Andrew found his brother, Peter, and said, 'we have found the Messiah'.

On the third day after His ministry began, Jesus went to a wedding in Cana of Galilee. The wine ran out. Jesus' mother told Him, 'They have no more wine'. Jesus replied, 'My time has not yet come'. Evidently she knew something others didn't. Anyway, Jesus worked His first miracle, that of turning water into wine.

When it was almost time for the Jewish Passover (His first after starting his ministry) Jesus went to Jerusalem (2:13).

In the temple courts He saw men selling cattle and exchanging money. He made a whip out of cords and drove all out from the temple area, scattered the coins and overturned the tables. (This was His first time to do this).

Many people saw His miraculous signs and believed in Him (John calls His miracles 'signs').

A man named Nicodemus (a member of the Jewish ruling council) came to Jesus at night.

He said, 'Rabbi, we know you are a teacher come from God. No one could do these things if God were not with him'.

Jesus told him, 'no one can see the kingdom of God unless he is born again'. Nicodemus said, 'how can a man be born when he is old?' Jesus said he must be born of water and the spirit.

Jesus said, 'for God so loved the world that He gave His only begotten son, that whosoever believes in Him shall not perish but have eternal life. God did not send His son to condemn the world, but to save the world'.

John had moved into the Judean countryside and was baptizing at Aenon near Salim. Some came to him and said, 'that man you testified about on the other side of the Jordan is baptizing and everybody is going to Him'. John said, 'I told you I am not the Christ, but I was sent ahead of Him. He must become greater, I must become less'. It was not Jesus who baptized, but His disciples (4:2).

Jesus was tired and was resting by Jacob's well in Samaria while His disciples went into town to buy food. A Samaritan woman came to the well to draw water and Jesus asked for a drink. She said, 'you are a Jew and I am a Samaritan'. (Jews did not associate with Samaritans).

Jesus told her she had had five husbands and the man you have now is not your husband. She told Him she could see He was a prophet. She told Jesus she knew the Messiah, called Christ, was coming. Jesus told her *He* was the Christ. The disciples were surprised to see Him talking with the woman. She left her water jar, went back and told the people, 'come see a man who told me everything I ever did'. They followed her. He stayed there two days and many became believers.

After this, He went to Galilee and visited Cana where He healed a child of fever. This was His second miracle in Galilee (4:54).

Jesus went to Jerusalem to another feast (probably Pentecost, 50 days after Passover). There was a pool near the sheep gate named Bethesda. A number of disabled people used to lie around it waiting for the stirring of the water. (From time to time an angel would come down and stir up the water. The first one into the pool would be cured). He had been an invalid for 38 years. He said while he was trying to get in someone goes ahead of him (5:1-9). Jesus said, 'Get up, pick up your mat and walk'.

When Jesus would heal on the Sabbath, the Jews would persecute him. He said, 'my Father works, and I too am working'. They said, 'not only is He breaking the Sabbath but He is even calling God His father'. He said, 'By myself I can do nothing. I seek not to please myself but Him who sent me. I have come in my Father's name'.

The Jewish Passover was near and there were big crowds there. (This is His 2nd Passover since starting His ministry). This is also the time period when He fed the 5,000 and walked across the lake on the water. When they found Him on the other side of the lake they said, 'when did you get here?'

Sometimes it was hard to know what Jesus was talking about like this: I am the bread of life; He who comes to me will never thirst. I have come down from heaven not to do my will, but to do the will of Him who sent me. They said, 'is this not Jesus, the son of Joseph, whose father and mother we know?' (His father was alive at this time).

Upon hearing many of His hard teachings, some disciples turned away from following Him. Jesus asked the 12, 'Do you want to leave too?' Peter answered, 'Lord, to whom shall we go? You have the words to eternal life'.

Jesus' own brothers did not believe Him to be the Christ at this time, but later did (James and Jude, 7:5).

Jesus said, 'I am with you for only a short time, and then I go to the One who sent me. You will look for me but you will not find me. And where I am you cannot come'. (They couldn't figure this out either). We know, after the fact, that He ascended back to heaven.

The guards of the temple said, 'no one ever spoke the way this man does' (7:46).

Early the next morning Jesus went back to the temple courts. The rulers brought in a woman caught in adultery. 'Moses commanded us to stone such women. What do you say?'

Jesus bent down and started writing on the ground. He said, 'if any one of you is without sin, let him be the first to throw a stone'. They began to leave one by one. He asked her, 'has no one condemned you?' She said, 'no one sir'. 'Then neither do I; go and leave your life of sin'.

Jesus said He was the light of the world. Whoever followed Him would never walk in darkness. Christians are also the light of the world. Even children sing, This Little Light of Mine. (Matthew 5:14)

Jesus said, 'you will know the truth and the truth will set you free. If the Son sets you free, you will be free indeed'.

Some more things Jesus said were hard for them to understand: If anyone keeps my word, he will never see death and, before Abraham was born I am (8:51, 58).

John wrote the whole ninth Chapter about a man born blind. Some thought he was blind because of sin. In this case, Jesus said it happened so that the work of God might be displayed in his life.

Jesus spit on the ground, made some mud, put it on the man's eyes and told him to go wash in the pool of Siloom. This was on a Sabbath and the Pharisees investigated, trying to find out who healed him. Unable to, they sent for his parents. They said, 'ask him, he is of age'. They sent for the man again. He said, 'one thing I know: I was blind but now I see'.

'We know that God does not listen to sinners. He listens to a Godly man who does His will'. They threw him out. When Jesus heard about this, He appeared to Him and revealed who He was.

The Good Shepherd

Jesus said He was the good shepherd. The good shepherd lays down his life for his sheep. They know his voice and will not follow a stranger. (Do we know His voice?)

He said He had other sheep – that He must bring them also (He was referring to the Gentiles).

The Death of Lazarus

Lazarus lay sick. Mary and Martha sent word to Jesus saying, 'Lord, the one you love is sick'. He waited two days then said to His disciples, 'Let us go back to Judea'. They reminded Him the Jews had tried to stone Him there (10:31-33).

He told them Lazarus was dead. 'Let us go to him'. When He arrived, Lazarus had been in the tomb four days. Bethany, where they lived, was less than two miles from Jerusalem and many Jews had come to comfort Mary and Martha.

Martha went to meet Jesus. She said, 'Lord, if you had been here my brother would not have died'.

Jesus said, 'Your brother will rise again'.

Martha said, 'I know he will rise in the resurrection'. Martha went inside and told her sister, 'the Teacher is here and is asking for you'. Mary got up quickly and went to meet Him. She fell at His feet and said, 'Lord, if you had been here my brother would not have died'.

Jesus said, 'where have you laid him?' Jesus wept (John 11:35). When they got to the tomb, Jesus said, 'Take away the stone'.

Martha said, 'by this time, there is a bad odor'.

Jesus said, 'did I not tell you that if you believed, you would see the glory of God?' He called out in a loud voice, 'Lazarus, come out!'

He came out with his burial clothes on him. Jesus said, 'Loose him and let him go' (KJV).

The Pharisees called a meeting. They said, 'If we let him go on like this, everyone will believe in Him. The Romans will take away our place and nation'.

Caiaphas, the high priest, spoke up. 'It is better for one man to die for the people than the whole nation to perish'.

From that day on, they plotted to take Jesus' life. Jesus withdrew from the public and went to a place called Ephraim near the desert.

It was about time for the Passover (His third). People were wondering if he would come. The chief priests had given orders if anyone found out where he was to report it, so they could arrest Him.

Jesus Anointed at Bethany

Six days before the Passover, Jesus arrived at Bethany at the home of Lazarus, Mary and Martha. A dinner was being given in his honor. Martha served, Lazarus reclined at the table with Jesus and Mary took about a pint of pure nard (an expensive perfume) and poured it on Jesus' feet and wiped His feet with her hair. Judas Iscariot objected. He said, 'why wasn't this perfume sold and the money given to the poor?' It was worth a year's wages.

John said Judas didn't say this because he cared for the poor but because he was a thief. He kept the money bag and used to help himself to what was put into it.

Jesus said, 'you will always have the poor among you, but you will *not* always have me'.

Jesus made His triumphant entry into Jerusalem riding on a young colt. It had not been long since Lazarus was raised and the word was traveling fast. Some Greeks had come to the Passover feast. They came to Philip and said, 'Sir, we would like to see Jesus'.

Jesus said, 'The hour has come for the Son of Man to be glorified'.

Jesus observed three Passovers:
2:13 (about a week into His ministry)
6:4 (1 year later)
13:1 (last)

Many, even after seeing or hearing about all these miraculous signs, still did not believe.

Many leaders believed but would not confess for fear they would be put out of the synagogues.

Jesus said, 'when a man believes in me, he also believes in the one who sent me'. He said He spoke what the Father commanded Him to say.

Jesus Washes His Disciple's Feet

It is now Thursday, just before the Passover feast. The evening meal was being served. Judas had already agreed to betray Jesus.

Jesus took off His outer clothing and wrapped a towel around His waist. He poured water into a basin and began to wash the disciples' feet, drying them with the towel. Peter didn't want Him to wash his feet but consented when Jesus said, 'unless I wash your feet, you have no part with me'.

As they were eating, Jesus said, 'he who shared my bread, has lifted up his heel against me'. When they asked who it was, He said, 'the one I give this piece of bread to, when I have dipped it in the dish'.

He told Judas, 'what you are about to do, do quickly'. (Some thought He was telling Judas to buy something for the feast, or to give to the poor). As soon as Judas had taken the bread, he went out and it was night.

After Judas left, Jesus said to His disciples 'my children, I will be with you only a little longer. Where I am going, you cannot come. A new commandment I give you: Love one another. By this, all men will know that you are my disciples, if you love one another.

I go to prepare a place for you. I will come back and take you to be with me that you also may be where I am... No one comes to the Father except through me'.

The Holy Spirit

'I will ask the Father and He will give you another counselor, to be with you forever–the Spirit of Truth. The Counselor, the Holy Spirit, whom the Father will send in my name, will teach you all things and will remind you of everything I have said to you'.

The Vine and the Branches

Jesus is the vine and we are the branches. If a branch is cut off, it can bear no fruit. We must be 'in' the vine (the church).

The World Will Hate Us

'If the world hates you, keep in mind that it hated me first. If they persecute you – they persecuted me also. They hated me without a reason. When the Spirit of truth comes to you, you must testify, for you have been with me from the beginning. A time will come when anyone who kills you, will think he is offering a service to God. It is for your good that I am going away. Unless I go, the Counselor will not come'.

Grief Will Turn to Joy

'You will weep and mourn while the world rejoices. A time is coming when you will be scattered. You will leave me all alone, but my Father will be with me. In the world you will have trouble, but take heart! I have overcome the world'.

The whole seventeenth Chapter is a prayer Jesus prayed before His apostles. He said He had brought His Father glory on earth by completing the work He gave Him to do, He had revealed God to those He gave Him. None had been lost, except the one doomed to destruction (Judas). He asked God to protect the apostles from the evil one (Satan). His prayer was not for them alone, but also for those who would believe in Him through their message. He prayed that they would all be one as He and His Father were one. He wanted the apostles to be with Him and see His glory.

Jesus Arrested

Jesus and His disciples went to the garden of Gethsemane (Mark 14:32). John doesn't name the place.

Judas rightly guessed where He would be, as He went there often. He brought a crowd armed with torches, lanterns and weapons.

Jesus went out and asked them, 'who is it you want?' They said, 'Jesus of Nazareth'.

Peter drew his sword and cut off the ear of the high priest's servant. Jesus commanded Peter, 'put your sword away!'

The first one they brought Him to was Annas, the father-in-law of Caiaphas, so he went with Jesus into the courtyard, but Peter had to wait outside. After John spoke to the girl on duty, they let Peter in. She asked him if he was one of the disciples and he denied it as he stood by the fire, warming himself.

Jesus Questioned

The high priest questioned Jesus about His disciples and His teaching. He said He had spoken openly and in synagogues and the temple, where the Jews came together. 'Why question me? Ask those who heard me'.

One of the officials struck Him in the face. He said, 'Is this the way you answer the high priest?'

Annas sent Him to Caiaphas, then early Friday morning to the Roman governor, Pilate. He told them to judge Him by their laws. They said they had no right to execute anyone (they stoned).

Pilate personally questioned Jesus. He asked Him if He was the King of the Jews and what He had done. Jesus told him His kingdom was not of this world.

Pilate went out and told them He had no basis for a charge against Him. They always released a prisoner at the time of Passover. They didn't want Jesus released and asked for Barabbas. Pilate took Jesus and had Him flogged. Twice more, Pilate told them he found no basis for a charge against Him but finally handed Him over to them to be crucified. The sixth hour spoken of in 19:14 was Roman time (6 AM). He was crucified at 9AM (Mark 15:25) and hung on the cross until 3 PM (Mark 15:34-37). It took six hours.

Pilate had a sign written in Aramaic, Latin and Greek. It read: *Jesus of Nazareth, the King of the Jews.* The chief priests objected, but Pilate answered, 'what I have written, I have written'.

Luke recorded three things Jesus said on the cross. John records four more:
1. Dear woman, here is your son (to Mary)
2. Here is you mother (to John). He took her to his home
3. I am thirsty
4. It is finished

The next day was a special Sabbath. It was also Passover. The Passover went by the day of the month and sometimes fell on Saturday. They wanted them down from the cross before 6 PM because their day started then.

They went to break their legs (to hasten their death) but Jesus was already dead, so they pierced His side. This fulfilled the scripture that not one of His bones would be broken (Ps. 34:20).

Joseph of Arimathea asked Pilate for His body, accompanied by Nicodemus. They brought about 75 pounds of spices and wrapped His body using the spices and strips of linen. He was buried in a new tomb in a nearby garden.

The Empty Tomb

Early on the first day of the week, Mary Magdalene (John makes no mention of the other women or their spices) went to the tomb and found the stone removed. She came running to Peter and John. She said, 'they have taken the Lord out of the tomb and we don't know where they have put Him'. John outran Peter and reached the tomb first. He saw the strips of linen, but did not go in. Peter went in. The burial cloth that was around Jesus' head was folded by itself, separate from the linen.

The disciples went back to their homes, but Mary stood outside crying. She bent over to look inside and saw two angels seated where Jesus' body had been. They asked her why she was crying. She said, 'they have taken my Lord away and I don't know where they have put Him'.

As she turned around, she saw Jesus but did not realize it was Him until He said, 'Mary'.

He told her He had not yet returned to the Father. 'Go to my brothers and tell them I am returning to my Father and your Father, to my God and your God'.

She went and told the disciples, 'I have seen the Lord!'

That evening the disciples were together with the door locked. Jesus came and stood among them saying, 'peace be with you'. He showed them His hands and side. They were overjoyed.

Thomas was not with the rest. When they told him, he said he would not believe it until he had put his finger where the nails were. A week later, the Lord came back and told Thomas to do this. He didn't need to. That's why he's known as 'doubting Thomas'. Jesus told him, 'Because you have seen me, you believe. Blessed are those who have *not* seen and yet have believed'. John said the things recorded in this book (of John) were written that we may believe that Jesus Christ is the Son of God.

Later, Jesus appeared to seven people who had gone fishing in the Sea of Galilee at night. Again, they caught nothing. Early the next morning, Jesus stood on the shore and called out to them, asking if they had no fish. They answered no. He told them to throw out their nets on the right side and they would find some. When they caught a large number, as before, they realized it was the Lord. Peter jumped into the water (he couldn't wait).

When they landed, they saw a fire of burning coals with fish on it and some bread. The boat was full of large fish (153). Jesus said, 'come and have breakfast'. This was his third time to appear to them after His resurrection.

When they had finished eating, Jesus asked Peter, 'do you truly love me more than these?' He said, 'Yes, Lord. You know that I love you'. Jesus said, 'Feed my lambs'. He asked this three times.

Jesus told Peter, 'when you are old you will stretch out your hands and someone else will dress you and lead you where you do not want to go'. (This was to indicate what kind of death Peter would glorify God).

Peter saw the disciple Jesus loved following and said, 'Lord, what about him?'

Jesus said, 'If I want him to remain alive until I return what is that to you?'

John said Jesus did many other things, that if they were written down he supposed the whole world couldn't hold them. These four gospels are very similar but it takes all four to get the full picture of Jesus' ministry.

Ex: John writes nothing about Jesus' ascension.

Acts

A Review

Acts was written by Luke, not an apostle but a fellow worker with Paul. He was called 'the beloved physician' (Col. 4:14). He also wrote Luke. He referred to himself as 'we' to indicate his presence when things happened. As a doctor, he was granted a Roman citizenship. Luke was with Paul during his two year imprisonment in Rome (Acts 28:16). In Paul's letter he wrote: Only Luke is with me (2 Timothy 4:11).

Luke relates events that happened before Christ's death in his gospel and after his death in Acts (the spread of the gospel).

The book centers mostly around two of the apostles. The first 12 Chapters are about Peter and the remaining 16 Chapters are about Paul (mostly).

After Jesus' resurrection, He had appeared to His followers over a period of 40 days. He told them not to leave Jerusalem.

The Passover Feast and the Pentecost (when Jews would again come to Jerusalem) were 50 days apart (Lev. 23:15, 16).

This was the time Jesus picked to establish His church. Peter had previously been given the 'keys to the kingdom' after his confession that Jesus was the Son of God (Matt. 16:17-19).

On the day of Pentecost, the apostles were all in one place. Suddenly the sound of a mighty wind came from heaven and what seemed to be tongues of fire came to rest on each of them. They began to speak in tongues (languages). The people all heard in their own language. At that time there were Jews there from 15 nations, every nation under heaven (2:5).

Peter rose up and spoke: He told them this was what the prophet Joel had written about (Joel 2:28-32). He said this same Jesus they had crucified was the Christ (Acts 2:36).

They were cut to the heart and asked what they could do. Peter told them to repent and be baptized in the name of Jesus Christ for the remission of their sins and they would receive the gift of the Holy Spirit. The promise was to them, their children and *all* who were far off – all whom the Lord would call (Acts 2:38).

About 3,000 believed that day and were added to their number. Later it had grown to 5,000 (4:4).

Sprit

When God formed Adam (man) from the dust of the earth, He breathed into him 'spirit' or life. When we die, the spirit returns to God who gave it, and we are but a lifeless form (Eccl. 12:7, 1 Cor. 5:3).

When we are baptized, we receive the gift of the Holy Spirit, that is, we have a new spirit of love, joy, hope, etc. (Not a sinful spirit, Rom. 8:2-9, I Cor. 2:12).

The apostles, on the day of Pentecost, received a much greater measure. All the things Jesus had been teaching them were brought to their remembrance and they understood it all (Acts 2:4, 1 Cor. 2:10-16). They were able to work miracles as He had done (Acts 3:6).

The apostles could pass this ability on to others, but after their death, there is no record of anyone else being able to do this (2 Timothy 1:6).

The Holy Spirit is the third person of the 'Godhead' – God, Jesus and the Holy Spirit, who work as a team (one) in heaven (John 4:24, Rom. 8:26, Matt. 28:19).

Old Testament

Certain people in the Old Testament also received the Holy Spirit at times. (Jud. 6:34, Isa. 61:6, 1 Sam. 16:13, Lu. 4:18; the New Testament did not start until the day of Pentecost, Acts 2).

The Fellowship of Believers

They devoted themselves to the apostle's teaching, to fellowship, to breaking of bread and prayer. The believers were together and had everything in common. The Lord added to their number daily those who were being saved.

One day as Peter and John were going to the temple, a crippled man was being carried to the gate called Beautiful to beg. He asked them for money. Peter said, 'look at us. Silver and gold I do not have, but what I have I give you. In the name of Jesus Christ of Nazareth, walk'. Instantly, the man began to walk. The people were astonished.

Peter Speaks Again

People came running to them in a place called Solomon's Colonnade. Peter said, 'why does this surprise you so, as though it was by our own power we made this man walk? It was by faith in the name of Jesus – the one you handed over to be killed (though Pilate had decided to let Him go). You killed Him, but God raised Him from the dead. We are witnesses of this. I know you acted in ignorance, but God fulfilled what had been foretold through all the prophets'.

Before the Sanhedrin

The rulers were disturbed because Peter and John were proclaiming the resurrection and put them in jail overnight. The next day they asked them (in front of a lot of rulers), 'by what power or name did you do this?'

Peter said, 'It is by the name of Jesus Christ of Nazareth, whom you crucified but whom God raised from death, that this man stands before you healed'. There was no denying the man had been healed so they told them not to speak anymore in the name of Jesus. They said, 'we cannot help speaking about what we have seen and heard'.

After this, they went back to their own people and prayed. The place was shaken; they were filled with the Holy Spirit and spoke boldly.

Shared Possessions

The believers were of one heart and mind, no needy persons among them. From time to time, those who owned houses or land sold them and brought the money to the apostles. One that did this was Barnabas. A man and wife named Ananias and Sapphira sold a piece of property, kept back part of the money and brought the rest to the apostles. They must have pretended they gave all, because Peter said, 'didn't it belong to you, and wasn't the money at your disposal? You have lied to God'. He fell down dead. Three hours later, his wife came in and verified his story. She too fell down dead. Great fear seized the whole church. (Even though Jesus was in heaven, He knew what was going on on earth.

The apostles continued to heal people as Jesus had and more and more men and women believed. The streets were filled with people wanting to be healed.

Jailed Again

Again the rulers put the apostles in the public jail, but during the night an angel opened the door and brought them out.

He told them to go to the temple courts and tell the people the full message of this new life.

The next morning when the rulers went to the jail, they found it locked with the guards at the door, but the apostles were gone. They found them in the temple courts teaching.

They said, 'we gave you strict orders not to teach, yet you have filled Jerusalem with your teaching and are determined to make us guilty of this man's blood'.

Peter said, 'we must obey God rather than men'. Gamaliel, a teacher of the law who was honored by the people, asked that the men be put outside. He addressed the rulers, 'men of Israel, consider carefully what you intend to do to these men. Other men have claimed to be somebody and it came to nothing. If this activity is of human origin, it will come to nothing, but if it is from God, you will not be able to stop them; you will only find yourselves fighting against God'.

This speech persuaded them. They had them flogged, ordered them to quit speaking and let them go. They never stopped.

The Choosing of the Seven

The apostles were like Moses, they needed some help (see Ex. 18:13-26). The number of disciples was increasing and taking a lot of the apostles' time to see to the daily distribution of food. The apostles told the brothers to choose 7 men from among them, who were full of the Spirit and wisdom to attend to this, leaving the apostles time to devote to prayer and the ministry.

They chose Stephen, Philip, Procorus, Nicamar, Timon, Parmenas and Nicolas from Antioch (a convert to Judaism). The apostles prayed and laid their hands on them.

A large number of priests became obedient to the faith.

Stephen Seized

Stephen, one of the seven did great wonders and signs among the people. Some men who were not from Jerusalem began arguing with Stephen, but were not able to stand up against his wisdom. They brought him before the Sanhedrin and said, 'this fellow never stops speaking against this holy place and the law. We have heard him say this Jesus of Nazareth will destroy this place and change the customs Moses handed down to us'.

The high priest asked him if the charges were true. Stephen started with the call of Abraham and reviewed the *entire* history of the Jews (Chapter 7). He said, 'you are just like your fathers: you always resist the Holy Spirit! Was there ever a prophet your fathers did not persecute? Now you have betrayed and killed the righteous one and murdered Him'.

When they heard this, they were furious and gnashed their teeth. Stephen looked up to heaven and saw the glory of God and Jesus standing at His right hand. When he told them this, they covered their ears and yelled at the top of their voices.

They dragged him out of the city and began to stone him, laying their clothes at the feet of a young man name Saul.

The Church Persecuted

On that day, a great persecution broke out against the church at Jerusalem, and they were scattered (except the apostles). Some went to Samaria. Philip went there and proclaimed the Christ and healed. There was great joy in that city.

There was a man there named Simon who practiced sorcery. When he heard Philip, he believed and was baptized. When the apostles in Jerusalem heard that Samaria had accepted the word of God, they sent Peter and John to impart the Holy Spirit. When Simon saw that the Spirit was given by the laying on of the apostle's hands, he offered them money to give him this ability. Peter said to him, 'may your money perish with you, because you thought you could buy the gift of God. Repent and pray. Perhaps he will forgive you'.

Simon said, 'Pray to the Lord for me'.

Philip and the Eunuch

An angel of the Lord told Philip to go south to the road that went from Jerusalem to Gaza. He met an Ethiopian eunuch, an important official of Candace, their queen. He had been to Jerusalem to worship. (He must have been a convert of the Law of Moses). He was on his way home and was reading in the book of Isaiah. Philip ran up to him and asked him if he understood what he was reading. He said, 'how can I unless someone explains it to me?' He invited Philip to come up and sit with him in his chariot. The scripture was Isaiah 53:7, 8

'He was led like a sheep to the slaughter, and as a lamb before the shearers is silent, so He did not open His mouth.
In His humiliation He was deprived of justice. Who can speak of His descendants? For His life was taken from the earth'.

Peter began with that scripture and taught him about Jesus. At that exact moment, the eunuch said, 'look, here is water, what doth hinder me to be baptized?' (KJV). Philip said, 'If you believe with all your heart you may'. He answered, 'I believe that Jesus Christ is the Son of God'.

He gave orders to stop the chariot. Both he and Philip went down into the water and Philip baptized him. The Spirit caught Philip away and the eunuch went on his way rejoicing. Philip found himself at Azotus and continued preaching in the towns until he reached his own home in Caesarea (see 21:8).

Saul's Conversion

Because of the great persecution, after the stoning of Stephen, many disciples fled to Damascus (150 miles away).

Saul went to the high priest and asked for letters to take to the synagogues in Damascus so that, if he found any there who belonged to the Way, he could bring them back to Jerusalem as prisoners. As he drew near Damascus, suddenly a bright light from heaven flashed around him. A voice said, 'Saul, Saul, why do you persecute me?' Saul asked, 'who are you, Lord?' 'I am Jesus, whom you are persecuting. Go into the city and it will be told you what you must do'. Saul was struck blind. They had led him to the house of Judas on the street called Straight. For 3 days he was blind, did not eat or drink and continued in prayer.

Ananias was told, in a vision, to go to him and restore his sight. Ananias had heard about Saul and the harm he had done, but when the Lord told him Saul was a chosen vessel, he went.

Something like scales fell from his eyes. He was baptized and ate some food. At once he began to preach in the synagogues of Damascus. The ones who heard him were astonished. Galatians 1:7, 8 says he did not go to Jerusalem until after three years. The church enjoyed a time of peace and grew.

In Joppa there was a disciple names Dorcas who was always doing good and helping the poor, but she became sick and died. When the disciples heard Peter was in a town nearby, they sent for him. She was laid out in an upstairs room. When Peter arrived the widows stood around him crying and showing him clothing she had made for them. He sent them out of the room and got down on his knees and prayed. He said, 'Tabitha (Dorcas) get up'. She opened her eyes and he took her by the hand and presented her alive. It caused many other people to believe. He stayed in Joppa for some time with a tanner named Simon.

Cornelius

While Peter was there, a centurion named Cornelius had a vision. He was a good God-fearing and benevolent man. He was told to send men to Joppa and bring back a man called Peter. He was staying with Simon the tanner, whose house was by the sea.

During the meantime, Peter also had a vision. He had gone up on the roof to pray. He became hungry but while the meal was being prepared, he fell into a trance. He saw a large sheet being let down to earth with all kinds of unclean animals in it. A voice said, 'Get up Peter, kill and eat'. Peter said he had never eaten anything unclean (see Lev. 11). They voice said, 'do not call anything impure that God has made clean'. This happened three times.

While Peter was still thinking about the vision, the men Cornelius had sent arrived. The Spirit told Peter to go with them. Peter invited them in and the next day they left for Caesarea, where Cornelius lived. Some of the brothers went along. When they arrived, they found a large number of people gathered to hear what Peter had to say. First, he said it was against the Jewish law to visit or associate with a Gentile, but God had shown him that he should not call any man impure or unclean (or animals either).

Peter said he realized that God accepts men from every nation, who fear him and do what is right. He told them about John the Baptist, how God had anointed Jesus with the Holy Spirit and how He had gone about doing good, how they had killed Him, how He had been raised the third day, how He had commanded His disciples to continue to preach that everyone who believes in Him receives forgiveness of sins through His name.

While Peter was still speaking, the Holy Spirit came on all who heard. The people who had come with Peter were astonished that the Holy Spirit was poured out even on the Gentiles.

Peter said, 'can anyone forbid these people from being baptized that have received the Holy Spirit, just as we have?'

Peter Explains

When the Jewish brothers heard that the Gentiles had received the word, they criticized Peter. Peter related all that had happened and that six brothers had also gone with him. He said, 'who was I to oppose God?' After hearing him out, there were no further objections and they praised God. Peter had the 'key to the kingdom' to the Gentiles also.

Antioch

Another place Christians went to after the stoning of Stephen was Antioch. At first they taught the Jews only, then some men came and preached to the Greeks also and a great number believed.

This reached the ears of the church in Jerusalem and they send Barnabas to Antioch. Now, Barnabas was one who sold a field to help feed the early church and also brought Saul to the apostles and told them of his conversion when he first returned to Jerusalem (4:34-37, 9:26-27). Barnabas went to Tarsus to look for Saul. He brought him to Antioch where they worked together for a full year. The disciples were called Christians first at Antioch. (Isaiah said in 62:2 'you will be called by a new name that the mouth of the Lord will bestow').

Some prophets came from Jerusalem to Antioch. Through the Spirit, they predicted a severe famine would spread over the entire Roman world. This happened during the reign of Claudius (Josephus recorded it happened in 46 AD). A gift was sent to Jerusalem by Barnabas and Saul to aid in the famine (Ch. 11).

Peter Escapes Prison

King Herod started arresting those who belonged to the church. He had the apostle James put to death. He arrested Peter also during Passover with the intention of bringing him to trial after the Passover. He was sleeping between two soldiers bound with chains with guards at the entrance.

An angel appeared and woke Peter telling him to get up. His chains fell off. He put on his clothes and followed the angel. After some distance the angel left him. When he realized it was real, not a vision, he went to the home of John Mark's mother. People had gathered there to pray. A servant girl named Rhoda answered the door. She recognized his voice but when she went to tell the rest they didn't believe her. He kept on knocking until they opened the door. He told them about what had happened and asked that they tell James (the brother of Jesus) and the brothers. He left for another place. Herod executed the guards.

Herod's Death

After persecuting Christians, he was struck down because he boasted of things he had done and did not give praise to God. This was the Herod called Agrippa. (Josephus said he helped other countries by giving them grain, Chapter 12).

Barnabas and Saul

In the church at Antioch there were prophets and teachers. The Holy Spirit said, 'set apart for me Barnabas and Saul for the work I have called them'. They set out on what we refer to as the 'first missionary journey'. John Mark was also with them. Saul is now being called Paul. They went to a place called Psidian Antioch and entered the synagogue, where they were asked to speak. Paul stood up and gave a summary of Jewish history (13:16-37). He ended by telling them the people of

Jerusalem and their rulers did not recognize Jesus and unknowingly fulfilled the words of the prophets but God raised him from the dead.

The people at the synagogue invited them to speak further on these things the next Sabbath. The next Sabbath, almost the whole city was there. The Jews were jealous and talked against what Paul was saying. He said, 'we had to speak the word of God to you first – since you reject it, we now turn to the Gentiles'. The Gentiles were glad and the word spread through the whole region. The Jews expelled them from that region.

In Iconium, Paul and Barnabas went to the Jewish synagogue. A great number believed but the city was divided. They discovered a plot to stone them and left.

At Lystra they healed a man lame from birth, and the people called them gods. They said, 'we are only men, human like you'. Some Jews came from Antioch and won the crowd over. They stoned Paul and dragged him outside the city, thinking he was dead but he was not.

They turned back and passed through the town again on their way back to Antioch. They told them, 'we must go through many hardships to enter the kingdom of God'. They also appointed elders in each church. At the end of their first missionary journey, they reported all that God had done through them to Antioch, their sponsoring church.

The Council at Jerusalem

Some men from Judea came to Antioch and were teaching: 'unless you are circumcised, according to the custom taught by Moses, you cannot be saved'. This brought on a sharp dispute. Paul and Barnabas and some others were appointed to go up to Jerusalem to discuss this question.

Peter addressed the assembly. He said, 'brothers, you know that some time ago, God made a choice among you that the Gentiles might hear, from my lips, the message of the gospel.

He made no distinction between us and them. Why do you want to put this yolk on them? We should not make it difficult for them'.

They wrote a letter and sent two of the brothers there; along with Paul and Barnabas to confirm it. The content of the letter:

It seemed good to the Holy Spirit and to us not to burden you with anything beyond the following requirements: You are to abstain from foods sacrificed to idols, from blood, from the meat of strangled animals and from sexual immorality. You will do well to avoid those things.   Farewell.

The people read the letter and were glad.

Paul and Barnabas Disagree

After being in Antioch a while, Paul said to Barnabas, 'Let us go back and visit the brothers where we preached and see how they are doing'. Barnabas wanted to take John Mark (he left them on their first journey, 13:13). Paul did not want to take him, so they split up. Barnabas took Mark and Paul chose Silas.

When Paul got to Lystra, he wanted to take with them a young man named Timothy. His mother was Jewish, but his father was a Greek. Paul circumcised him because of the Jews who lived in that area.

Paul had a vision. A man from Macedonia was begging him to 'come on over and help us'. They got ready and left at once, arriving at Philippi. There was no synagogue there so they went down to the river. Some women were gathered there. One was named Lydia, a dealer of purple cloth from Thyatira. (There needed to be ten Jews in a town for a synagogue). Lydia invited them to stay at her house.

As they were going to a place of prayer, a slave girl, who was a fortune teller, kept following them and saying, 'these men are servants of the Most High God; who are telling you the way to be saved'. Paul commanded the spirit to come out of her. When her owners lost their way to make money, they dragged Paul and Silas before the rulers and they were stripped and beaten and thrown into prison.

About midnight Paul and Silas were praying and singing to God. The other prisoners were listening. Suddenly there was a violent earthquake. When the jailor woke up and saw the prison doors open and the chains loose, he was about to kill himself, thinking the prisoner had escaped.

Paul shouted out, 'don't harm yourself we are all here!' He said, 'sirs, what must I do to be saved?' They replied, 'believe in the Lord Jesus'. They spoke the word of the Lord to him and his house. He washed their wounds; then the family was baptized. He brought them into his house and set a meal before them. The next morning, the magistrate came and told them they could leave. Paul said, 'they beat us publicly without a trial, even though we are Roman citizens. Let them come and escort us out. After that, they went to Lydia's house, then left town'.

The next place they went was Thessalonica. There was a Jewish synagogue there. Paul went there for the next three Sabbath days teaching about Christ. Some Jews were persuaded and a large number of Greeks, but as usual the Jews stirred up people and they had to leave as soon as it was night.

The next place they went was Berea. They had a synagogue. Luke wrote the Bereans were nobler than the Thessalonians. They searched the scriptures daily to see if what Paul said was true. Many believed, both Jews and Greeks. The Jews from Thessalonica went there too and stirred up a crowd. Paul left and went to Athens. Silas and Timothy were to join him.

Athens

While waiting for Silas and Timothy, Paul looked around and saw that it was full of idols. He spoke in the synagogue with the Jews and in the marketplace. Some thought he was talking about a foreign god.

He was brought to the Aeropagus (Mars Hill) where they like to listen to new ideas. In his looking around, Paul had seen this inscription: <u>To an Unknown God</u>. Paul used this as his sermon (a very eloquent one).

'This is the God I'm going to tell you about. He is the God who made the world and everything in it. He does not live in the temple made by hands. From one man he made very nation and decided the exact places they should live. In Him we live and move and have our being. We are His offspring; the divine being is not made by man's skill. In the past, God overlooked ignorance, but now He commands all people to repent. He has set a day when He will judge the world'.

When he talked about the resurrection of the dead, some sneered. Others wanted to hear him again. A few believed, one being Dionysius, a member of the Aeropagus.

Corinth

Next, Paul went to Corinth, another city in Macedonia. He met Aquila and his wife Priscilla. He was a tentmaker as was Paul so he stayed and worked with them. They formerly lived in Rome but Emperor Claudius had ordered the Jews to leave about 49 AD. When Silas and Timothy arrived, he devoted himself entirely to preaching. First to the Jews, but after their opposition, he shook out his clothes and said, 'from now on I will go to the Gentiles'.

One night Paul had a vision from the Lord. He told him to not be afraid; to continue on as he had many people in this city. He stayed in Corinth a year and a half.

Priscilla, Aquila and Apollos

Leaving Corinth, Paul set sail for Syria with Priscilla and Aquila. (He had his hair cut off because of a vow). He left them at Ephesus and promised to come back, if it was the Lord's will. After returning to Antioch, he set out again on his third journey and did not return to Ephesus.

During the meantime, a man named Apollos had come to Ephesus. He was well-versed in the scriptures but knew only the baptism of John. When Aquila and Priscilla heard him, they invited him into their home and explained the way of God more adequately. Paul found some more disciples who had only been baptized by John's baptism. He told them John's baptism was for people to believe in the one coming after him (Jesus). They were baptized in the name of Jesus. Paul imparted the Holy Spirit on them. There were 12. He stayed in that area two years. All the Jews and Greeks who lived in the province of Asia heard the word of the Lord and God did many miracles through Paul.

Paul decided to go to Jerusalem, passing through Macedonia and Achaia on the way. Before he left, a great disturbance arose about 'the way'. A silversmith named Demetrius called a meeting of his craftsmen. He said, 'men, you know we receive good income from this business, but this fellow, Paul, says man-made gods are no gods at all. There is danger of us losing our trade...'

The craftsmen were furious and began shouting 'Great is Artemis of the Ephesians!' and the assembly was in confusion. This went on for about two hours. Finally, the city clerk quieted them by saying if they had a grievance they should go through the courts and that they were in danger of being charged with rioting. Paul told them goodbye and went to Greece where he stayed three months.

On the first day of the week, Paul and his party were at Troas. They had come together to break bread (observe the Lord's Supper, Mark 14:22-25). He was to leave the next day so he talked for a long time. A young man named Eutychus was sitting in a third story window. He went to sleep and fell to the ground, dead. Paul raised him, went back upstairs and continued speaking until daylight.

Paul wanted to get to Jerusalem by Pentecost so when he arrived at Miletus, he sent for the elders of the church at Ephesus to meet him there.

He told them he was compelled to go to Jerusalem, but also that the Spirit warned him that prison and hardships would await him there. He told them they would never see him again. He told them to keep watch over the flock (church) the Holy Spirit had made them overseers. He said after his departure, savage wolves would come in, even among their own number. He said his own hands had supplied his needs and that of his companions. He knelt down and prayed and they all wept (Ch 20).

All along the way if possible, Paul would visit with the disciples a day or two; some pleaded with him not to go to Jerusalem. Upon arriving at Jerusalem, they were received warmly and he went to see James (the Lord's brother) and the elders.

After only seven days, some Jews from Asia saw Paul at the temple and stirred up the crowd. They shouted, 'this is the man who teaches all men everywhere against out people, our law and this place'.

They drug him from the temple and were trying to kill him. The commander came up and arrested him. He thought by the commotion he was someone else. Paul asked to speak and was granted permission. He spoke in Aramaic (Hebrew). He told them he was born in Tarsus, but was brought up in Jerusalem and trained under Gamaliel. He said he persecuted the 'way'. He related his conversion (22:3-21).

The crowd listened until he said, 'the Lord said to me, 'Go, I will send you far away to the Gentiles'. Then they started shouting again. The commander was going to have him flogged until Paul asked, 'is it legal to flog a Roman citizen who hasn't been found guilty?' After this they sent him to Caesarea by cavalry. The governor said he would hear his case when the accusers got there.

Trial Before Felix (52 – 60 AD)

Five days later Ananias, some elders and a lawyer came down and brought charges. They said, 'We have found this man to be a troublemaker, stirring up riots, among the Jews, all over the world'.

The governor motioned for Paul to speak. He said, 'I admit that I worship the God of our Fathers as a follower of the Way, which they call a sect. I have the same hope in God as these men, that there will be a resurrection of both the righteous and the wicked. I was ceremoniously clean when they found me in the temple'.

Felix was well-acquainted with the Way and adjourned the proceeding until the commander came. He kept Paul under guard but allowed his friends to take care of his needs. Several days later, Felix and his wife Drusilla sent for Paul and listened as he spoke about faith in Jesus Christ and the judgment to come. He was afraid and said, 'That's enough for now, when I find it convenient, I will send for you'.

He was hoping Paul would offer him a bribe so he sent for him frequently and talked with him. After two years had passed, Felix was succeeded by Festus. Wanting to grant a favor to the Jews, he left Paul in prison (Chapter 24). Three days after taking over, Festus went to Jerusalem. The Jewish leaders requested Paul be transferred to Jerusalem. He said, 'He is being held at Caesarea. Let the charges be pressed there'.

After eight or ten days, he went to Caesarea and had Paul brought before him. Jews from Jerusalem were there, making charges they could not prove. He asked Paul if he was willing to go to Jerusalem. He said he was not guilty and appealed to Caesar.

Festus Consults King Agrippa

King Agrippa and his sister, Bernice, came to show their respects to Festus, the governor. They discussed Paul's case. Festus said he was not charged with a crime, but some dispute about their religion and about a dead man named Jesus, who Paul claimed was alive. 'I was at a loss how to investigate such matters'. Agrippa said he would like to hear Paul.

Paul Before Agrippa (a Jew)

The next day, Agrippa and Bernice came with great pomp. Paul was brought in. Festus said, 'King Agrippa, the whole Jewish community has petitioned me about him in Jerusalem and here in Caesarea. They said he should not live, but I found he had done nothing deserving of death. I didn't know what to write to Rome about. I think it unreasonable to not specify charges against him'.

Agrippa said to Paul, 'you have permission to speak'.

Paul said he considered himself fortunate to make his defense before Agrippa because he was well acquainted with the Jewish customs. He told him of his previous life as a Pharisee and how he too opposed Jesus. He told about his conversion on the road to Damascus and that he was not disobedient to the heavenly vision.

'I am saying nothing beyond what the prophets and Moses said would happen'.

Festus shouted, 'you are out of you mind Paul! I'm convinced that none of this has escaped King Agrippa's notice'.

'It was not done in a corner', Paul continued. 'King Agrippa, do you believe the prophets? I know you do'. Agrippa said, 'Do you think in such a short time you can persuade me to be a Christian? Festus' he said, 'this man could have been set free if he had not appealed to Caesar'.

Paul Sails from Rome

Paul, Luke and Aristarchus, a Macedonian, all boarded ship and set out on their trip to Rome. From the first, the winds were against them. They landed at Myra and changed ships to an Alexandrian ship sailing for Italy. Much time had been lost. Sailing was not safe between September and March 15th. Luke said by now it was the Fast (the Day of Atonement). Paul warned them that the voyage would be disastrous but since the harbor of Fair Havens was not suitable to winter in, they decided to sail on.

The Storm

A gentle wind began to blow and before long, a hurricane wind began. The ship was driven along as the wind took it. They began to throw the cargo overboard, then the tackle. There was no sun or stars for many days and they had given up hope. They had gone a long time without food. Paul took charge. He said no life would be lost but the ship would be destroyed. He said an angel had stood beside him during the night and told him not to be afraid, that he would stand trial before Caesar.

On the fourteenth night they were being driven across the Adriatic Sea. They could tell they were nearing land. Paul urged everyone to eat. There were 276 people on board. When daylight came, they saw a bay with a sandy beach so they headed for it but struck a sandbar and ran aground. Everyone was spared.

The island was Malta and the natives were kind. They built a fire because it was raining and cold. As Paul was helping pile brushwood on the fire, a snake fastened itself on his hand. They said, 'This man must be a murderer, he escaped the sea but justice has not allowed him to live'. When he shook the snake off into the fire and nothing happened to him, they said he was a god.

The chief official of the island was Pubbius. He was very hospitable. Hs father was sick and Paul healed him, then the rest of the sick on the island were cured. They were there 3 months, and then left in a ship that had wintered there from Alexandria.

The brothers in Rome had heard they were coming and traveled some distance to meet them. In Rome, Paul was allowed to live by himself, with a soldier to guard him.

After being there three days, he called together the leaders of the Jews. He told them he had done nothing wrong. That he was arrested in Jerusalem and handed over to the Romans and that he was there because he had appealed to Caesar.

They said they had not received any letters or heard anything bad about him, 'But *we* want to hear what your views are'. From morning until evening, he explained to them the kingdom and tried to convince them about Jesus. Some were convinced but others were not. For two whole years he stayed in his own rented house and taught boldly.

He was probably released about 63 AD because of a defaulted case. He was re-arrested later and probably killed by Nero about 65 AD.

While in Rome, he wrote four epistles: Ephesians, Colossians, Philemon and Philippians. He went on three missionary journeys.

1st journey – Chapters 13 and 14
2nd journey – Chapter 15:22 – 18:22
3rd journey – Chapter 18:23…

Some of Paul's special helpers:

Barnabas	Luke	Silas
Timothy	Epaphraditis	Apollos
John Mark	Priscilla	Aquila

Romans

A Review

Written by Paul about 56-58 AD from Corinth during his third missionary journey. (He stayed there a year and a half, Acts 18:11). He did not establish the church at Rome. It was not addressed to 'the' church at Rome, but to the 'saints'. They most probably had small groups of Christians meeting all over the Capital city. This would have been during the reign of Nero (54-68 AD).

Emperor Claudius had ordered the Jews to leave Rome in about 49 AD (Acts 18:2), but at this time of writing, the churches in Rome were made up of both Jews and Gentiles.

Paul had long desired to visit Rome and had some kinfolk there. (Andronicus, 16:7, Junias and Herodion 16:11. Paul mentions 29 people and/or households in Chapters 16. Nine were women).

Tertius did the writing for Paul (16:22).

Gaius was his host (16:23).

One reason Paul wanted to go to Rome in person was so that he could impart some spiritual gift on them. (Only an apostle could pass this on, 2 Timothy 1:6).

Paul said he was not ashamed of the gospel of Christ (the death, burial and resurrection of Christ, Mark 16:15, 16). He said it was the power of God for the salvation of everyone who believes: first to the Jew, then for the Gentile (1:16).

He said since the creation of the world, God's invisible qualities have been clearly seen, but mankind did not glorify Him nor give thanks to Him (1:20, 21). He says we have no excuse.

Paul said when we pass judgment on someone and we do the same things they are doing, we condemn ourselves (2:1-3).

God will give to each person according to what he has done, and he does not show favoritism (2:11).

The Gentiles did not have the law, but when they did by nature, things required by the law, they were a law for themselves (2:14). Under the law, the Jews were circumcised but if they broke the Law, it would be of no avail. Now, circumcision is of the heart.

Paul asks, 'what advantage is there in being a Jew?'
1. They were entrusted with the very words of God, the Old Testament
2. God is true, He keeps His promises whether man does or not
3. The purpose of the Law was to reveal sin. (Where there is no law, there is no sin, 5:13).

Through the law, we become conscious of sin. Now, righteousness comes through faith in Jesus Christ to all who believe.

Abraham lived before the Law was given. He believed and obeyed God and it was credited to him as righteousness, even before he was circumcised. Against all hope, he believed.

Through one man, sin entered the world and death because of sin. Through one man, Jesus Christ, because of His death on the cross we can have reconciliation to God. Baptism represents a death, burial and resurrection of our old life. We arise to lead a new life, free from sin.

We could liken Christianity to marriage. That first law died, freeing us from it and now we are marred to another (Christ). We have been released from the law to serve in a new way.

The Struggle

When the law says, 'don't do it', our mind wants to do it (verse 15). There is a constant struggle against sin. When I want to do good, evil is right there with me. Who will rescue me? Jesus Christ our Lord.

There is now no condemnation for those who are in Christ Jesus, because the law of the spirit has set me free from the law of sin and death (8:1). Forgiveness is the Christian's comfort. The mind controlled by the Spirit is life and peace, if the spirit lives in you. If anyone does not have the Spirit of Christ, he does not belong to Christ. This Spirit that lives in me helps me conquer the desire to sin and gives me hope. We are God's children and fellow heirs with Christ. The Holy Spirit also helps us. Sometimes we don't know how or what is best for us to pray for, but the Holy Spirit searches our hearts and intercedes for us (8:26, 27). We know that in all things, God works for the good of those who love Him. If He is for us, who can be against us?

Christ is now at the right hand of God interceding for us. We are more than conquerors through Him who loves us.

Neither life nor death, neither angels nor demons, neither the present nor the future, nor any powers, neither height nor depth nor anything else in all creation, will be able to separate us from the love of God that is in Christ Jesus our Lord.

God's Choice

Paul grieves over his fellow Jews – the ones who received the covenants, the temple worship, the promises, the patriarchs, and the ancestry of Christ. It was not because God's word had failed. Not all who descended from Abraham are Abraham's children. They are still in unbelief (Chapter 9). God will always choose those who choose Him.

Paul said his heart's desire and prayer to God was that the Israelites may be saved. He said they were zealous, but their zeal was not based on knowledge.

Anyone can be saved who so chooses. There is no difference between Jew and Gentile (10:12). God did not reject

Israel; they rejected Him (11:2).   Isaiah wrote, 'all day long I have held out my hands to a disobedient and obstinate people'.

Paul wrote in Chapter 11 that they did not fall beyond recovery. Even though we fall, we can rise again. If one doesn't want the blessings of God, it's up to him. God will not force him, we are of free will.

To the Gentiles: If some of the branches have been broken off and you have been grafted in, do not boast.   They were broken off because of unbelief. If God did not spare the natural branches, He will not spare you either. God is able to graft them in again.

Chapter 12 says we are to offer our bodies as living sacrifices, holy and pleasing to God. Members have different abilities.

Some good qualities a Christian could exhibit are:

A sincere love for good, hating evil.
Honoring one another above ourselves.
Being joyful, patient, faithful in prayer, sharing and hospitable

Some qualities we are not to exhibit:

Do not curse, do not be proud
Do not be conceited, do not take revenge
Do not be overcome by evil, but overcome evil with good

Do what is right in the eyes of everybody. If it is possible, as far as it depends on you, live at peace with everyone.

'If your enemy is hungry, feed him; if he is thirsty, give him something to drink. In doing this, you will heap burning coals on his head'.

Christians are to obey the laws of the land, unless they violate God's laws. There is no authority except what God has established. He who rebels against the authority is rebelling against what God has instituted. Rulers hold no terror to those who do right, but if you do wrong, be afraid.

Give everyone what you owe them (taxes, respect or honor). All the commandments could be summed up in this one rule:

Love your neighbor as yourself.

Love does no harm to its neighbor. Our salvation is nearer than when we first believed.

Special Days

Don't pass judgment on disputable matters. (Things that would not cause you to be lost) We have leeway here, but if you think it's wrong, don't do it.

One man considers one day more sacred than another; another man considers every day alike.

Under the law, they had a lot of special days. Certain meats were forbidden to eat. There were people they were not to associate with and a lot of things hard to keep, like travel on the Sabbath. These things were done away with under the Christian age. None of these made them a better person. It made them more conscious of their outward activities rather than the heart.

The first day of the week (Sunday) was when they came together to break bread, John was 'in the spirit' on the Lord's Day (Rev. 1:10). The Lord arose on the first day of the week and the church was established on the first day of the week. If any day is special now, it would be the first day of the week, but even on that day, it is not like the Sabbath, where they could do no work. It seems left up to us if we want to celebrate certain days (Chapter 14). Special days and foods don't seem to benefit us so far as our salvation is concerned.

If either one would be a stumbling block to a weak brother, don't do it. Let us make every effort to do what leads to peace and edification. Everything that is not of faith is sin.

Paul said, 'we who are strong ought to bear the failings of the weak and not to please ourselves'. He said even Christ did not please Himself.

Paul said it had always been his ambition to preach the gospel where Christ was not known so he would not be building on someone else's foundation. For many years, he wanted to go to Rome and to Spain.

As he is writing this letter, he says he is on his way to Jerusalem to take a contribution to the poor from Macedonia and Achaia. He said they were pleased to do it, because they had shared in Jesus' spiritual blessings. He did get to go to Rome, but not as a free man. When he arrived in Jerusalem, it wasn't long until he was arrested.

In Ananias' vision, the Lord told him Paul was a chosen instrument to carry his name before the Gentiles, kings and the people of Israel (Acts 9:15, 16).

In explaining his conversion, Paul appeared before all the rulers in the Jerusalem area; then for two full years in Rome, after he had appealed his case to Caesar (Acts 28:19, 23, 30). Boldly, and without hindrance, he taught the kingdom of God and the Lord Jesus Christ.

This letter may have been sent to them by Phoebe (16:1). He urged them to watch out for those who caused division and keep away from them.

1 Corinthians

A Review

1 Corinthians was written about 55 AD from Ephesus (16:8). Paul had gone to Corinth from Athens in the early fifties. That is where he met Aquila and Priscilla, who were Jews. (Claudius had ordered all the Jews to leave Rome in 49 AD).

He probable met them at the Jewish synagogue. They were tentmakers, as was he. He stayed and worked with them through the week and on the Sabbath taught in the synagogue. Later, when Silas and Timothy joined him, he devoted himself to full-time preaching (Acts 18:1-5).

Paul stayed in Corinth a year and a half. This was on his second missionary journey. He was thankful for them. He said his testimony had been confirmed in them and they did not lack any spiritual gift.

Divisions

Paul had gotten some reliable information from the household of Chloe that there were quarrels among them. Some were saying, 'I follow Paul', another, 'I follow Cephas (Peter)', another 'I follow Apollos', and yet another, 'I follow Christ'.

He wrote, 'Is Christ divided? Was Paul crucified for you, were you baptized into the name of Paul? I appeal to you, in the name of our Lord, to agree with one another so that there be no divisions among you; that you be perfectly united in mind and thought'.

He asked them to think of what they were when they were called. Not many were wise (by human standards), not many influential or of noble birth. He said when he came to them it was not with eloquence. He resolved to know nothing while he was with them, except Jesus Christ and Him crucified. His preaching was not with wise and persuasive words.

Wisdom From the Spirit

It is written in Isaiah 64:4:
'No eye has seen, no ear has heard, no mind has conceived
What God has prepared for those who love Him.'

Paul said the rulers of this age did not understand this, but it had been revealed to him by the Spirit and they still were not ready for it. He said he, Peter, and Apollos were only servants. They planted but God made it grow. They were all fellow workers. No man can lay a foundation other than the one already laid. We are God's temple (dwelling place) and God's spirit lives in us.

Even the apostles are servants of Christ that were entrusted with the secret things of God. Paul said often he was hungry, thirsty, homeless and ill-treated.

He said he was sending Timothy, his son (in the gospel) to remind them of his way of life; that if it was the Lord's will, he would come soon. He wanted to come to them in love, not with a whip.

Immoral Brothers

It was reported there was sexual immorality among them. A man had married his father's wife (step-mother). This goes back to Leviticus 18:8. Instead of grieving over it, they were accepting it. Paul said:
'When you are assembled in the name of our Lord
Jesus and I am with you in Spirit and the power of our
Lord Jesus is present, hand this man over to Satan, so

that the sinful nature may be destroyed and his spirit saved on the day of the Lord'. 1 Corinthians 5:4, 5

Paul said he had written them in his letter (another letter?) not to associate with sexually immoral people–he said this did not mean the people of the world, but one who calls himself a brother that is sexually immoral, greedy, an idolater, a slanderer, a drunkard or a swindler. With such a man do not even eat (Ch 5).

Lawsuits Among Believers

Paul wrote if there was a dispute among them, do not take it before the ungodly for judgment. Let men from the church judge the dispute. He said, 'why not rather be wronged?' He said some of them had been sinful, but they had been washed, sanctified and justified in the name of the Lord (through baptism for forgiveness of sins, Acts 22:16).

Marriage Chapter 7

Paul said the body is not meant for sexual immorality. The body is the temple of the Holy Spirit. He said since there was so much immorality (Corinth was known for its immorality), each man should have his own wife and each woman her own husband, and they should not deprive each other except by mutual consent for a short time. He said he wished that all men were as he was (single) but it was better to marry then to burn with passion.

He said a wife must not separate from her husband but if she does, she is to remain unmarried or else be reconciled. If a husband or wife is married to an unbeliever and he or she is willing to live with them, they must not divorce. If the unbeliever leaves, the believer is not bound in such circumstances. How do you know whether you might be able to save you mate?

Each person should remain in the situation he was in when called. Because of the present crisis (Christians were being persecuted by Nero) it would be better to remain unmarried, but if they did, they did not sin. He said the time was short (war was looming) and he would like for them to be free from concern. If you have a wife and family, your interest is divided.

Paul said a woman is bound to her husband as long as he lives, but if he dies, she is free to marry anyone she wishes, but he must belong to the Lord. Paul said she would be happier if she stayed single. (It would depend on the circumstances, Ch 7).

Food Sacrificed to Idols

In the world at that time, there were many 'gods', but for a Christian, there is only one God. At that time, they offered food as a sacrifice to idols. Paul says they should not eat it; not because of themselves, but because it may wound a weak conscience. He says food does not bring us near God. We are no worse if we eat and no better if we do.

The Apostle's Rights

Paul writes: 'Who serves as a soldier at his own expense? Who plants a vineyard and does not eat of its grapes? Who tends a flock and does not drink of its milk?

If we sow spiritual seed, is it too much to reap a material harvest? Those who work in the temple get their food from the temple. Those who serve at the altar share in what is offered on the altar. In the same way, the Lord has commanded that those who preach the gospel should receive their living from the gospel' (Matt. 10:10, Luke 10:7).

Because Paul and Barnabas worked and at times supported themselves, some probably thought they were not real apostles. He said, 'don't we have a right to food and drink? Don't we have a right to take a believing wife along with us, as do the other apostles and the Lord's brothers and Cephas (Peter)?' He said he did it to win as many as possible.

Warnings From Israel's History

Our forefathers all passed under the cloud and through the sea. They ate the same spiritual food. That 'rock' that guided them was Christ. With most of them, God was not pleased. They engaged in pagan revelry, committed sexual immorality. In one day, 23,000 died. These things were recorded as warnings for us. No temptation has seized you except what is common to man, but the Lord will not let us be tempted beyond what we can bear, but has provided a way out.

The Lord's Supper

The *cup* is a participation of the *blood* of Christ.
The *bread* we break is a participation of the *body* of Christ.

The Covering of the Head

The head of every man is Christ.
The head of ever woman is man.
The head of Christ is God (11:3).
To honor God, a man ought *not* to cover his head. The woman should, but her hair is a natural covering. To a man, long hair is a disgrace, but to a woman it is her glory.

More on the Lord's Supper

When you come together, it is not the Lord's Supper you eat. It seemed as if they were making a meal of it, and not even waiting until everyone got there.

Paul said he received from the Lord what he passed on. (He was not there).

On the night He was betrayed, He took bread, gave thanks and broke it. He said, 'this is my body – do this in remembrance of me'.

After supper He took the cup saying, 'this cup is the new covenant in my blood; do this, whenever you drink it, in remembrance of me. Whoever eats the bread or drinks the cup of the Lord in an unworthy manner will be guilty of sinning against the body and blood of the Lord. If anyone is hungry, he should eat at home'.

Spiritual Gifts

Each person had different gifts and abilities. The church is like the body. The eye does one thing, the hand another. When one part suffers, the whole body suffers. So it should be with church members. One might speak with tongues (languages), one teach, one lead singing, one pray, one cook, one make people feel welcome –it takes the whole body of members to do the work. The church is the body of Christ.

Love

Though I speak with the tongues of men and angels, and have not love, I am become as a sounding brass or a tinkling cymbal.

And though I have the gift of prophesy, and understand all mysteries, and all knowledge; and though I have all faith so that I could remove mountains, and have not love, I am nothing.

And though I bestow all my goods to feed the poor, and though I give my body to be burned and have not love, it profiteth me nothing.

Love suffereth long and is kind. Love envieth not; it wanteth not itself, is not puffed up;

Does not behave unseemly, seeketh not her own, is not easily provoked, thinketh no evil;

Rejoiceth not in iniquity, but rejoiceth in the truth;

Bareth all things, believeth all things, hopeth all things, endureth all things.

Love never fails, but where there be prophecies, they shall fail; where there be tongues, they shall cease; where there be knowledge it shall vanish away.

For we know in part and we prophesy in part.

But when that which is perfect is come, that which is in part shall be done away.

When I was a child, I spoke as a child, I understood as a child, I thought as a child: but when I became a man, I put away childish things.

For now we see through a glass, darkly; but then, face to face. Now I know in part, but then shall I know, even as I am known.

And now abideth faith, hope, love, these three but the greatest of these is love. (KJV)

In heaven there will be no need of faith, because we will know. There will be no need of hope, because that hope will be realized. What remains will be love.

Tongues

There are many languages in the world and God created them all, when people were trying to build the tower of Babel (Gen. 11:7-9). God understands them all and people can talk to Him, but in the church, Paul said not to speak in a foreign language unless it is interpreted (14:1-39).   It would not be understood by the people.

The worship should be orderly with one person speaking at a time. In the worship service, where men are present, the women are not to speak (lead). If it is not worship (class discussion) she can (Acts 18:26).

The Resurrection of Christ

Paul reminds the Corinthians of the gospel he preached to them: the death, the burial and the resurrection of Jesus.

He does not mention the women Jesus appeared to, but says He appeared to Peter, then the twelve, then 500 brothers at the same time, then James (His brother), then all the apostles and last of all to Paul (15:5-8).

Paul said if Jesus was not raised, all their teaching was useless. He has been raised! In Adam all die, in Christ all will be made alive.

Some may ask, 'what kind of body will we have?' 'Take a seed that is planted. When it comes forth from the ground, it is a live plant, totally different. So will we be. It won't be flesh and blood, but will be imperishable'.

When the end comes, Jesus will hand the kingdom over to God the Father. Even the Son Himself will be subject to God.

The Collection

A collection of money is to be taken up on the first day of the week in keeping with the income made that week (16:1, 2).

Paul asks them to accept Timothy when he comes and to be men of courage (4:17).

2 Corinthians

A Review

2 Corinthians is a follow-up letter written by Paul, probably within a year of his first letter (about 56 AD). Timothy has returned from his visit to Corinth. In Paul's first letter, he addressed problems such as: divisions, fornication, purity and marriage, foods sacrificed to idols, the rights of an apostle, covering of the head, spiritual gifts, love, tongues, the resurrection and the collection. Paul said God comforts us in all our troubles so that we can comfort others. In this letter, he expresses his joy at the good news of their progress. He further instructs them in the treatment of the offender so as to bring about reconciliation between the two.

Other problems had arisen, like opposition to Paul's authority. He reminds them of all the things he has suffered in Asia (Acts 19). He said it was almost beyond his ability to endure (1:8-10). He had planned to visit Corinth (1 Cor. 16:5, 6) but said it was in order to spare them that he did not return (1:23).

He made up his mind that he would not make another painful visit to them (2:1). He said he had written them out of great distress and anguish of heart. He said the punishment inflicted on him (the man who had his father's wife) was sufficient. Now he tells them to forgive and comfort him so that he won't be overwhelmed by excessive sorrow.

We don't want to run them off but to have them repent and feel loved again. Paul said they were the aroma of Christ to those being saved. Paul says in 2:17, 'unlike so many, we do not peddle the word of God for profit. It was happening that far back (20 years from the beginning of the church). He says even today, the same veil remains when the old covenant is read. Only in Christ is it taken away (3:14).

The god of this age (Satan) has blinded the minds of unbelievers so that they cannot see the light of the gospel. Paul said he had been hard pressed on every side, but not crushed; perplexed but not in despair, persecuted but not abandoned; struck down but not destroyed (4:8, 9). Though outwardly we are wasting away, yet inwardly we are being renewed day by day.

As we grow older, our outward body is growing weaker, but the inward is being prepared for the next life (heaven).

Paul said he would prefer to be away from the body and at home with the Lord, but since he knows what it is to fear the Lord, he tries to persuade men. He said we are Christ's ambassadors. God makes His appeal through us (5:20).

Again in Chapter 6, Paul relates his many hardships. He says, 'do not be yoked together with unbelievers for what do righteousness and wickedness have in common?' Paul says in Chapter 7 he realized his first letter had hurt them for a little while, but was happy it had led them to repentance. They had proved themselves to be innocent in this matter.

He told the Corinthians the Macedonian churches had been very generous in their giving, even with their poverty. He asks the Corinthians to be generous also. He said the gift should be according to what one has, not according to what he does not have (8:2 and 12). Titus was to pick up this offering. It was to be taken to Jerusalem, not for their support.

(There had been an earthquake in the reign of Claudius with widespread crop failures and the prophet Agabus had announced a famine, Acts 11:28). Combined, this is why they were in need.

Paul said whoever sows sparingly will reap sparingly and whoever sows generously will reap generously (9:6).

He who supplies seed to the sower and the bread for food (God) will also supply and increase your store of seed and enlarge the harvest of your righteousness.

Paul may have been a better writer than he was a speaker. He said, some said his letters were weighty and forceful, but in person he was unimpressive. He said he may not be a trained speaker but he did have knowledge.

Paul did not want to be a burden to any church. He said there were deceitful workmen masquerading as apostles of Christ. He said, 'no wonder, for Satan himself masquerades as an angel of light'.

Again Paul relates the hardships he had suffered: floggings, beaten with rods, stoned, shipwrecked...in danger from rivers, bandits, his own countrymen, from the Gentiles, false brothers. He said he had labored and toiled, gone without sleep, known hunger, thirst and cold. Besides everything else, he faced daily the pressure of his concern for all the churches.

Paul said that 14 years ago (that would be about 42 AD) he was caught up to the third heaven. Whether it was in the body or out of the body, he didn't know. He was caught up to paradise and heard inexpressible tings that man is not permitted to tell.

He said to keep him from being conceited he was given a 'thorn in the flesh' to torment him. He said he pleaded with the Lord three times to take it away, but he said, 'my grace is sufficient for you, my power is made perfect in weakness'. He said the things that marked an apostle were signs, wonders and miracles which he had done among them.

He is readying to visit them for a third time and he's afraid he may not find them as he wants them to be and they may not find him as they want him to be. He wanted to straighten things up before he came, if not, he would not spare them.

Galatians

A Review

The church at Antioch of Syria sent Paul and Barnabas on their first missionary journey, where they established churches in Galatia: Antioch of Pisidia, Iconium, Lystra and Derbe (Acts 13:2 – 14:27). Paul must have written this letter before the council at Jerusalem (Acts 15).

Some men had come down from Judea and were teaching the brothers: unless you are circumcised, according to the custom taught by Moses, you cannot be saved (Acts 15:1).

Paul wrote in Galatians 1:6, 'I am astonished that you are so quickly deserting the one who called you and turning to a different gospel – which is really no gospel at all'.

He said, 'even if we, or an angel from heaven, taught any other gospel, other than the one we preached, let him be eternally condemned' (1:8).

Paul said the gospel he had taught them, he received by revelation from Jesus Christ (1:12). He said he did not consult any man (didn't need to) nor did he go to Jerusalem to see those who were apostles before he was. He went to Arabia (where Mt. Sinai is).

Three years later, he went up to Jerusalem to get acquainted with Peter and stayed with him 15 days. He also saw James, the Lord's brother. He was unknown to the churches of Judea, but they had heard the report that the man who formerly persecuted us is now preaching the faith, he once tried to destroy.

Fourteen years later, he went to Jerusalem again, taking along Barnabas and Titus. This trip was to take aid during the famine (see Acts 11:27-30).

They met privately with the three men who seemed to be the leaders in the Jerusalem church: Peter, James (the Lord's brother) and John.

They related to them all that had been happening among the Gentiles. Peter had already carried the gospel to the house of Cornelius, a Gentile (see Acts 10).

They saw that Paul had been entrusted with the task of preaching the gospel to the Gentiles, as Peter was to the Jews. The apostles in Jerusalem gave Paul and Barnabas the right hand of fellowship.

Peter Visits Antioch

Peter went to visit the Gentile church in Antioch and was eating with them, until some men arrived who were Jews. Then he began to draw back and separate himself. Paul opposed him to his face. He said we Jews know that a man is not justified by following the law, but by faith in Jesus Christ.

He wrote the Galatians that all those who believe are children of Abraham. Foreseeing this, the Lord told Abram, 'All people on earth will be blessed through you'. (Jesus is in the lineage of Abraham, Gen. 12:3).

Paul said the law, introduced 430 years later, after the promise of Abraham, was because of transgressions (see Gal. 3:17-19 and Gen. 15:13). It was intended to lead us to Christ (3:24).

If we belong to Christ, we are Abraham's seed and heirs according to the promise (3:16, 29).

Paul asked the Galatians, 'Do you want to be enslaved again? You are observing special days, months, seasons and years. I fear for you, that I have wasted my efforts on you'.

He said it was because of an illness that he first preached the gospel to them. He said, 'if you could have, you would have torn out your eyes and given them to me'. He doesn't say when this happened, but it may have been when he was stoned and left for dead in Lystra (Acts 14:8-20). After that he left for Derbe the next day.

Judaism

The Jews were trying to win back the Christians to Judaism or, at least, to partially keep the law. Paul used the story of a slave woman and a free woman to show them we are children of the free woman. He told them not to be burdened again by a yoke of slavery (5:1).

He said those who were trying to be justified by the law have fallen from grace. In Christ, neither circumcision nor uncircumcision has any value. He said the entire law is summed up in a single command: Love your neighbor as yourself.

If someone is caught in a sin, you who are spiritual should restore him gently (6:1). Carry each other's burdens and you will fulfill the law of Christ.

As we have opportunity, let us do good to all men, especially those who belong to the family of believers (6:10).

Ephesians

A Review

Ephesians is a general letter applicable to Christians everywhere (Gentiles). No reference is made to the Old Testament scriptures. It was written by Paul while he was a prisoner in Rome (1:1, 3:1). He also wrote Philemon, Colossians and Philippians during this two year period.

God had planned, from the creation of the world, to send His son to redeem mankind (1:4-7). He did not include the Gentiles in the beginning of the gospel. They are now included, bring brought together through the blood of Christ.

He destroyed the barrier when he died on the cross; when the veil of the temple was rent in two (Luke 22:45).

He created in Himself *one* new man out of two, destroying the barrier, the law. God appointed Jesus to be head over everything to the church. In times past, this was a mystery. This mystery is: through the Gospel, the Gentiles are heirs together in the promise in Jesus Christ. We are all one in Christ, fellow citizens.

Paul wrote there was one body, one hope, one Lord, one baptism and one God and Father of all (4:4-6). Christ is able to do immeasurably more than we can ask or imagine (according to the power that is at work within me).

Paul wrote that Christ *descended* to the lower parts of the earth and then *ascended* far above all heavens (4:9, 10).

He gave some to be apostles, some prophets, some evangelists, some pastors and teachers so that we may be built up in Christ and reach unity in the faith, speaking the truth in love.

He wrote the Gentiles that they must not live as they once did, but to put off their old self and have a new attitude of mind.

Ex: Put off falsehood, in anger do not sin, do not steal, don't let unwholesome talk come out of your mouths, be kind, compassionate and forgiving. There must not be even a hint of sexual immorality, impurity, obscenity, foolish talk or coarse joking. They must live as children of light, continually walking and thinking of right (4:17 – 5:13).

He said it is shameful even to mention what the disobedient do in secret. He said to speak to one another with psalms, hymns and spiritual songs. Sing and make music in your heart to the Lord, always giving thanks to God the Father for everything, in the name of our Lord, Jesus Christ (5:19, 20).

Wives and Husbands

Wives, submit to your husbands as to the Lord.   The husband is the head of the wife as Christ is head of the church.

Husbands love your wives as Christ loved the church and gave himself up for her. He who loves his wife loves himself. For this reason a man will leave his father and mother and be united to his wife, and the two will become one flesh (5:22-31).

Children are to obey their parents in the Lord, for this is right. Honor your father and mother that you may enjoy a long life on the earth. (This is the first commandment with a promise, Deut. 5:16).

Slaves and Masters

(Employers and employees) Serve wholeheartedly, as if you were serving the Lord. The master of both is in heaven and he does not show favoritism.

Our Armor

We are to 'put on the armor of God so that we will be able to stand strong against the forces of evil'. The armor is the word of God.

Paul also wants us to continue in prayer. It is good to stay informed about what is going on in area churches. Things like: gospel meetings, writings, TV programs and word of mouth (6:21, 22).

In this area, the Magnolia Messenger helps us do this.

Tychicus is mentioned several times in Paul's writings as his messenger or representative.

Ephesus is where the temple of Diana, which was regarded as one of the ancient wonders of the world, was located. Paul stayed and taught in Ephesus two years (Acts 19:10).

Philippians

A Review

Written by Paul while in a Roman prison (verses 12-14, 4:22). Timothy and Epaphroditus were with him (1:1, 2:19, 25-30). Philippi was once a great city with much gold. It was the headquarters of the famed Roman highway (The Ignation Way). It was 500 miles long (Encyclopedia Britannica, Vol. 1 page 134).

The church at Philippi was established on Paul's second missionary journey. He had a vision during the night of a man saying, 'come over to Macedonia and help us'. This is referred to as the 'Macedonian Call' (Acts 16). There was no synagogue there. His convert was Lydia, a dealer in purple cloth. She was converted by a river and Paul stayed at her house. When Paul and Silas were put in prison, they were praying and singing at midnight when there was a violent earthquake and because they did not escape, they were able to teach the jailor and his family.

This Philippian church brought Paul great joy, and he longed to see them, but also said his chains had served to advance the gospel. The important thing was that Christ was preached. He said, for him to live is Christ and to die was gain.

He told them whatever happens, to conduct themselves in a manner worthy of the gospel of Christ. He said Jesus was in very nature God, but He made Himself nothing, taking the very nature of a servant. God exalted Him and gave Him a name that is above every name, that every knee should bow to Him and every tongue confess that He is Lord.

Paul was planning to send Timothy to them soon to see how they were doing and he hoped to come soon himself (2:24). They had sent Epaphroditus to help take care of Paul, but he became ill and almost died. Paul was sending him back home (2:19-30). You might say, 'why didn't Paul heal Epaphroditus?' This power to heal, that the apostles had, was for the unbelieving to show they were from God, not for their own convenience.

Paul was first arrested when he went to Jerusalem. He was warned by the Holy Spirit that he would have trouble there, but was determined to go (Acts 20:33, 21:10-14). He was arrested there in 57 AD and stayed in prison in Caesarea 2 years, explaining his conversion to all the officials there before appealing his case to Caesar. He was sent to Rome where he was in prison two more years.

He was not idle by any means. Everywhere he went, he taught. He received all who came to him there and wrote letters to four churches (Acts 28:16-31). He was probably released in 61 or 62 AD. By making his defense, he was able to tell the story of Jesus in many 'high places' (see Acts 9:15).

Paul said he forgot what was behind and pressed on toward the goal (heaven). He said to not be anxious about anything but to present our requests to God. The peace that passes understanding will guard our hearts and minds in Christ Jesus.

He said, 'whatever is true, noble, right, pure, lovely or admirable – if anything is excellent or praiseworthy, think about such things'.

He said the Lord would transform our lowly bodies so that they will be like His glorious body (3:20, 21).

He said in the early days, when he set out from Macedonia they were the only church who shared with him in giving.

Things that indicate Paul was released from prison in Rome (the first time):

1. He awaits release and plans to go to Colossae (Philemon 1:22).
2. He visited Ephesus where he left Timothy to supervise the churches while he went on to Macedonia (1 Tim. 1:3).
3. He visited Crete and left Titus to supervise what was left unfinished. The only record of him being near Crete was when he was en route to Rome (Titus 1:5).
4. He went to Troas where he may have been arrested the second time (2 Tim. 4:13).

Paul's Letters

1. Second missionary journey:
   Galatians (49), 1 and 2 Timothy (51), 1 and 2 Corinthians (56), (57), Romans (58).
2. First imprisonment: (in Rome)
   Ephesians, Philippians, Colossians, Philemon (60-62)
3. After his release:
   1 Timothy (63), Titus (65)
4. Second imprisonment;
   2 Timothy (66)

(Nero in power 54 – 68 AD)

Colossians

A Review

This letter was written by Paul during his two year imprisonment in Rome (4:3). He did not establish this church. Epaphras did in about 60 – 61 AD (1:7). While in prison, in his own rented house, Paul welcomed all who came to see him (Acts 30-31). This must have served as his headquarters.

In this letter, he writes of many workers. Some were in prison, others he was sending out to work in the kingdom.

Timothy (was with him, 1:1)

Tychicus (was being sent to Colossae, 4:7, 8)

Onesimus (was being sent to Colossae, Philemon 1:8-11. (He was the run-away slave being sent back and maybe joined by Paul later)

Aristarchus (a fellow prison, 4:10)

Mark
Justus } (fellow Jews with Paul)

Epaphras
Luke } (sent greetings, 4:7-14)
Demas

Epaphras either visited Paul in Rome or was a fellow prisoner there (Phil. 23). Evidently, he had told Paul of the error being taught in Colossae and asked for his help.

First, Paul told them he had heard of them through Epaphras and that he had been praying for them; that they would live a life worthy of Jesus and would be growing and bearing fruit. He was glad they would be sharing in the inheritance of the saints.

Christ's Supremacy

Paul wrote that Christ was the image of the invisible God, that all things were created by Him and for Him. He is the head of the body, the church.

Once you were alienated from God, but have been reconciled by Christ's death, if you continue in faith. This is the gospel you heard and has been proclaimed to every creature under heaven (1:23).

Paul's Labor

Paul said he had become a servant of the commission given to him by God, to make known to the Gentiles the riches of this mystery which is: Christ in you, the hope of glory.

He said even though he had not met them, he was struggling for them as well as the church at Laodicea, that no one should deceive them by fine-sounding arguments.

Freedom from Human Regulations

He said to continue living in the faith as they were taught, not by human traditions or circumcision, which was done by the hands of men, but circumcision of Christ (when they were baptized and put off the old life). He took away the written code, nailing it to the cross. He told them not to be judged by what they ate or drank or special days.

Holy Living

He told them to set their hearts on things above, where Christ is seated at the right hand of God.   You must rid yourselves of such things as anger, rage, malice, slander and filthy language and put on the new self: compassion, kindness, humility, gentleness and patience.

Forgive as the Lord forgave you, but above all, put on love. We were called to peace. He told them to sing psalms, hymns and spiritual songs.

This letter is much like the letter to the Ephesians. He told them, the Colossians, to also submit to their husbands, husbands love your wives and children obey your parents and slaves obey your masters as working for the Lord.

Paul asks them to pray for him also, that a door may be opened to proclaim the message. He said that Tychicus would tell them all the news about him, that he would be coming with Onesimus (our faithful and dear brother, who is one of you).

Paul instructs the church at Colossae to pass on this letter to the church at Laodicea and for them to read the letter he had written to them (swap).

Colossae was 11 miles from Laodicea.

1 Thessalonians

A Review

1 Thessalonians was written by Paul on his second missionary journey, about 51 AD; most probably from Corinth as he was there about one and one-half years (Acts 18:11).

Paul had gotten what we refer to as 'The Macedonian Call' in a vision while at Troas. Macedonia is now called Europe. Paul and his companions, Silas and Timothy, started churches in several large cities there: Philippi, Thessalonica, Berea, Athens and Corinth (Acts 16:8 – 18:17).

Thessalonica was the capital and the largest city. It had a synagogue. On three Sabbath days, Paul went there and proclaimed Christ using the scriptures (the Old Testament). It was a mixed group and the Jews started a riot so they had to leave after a short while. Even with that short stay, quite a few people believed: Jews, Greeks and prominent women (Acts 17:1-9). This is the church Paul is writing this letter to.

Even though he was not there long, he was very pleased with them and said they had become a model to all the believers in Macedonia and Achaia. He said they had turned from idols to serve the living and true God.

He had strong opposition there, but dared to preach the gospel in spite of it. He was not trying to please men, but God. He said they worked night and day in order not to be a burden to them and were gentle among them, like a mother caring for her little children. He said they became imitators of God's church in Judea. They suffered from their countrymen like those churches suffered from the Jews. They killed Jesus and the prophets and drove Paul out to keep him from speaking to the Gentiles so that they too, could be saved.

Longing to See Them

Paul said when they were torn away from them, after such a short time (in person but not in thought) he wanted to return, but Satan stopped them. When he could stand it no longer, he sent Timothy to find out about their faith.

He was afraid his labors might have been in vain, but when Timothy brought back a good report, he was filled with joy.

Living to Please God

He urged them to continue to grow and to lead holy lives, to mind their own business, to work with their own hands and thereby win the respect of outsiders (4:11, 12). It is God's will that they should be sanctified (set apart).

The Coming of the Lord

Paul explains more perfectly what will happen when the Lord returns. First, he told them not to grieve for those who die in the Lord, like they would for those who have no hope.

We believe that Jesus died and rose again and will take with Him to heaven those that have died 'in' Him (when He comes back).

This is the order it will happen:

The Lord will descend from heaven with a shout with the voice of the archangel and with the trump of God.

The dead in Christ (believers) will rise first.

The living believers will be caught up together with them in the clouds to meet the Lord in the air and so will we ever be with the Lord forever. (He will not put foot on this earth).

Christians will not be surprised because they will recognize the signs. We belong to the day. Whether we are awake (alive) or asleep (dead) we will live together with Him.

(For more on the coming back of the Lord see 1 Corinthians 15:35-54.)

In ending, Paul urges them to respect the elders, who are over them, and to hold them in highest regard because of their work.

He told them not to be idle. (It seems like they may have been looking for the Lord to return soon; by being idle).

Paul told them to give thanks in all circumstances and to have this letter read to all the brothers.

2 Thessalonians

A Review

2 Thessalonians was written by Paul on his second missionary journey from Corinth, shortly after the first letter. He was still encouraged by their faith and their desire to learn more. Its main purpose was to make clearer things concerning the coming of Christ.

He wanted to them to feel safe in the fact that the believing righteous would be saved and go to heaven to be with Jesus, but just as sure, those who do not obey, the unbelieving, will be punished with everlasting destruction and shut out from the presence of the Lord (1:9).

It seems someone had written them a letter and signed Paul's name saying the day of the Lord had already come. He told them not to let anyone deceive them. He said in all his letters he writes a greeting by his own hand (3:17).

Lawlessness

Paul wrote the Lord will not come until a rebellion occurs (2:3); a falling away or a leaving of the truth. It might be from persecution, false teachers, temptations, worldliness, or not enough knowledge.

He wrote that iniquity was already at work. This is Satan's lie: Believe me, not God. Most people will.

Paul said, if we do not believe the truth, God will send us a strong delusion that we may believe the lie and be damned (2:11).

There are untold numbers of anti-Christ's in the world. Anyone who is not 'for Christ' is against Him. Jesus Himself said in the Sermon on the Mount, 'straight is the gate and narrow is the way which leads to life, and few there be that find it' (Matt. 7:14). He also said to watch out for false prophets. They come to you in sheep's clothing, but inwardly they are ravening wolves (Matt. 7:15).

Paul also said in Acts 20:29 that after his departure, wolves would enter in among them, not sparing the flock. Of their own selves, men would arise and draw disciples after them.

He wrote Timothy the time would come when men would not endure sound doctrine (2 Tim. 4:3-5).

Timothy never wrote a letter (that we have) but I'm sure he really had a hard time keeping the churches that were entrusted to him pure after Paul's departure.

Many anti-Christs of renown have arisen in the world. The Catholic religion had probably made more changes than any 'Christian' religion. The unbelieving Jews still flourish, communism and atheism abound. Mohammed, Stalin, Hitler, the Arabs of today…

The church itself is not walking the straight line, in some instances. We will always have to be on guard and not grow weary. It will never be easy, but the reward will be worth it.

Things will grow worse as time progresses but Jesus Himself says it will be an ordinary day when He comes, but make no mistake; every eye will see Him and we will *know* what is taking place (comment by author).

Paul told them to stand firm and hold to the teaching we passed on to you by word or by letter.

Again, Paul condemns idleness. He had admonished them about this in his first letter (1 Thess. 5:14). In this letter, he *commanded* them to work. In 3:6-15, he told the members to keep away and do not associate with those who are not working so they would feel ashamed. He said, 'if a man will not work, he shall not eat'.

Some, in our generation, have set a date when they thought Jesus was coming, sold their property and gone to a waiting place, but only God knows when that day will be.

1 Timothy

A Review

Background:

Timothy was the son of a Greek father and a Jewish mother named Eunice (2 Tim. 1:5). His grandmother was named Lois and was also Jewish. They were faithful to the Jewish religion and taught Timothy.

Paul refers to him as his son in the faith. (He was probably converted by Paul on his first missionary journey). They met later at Lystra, where Timothy lived, while Paul was on his second missionary journey.

Paul wanted to take him, along with Silas, on their trip. Paul circumcised Timothy (Acts 16:1-3). Not because he needed to, but because of the Jews who knew him. The brothers at Lystra spoke well of him.

When this letter was written, Paul had sent Timothy to Ephesus, where there seemed to be a need for authority and further teaching. It was probably in 62 or 63 AD, after Paul's release from the Roman prison.

Ephesus was in Asia. In fact, it was one of the seven churches of Asia that John wrote to when he was on the island of Patmos (Rev. 2:1-7). They had forsaken their first love when John wrote about 5 years later.

The great Roman fire was July 19, 64 AD. After that, Nero really started persecuting Christians. The Roman-Jewish war started in 66 AD. They were out of that area by then.

Warning Against False Teachers

False doctrines were already being taught. Timothy was to correct this (1 Tim. 1:3-11). Paul said he was once a blasphemer, a persecutor and a violent man, but was shown mercy because he acted in ignorance. He said Jesus came into the world to save sinners.

Paul urged that requests, prayers, intercessions and thanksgiving be made for everyone–kings and those in authority, so that we would be able to lead peaceful and quiet lives. He said there was one mediator between God and men, Jesus Christ, and to pray in faith.

Women

Paul instructs women to dress modestly–let her beauty be her good deeds. He also says the women are not to teach when men are present or to have authority over them.

Paul said Adam was deceived, that Eve was, and a sinner, but she would be saved through child-bearing if they are taught to obey the Lord.

Elders and Deacons

In Chapter three, Paul presents the qualifications of elders and deacons. He says it is a good work, a sacrifice, but the love of saving souls should be the motivation.

Elders:
Must be above reproach
The husband of one wife
Temperate, self-controlled, respectable and hospitable
Able to teach
Not given to drunkenness

Not violent, gentle, not quarrelsome, not a lover of money
He must manage his own family well (if he can't manage his own family, how can he take care of God's church?)
He must not be a recent convert
Must have a good reputation with outsiders

Deacons:
Men worthy of respect
Sincere, not indulging in much wine
Not a pursuer of dishonest gain
Keep hold of the faith
One wife and obedient children

Wives:
Women worthy of respect
Not malicious talkers
Temperate and trustworthy
(1 Timothy 3:1-12)

These instructions were so people would know how to conduct themselves in God's household. Notice: these qualities were to be evident *before* they were appointed leaders.

To Timothy

The Spirit says in later times some will abandon their faith and follow deceiving spirits such as: forbidding people to marry and abstaining from certain foods. Have nothing to do with myths and old wives' tales.

Paul told Timothy physical training is of some value, but godliness has value for all things; in this life and the life to come (4:8). He told him not to let anyone look down him because he was young, but to set an example for the believers in speech, in life, in love, in faith and in purity.

Widows, Elders and Slaves

Paul told Timothy not to rebuke an older man harshly, but exhort him as if he were his father, treat the younger men as brothers, older women as mothers and younger women as sisters.

If a widow has children or grandchildren, they should take care of her for: 'if anyone does not provide for his relatives, he has denied the faith and is worse than an unbeliever' (5:8).

If a widow has no one to take care of her, she should not be taken care of by the church unless:

- She is over 60 years old
- Has been faithful to her husband
- Is well-known for good deeds, such as, bringing up children, showing hospitality, washing the feet of the saints, helping those in trouble and devoting herself to all kinds of good deeds.

The younger widows should marry, have children, and manage their homes...

Do not accept an accusation against an elder unless brought by two or three witnesses.

Stop drinking only water; use a little wine because of your stomach and your frequent illnesses.

The ones under slavery should show their master respect, especially if they are brothers. We brought nothing into the world, so we can take nothing out of it. The love of money is a root of all kinds of evil (6:10). Some people, eager for money, have wandered from the truth.

Paul's Charge to Timothy

- Fight the good fight of the faith

- Take hold of the eternal life to which you were called (when you made your good confession in the presence of many witnesses. Paul must have been a witness)

- Command those who are rich, in the present world, not to be arrogant but do good, be generous and willing to share. In this way they will lay up treasure for themselves

- Guard what has been entrusted to your care

2 Timothy

A Review

This is Paul's last known letter (4:6). It was written from Rome during a second imprisonment, about 67 AD. The Jewish war was going on. It started in 66 AD and lasted 3 ½ years until 70 AD. (It was not being fought in Rome, but in the Jerusalem area).

Paul was beheaded in May or June of 68 AD. Nero committed suicide the same year on June 9, 68 AD (according to Josephus).

You could see how much Paul loved Timothy, calling him his 'dear son'.

After Paul's release from his first imprisonment, he was free several years. At the time of this writing, he knew this would be it, that his departure was near (4:6). He had some last things to say to his beloved Timothy.

1. He wanted to exhort him in his ministry there at Ephesus, where he had been sent. He wanted him to know he loved, missed and wanted to see him. He reminded him of the gift that was passed on to him by the laying on of Paul's hands (1:1-6).

   Paul was not ashamed of his bonds and didn't want Timothy to be either, saying God did not give us a spirit of timidity (1:7).

   He asked that Timothy keep, as a pattern, the sound teaching he had heard from him and to pass on this same teaching to reliable men who would be able to teach others also (2:2). Paul told Timothy to do his best to present himself to God, as a workman who correctly handles the word of truth.

2. Paul wanted to warn Timothy of coming troubles, both inside and outside the church (Chapters 2 and 3).

   He said the Lord's servant must not quarrel. He said in the last days, perilous times would come. Things like: lovers of self, lovers of money, boastful, proud, abusive, disobedient to parents, ungrateful, unholy, without love, unforgiving, slanderous, without self-control, brutal, not lovers of good, treacherous, rash, conceited and lovers of pleasure rather than lovers of God (3:1-4).

   Paul said all who lead godly lives will be persecuted (3:12).

   He said all scripture is useful in making the man of God complete and equipped for every good work.

   He gave him this charge: Preach the word; be prepared in season, out of season, correct, rebuke with all longsuffering and doctrine. Do the work of an evangelist (4:5).

   Paul said he had finished the race, he had kept the faith. He knew there would be a crown of righteousness awaiting him at 'that day'. The promise is to all who would be faithful.

3. Paul told Timothy to come to visit him in prison and bring his cloak, scrolls and parchments (Chapter 4). Also, to bring Mark with him. He said only Luke was with him. Luke was with him until the end.

   He wrote the gospel of Luke and Acts. The cloak, scrolls and parchments, left at Troas, seems to indicate Paul was arrested suddenly without any belongings.

   He also wanted Timothy to come before winter (he would need his cloak, winter of 67-68 AD).

   He may have wanted to personally give his books and parchments to one of his beloved helpers

Titus

A Review

Written by Paul in 63–64 AD after 1 Timothy. Titus was a Gentile. He most probably was converted by Paul (1:4). He accompanied Paul when he carried the offering to the poor saints in Jerusalem (2 Cor. 8:16) from the Gentile churches. He was a young man like Timothy who Paul was training to carry on the work after him. At the time of this letter, Paul had left him in Crete to set in order things that were lacking, namely ordaining elders in every city (where there were churches).

1. Crete is first mentioned on the day of Pentecost as having Jews present the day the church was established (Acts 2:11).
2. When Paul was being sent to Rome for trial, his ship passed by Crete (Acts 27:7-13).
3. After Paul's Roman imprisonment, he visited Crete and left Titus there to continue the work.

Crete was a large island southeast of Greece. When the people went home after Pentecost, they most probably took the gospel to their fellow Cretans. The Cretans had a bad reputation but salvation can change us into a new person (Titus 1:11, 12): Regenerate our sinful nature into a righteous one (2:11-14, 5-7).

In Titus 2:15, Paul writes Titus to encourage and rebuke (with all authority). It doesn't say so, but implies Paul laid his hands on Titus as he did Timothy because one of the main things he was to do was to appoint elders and bishops in every town (church) (verses 6 and 7).

The qualifications in Titus are not as thorough as the ones in 1 Timothy 3:1-7 because he doesn't mention deacons or their wives. Qualifications in Titus:

Blameless
Husband of one wife
Having faithful children
Not accused of riot or unruly
Not self-willed
Not soon angry
Not given to wine
No stiker
Not given to filthy lucre (money)
A lover of hospitality
A lover of good men
Sober
Just
Holy
Temperate
Holding fast the faithful words he has been taught that he may be able to exhort and convince the naysayers.

Some things Paul wrote Titus to instill in different members and would apply to any Christian are these:

Aged men, be sober, grave, temperate, sound in faith, charity and patience.

Aged women, behavior that becometh holiness, not false accusers, not given to much wine, teachers of good.

Young women, be sober, love their husbands, love their children, be discreet, chaste, keepers at home, good, obedient to their own husbands.

Young men, likewise be sober minded, showing a pattern of good works, uncorrupt in doctrine, grave, sincere, sound in speech, that no evil thing he said of them.

Servants, be obedient to their masters – please them well in all things, not answering again (don't talk back), don't steal from them, be trustworthy (2:1-10).

Paul wrote the grace of God has appeared all men (everybody). He wrote Titus to avoid foolish controversies, genealogies, arguments and quarrels about the law. He said after warning a divisive person twice, to have nothing to do with him (3:9, 10).

Paul had intended to winter at Nicopolis (3:12). Where this is and where he was last arrested we don't know. He wrote Timothy he had left his cloak at Troas (2 Tim. 4:13).

Philemon

A Review

Written by Paul while in a Roman prison where he had been for the past two years but was expecting to be released soon (62 – 63 AD). This was a personal letter to Philemon and perhaps his wife and son (1:2). It concerned his slave, Onesimus, who had run away and perhaps stolen some money to do so (1:18, 19). Paul would repay. Sometime while Paul was in prison, he had met Onesimus and had taught the gospel to him (1:10).

It doesn't say where Philemon lived in this letter, but in Colossians 4:9 it says he as one of you (Colossae). Also, when he was sent back (under Roman law it was necessary to return a runaway slave), he was accompanied by Tychicus along with the letter and also one to the Colossians (Col. 4:7-9). This may have been partly for Onesimus' protection while traveling. Paul says Onesimus is now a dear brother.

1. The gospel is for everyone, slave or free
2. A slave does not become free because he has been baptized, neither people in prison today
3. No man is too lowly to be taught
4. We should forgive those who sin against us, if they repent and ask us. Paul could have ordered Philemon to accept Onesimus back but appealed to him on the basis of love.

Hebrews

A Review

We cannot be certain of the writer of this book nor the date. We can be certain that he had a thorough knowledge of the Old Testament and most probably was Jewish, through when inspired by God, it doesn't matter.

Chapter 13:23 refers to Timothy's release. Verse 24 shows it was written from Italy. The end of the letter, 'grace be with you all, amen', was the way Paul concluded his letters (see Rom. 16:20, I Cor. 16:23, 2 Cor. 13:14, Gal. 6:18, Eph. 6:24, Phil. 4:23, Col. 4:18, I Thess. 4:28, 2 Thess. 3:18, 1 Tim. 6:20, 2 Tim. 4:22, Titus 3:15, Phil. 25). As to the date, Jerusalem was still standing (8:4, 10:8 and 11). The temple sacrifices were still going on.

Hebrews 2:3 says: how shall we escape if we ignore such a great salvation? That which was first announced by the Lord, was confirmed to us by those who heard Him. Paul declares that his apostleship came directly from a vision from Jesus (Acts 9:1-6, 22:1-21, 26:9-19).

The dictionary says to confirm is to acknowledge with definite assurance, to add strength, prove, validate… 2:4 goes on to say, 'God, also bearing them witnesses, both with signs and wonders, miracle, gifts of the Holy Spirit…'

Also, Paul had nothing to do with teaching the Jews in Jerusalem in the beginning. By writing to them, the letter might carry more weight if no name was attached. Personally, I lean toward Paul as the author.

The reason, it seems, for writing to the Hebrews was because of the danger of leaving the church and going back into Judaism. They were being persecuted. Stephen had been killed, some had lost their property, some had to meet in secret. Of course even in the best of times, people leave.

Hebrews can be separated into seven discussions:
1. Christ better than angels (1:1, 2 and 18).
2. Christ better than Moses (3:1-4, 13).
3. Christ better than the High Priest (4:14, 7:10)
4. Christ author of a better covenant (7:11 – 8:13)
5. Christ, a better sacrifice (9:1-10, 39).
6. Christ proves better blessings (11:1-40)
7. Christ expects better service (12:1-13, 25).

(1) Christ Better than Angels

God, having of old time, spoken unto the fathers by the prophets in diverse portions and in diverse manners, hath at the end of these days spoken unto us in His Son…

Christ is a part of the godhead; active in the creation. He became flesh and lived on earth. After finishing what He came to do, He is now seated at God's right hand.

Angel's are servants of God; Christ is the Son of God (1:14), equal with God. Angels are ministering spirits sent forth to do service for the sake of those that shall inherit salvation (vs 14).
1. They bear away the souls of the righteous in death (Luke 16:22)
2. They aid in bringing salvation to the lost (Acts 10:3). (They do not personally teach.)
3. They watch over little children (Matt. 18:10).
4. They rejoice when sinners repent (Luke 15:7).
5. Worshipping them is forbidden (Col. 1:18).
6. They are not mediators, only Jesus is this (1 Tim. 2:5).

Although Christ became a little lower than the angels while on earth, so he could die like a man (angels do not die), after his death, God put all things in subjection to Him (2:7). His death was necessary for the redemption of man because He was made sin for us, our atonement.

The Law of Moses never provided forgiveness except from year to year, but through Christ's death on the cross, it provided a continued forgiveness.

(2) Christ Better than Moses

Moses and Christ had similar backgrounds. Both were Israelites, left high stations in life to perform a mission, both were rejected, both completed their mission and both used miracles to show they were from God, among other similarities.

As angels are servants, so was Moses. Jesus is a Son. Like the Israelites under Moses, the new Christians were in danger of falling away because of the deceitfulness of sin and unbelief; causing them to wander 40 years and to lose a whole generation of people.

(3) Christ Better than the High Priest

Having a great high priest who has passed through the heavens…The Levite priest passed through curtains in the tabernacle.

Leviticus 16 details the duties of the high priest. Under the Law of Moses on the Day of Atonement, he wore special linen garments that were kept in the sanctuary. It required four sacrifices: a bull, for a sin offering and a ram for a burnt offering for his own family. After this, of the two male goats that were left, one was chosen by lot and killed. Its blood was sprinkled on the mercy seat to make atonement for the sins of the people. The remaining goat (called the scapegoat) had the high priest's hands laid on its head, confessing the sins of the people and driven off to an uninhabited place.

Then the high priest bathed himself and washed his clothes before entering the camp. The bull and goat were carried outside the camp and completely burned. This happened only one day in the year, Atonement Day.

Hebrews 4:15 says we have not a high priest that cannot be touched with the feeling of our infirmities, but one that has been tempted in all points like we are. Verse 16 says to draw near with boldness unto the throne of grace, that we may receive mercy and find grace to help in time of need. Christ is the high priest.

Priests from Aaron died and a new priest would have to take his place but Christ will never be interrupted, as He will last forever.

He could not have been a priest on earth because he came in the line of Judah. The Levites were the earthly priests. He was said to be after the order of Melchezedek. He came before the Law and was picked by God. We know nothing of his lineage. Christ is the high priest of a new covenant, not like the old one. Christians are priests. We can go to our high priest, Jesus, anytime in prayer, repenting and He will interceded for us to God. He will forgive us and remember our sins no more.

The Hebrews had not grown as much as they should have, being content with the first principles of the gospel (Chapter 6). They should have been teachers, but instead needed to be taught again. Peter referred to young Christians as 'newborn babes'.

Spiritual growth comes with Bible study, meditation, prayer, faithfulness and overcoming struggles with temptation. The goal of a Christian is to reach perfection.

Some of the First Principles We Should Know

1. *Faith* – without it, no one can please God.

2. *Repentance* – a condition of forgiveness
3. *Baptism* – a burial in water (representing the death, burial and resurrection of Christ). This is when our sins are washed away and we get into Christ. God adds us to His church and writes our names in the book of life in heaven. A new life must follow.
4. Another fundamental thing we must believe is: Jesus Christ is the Son of God and that He was raised from the dead. Without the resurrection, our faith is in vain.
5. Another thing we should know is that the laying on of hands by the apostles would cease because the apostles were the only ones who could pass on miraculous abilities (Acts 8:18). When they died, that was the end of it.
6. Heaven and hell; one day Jesus will return and all nations will appear before Him in judgment (Matt. 25:31) (from the beginning of creation).
7. We should know that there is no other way. As under the law, if it was not kept, they were doomed. Under Christ it's the same. There is no more sacrifice for sin. His way is the only way. God will forgive any sin if we repent and turn back to Him, but if we leave Him, He will let us. He does not force obedience.

(4) Christ is the Author of a Better Covenant

The law was temporary. It made nothing perfect. On the other hand, Jesus is perfect and He's always there for us. He *daily* intercedes for us, not yearly.

God always has a pattern for everything. The plan of salvation has a pattern. The worship has a pattern. Christian living has a pattern. Prayer has a pattern. Singing has a pattern. Giving has a pattern. The family has a pattern. Preaching has a pattern. It was the same in the Old Testament–the ark, the temple, the worship had a pattern.

The law was added because of transgressions until the seed should come (Gal. 3:19). 'The time is coming when I will make a new covenant...I will put my laws in their hearts...I will forgive their wickedness and remember their sins no more'. By calling this covenant new, He has made the first one obsolete and what is obsolete and aging will soon disappear. (He would soon cause the temple worship to disappear altogether. We know the temple fell in 70 AD).

(5) Christ Provides Better Sacrifices

We no longer have to offer all those bulls and goats. Jesus gave His life – offered His own blood for us. We don't have to go to the feasts, taking all those animals for sacrifice.

How does our spirit come in contact with the blood of Christ? Christ shed His blood when He was crucified. Romans 6:3 says, 'all we who were baptized into Christ were baptized into His death'. When Christ died and became the mediator of a new covenant, He also set them free from the sins committed under the first covenant (9:15). He died for everybody.

The sacrifice of Christ was for the removal of our sins. It was God's way of reconciling us to Him. 'God so loved the world that He gave His only begotten Son that whosever believeth on Him should not perish but have eternal life' (John 3:16).

The writer of Hebrews calls on us to persevere. Not forsaking the assembling together as the manner of some is, but exhorting one another; and so much the more, as you see the day approaching (10:25).

The early Christians assembled on the first day of the week (the Lord's Day). Sometimes they had to meet at night but never-the-less on the first day of the week. Some were forsaking the worship then and needed to be encouraged as now.

Some try to make 'the day' something else, but we know when the Lord's Day is. No one knew when Jerusalem was going to be destroyed or when the judgment is drawing near. Heaven is reached by a lifetime of patient and faithful service.

(6) Christ Provides Better Blessings

Hebrews Chapter 11 is called the 'faith Chapter'. 'Faith is being sure of what we hope for and certain of what we do not see' (11:1).

(The mind is thoroughly convinced). We believe there is a God. That everything was created by Him, that the godhead comprises God, Jesus and the Holy Spirit. That Jesus came to earth, was crucified and rose from the dead and is coming again to receive us unto Him in heaven.

Chapter 11 lists many men of faith that caused them to act on it.

1. Abel offered a pleasing sacrifice (Gen. 4:10)
2. Enoch walked with God (was translated) (Gen. 5:24)
3. Noah built an ark to save his family from things not seen (Gen. 5 – 10).
4. Abraham (and Sarah) is called the father of the faithful. He left his home and went to an unknown place, offered his promised son as a sacrifice, and believed in the resurrection (Gen. 12 – 25).
5. Isaac passed on the blessing to his sons (Gen 25 – 28).
6. Jacob blessed Joseph's sons… (Gen. 27 – 35).
7. Joseph, 'God will bring you out of this place. Carry my bones with you to the land God swore to give you' (Gen. 50:24, 25, Gen. 39 – 50).
8. Moses, when he was grown up refused to be called the son of Pharaoh's daughter, choosing to suffer ill treatment with the people of God. He believed in the promises to Abraham and the heavenly reward (Ex. 2)

9. The Israelites (by faith) passed through the Red Sea, marched around the walls of Jericho, trusted in Rahab (as she also trusted).

10. David (the only king of Israel in the list) showed faith by his humility, his penitence, his honor towards Saul. He wrote many prophecies and psalms.

11. Other prophets and leaders were Barak, Gideon, Samson, Jephthah, Samuel and the prophets… Some of the things they endured: through faith they conquered kingdoms, administered justice, shut the mouths of lions, escaped the sword, routed enemies in battle, raised the dead, endured torture, faced jeers and flogging, were chained, stoned, sawed in two, put to death by the sword, went about in sheepskins and goatskins, destitute, persecuted and mistreated.

A good example is Jeremiah, a prophet to Judah for 40 years before the Babylonian captivity. They had become unfaithful and God was about to bring a distant nation against them. Jeremiah wrote, 'to whom can I speak and give warning? Who will listen to me?' They even dug a pit for him and plotted to kill him. They ridiculed and mocked him, but he wrote, 'if I say I will not mention Him or speak any more in His name, His word is in my heart like a fire, shut up in my bones. I am weary of holding it in; indeed, I cannot'. The people did not heed his warning and Jerusalem was destroyed the first time in 586 BC.

Hebrews is reminding the Christians of the past, not wanting it to be repeated. None of these people of faith saw what had been promised in their generation. Together, with us, they will receive their great reward through the blood of Christ (2 Tim. 4:8). It reached back to the beginning of time and will continue on until the end.

(7) Christ Expects Better Services

Sometimes we need to be reminded of the hardships others have endured, the sacrifices they have made. Those Hebrews this letter is addressed to were familiar with the ones who had gone before. They needed to be reminded of how much better things are under the new covenant. They did not want to go back! If these witnesses could do it, we can.

Life is like a race, a struggle; put away everything that hinders us that we can. This race does not have one winner. All who endure are winners. Jesus, for the joy that was set before Him, endured the cross. He did it for us, for our salvation. We shall also reap, it we faint not. Trials make us stronger.

We must continue in Bible study, meeting together and prayer to stay strong. God doesn't bring trouble on us but allows it to happen. If life was too good here, we might not strive to get to heaven. Jesus said, 'blessed are you when people insult and persecute you…' (Matt. 5:11).

We are only sojourners on this earth. Our sufferings are only for a short time until we reach heaven and a place of rest. Jesus is the mediator of a new covenant a better covenant.

Thank you, Jesus.

James

A Review

Written by James; one of the Lord's half-brothers (Gal. 1:19). It is written to the twelve tribes scattered among the nations (Jews). It seems to have been written before the Gentiles received the gospel.

James grew up in a carpenter's home in Nazareth, as did Jesus (Matt. 13:55). He moved to Capernaum when Jesus began His ministry (John 2:12). At first he did not believe Jesus was the Christ (John 7:1-5). He was there on Pentecost (Acts 1:14). He was a leader in the Jerusalem church (Acts 15:13, 21:18). Josephus wrote James was martyred about 62 AD.

It seems like every sentence in James is important. It's almost as if Jesus himself was speaking as it is similar to the Sermon on the Mount (Matt. 5–7). The theme of both is perfection.

James and Jesus

1. Jesus said: be perfect, therefore, as your heavenly father is perfect (Matt. 5:48)

   James said: That you may be perfect and entire, lacking nothing (1:4)

2. Jesus said: If you have faith and doubt not…'

   James said: But let him ask in faith, nothing doubting (1:6-8)

3. Jesus said: Everyone that asketh receiveth (Matt. 7:8)

   James said: you have not because you ask not (4:2)

4. Jesus said: be not therefore anxious for the morrow, for the morrow will be anxious for itself (Matt. 6:34)

James said: whereas ye know not what shall be on the morrow (4:14)

There are many more similarities in the letter, but throughout, the teachings of Christ are easily seen.

James and Paul

There are also similarities to Paul's writing.

1. Paul said: the righteous judgment of God; who will render to every man according to his works (Rom. 2:6)
   James said: men are justified by works and not by faith only (2:24).

2. Paul said: I will come to you shortly, if the Lord wills (1 Cor. 4:19)
   James said: If the Lord wills, we shall live and do this and that (4:15).

3. Paul said: Neither give place to the devil (Eph. 4:27)
   James said: Resist the devil and he will flee from you (4:7)

4. Paul said: Be not fashioned according to this world (Rom. 12:2)
   James said: … the Christian should keep himself unspotted from the world (1:27).

It is also clearly seen that James and Paul taught the same things. Both were guided by the Holy Spirit.

Some Lessons We Should Take to Heart

1. Faith has no room for doubt

2. God allows us to be tempted but does not tempt us Himself. We must prove that we can persevere.

3. Be slow to speak and slow to anger. Anger does not bring about the good influence God desires and men need to see in us. Control our tongues!

4. Don't show favoritism. Christianity is not measured by our worldly possessions. The poor are not saved because of their poverty, neither are the rich condemned because of their wealth.

5. Some people claim to be saved 'by faith only'. Let's look back to our review of Hebrews Chapter 11. All the people of faith proved it by their actions. James mentions Abraham and Rahab. Salvation at the moment of faith is not a teaching; anywhere salvation is related.

   How do we get into Christ? We have to have faith alright, but we enter Him through baptism, which represents His death, burial and resurrection. This is the way Paul was taught after he was blind and praying for 3 days after his 'religious experience' on the way to Damascus (Acts 9:1-19).

   James said to humble ourselves before the Lord and He will lift us up (4:10).

6. James said what causes fights and quarrels among us is wanting something but don't get it (4:1, 2).

   Pursuing pleasures of this world is dangerous to our salvation. It crowds out Bible study, prayer, fellowship with Christians, takes away money that could be put to better use. It actually does not bring us the peaceful life we desire and the joy that being near to God brings us.

7. Suffering for the Lord and Christianity was going on then. James said we must be patient (ex. Job) and stand firm until the Lord's coming (5:7). He was aware of the coming destruction of Jerusalem. Jesus had told them about it in Matthew 24 and Luke 21.

8. James said a Christian can err from the truth. If we would be able to help restore that person it certainly would show an act of Christian love. Paul wrote, 'in doing this thou shall save both thyself and them that hear thee' (1 Tim. 4:16).

James doesn't claim to be anyone special or refer to Jesus except to say he was a servant of Jesus (James 1:1). Jesus made a special appearance to James after His resurrection, related by Paul (1 Cor. 15:7).

1 Peter

A Review

Written by the apostle Peter in the mid-60's. It was written to Christians scattered in Asia Minor. The places were represented in Jerusalem on Pentecost and heard Peter's sermon (Acts 2:9, 10).

Some Background of Peter From the Gospels

He was from Bethsaida on Lake Galilee.

He was a fisherman as was his brother Andrew. Andrew found his brother and told him, 'we have found the Messiah' (John 1:41).

He was told by Jesus to 'come follow me and I will make you fishers of men' (Matt. 4:19).

Jesus healed Peter's wife's mother of a fever (he was married) (Matt. 8:14).

He was made an apostle (Matt. 10:2).

Peter was the first to make the good confession (Matt. 16:13-18).

He was given the keys of the kingdom (Matt. 16:19).

He was present at the transfiguration of Christ, along with James and John (Matt. 17:1-5).

He cut off Malchus' ear (the servant of the high priest) when they came to arrest Jesus (John 18:10-12).

He denied Jesus 3 times before the crucifixion (Mark 14:66-72).

He ran (along with John) to see the empty tomb (John 20:1-10).

He was the first apostle to see Jesus alive after the resurrection (Luke 24:34).

Jesus told him to feed the flock of God (John 21:15-17).

He was present when the Lord ascended to Heaven (Matt. 28:16).

Some Background From Acts

Peter preached the first gospel sermon on Pentecost to Jews (Acts 2).

Peter preached the first gospel sermon to the Gentiles (Acts 9:43).

He received a 15-day visit from Paul (Gal. 1:18).

He raised Dorcas from the dead (Acts 9:39…)

He visited Antioch (Gal. 2:11-17)

He was accompanied by his wife as he traveled (1 Cor. 9:5).

He was an elder (1 Peter 5:1).

He was crucified (head downward) in Rome at the age of 75 by Nero (tradition).

As with James, Peter's writing sounds a lot like Jesus':

Peter: If you are reproached for the name of Christ, blessed are you (4:14).
Jesus: blessed are you when men shall reproach you…(Mt. 5:11).

Peter: Even baptism doth now save you (3:21).

Jesus: He that believeth and is baptized shall be saved (Mark 15:16).

Peter wrote to these Christians that they were strangers, or sojourners, in the world as did Abraham and Joseph feel they were. He wrote that even though we may suffer all kinds of trials in this short life, our hope and goal is the salvation of our souls (1:9). Peter was familiar with the prophetic writings and how they tried to figure out when the Savior might come (1:10, 11).

Peter said the plan to send Jesus was conceived before the creation of the world (1:20). Peter said the same Holy Spirit that spoke through the apostles and told them what to say also spoke through the Old Testament prophets. Peter said we should be holy in our manner of living if we want to see God because God will render to every man according to his works (Heb. 12:14). We should fear displeasing God.

He said we have been born again, we are a chosen people and to abstain from sinful desires. We are to submit to authorities and to show proper respect to everyone. If we should suffer unjustly and endure it, it is commendable because Jesus left us that example (2:13-23).

Peter also told us to be submissive to our husbands. If any are not Christians, they might be won by the good behavior of their wives. (People are watching us, especially outsiders). The good spirit of the inner man should be our adorning. The love we have for fellow Christians speaks volumes. We cannot be right with God if our earthly relationships are not right. He wants us to live in harmony with each other, be sympathetic, compassionate and humble.

Peter quoted this from Psalm 34:

Whoever would love life and see good days must keep his tongue from evil and his lips from deceitful speech. He must turn from evil and do good; he must seek peace and pursue it. For the eyes of the Lord are on the righteous and his ears are attentive to their prayers, but the face of the Lord is against those who do evil.

The Christian should not fear what others fear. Even though our bodies might be shattered, our souls can never be destroyed by man.

Peter said: 'The end of all things is near' (4:7).

John said: 'It is the last hour' (1 John 2:18).

John said: 'The time is near' (Rev. 1:3).

This is not speaking of the Lord's return as no one knows when that will be. Within 5 years of this writing, war had started between the Jews and Romans. It lasted 3 ½ years (66 - 70AD).

Nero was persecuting Christians, sending thousands to their deaths. The temple was burned with fire, the daily sacrifice was ended, and the priesthood was ended. This destruction ended the Jewish worship at the temple but not Christian worship. See Jesus' description of the events in Matthew 24:2-25 and Luke 21:20-24. These were the Jews who were still trying to keep the Law of Moses and would not accept Christ as the savior.

These things were probably revealed to Peter. The way he would die was (John 21:18, 19). Peter wrote if anyone should suffer as a Christian, let him not be ashamed (4:16). He was the only one to use this name as official.

The prophet Isaiah in 62:2 had written the children of God would be called by a new name, which the 'mouth of the Lord' would name.

Summary

We have a living hope, a hope the prophets could only glimpse. We are redeemed by Christ; planned before the foundation of the world.

We are His children.

I am told to be holy (because He is).

I am told to be self-controlled (because He is).

I am told to have a sincere love for my brothers and sisters in Christ, to crave the word so that I may grow spiritually and lead a good life.

I am free, but must keep the laws of the land.

I must submit myself to my husband and show him respect.

If I suffer for doing good, I'll be following Jesus' example. He wants a gentle and quiet spirit.

He looks on the inside, not outward adorning.

I must be able to give Bible answers concerning my faith.

I must look after my brothers and sisters in the faith and in the church.

I can cast all my anxieties on Jesus for He cares for me and wants me.

[Along with 1 Peter, Coffman's Commentary on Peter and other parts of the Bibles were reviewed (the gospel and Acts) plus personal comments. C.W.]

2 Peter

A Review

This second letter of Peter's was written a year or so after his first letter (64-67) and a short while before his death (see 1:13, 14). He calls himself Simon Peter, the name Jesus had given him (Mark 3:16). It was written to the same people his first letter was written to – those of 'like precious faith' (1 Peter 1:1, 2 Peter 3:1).

Peter wanted to bring to their remembrance the things they had been taught and to make every effort to add to their faith things like virtue or goodness, knowledge, self-control, perseverance, godliness, brotherly kindness and love. These things would make their calling and election sure.

Jesus had foretold Peter what manner of death he would have (John 21:18, 19). He said he was an eye-witness of His majesty, referring to the time he, James and John went with Jesus on the Mount of Transfiguration and heard God speak these words: 'this is my beloved Son, in whom I am well-pleased'.

Peter said no prophesy of scripture was of private interpretation, but was delivered by men as the Holy Spirit moved them. Even then, though, there were false prophets and there will be false prophets (teachers) among us today. They will bring destruction on themselves and those that follow their teachings. Peter said they would do this through covetousness (money).

Peter said God did not spare the ancient world that sinned, did not spare Sodom and Gomorrah, did not spare the angels and will not spare those today who sin. He said God knows how to deliver the godly out of temptation and to keep the unrighteous under punishment unto the day of judgment.

Between death and the judgment, there is a division between the righteous and the wicked (Luke 16:19-21). We're not given much information on this. Peter says there are those who were once in the right way and went astray. He said they were worse off than in the beginning (2 Peter 2:20, 21).

The third Chapter talks about the second coming of the Lord. Christianity is all about the second coming; the resurrection of the dead and the final judgment. People still tend to doubt it, even after the flood.

It seems to us that things will continue on forever as they are. How could the heavens pass away and melt with a fervent heat? Our generation can understand how this could happen. When the old prophets spoke of this, when Jesus spoke of it, and now Peter, there had been no atomic bomb blast. Now, we can see how it could happen. Jesus knew how it could happen when He said, 'Heaven and earth shall pass away, but my word shall not pass away' (Matt. 24:35).

The Lord foretold the destruction of Jerusalem, the temple and the Jewish way of life (Matt. 24). He also said, 'many false prophets shall arise and shall deceive many, but he that shall endure unto the end will be saved'. The Lord is long suffering, not wanting any to perish or be carried away by the error of the wicked. We need to be well informed so we will know how to withstand any false teaching so that we'll be found blameless at His coming.

1, 2 and 3 John

A Review

Written by the apostle John, the brother of James and son of Zebedee. Please read the review of the gospel of John for a more complete review of John the man. The gospel was written by one who was there, who saw and touched him, that we may believe. These other epistles were written to assure us of that salvation. This letter, as well as all the books of the New Testament, was written before 70 AD. Nowhere is it written about as having already happened.

God is Light

God is light. In Him is no darkness at all. If we walk in the light, we have fellowship with Him. God sent His son, Jesus, to die for us as a sacrifice for our sins, once. If we believe Him to be the Christ, confess Him, repent of our sins, are baptized into Him and faithfully keep His commandments, we will be walking in the light. His blood will continually cleanse us from our sins.

If we continue to lead sinful lives, we can have no fellowship with Him, no assurance, no forgiveness. Whoever claims to live in Him must walk as Jesus did. If we (or I should say *when* we) sin, Jesus will speak to the Father on our behalf. The goal of the Christian is to stay free of sin. Keeping the commandments is the test: walking in the light, following the truth, obeying the word. This is how we can know that we are 'in Him', if we keep His word (5:13).

No matter how much faith we have, it will avail us nothing if we don't have love for our brothers (2:9-11). We are to love our brothers but not the things of the world – the lust of the eyes, the lust of the flesh and the pride of life. These things will all pass away but the love of God lasts forever (2:16, 17).

Anti-Christ's

What John calls 'anti-Christ's', others call false teachers (2 Peter 2:1, 2). John said the anti-Christs are the ones who deny that Jesus is the Christ. Some were once Christians who had left the faith (2:19).

John said in 2:18, 'it is the last hour'. People were trying to deceive, most of the Jews were hanging on to the Law of Moses, not believing in Jesus as the Christ. The time was drawing near for something drastic (the destruction of the temple and the un-believing Jews). He is writing this, hoping they will not be led astray (2:26).

Children of God

Behold what manner of love the Father hath bestowed upon us, that we should be called children of God. All of us were created in God's image in the beginning.

Now, believers are children of God. In the resurrection, we shall be like Him and see Him like He is (3:2).

To be part of this, we must be purified just as He is pure. We cannot do this on our own. We must abide in Him (3:6). If we abide in Him, we won't want to do sinful things. If we do sin, He is faithful to forgive us through repentance and prayer (3:9).

Character of a Christian

A profession of faith will be shown in a Christian's behavior. John said to marvel not, if the world hates us (3:13).

Josephus wrote that not only did Cain kill his brother Abel, but that he was evil in other ways. We are often hated for doing good, but we should do good anyway. We should avoid things that would cause hostility but a good life in itself is a reminder to them.

A stingy person would be a bad example to the world. We must do more than talk, but show our love by deeds (3:18). A Christian should have a good conscience. If we feel reluctant to do something, we probably shouldn't (3:19, 20). If we have a clear conscience we can go boldly to God.

Greater is He that is in you than he that is in the world (the indwelling of God is greater than anything Satan can teach, 4:4).

Faith and Love

John quotes Jesus in 5:2, 'if you love me, you will keep my commandments'. He said His commandments were not grievous.

John said, 'these things have I written unto you, that ye may know, that ye have eternal life...' (5:13).

God does not ignore our requests in prayer. We can pray for a sinful brother. We can pray for illnesses. We can pray for physical needs. We can pray for material blessings or whatever our daily needs are (3 John 2).

We can be confident that we will be saved if we continue in faithfulness. (3:14, 18 and 19, 24), (4:13, 16-18), (5:18-20).

Second John

The elder to the elect Lady and her children probably means the older John to the church and members. (Whether to one family or the whole family, the message is the same.)

He rejoiced that some were walking in the truth, but, many deceivers are gone forth in the world. He calls them anti-Christ's. He warned us not to be deceived and not to give them any encouragement.

It reminds me of what God told Joshua, '...Do not turn to the right or to the left' (Joshua 1:6-8). He said if anyone comes to you and brings not this teaching, receive him not in your house and give him no greeting (verse 10).

Third John

Written by the same John as 1 and 2 John. The letter is addressed to Gaius, an individual, whom he called 'beloved'. He prayed that, in all things, Gaius would prosper and be in health, even as his soul prospered (verse 2).

Christians needed to be in good health and prosperity, to be hospitable, to aid in good causes and to help the traveling preachers then.

Some of the brethren had given a good report of Gaius. John had probably taught him because he wrote, 'greater joy have I none than this, to hear of my children walking in the truth' (living faithfully).

Verse 7…taking nothing of the Gentiles. People who are not Christians are not expected to give, even now. Afterwards, they are expected to be fellow workers.

Diotrephes did not receive John (verse 9) and probably others, plotting against them (gossiping maliciously).

John was planning to go to that church soon. I wonder how he dealt with Diotrephes. John, the disciple Jesus loved, lived into his nineties and died a natural death. The rest were killed.

<u>Jude</u>
A Review

Written by Jude, the half-brother of Jesus.

'Is not this the carpenter's son? Is not his mother called Mary? And his brethren James and Joseph and Simon and Judas and his sisters?... (Matt. 13:55, 56).

This letter was written to Christians, to exhort them to earnestly contend for the faith. 'The' faith is referring to the requirements of Christianity:

1. Faith that Jesus is the Son of God (Rom. 10:17).
2. Repentance, turning away from sins (1 Cor. 7:10).
3. Confession of that faith before men (Rom. 10:10).
4. Baptism forgives our sins and puts us 'into Christ' (Acts 2:38, 41).
5. We must continue to lead Christ centered lives, following the examples of the early Christians (Acts 2:46, 47).

Jude was very concerned because 'certain men' were creeping in and leading these new Christians astray. He uses three examples they were familiar with, that were once saved, but later destroyed because of their unbelief.

1. The Israelites that were led out of Egypt (Num. 14:28-35).
2. Sodom and Gomorrah (Gen. 19:1-29).
3. Angels that sinned (Rev. 12:7-12).

He also names three people as wicked men who were punished.
1. Cain (Gen. 4:1-12)
2. Balaam (Rev. 2:14)
3. Korah (Num. 16)

Even as far back as Enoch (Noah's great-great-grandfather) he prophesied, 'the Lord is coming with thousands of His holy ones to judge everyone, and to convict all the ungodly of all the ungodly acts they have done in the ungodly way, and of all the harsh words ungodly sinners have spoken against Him'.

Jude said all the apostles warned of these false teachers that would come, walking after their own lusts and for money. Jude said perhaps some can be rescued – snatched from the fire (verses 22 and 23).

He said we should keep building ourselves up in the faith and prayer. Jesus is able to keep us from falling and present us faultless before God (verse 24)

Revelation

A Review

Written by the apostle John, brother of James and son of Zebedee. He also wrote the gospel of John, 1, 2 and 3 John. Now, as
probably the last apostle living, he is writing the last revelation
from God. It is to show His servants what must soon take place
(1:1-3).

He first talks about the second coming. He said Jesus is
coming with clouds and every eye will see Him, even those who
pierced Him (1:7).

At this time, persecution had been going on, starting with
Nero. John was on the island of Patmos. It was a Sunday, the
Lord's Day. He said he was in the Spirit (probably worshipping)
when he heard a loud voice like a trumpet which told him to
write on a scroll what he saw and send it to the seven churches
of Asia. They all had some good in them, but lacked things that
would make them acceptable.

The one speaking was Jesus (1:17-20).

The Seven Churches

Ephesus; forsaken their first love.

Smyrna; they will suffer persecution.

Pergamum; some were following false teaching.

Thyatira; they were tolerating a woman who was immoral and
misleading some.

Sardis; had a reputation of being alive but were dead. A few
were living right.

Philadelphia; you have little strength, yet you have kept my word and have not denied my name (3:8). I will keep you from the hour of trial… (3:10).

Laodicea; neither cold nor hot… I am about to spit you out of my mouth (3:15, 16).

It seems as if Jesus is trying to straighten out these churches, as soon the Christians will be fleeing from Galilee and Jerusalem to other locations [C.W.].

Chapters 4 Through 19

John was taken in a vision to Heaven itself where God and Jesus and innumerable angels were. Jesus spoke again and said, 'come up here and I will show you what must take place after this' (4:1). Jesus opened the first of the seven seals (6:1).

The Seven Seals

First seal: a white horse. He rode out as a conqueror bent on conquest (6:2).

Second seal: a red horse. Its rider was given power to take peace from the earth and to make men slay each other (war).

Third seal: a black horse. He was holding a pair of scales. A voice said, 'a quart of wheat for a day's wages, and three quarts of barley for a day's wages, and do not damage the oil and the wine' (6:6) (famine).

Fourth seal: a pale horse. They were given power over a fourth of the earth to kill by sword, famine and plague and by the wild beasts of the earth (6:7, 8).

Fifth seal: souls that had been slain because of the word of God and the testimony they had maintained. They called out in a loud voice, 'how long...until you avenge our blood?' They were told to wait a little longer (6:9-11).

Sixth seal: an earthquake – everything removed from its place. The people of the earth hid. The great day of wrath had come (6:12-17).

After this, John saw a vision of the saved. There was a great multitude no one could count, from every nation, tribe, people and language. They were wearing white robes – never again will they hunger, never again will they thirst (7:16). God will wipe away every tear from their eyes (7:17).

Seventh seal: There was silence in heaven for about half an hour. An angel with a golden censer offered the prayers of all the saints on the golden altar before the throne.

The Seven Angels

The seven angels who had seven trumpets prepared to sound them (8:6). If the trumpet does not sound a clear call, who will get ready for battle? (1 Cor. 14:8).

First angel: a third of the earth was burned up.

Second angel: a third of the sea turned to blood.

Third angel: a third of the water turned bitter and people died from them.

Fourth angel: a third of the sun, moon and stars turned dark.

Fifth angel: locusts were sent down to torture those who did not have the seal of God on their forehead (for five months). Locusts' life span is five months. The battle for Jerusalem lasted 5 months. Locusts represent the Roman armies.

Sixth angel: a third of mankind was killed by smoke and sulfur. John saw another mighty angel. He said, 'there will be no more delay! In the days when the seventh angel is about to sound his trumpet, the mystery of God will be accomplished, just as He announced to His servants, the prophets'. Measure the temple and count the worshippers there. They will trample on the holy city for 42 months (3 ½ years). Bodies will lie in the street of the great city (Jerusalem) where their Lord was crucified. They will be refused burial (there were too many). At that very hour, a severe earthquake came and collapsed a tenth of the city. The temple covered a tenth of the city (Jerusalem).

Seventh angel: After the seventh angel sounded his trumpet, voices were heard to say: the kingdom of the world has become the kingdom of our Lord and His Christ (11:5). There was no more temple after this.

Prophesies

Daniel 12:11

'From the time that the daily sacrifice is abolished and the abomination that causes desolation is set up, there will be 1290 days (3 ½ years: the length of the Jewish–Roman war).

Jesus; Matt. 24:15-22, Luke 21:20-32

'When you see standing in the holy place 'the abomination that causes desolation' spoken of through the prophet Daniel... let those that are in Judea flee to the mountains... there will be great distress, unequalled from the beginning of the world until now – and never to be equaled again...'

Josephus, the Jewish Historian

The Jewish – Roman war began in the twelfth year of the reign of Nero. A great persecution had started when he accused Christians of setting fire to Rome in AD 64 (6:4). Killing was going on everywhere (6:2). This is what they did to every village: kill, plunder and burn in the areas of Galilee, Samaria and Judea.

Vespasian was in charge of the war until Nero committed suicide in 68 AD. After that, he was made emperor and his son, Titus, took over the war effort. During this time, there was a six month interval before the siege of Jerusalem began. This gave the Christians time to leave as Jesus had suggested in Matthew 24.

The Feast of Unleavened Bread, or Passover, had come and the gates of the temple were opened to the Jews who had come to celebrate as usual. This feast lasted a week. The people who came brought animals to sacrifice and provisions for the week. They were those Jews who were still keeping the Law of Moses, not Christians.

Once they were inside the temple area and the Roman army surrounded them, they were forced to stay inside. Their food ran out and famine killed whole houses. The city was full of dead bodies, too many to bury (11:8, 9). Birds ate their flesh (19:17, 18, 21).

They were given opportunity to leave by Titus buy few did (Josephus). Finally on August 6, 70 AD the temple was burned. The war began in April of 66 AD and ended in August of 70 AD, a total of 3 ½ years.

The number killed in Jerusalem was 1,100,00 and 97,000 captured. This exceeded all destruction in war that had ever been (Josephus).

When John wrote Revelation, none of this had happened yet. Revelation 11:8 says, 'Their bodies <u>will</u> lie in the street of the great city (Jerusalem)…where also their Lord was crucified'.

Also, the temple was still standing. In Revelation 11:1, 2 John was given a measuring rod and told to <u>measure the temple and the altar and to count the worshippers there</u>.

There is no doubt this book, as well as all the other writings in the New Testament were written before 70 AD.

Chapter 12, Satan

The unbelieving Jews were greatly diminished after the war but Satan is still at work. He tried to tempt Jesus and he's at work in the church. When there was war in heaven and he and his angles were hurled to earth, he was filled with fury because he knows his time is short (Chapter 12).

The first great enemy of the church is Satan, who makes himself look like an angel of light (2 Cor. 11:14, 15).

Chapter 13, World Powers

The seven previous world powers that were hostile to God and His people:

1. Egypt
2. Assyria
3. Babylon
4. Medo-Persia
5. Greece
6. Rome
7. Catholicism?

The Roman Empire came to an end in 476 AD. The head of the Roman Catholic Church is still in Rome. It still has followers in every tribe, people, language and nation (13:7). It placed a man as head of the church. It took the written word away from the common man, took away the wine, tortured countless saints during the Spanish Inquisition, introduced graven images, invent-ted purgatory, sold the right to sin, forbade marriage (to some), changed baptism and other things. Whatever rule the Christian lives under, he must follow Christ in the way taught in the Bible. Christianity cannot be defended by force as when Peter drew his sword and cut off Malchus' ear (Matt. 26:51, 52, John 18:10, 11). [666 = evil, 777 = good]

Chapter 14

Again, John was drawn to heaven. The faithful were there, those who had kept themselves pure and blameless. They were singing a new song. Later, he saw an angel flying in mid-air. The angel said to, 'proclaim the gospel to all who live on the earth' (14:6).

Another angel said, 'fallen is Babylon (Jerusalem) the great' (14:8). A third angel said, 'If anyone worships the beast (Roman government) he too will drink of God's wrath' (14:9-11).

A voice from heaven said, 'write: blesses are the dead who die in the Lord. They will rest from their labor, for their deeds will follow them' (14:13). No one ever died in the Lord who was not 'in Him' before they died [C.W.].

Next, John saw on a white cloud, 'one like a son of man' with a sharp sickle in his hand. Another angel called out, 'the time has come to reap' – both the saved and the lost (14:14-20).

Chapter 15, God's Wrath is Completed

With the last seven plagues, God's wrath is completed. Those who had been victorious sang the song of Moses and the Lamb (vs 3).

Chapter 16

Seven angels poured out seven bowls of wrath upon the earth. After that, there was a severe earthquake. Babylon (Jerusalem) received the fury of this wrath.

Chapter 17

One of the angels who had the seven bowls said to me, 'come I will show you the punishment of the great prostitute (Jerusalem)'. It is also called Babylon and Rome is called the Beast. (Once Jerusalem had been the holy city, God had chosen to put His name, 2 Sam. 7:13).

The time frame this is written in and the time is near (1:3) is found in (Chapter 17:10, 11).

There are also seven kings. Five have fallen, one is, the other has not yet come; but when he does come, he must remain for a little while. The beast, who once was and now is not, is an eighth king. He belongs to the seven and is going to his destruction.

Roman Empire and her Kings:

1. Augusts Caesar   27 BC – 14 AD
2. Tiberius (crucified Jesus) 14 – 37
3. Caligula (Caius)   37 – 41
4. Claudius (famine)   41 – 54
5. Nero (fire in 64)   54 – 68 (suicide)
6. Gabba (is)   68 – 69 (murdered)
7. Otho   69
8. Vitllius   69
9. Vesparian (during war)   69 – 79
10. Titus (a son)   79 – 81 AD
11. Domitian (a son)   81 – 96

God has put it into their hearts to accomplish His purpose… until His words are fulfilled (17:10, 11).

Chapter 18, The Fall of Babylon (Jerusalem)

The kings of the earth committed adultery with her. The merchants of the earth grew rich from her excessive luxuries (verse 3).

Then I heard another voice from heaven say, 'come out of her my people…' (verse 4). In one day, her plague will overtake her; death, mourning and famine. She will be consumed by fire (verse 8).

The merchants of the earth will weep and mourn over her because no one buys her cargoes anymore (verse 11). When they see the smoke of her burning, they will exclaim, 'Was there ever a city like this great city?' (verse 18).

Rejoice, saints and apostles and prophets! God has judged her for the way she treated you (verse 20). In her was found the blood of prophets and of the saints (verse 24).

Chapter 19, Hallelujah!

After this, John heard what sounded like the roar of a great multitude in heaven. They shouted 'hallelujah!' (verse 6).

The wedding of the bride (the church) has come...Blessed are those who are invited to the wedding supper of the Lamb (verse 9).

When Jerusalem was destroyed, there was also a great supper but their flesh was left for birds to eat (verses 17 and 21).

Chapter 20

Christians and those faithful from the beginning will reign with Christ. The unfaithful will be tormented day and night forever.

John saw a great white throne. Earth and sky was gone. The dead were standing before the throne and the books were opened, including the book of life. The dead were judged by what was recorded in the books (see Acts 2:41, 47 and Phil. 4:3).

The sea gave up its dead. Death and Hades gave up its dead. If anyone's name was not found written in the book of life, he was thrown into the lake of fire.

Chapter 21, The New Jerusalem

John saw a new heaven and a new earth, for the first heaven and the first earth had passed away as well as the sea. The old order of things had passed away. God will dwell with men. He who overcomes will inherit this.

Hebrews 12:22-24 says, 'you have come to Mount Zion, to the heavenly Jerusalem, the city of the living God. You have come to thousands upon thousands of angels in joyful assembly, to the church of the first born, whose names are written in heaven. You have come to God, the judge of all men, to the spirits of righteous men made perfect, to Jesus the mediator of a new covenant...

The city was four-square, the street pure gold, the walls had every kind of precious stones. The glory of God gives it light. There will be no night there. Nothing impure will ever enter it.

Chapter 22, The River of Life

The river of life will flow from the throne down the middle of the street. The tree of life will be there. We will see the face of God.

John wanted to fall down and worship the angel that had been showing him these things, but he said, 'I am a fellow servant with you. Worship God!' He told John, 'Do not seal up the words of the prophesy of this book, because the time is near'.

Jesus spoke, 'I, Jesus, have sent my angel to give you this testimony for the churches...' (22:16).

Come, whoever is thirsty, let him come and whoever wishes, let him take the free gift of the water of life (22:17).

Warning: If anyone adds anything (to the prophesy of this book) God will add to him the plagues described in this book. If anyone takes away, God will take away from him his share in the tree of life and in the holy city (22:18, 19).

This review of Revelation was taken from the New International Version, Coffman Commentaries, the book of Josephus and personal views.

A Message From the Author
What Christ Means in My Life

From a child, I've been fortunate to have been raised in the Lord's church.

Preachers in the past preached plain, factual sermons, really emphasizing the things we *must do*, using the Bible as the only authority and that we should not change it in any way. I never gave any thought to checking out other religions, because there was no doubt on my part.

My learning was by sermons, Bible classes and through the influence of my father and grandmother. When I was young, I never read the Bible myself.

I was baptized first at about age 12. I believed Jesus to be the Son of God, but thought I had to lead a sinless life. I thought that if I should die with *any* sin, I would be lost.

This is true, but I never realized the forgiveness through prayer a Christian has.

When I was about 17 years old, I was re-baptized, having come to a better understanding of how forgiveness works; that instead of fear, we can have assurance. Baptism and faith in God's son is just the beginning of Christian life.

Because I am 'in Christ' my past sins are forgiven. I have a new start in life. I have confessed Him before men. Now, I must confess Him by my manner of life. Because I am now 'in Christ', I have many spiritual blessing.

1. His Holy Spirit dwells in me (Acts 2:38).

2. The Lord has added me to His church (Acts 2:41).

3. All spiritual blessings are in Christ (Eph. 1:3-5).

4. I have the promise of a heavenly home, if I remain faithful.

5. God will hear and answer my prayers (1 John 5:13, 14).

6. Jesus and the Holy Spirit make intercession to God for me.

7. There is now no condemnation if I continue to live right (Romans 8:1).

8. Our name is written in the book of life (the most important thing that can happen).

Baptism represents a death and burial of our old life. We arise to live in a new life, free from sin. I am now His daughter. His spirit lives in me. Jesus and the Holy Spirit help me conquer the desire to sin. Even though I should fall, I can rise again (Romans 11).

No one accidently grows into the type of person that pleases God. Just because our past sins are forgiven doesn't mean we won't be tempted to sin or escape the consequences of it. We should grow spiritually just as we grow physically.

We should assemble weekly with other Christians.

We should partake of the Lord's Supper weekly.

We should worship in Spirit and in truth.

We should lift our voices in praise.

We should give cheerfully of our means.

We should humble ourselves in prayer.

We should love our brother – not only on Sunday, but as a way of life.

If we should sin against anyone, we should go to them and make things right, for if we don't forgive our fellow man, God won't forgive us.

We are not to love the things of the world, not seek after riches – but be moderate in all things.

We are to be good stewards of our possessions and work as unto the Lord.

We should lead a life filled with prayer. This could be upon rising and before going to sleep, at meals, at set times or odd times, before a trip, when we're thankful, when we're discouraged, aloud or in silence. Just a few words, or at length and often. The Lord doesn't care about beautiful words but beautiful hearts.

If we truly repent, and do not repeat the sin, there is no need to ask for forgiveness over and over for the same thing. To me, that would show doubt that we've not been forgiven, as promised.

Don't look back, look forward. Knowing we've been forgiven will remove our guilty feelings and make us free.

God wants us to be happy and productive, not sad and shamefaced. We read in Romans 8:28, 'to them that love God, all things work together for good'. That does not mean that we won't have troubles and disappointments in this life, but if we believe this, it will give us peace of mind. We will feel like God has a purpose and plan for us.

One of my favorite verses is this: '*For the eyes of the Lord range throughout the earth to strengthen those whose hearts are fully committed to Him*' (2 Chron. 16:9).

Christianity is kind of like growing a crop, with age being the ripened fruit. To a Christian, the most contentment comes at the end of life.

You love home, you don't strive for *things*, you don't *need* clothes or furniture, you put your trust in God, looking to your reward.

Once, an older woman told me, 'there'll come a time in your life when you will feel very calm'. At that time, I thought this strange but I pondered it in my heart like Mary did. Sure enough that time came. We will have pains and sickness, but this is probably a preparation for heaven.

Many of us feel like our usefulness is over, that we've done all we can. Our outward man may be, but our inward man is growing ever closer to God.

Age means experience. We know the promises of God. There's no guessing, no doubting. Our eyes are fixed on the goal.

The Christian life is the best kind of life, even if this life was all there was. All these blessings I feel in my life can be anyone's. The Lord will give us peace of mind, be our constant companion but these blessings will only come to those who are 'in Christ'.

It's very important to know the truth. A knowledge of God's word will give us assurance, because we know it will not change. I wanted to write this review of the Bible to try to help us all understand what the will of God is.

God bless the reader,

Carrie Wall

About the Author

Carrie Wall was born near Vernon, AL and grew up in the Columbus, MS area on a farm.

She has been married to Tommy Wall since 1949 and is the mother of six children, ~~twelve~~ *14* grandchildren and ~~three~~ *13* great-grandchildren. At first, Carrie was a stay-at-home mom while her husband taught school. She later started a drapery business which she owned and operated for forty years.

Over the years, they have lived in: Holcomb MO, Thibodaux LA, Starkville MS, Kosciusko MS, and Abilene TX. They are now retired and living in ~~Amory~~ MS. *Laurel*

Carrie has also written: <u>From The Beginning</u>, <u>The Long Journey</u>, <u>My Life</u> (a biography), <u>People of The Bible</u>, and <u>Memories of Home</u> (a cookbook).

Carrie would like to hear from you. Please mail your feedback and/or inquiries about this book or others she's written to:

A Review of the Bible
Attention: Carrie Wall
~~809 Town and Country Lane~~ *3 Mar Rue Dr.*
~~Amory, Mississippi 38821~~ *Laurel, MS. 39440*

ph. 662-315-3276